GLOBALIZATION

THE READER

GLOBALIZATION

THE READER

Edited by

John Beynon

and

David Dunkerley

ROUTLEDGE
NEW YORK

Published in America in 2000
Routledge
29 West 35th Street
New York, NY 10001
www.ROUTLEDGE-NY.com
By arrangement with
THE ATHLONE PRESS

British Library Cataloguing in publication Data
A catalogue record for this book is available from the British Library

Library of Congress Cataloging-in-Publication-Data
Globalization: the reader / edited by John Benyon and David Dunkerley
    p. cm
  Includes bibliographical references and index.
  ISBN 0-415-92922-9 (pbk.)
  1. International economic relations. 2. Globalizaiton. 3. World politics –
1989— 4. Economic history – 1990— I. Benyon, John. II. Dunkerley,
David.
HF1359 .G594 2001
303.48′2—dc21   00-044645

Typeset by Florence Production Ltd, Stoodleigh, Devon
Printed and bound in Great Britain

CONTENTS

LIST OF EXTRACTS

Part B   GLOBAL CULTURE   77

Part B2 GLOBAL CONSUMERISM, TOURISM AND IDENTITY 141

Part C1   GLOBALIZATION, MEDIA AND COMMUNICATION   165

Part C2   THE GLOBAL IMPACT OF NEW TECHNOLOGIES   205

Part D GLOBALIZATION AND THE POLITICAL ECONOMY 231

GENERAL INTRODUCTION

1 A PARABLE OF OUR GLOBAL TIMES

Just as we were about to deliver our manuscript to the publisher, something happened which is a highly appropriate scene-setter for a book on globalization (and one which, while it addresses cultural, political and economic aspects of globalization, nevertheless underlines the key role being played by global media, in particular the new communication technologies).

1.1 'I LOVE YOU'

Just after midnight on Thursday, 4 May 2000, the virus control centre of Message Lab (a firm in Cirencester, England, specializing in computer 'bug-busting') intercepted a copy of an e-mail on the subject of 'I Love You' with an attachment 'Love-Letter-For-You'. At first there seemed little out of the ordinary: like other 'cyber-bugs' it was activated by opening its e-mail and then posted itself to all the addresses in the address book. Hours later vague worry became real fear as the newcomer's virulence became apparent. By 7 am UK time, eight copies had been spotted; by 8 am, 462; and by 9 am, over 3,000. An hour later the US awoke to the problem as its Federal computer monitoring unit registered the first sighting at 5 am Eastern time. By then people all over Europe had opened their e-mails and so sent the virus in every direction – the same thing was also happening in America. By midday UK time

tens of millions of computers world-wide had been disabled, among the victims were the UK House of Commons, US Congress, White House, Pentagon, the CIA, NASA, Microsoft, Time-Warner, Ford Motor Company and Merrill Lynch. In the UK alone it was estimated that over 50 per cent of all businesses were affected and the situation in other countries (for example, Germany) was worse. Many even closed down (for example, Nestlé, the giant food group, sent its workers home). The loss of business revenue was enormous and, added to the clean-up costs, was estimated not in millions, but in billions of dollars.

The author of the virus (thought to be, at the time of writing, a young Filipino computer buff in Manila) not only had the technological expertise to write a program capable of paralysing untold millions of computers world-wide, but sufficient insight into the human psyche to understand how to lure the maximum number of victims into the trap. We all, it seems, like to be loved and, as the editorial of the UK's *Daily Telegraph* commented:

All over the world, people switched on their computers to find messages waiting for them purporting to come from people they knew, each labelled 'I Love You'. Hearts thumping, over-weight Senators in the American mid-West, sharp-faced bankers in Zurich, Ministers of the Crown at Westminster, acne-ridden boys and girls in the suburbs of Sydney, all eagerly clicked open the file and then its personal attachment, desperate to read more, so that within a matter of hours the 'love-bug' had spread to the four corners of the globe, eating up files and bringing cyber commerce to a standstill.

It truly is a parable for our 'global times' in that it illustrates both the strengths and possibilities, weaknesses and dangers, of our (that is, humankind's) increasing dependence upon the new communication and information technologies operating on a global scale, but 'operationalized' in a local context.

1.2 OUTLINE OF ISSUES AND DEBATES

'Globalization' is one of the most frequently used 'buzzwords' of today, repeatedly on the lips of politicians, academics, economists, media and marketing people, television executives and environmentalists, among others. Meanwhile, globalization has become a major topic of study in universities, especially in cultural, media and communication studies; sociology; international studies; and in newly emerging areas (especially at Masters' level) like global studies. It is not surprising, therefore, that the literature on it is expanding at an ever-increasing rate. This Reader reviews the principal issues and debates surrounding globalization, with particular reference to cultural globalization, and makes available to students a wide variety of ideas and perspectives it would otherwise be difficult for them to obtain (taking into account the prohibitive cost of books and the constraints on text and journal availability in even the best endowed academic libraries).

As we have already seen, riding on the back of ever-more-effective communication technologies with a 'global reach', contemporary globalization has undoubtedly changed the relationship between time and space and, in the process, rendered the world a more compressed place. But opinions as to its consequences are sharply divided, especially in respect of cultural globalization. It is proposed by some as a thoroughly progressive and liberating phenomenon, opening up the potential for greater human connectedness and the spread of human rights, democracy, health care and improved inter-cultural under-

standing world-wide. Here, for example, is Beck (2000) on the collapse of the former Communist eastern bloc:

> The Iron Curtain and the military counter-espionage service dissolved into nothingness in the television age. Television advertising, for example, (which is often scorned by cultural criticism in the West) changed in an environment of shortage and regimentation into a fused promise of consumption and political freedom. (p. 66)

Conversely, it is widely attacked as heralding in a new and voracious phase of Western capitalism and the imposition of Americanized culture (in the form of television, videos, pop music, films and adverts and other Western goods) on vulnerable communities unable to protect themselves from the sheer volume and intensity of foreign imports. The talk is of electronic imperialism through the unequal flow of media, such as entertainment (building on English's unique position as a global language) from America as the world's sole superpower and the growing disparity between the world's (technology-owning) 'information rich' and 'information poor'.

The eradication of cultural difference, which some allege is taking place, is seen to be to the advantage of Western capitalism and to the detriment (both culturally and economically) of the 'colonized' local. Schiller (1976; 1985; 1991; 1996) is strongly of this view, arguing that Western countries dominate economic and technological resources, so much so that the developing world is doomed to remain at the margins of the global economy. Multinational corporations control the global market and exploit cheap labour and resources wherever they can be located. Both Harvey (1989) and Jameson (1984; 1991), for instance, view the proactive opening up of new global markets and commodification of culture and consumption as the hallmark of 'late capitalism' in its 'postmodern phase'.

What is of particular concern is the concentration of ownership of global media production and transmission in the hands of a small number of (mostly American) corporations. For example, the past two decades have witnessed a huge expansion of the pop music industry, including the development of pop videos and the MTV 24-hour music channels in America, Europe and Asia. Communication satellites now embrace the planet and pop music circumvents national boundaries. But 70 per cent of all pop music is produced and distributed by a handful of huge, multinational corporations that integrate production, transmission and promotion, thus ensuring that Michael Jackson's and Madonna's voices and faces are everywhere: on television, video and film; on CDs; in magazines and newspapers; in magazines and advertisements; on radio and cassettes; and emblazoned on baseball caps and T-shirts (Negus, 1992; 1996).

What is undeniable is that globalization, in one form or another, is impacting on the lives of everyone on the planet, whatever their age, class, ethnicity, gender or wherever they live. It is changing consciousness, too, as everyone everywhere becomes more globally aware and oriented. In this sense globalization might justifiably be claimed to be the defining feature of human society at the start of the twenty-first century. Its impact may be *direct* (as in the case of people in a township in Soweto, South Africa, watching American and British televised 'soaps'), or *indirect* in that the clothes you wear, although Western in style, have probably been made elsewhere else. For example, an important aspect of globalization is that many non-Western economies are hugely dependent on the making of Western goods for the Western market: 40 per cent of Levi jeans (one of the great symbols of America) are manufactured in Tunisia, 30 per cent in Turkey, and 30 per cent in the UK. Indeed, in terms of the global fashion industry, countries like Taiwan, Bangladesh, South Korea, Hong Kong and China have become mass producers of clothes for the West (Craik, 1994).

1.3 STRUCTURE OF THE BOOK

- First, in what follows we set out to answer three questions:
    - what is globalization? (Section 2);
    - what is global culture? (Section 3);
    - what is cultural globalization? (Section 4).
- Second, we examine the case for and against cultural homogenization and hybridization (Section 5).
- Third, we critically review debates concerning global media and media imperialism (Section 6).
- We conclude the General Introduction in Section 7 by looking in some detail at a small selection of leading commentators on global culture and postmodernism (David Harvey, Jean Baudrillard and Paul Virilio); and on globalization (Roland Robertson and Arjun Appadurai).
- In each of the four Parts we focus on Globalization: in Part A, globalization and society; Part B, globalization and culture; Part C, globalization, media and technology; and conclude by contextualizing globalization in Part D, globalization and the political economy. Each part consists of a brief introduction, followed by carefully selected extracts from writers who have something informative, insightful, stimulating or provocative to say about the topic in question.
- Finally, we end with a list of questions arising out of both the General Introduction and the four Parts. We hope these prove useful to those students who use the Reader on an independent study basis.

2 GLOBALIZATION

In addressing the question 'What is globalization?' below, first, the antecedents of globalization are examined; second, this is done in the light of changes to the global political economy; and, third, the symbiosis between globalization and postmodernity is explored. Issues raised in this section are amplified in Parts A and D below.

2.1 WHAT IS GLOBALIZATION?

There are three possibilities concerning the origins of globalization, which Waters (1995) summarizes as follows:

- that a form of globalization has been in progress throughout history (for example, the unrecorded, prehistoric movements of people across the planet);
- that it is an outcome of capitalism in the modern period;
- that it is more recent, the product of the 'disorganized capital' of post-industrialism and post-modernity.

Addressing these three possibilities shapes the content of this section. But before proceeding any further a definition of 'globalization' is called for. This is not easy as commentators are far from agreed on its nature, impact or possible outcomes. Both Giddens (1990) and Wallerstein (1979; 1984), for example, are somewhat ambivalent about any long-term benefits it may hold for the human race. The former sees a world market for capital, commodities, labour and communications as having developed, with deadly weaponry and sophisticated surveillance technologies truly global in their reach. It is perhaps for this reason that all that can be said with any certainty is that globalization points towards a highly unpredictable future. Similarly, the latter's functionalist 'world systems theory' presents a world increasingly dominated by capital controlled by the West. Meanwhile, Jameson (1998) is of the opinion that, given its complexity, it is not yet possible to come up with anything like a comprehensive definition of globalization. Others point to its paradoxes in that although capitalist is centralizing in character, nevertheless (to quote Chomsky, 1993; cited in Wilson and Dissanayake, 1996, p. 1): 'all around the world there's much more involvement in grass roots organisations, regionalism and moves towards developing more local autonomy'. It is this contradictory character that makes defining and theorizing globalization so perilous, along with the fact that it crosses the boundaries of conventional academic disciplines, an issue emphasized by Jameson (op. cit., 1998) when he writes that it is:

the intellectual property of no particular field, yet seems to concern politics and economics in immediate ways, but just as immediately culture

and sociology, not to speak of information and the media, or ecology, or consumerism and daily life. (p. xi)

Beck (op. cit.) usefully distinguishes between 'globality', 'globalism' and 'globalization':

'globality' refers to the fact that we are increasingly living in a 'world society' in the sense that 'the notion of closed spaces has become illusory . . . from now on nothing which happens on our planet is only a limited local event'. (pp. 10–11)

'globalism' is the view that the 'world market' is now powerful enough to supplant (local and national) political action;

'globalization' is the blanket term to describe 'the processes through which sovereign national states are criss-crossed and undermined by transnational actors with varying prospects of power, orientations, identities and networks'. (p. 11)

However, it is already clear that, first, the relationship between 'the global' and 'the local' is becoming increasingly varied; and second, different 'locals' appear to react differently to different experiences of 'the global'. Giddens (op. cit.) skates over this when he defines globalization as 'the intensification of world-wide social relationships which link distant places in such a way that local happenings are shaped by events occurring many miles away and vice-versa' (p. 64). Also, as Spybey (1996) usefully reminds us, the influence of globalization operates not just on the large scale but, also, penetrates 'the significant, the routine and the most intimate aspects of life' (p. 5).

Indeed, it is this aspect which is noted by Robertson (1990; 1992), who regards the 'inside-the-head', phenomenological aspect of the relationship between the individual and the global as being central to understanding globalization. He employs the terms 'globality' and the 'global human condition' to describe a globe-oriented perspective: that is, a growing awareness in people's minds everywhere of the world conceived, not so much as a unified whole, but as a loose entity. He also points to some of the paradoxes of globalization noted above. For example, at a time of an accelerating 'coming together', widely associated with globalization, there is a simultaneous 'fragmentation'. For example, while nations are seeking to co-opt states and regions, many of these are seeking to advance their own concepts of nationhood. Nations are composed of groups whose common identity is based on a generally shared belief in a core notion of nationhood; and these constructions of nationhood appear to be steadily increasing and are regularly crossing state boundaries. In the 'new global order', nations and state are often in conflict in that more and more 'nations' appear to be threatened with disintegration. Examples would be the tension between Spain and the Basque separatists; Canada and the Quebecois; Sri Lanka and the Tamil Tiger separatists; and India and the Sikhs of Kashmir. Some even see the unity of the UK jeopardized by the establishment of a devolved Scottish Parliament and Welsh Assembly. Meanwhile, diasporas across the world continue to construct 'imagined communities' (Anderson, 1983) that traverse geographical borders. Indeed, Robertson (op. cit.) interprets such surges in local, regional and nationalistic pride and the push for nationhood as being very much part of the globalizing process. Rather than being about unity, globalization would appear to be about increasing diversity simultaneously operating at a number of levels.

Lash and Urry (1987; 1994) see post-Fordist 'disorganized capital' characterizing globalization, having replaced old Fordist 'organized capital'. They present the hallmarks of contemporary globalization as:

- more inter-state connections and the decreasing effect of state policy;
- the development of increased transnational communication and activities;
- a decline in the importance of the nation state;
- the emergence of global political, economic and cultural organizations and bureaucracies;
- the emergence of what King (1990) aptly terms 'global cities' (like London, New York, Paris and Tokyo) as local sites of global interaction;

- a huge increase in the flows of commodities and cultural products;
- and the world-wide spread of Western-style consumerism.

These ideas are expanded upon by Waters (op. cit.), who characterizes globalization as '. . . a social process in which the constraints of geography on social and cultural arrangements recede and in which people become increasingly aware that they are receding' (p. 3). He goes on to predict that in the future,

territoriality will disappear as an organising principle for social and cultural life . . . it will be a society without borders or spatial boundaries. In a globalized world we will be unable to predict social practices and preferences on the basis of geographical location. Equally, we can expect relationships between people in disparate locations to be formed as easily as relationships between people in proximate ones. (p. 3)

He holds that a number of features can now, with confidence, be held to mark out contemporary globalization:

- *Increasing speed and volume.* Speed of movement (whether by travel or via communicational technology) and the volume of goods, messages and symbols in circulation have massively increased. Although a 'globalizing tendency' has been gaining in force since the sixteenth century, it has now greatly accelerated and, in addition, works simultaneously on a number of levels (for example, economic, political, cultural and individual).
- *Shrinking space.* Space is increasingly expressed in time of travel or communication and appears to shrink as travel and communicational time decreases. Instantaneous telecommunication adds to this sense of global 'shrinkage', so much so that Waters (op. cit.) speaks of 'the phenomenological elimination of space and the generalisation of time' (p. 63). Globalization operates on the basis of messages, images and symbols that have been freed of spatial constraints. Giddens' (op. cit.)

term 'distanciation' encapsulates the way in which time has now been divorced from space. 'Distanciated networks' of interdependence are features of the global age, given that national politics and economics can no longer stand alone. Moreover, the increased movement of peoples across the face of the planet, coupled with the advent of new communication technologies, has resulted in social relations being 'disembedded' (that is. stretched across vast distances).

- *Permeable borders*. Political and geographical boundaries have been rendered permeable as greatly increased relations (whether through trade, tourism or electronically). The degree of interconnectedness between all nation states and the wider world is increasing. Events occurring in the latter now impinge upon the former to such a degree that total national autonomy or isolation is almost impossible to maintain. Economic, political and cultural change is now beyond the control of any national government, so much so that some commentators have talked, somewhat prematurely, of the 'death' of the nation state. While this process is far from complete, there does appear to be an inexorability about it, although it is somewhat premature yet to speak of a 'global society'. The fact is, however, that globalization affects everyone on the planet, so much so that it is hard, if not impossible, to escape its various influences. Satellite-beamed images and messages are available everywhere to anyone who has the means to receive them. Environmental pollution is evident world-wide, respecting neither geographical nor political boundaries: indeed, the depletion of the ozone layer and global warming is every bit a 'global phenomenon' as is the global economy or the presence everywhere of the ubiquitous Coca-Cola. While it is true that more people are now travelling further, faster and in greater numbers than ever before, we no longer have to move from home village, town or city to experience something of globalization.
- *Reflexivity*. People are, increasingly, orienting themselves to the world as a whole, regarding themselves as both 'locals' and 'cosmopolitans'.

Local sites everywhere have an increased opportunity to interact with the global; local businesses increasingly participate in global markets; and governments cannot risk becoming isolated. They must operate 'globally' in terms of the developing global economy; the increasing transnationalism of labour; the spreading of human rights; and environmental issues which are global in magnitude. Moreover, everyone is, in varying degrees, involved in the globalizing process: as much as it is a material thing (as measured in the millions of global financial transactions per minute, or the numbers of global brands available in the local supermarket), globalization is, also, personal in that people today are increasingly 'thinking globally' and are far more 'globally aware' than even in the recent past. Giddens (op. cit.), for example, points to the way in which we, as individuals, reproduce the global in our daily lives. He presents globalization as the essential component of what he terms 'reflexive modernity', characterized by an increasing flow of information, images, symbols and purchasable, 'lifestyle' identities.

- *Risk and trust*. Globalization increasingly involves everyone everywhere in a web of trust and risk, in that all of us have to place our trust in 'experts' and other unknown persons. Also, we place our faith in science and medicine, yet no one could foresee the advent of AIDS or CJD (the human equivalent of 'mad cow disease'). Similarly, each of us can be affected, either directly or indirectly, by something as apparently remote (and totally beyond our control) as the rise and fall in share prices in the New York, Tokyo or London stock markets.

Beck (1992) takes this theme further in ecological terms and labels the emerging global society as nothing less than the 'risk society'. In the past pollution was accepted as the necessary price to be paid for full employment and prosperity. The true magnitude of industrial modernism's destructive legacy in this respect is only now becoming fully evident. Moreover, the risks associated with global ecological threats are no longer anchored in localities: global warming, nuclear accidents and acid rain show no respect for geographical and political borders. It seems, too, that risks are multiplying: he refers to the 'boomerang effect' affects both perpetrators and victims: rich and poor alike are susceptible to the dangers resulting from damage to the ozone layer and the way in which steroids and fertilizers (used to increase productivity) return as toxins in the food chain. Ecological damage has both a local and global impact: as Beck (op. cit., 1992) expresses it, in the 'risk society everyone is pursuing a "scorched earth" policy against everyone else' (p. 38). While heavily polluting industries have been subjected to stringent regulations in the West, this is not always the case in the newly industrializing developing nations, which are willing to accept a higher level of risk in return for rising economic standards.

Commentators agree that the following are among globalization's most significant foundational factors:

- the expansion of trading relationships and the use of symbolic tokens, of which money is an obvious example;
- Copernicus' conception of the world as a globe;
- the invention of the mechanical clock, time measurement and global time zones;
- the invention of navigational aids and the steady advance of travel technologies (wind-powered or fuelled by coal, oil or diesel);
- the outward expansion of European institutions and culture;
- capitalism's insatiable drive to maximize profit leading it to 'go global' in its postmodern phase and to open up and exploit new markets with new products.

These points are explored further below. Historically, one of the most significant steps on the way towards contemporary globalization was the outward expansion of Europe from the late fifteenth century onwards and it is to this that we first turn.

2.2 THE OUTWARD EXPANSION OF EUROPE

The outward expansion of European institutions and culture stretches from the early voyages of the great navigators at the end of the fifteenth century through to the mass migration of European peoples across the Atlantic in the late nineteenth and early twentieth centuries. This is clearly a major precursor of globalization as we know it today.

In the 100 years following 1430 the globe was explored by the leading European maritime nations, in particular the Spanish, British, French and Portuguese. They developed an 'outward-looking-ness', whereas other powerful nations remained inward-looking, regarding the outside world as a hostile threat. Spybey (op. cit.) provides the example of the Chinese explorer Cheng Huo, whose voyages of exploration preceded the Europeans by a century but were held to be undesirable and eventually discontinued by his Emperor. This was in sharp contrast to Henry of Navarre, who established his famous school of navigation at Cape St. Vincent. Utilizing the technology of the caravel (in particular its highly effective triangular sail) and navigating by the pole star, his captains explored the West African coast. Thereafter they rounded the Cape of Good Hope and discovered the sea route to India. As a consequence, in the sixteenth century, Lisbon became the first 'world city'.

The journeying outwards of European navigators had a number of consequences:

- the expansion of geographical knowledge, with a placing of Europe at the centre of the then known world;
- the expansion of technical information as the European nations improved their techniques of marine construction and navigational skills. In the process they incorporated knowledge of sails (from India), the compass (from China), the astrolabe (from Islam) and gunpowder (from China);
- the emergence of what Spybey (op. cit.) terms a 'global consciousness' and which he defines as 'the capacity to conceive of the world as an accessible

and attainable whole that could be explored and was, indeed, available for exploitation by those who could achieve this' (p. 16);

- the growing sense of destiny and a mission to spread European culture, institutions and Christianity globally. European systems of trade, politics, administration, justice, government, military and worship were reproduced under colonization. Many colonized nations willingly adopted European ways, seeing the benefits of being part of an embryonic network of international relations;
- the international acceptance of European standards such as the Gregorian calendar and, later, the Greenwich meridian. The European concept of the nation state was also widely adopted and this, as Spybey (op. cit.) points out, was an important aspect of globalization;
- the appearance in Europe in the sixteenth century of produce never before seen (like spices, herbs, potatoes, tomatoes, green beans, peppers and chocolate) and which had a dramatic local impact among those who could afford them.

By the end of the eighteenth century a 'global ecumene' had emerged and by means of which European institutions were transplanted across the world. Throughout the nineteenth century and into the twentieth century the influence of the West intensified under the impact of railroads, industrialization and the imitation of European high culture and taste. Massive European migration to the New World and, later, Australia and New Zealand, was especially influential. Meanwhile, missionaries and European travellers began to extol the 'otherness' of exotic cultures, especially in the period 1850–80. World history was equated with European history and the advances of nineteenth-century and twentieth-century technology and science, along with literary and artistic achievement, were taken as ample 'proof' of European 'superiority' and a widespread belief that little could be learnt from the rest of the world. The European mind was held to be both more rational and creative than elsewhere outside Europe: 'elsewhere' (including the US) was regarded as unsophisticated at best and, at worst, barbaric.

2.3 HISTORICAL PERSPECTIVES ON GLOBALIZATION

The origins of globalization as we experience it today are varied and not easy to explicate. However, Giddens (op. cit.); Robertson (op. cit.) and Held *et al.* (1999) each have great insight in historically contextualizing globalization. We briefly look at each in turn.

(a) Anthony Giddens: 'The consequences of modernity' (1990)

For Giddens (op. cit.) globalization is directly allied to the development of modern societies, to industrialization and the accumulation of material resources, and is a continuation of modernity rather than a break with it. The contemporary period he terms 'high modernity', by which he infers that modernity has now moved into a global stage: society has become a 'world society' and the individual is confronted by social institutions that have become global. People everywhere cannot avoid coming into contact with the global through twentieth-century brand marketing, imagery and fashions. He identifies three factors in the nineteenth century that, in his opinion, have resulted in contemporary globalization:

- Nineteenth-century European nations' deployment of force to conquer tribal societies, colonize them and then establish ruling colonial communities.
- The comparative peace of the nineteenth century allowed the British in particular to invest resources in advancing colonial ambitions.
- Europeans' bureaucratic skills allowed them to develop diplomatic networks and transnational political and business agencies.

Although European states have regularly gone to war with each other, they have more often collaborated and, as a consequence, the nation state remains at the heart of contemporary globalization and its networks of international relations. Capitalism (with its aggressive competition for raw materials, production and constant search for new markets) has fuelled the pre-existing globalizing tendency. Finally, Giddens hopes, somewhat idealistically, that in the future globalization will result in a 'post-scarcity' economy; multi-level political participation; global demilitarization; and the use of high technology in ways that benefit all sectors of the human race.

(b) Roland Robertson: 'Globalization' (1992)

In contrast, Robertson (op. cit.) presents contemporary globalization as pre-dating modernity and the rise of capitalism. He argues that globalization in our time is qualitatively different from earlier manifestations in that modernization has accelerated globalization which has now permeated contemporary consciousness. Whereas most commentators see the world undergoing social compression since the sixteenth century, Robertson places the origins of globalization earlier and identifies five phases of globalization in Europe:

- *Phase 1, 1400–1750*: the germinal phase of global exploration, along with the spread of the Roman Catholic Church; the widespread adoption of the Gregorian calendar; the advent of mapping and of modern geography; and the growth of national communities and of the state system.
- *Phase 2, 1750–1875*: the emergence of internationalism in the form of international relations and exhibitions as non-European countries began to be admitted to the Europe-dominated 'international' society.
- *Phase 3, 1875–1925*: the 'take-off' phase of globalization, marked by globalizing tendencies such as communicational advances and increasing economic and political connections, along with cultural and sporting links (like the Olympic movement) and, from 1914–18, the first 'world' conflict.
- *Phase 4, 1925–69*: the struggle for dominance phase, with World War II and the splitting of the atom, as well as the founding of the United Nations and other organizations with a global remit.

- *Phase 5, 1969 to date*: the end of the Cold War; the moon landing and planetary exploration; the emergence of global institutions and global mass media; and world-wide debates around race, ethnicity, sex, gender, sexuality and human rights.

Today, European institutions no longer control the world and many of the old 'certainties' in place up to the 1960s no longer hold sway. Indeed, Robertson (op. cit.) believes that we may already have entered a sixth phase, one of global uncertainty, given the advent of AIDS; the rise of new diseases and pandemics; the re-emergence of old scourges in new forms (for example, tuberculosis and smallpox); global environmental hazards, the revival of ancient ethnic hatreds; the immense influence of the global media; increasing multiculturalism and polyethnicity; and the growth of Islamic Fundamentalism. The long-term outcomes of globalization are uncertain and, as he puts it, 'up for grabs'. But what makes contemporary globalization unique is that the world has moved from being 'in itself' towards being 'for itself' in that, increasingly, nations now engage more in a wide range of economic, military, cultural and political contacts and people everywhere have increasingly come to comprehend the world as 'one place' and to think, feel and act globally.

(c) Held *et al.*: 'Global transformations' (1999)

Held *et al.* (op. cit.) see contemporary cultural globalization as the latest manifestation of a set of historical processes. Examples of these are the pre-historic and historic migration of people; the global spread of the major world religions; the impact of the great Empires; the influence of powerful Western nation states and modern nationalism, including the outward expansion of Europe from the sixteenth century; the transnational flows of capitalism and of 'big' ideas (pertaining to science, liberalism, socialism, feminism, etc.); and, of course, the hegemony of English as a truly 'global language'. There are technological antecedents, too: for example, the development of the trans-Atlantic telegraph in the 1860s and cable communication across the British Empire by the 1880s.

Setting aside the pre-historical and pre-agrarian (about which, obviously, little is known) they look at four periods of globalization, each reflecting a particular arrangement of spatial, temporal and organizational circumstances. These are: the pre-modern; the early modern; the modern; and the contemporary:

- *The pre-modern (before 1500)*. 'Globalization' was interregional within Eurasia and the Americas, based on political and military empires and the movements of peoples into uncultivated areas.
- *The early modern (1500–1850)*. This was marked by the rise of the West and the movement of Europeans into the Americas and then Oceania. It was in the early modern period that world religions spread and exerted their most significant cultural influence, especially Christianity and Judaism, both of which attained a global distribution.
- *Modern globalization (1850–1945)*. This period witnessed an acceleration of global networks and cultural flows, dominated by the European powers, especially the British; and the great migration of European peoples to the New World. By the mid-nineteenth century European peoples, ideas and religions had transformed the Americas, with rapid developments in transport and communication technologies in the second half of the nineteenth century (for example, telegraphy, telephones, radio, railways, shipping, canals, etc.) making connections over large areas possible.
- *Contemporary globalization*. Everywhere the environment is degraded and new patterns of global migration have replaced the old. A worldwide system of nation states, overlaid by a combination of regional and global forms of regulation and governance, has emerged. Although still highly asymmetrical, contemporary globalization is less dominated by America and Europe:

> distributional patterns of power and wealth no longer accord with a simple core and periphery division . . . (and) . . . reflect a new geography of power and privilege which transcends political borders and regions, reconfiguring established international and trans-national hierarchies of social power and wealth. (p. 429)

But what really distinguishes contemporary globalization from anything that has gone before is the truly global impact of communications and transport which have increased the speed and volume of the circulation of images, symbols, goods and people. No state is disconnected from global telecommunication and the authors conclude that 'even though most people remain rooted in a local or national culture and a local place, it is becoming increasingly impossible for them to live in that place disconnected culturally from the world in which it is situated' (p. 369).

2.4 GLOBALIZATION AND THE CHANGING POLITICAL ECONOMY

At the outset of the twenty-first century it is manifestly clear that any sense of the West's previously assumed 'superiority' in the more interconnected 'globalized' world we now inhabit has disappeared. How has this come about?

- the world is no longer dominated by the Western military machine;
- the emergence of new global communicational technologies has facilitated the questioning of the previously taken-for-granted Western cultural superiority;
- the Eurocentric view of the world has been subverted and replaced;
- there has been a resurgence of Islam, based on oil money;
- the economic and manufacturing rise of Japan and of the Southeast Asia ('Tiger') economies;
- events in Eastern Europe in the late 1980s have had profound and lasting implications in terms of the 'ripple' effects on Western societies in particular.

The former tripartite distinction between the 'first world' (or 'free world' as it was frequently called), the 'second world' (comprising the former socialist societies of Eastern Europe) and the 'third world' (consisting of developing or non-aligned countries) lost its meaning after the events of 1989. The 'second world' disappeared and, at roughly the same time, several former developing countries (particularly in Southeast Asia) entered a phase of rapid economic growth. The speed of the changes in Eastern Europe was nothing short of breathtaking, with Hungary leading the way in February 1989, and with Poland, Bulgaria, East Germany, Czechoslovakia and Romania following by the end of that year. By early 1992 each of the former East European communist countries (including Albania) had moved towards democracy as a way of life.

These developments produced highly significant changes on the world stage to the extent that the political and economic character of many countries was changed in response to them. In this sense it is possible to distinguish forces of globalization operating in different contexts. Political globalization is evident as the former 'second world' countries have overwhelmingly chosen democracy and markets of a Western variety. Similarly, the economic developments of certain 'Pacific Rim' countries have led to political developments that again mimic arrangements familiar to the first world. Coupled with these dramatic political movements have been economic changes as the notion of a world economy has become more of a reality through global trading and capital markets and a clear move towards interdependency of separate economies. The political and the economic movements have been boosted and facilitated by technological changes, especially through information technology. In turn, it is possible to discern social and cultural changes resulting from the political, the economic and the technological. Taken together, these suggest very significant changes on a global scale, even a 'new world order' as claimed by former US President George Bush. The changes suggest that the traditional tripartite distinction no longer holds sway and that a high degree of convergence of societies, economies and political systems is well under way.

Such changes have led to suggestions that we are witnessing nothing less than the 'end of history' (Fukuyama, 1992). The apparent dominance of capitalism and democracy, it is argued, has meant that we are witnessing the end of ideological battles. Thus, fascism, communism and monarchism have no place in the postmodern world. The ideological struggle between capitalism and socialism is over, with the former having decisively defeated the latter. Liberal democracy is held up as the ultimate form of government and one being universally adopted. Does this, however, necessarily mean the end of history? Probably not, since liberal democracy has operated at the level of the nation state whereas the forces of globalization (whether they be economic, political, cultural, technological or whatever) are, by definition, global in their presence and impact and their consequences have yet to be fully understood and analysed.

We conclude by returning to what is undoubtedly the most comprehensive study of globalization to date, that by Held *et al.* (op. cit.), who are of the view that 'contemporary globalization is not reducible to a single, causal process, but involves a complex configuration of causal logics' (whether political, military, economic, migratory, ecological, or cultural). They raise two issues which are highly pertinent to our purposes here:

- First, while the processes of globalization may be uniting the globe physically, it is not necessarily inculcating a sense of global community and citizenship, a prerequisite for any future democratic global government. Indeed, some commentators see globalization intensifying conflict as nations seek to secure their own interests, so much so that 'growing nationalism and global inequalities reinforce cultural divisions and global fragmentation' (p. 451).
- Second, what kind of politics is required in the emerging global order? This is the question that Held *et al.* (op. cit.) raise when they ask 'what is the proper constituency and the proper realm of jurisdiction for developing and implementing policy with respect to health issues such as AIDS, narcotics, the management of nuclear waste,

military security, the harvesting of rainforests, indigenous peoples, the use of non-renewable resources, the instability of global financial markets and the management and control of genetic engineering and manipulation in animals and humans?' (p. 446).

2.5 GLOBALIZATION AND POSTMODERNITY

Jameson (op. cit.), one of the most influential and persuasive commentators, presents postmodernity as the latest stage of capitalism. Operating on a global scale, it is following what he terms the 'logic of late capitalism'. Indeed, the general consensus is that 'market capitalism' (approximately 1700–1850) gave way to modernism's 'monopoly capitalism' (1850–1945), which has now, in turn, given way to a 'late capitalism', characterized by multinational corporations' domination of an increasingly global marketplace. Postmodernity is capitalism in its post-Fordist guise, hungrily creating new opportunities, arenas and areas in which to operate, but still driven by profit. Empowered by new technology (which has transformed production and, in the process, changed the composition of the labour force) capitalism has moved from mass to flexible production based on lifestyle and niche marketing. Since the 1960s, in order to create new markets, capitalism has closed down (or relocated) old, 'smokestack' industries and outlawed what are regarded as outmoded working practices. It has, also, replaced traditional (modernist) 'high culture' with a new aesthetic, based on the 'image industries', in which 'desires' are created over 'needs' in order to bolster demand (for example, in fashion, pop music and lifestyle). Key to the dissemination of such consumerism is advertising and the media, in particular television, which now operate on a global basis and are predominantly (but not exclusively) in the hands of Anglo-American-owned corporations.

Postmodernity remains a highly contentious subject and many question whether 'postmodernity' *per se* (that is, as a distinct period following on from 'modernity') actually exists! However, writers such as Laclau and Mouffe (1985) and Hebdige (1989; 1990) have no doubts and maintain that postmodernity is the result of fundamental changes in social, economic and political processes (notably, as above, the shift from a Fordist economy to a post-Fordist one based on information technology, robotics, diversity, decentralization, differentiation and globalization). They maintain that in the advanced industrial economy the service sector will continue to grow over production *per se* and that global forms of organization will continue to develop at the expense of national ones.

Meanwhile, on the cultural front postmodernism is celebrated by many as the end of imperialistic modernism and the cultural styles and movements emblematical of the latter half of the nineteenth century and the first half of the twentieth century. It is seen to combat modernism's negative aspects and to celebrate, instead, the emergence of a more liberated era. This, many maintain, encourages novel connections; re-energizes values devalued by modernism; and is replete with exciting future possibilities. Huyssens (1984), for example, goes as far as to claim that postmodernism has forged a whole new 'postmodern sensibility' different from that of the preceding modernist period and marking the final end of the Enlightenment project. To support his argument he points to postmodernism's creativity and investment in new directions and alternatives to what has been.

Writers like Hebdige (op. cit.) are strongly of the view that postmodernism holds out the prospect of genuinely 'new times' and of a release of genuinely liberationist and democratic forces. Because of improved global communication (for example, the Internet) local groups now have the capability to combine globally. As confirmation of these 'new times', others point to the advent of radically different 'new age' family structures and beliefs (Thompson, 1992). At the same time various groups (youth, ethnic, gay/lesbian, etc.) have used fashion and music to forge new lifestyles and identities (Simon, 1996).

Responses to postmodernism tend to polarize into two distinct camps:

- 'a liberating phoenix', a celebration of a release from the old class politics of modernism and the promise of a democratic, 'free', pluralistic, post-industrial, post-class society of multiple lifestyles riding on the back of a diversity of cultural codes and discourses;
- 'an old dog in new clothes' and little more than the development of niche marketing and flexible specialization, increased commodification and packaging, a follow-on stage of modernism maybe, but still adhering to the old, exploitative ways of capitalism.

3 GLOBAL CULTURE

The globalizing of culture is not new: what is different is both the nature of 'global culture' and the processes of contemporary cultural globalization that are driving it. We address both these issues below and they are further amplified in Parts B1 and B2.

3.1 WHAT IS GLOBAL CULTURE?

'Culture' is widely recognized as extremely difficult to define adequately. This is not the place to explore this matter except to say that the term 'global culture' is, similarly, just as difficult to define. Indeed, some are reluctant to associate the term 'culture' with what they regard as the banal nature of the media and consumerist products being circulated around the world by the West. Others see this reluctance as reminiscent of the 'high' versus 'low' culture debate of the past, with the former (elitist) being seen as superior to the latter (mass). Yet others seek new ways to describe what they regard as a new cultural phenomenon, one that should not be lumbered with the baggage of the past. Indeed, Robertson (1992) warns that it is a mistake to 'carry into the study of globalization the kind of view of culture that we inherit from the conventional analysis of the national society' (p. 112).

But is it possible to say that something readily identifiable as 'global culture' actually exists and, if

so, what is it? Among the most obvious and tangible forms of cultural globalization are the products of the Western media: television (with its capacity for instantaneous transmission via satellite); global icons like Michael Jackson and Madonna; the global proliferation of products like Coca-Cola and McDonald's; and a wide range of Western consumer goods. However, the reception and impact of these cultural goods is hard to gauge. This raises a further set of issues because those who may agree it does exist need not necessarily agree as to its composition or value. Is it just a *mélange* of disparate components (Smith, 1990) or, in fact, something coherent and substantial (Rieff, 1993; Madsen, 1993; Axtmann, 1997)? Perhaps it is easier to start by briefly stating what global culture is generally believed not to be, namely similar to national cultures. Hall (1992) takes this line: in his view there are as yet no global equivalencies to the ethnic cores (composed of a patchwork of competing national myths, legends memories, stories, symbols, events and heroes, etc.) sedimented within national consciousness and which give identity to a nation and its people. In comparison, global culture is held to be mainly a recent media-driven construct. Local and national cultures have strong emotional connotations for large numbers of people, but global culture is bereft of such 'ethnic-based' appeal. While global culture can certainly draw upon folk and national cultures, it is not (yet) based on shared global stories and memories. In this sense it is 'memory-less', syncretistic and dependent upon the profit-seeking production of mass-mediated signs and symbols (Perry, 1998). Whereas local culture is closely tied to place and time, global culture is free of these constraints: as such it is 'disconnected', 'disembedded' and 'de-territorialized', existing outside the usual reference to geographical territory (Featherstone, 1990; 1995).

In what terms do those who confidently talk of 'global culture' conceive it? Robertson (1992, p. 114) argues that 'global culture' is now 'just as meaningful as the idea of national and local culture'. More than ever before we are witnessing the interpenetration of cultures as nations come under intense pressure to connect what he terms 'inwardness and outwardness' (for example, in the case of the 'closed' nature of contemporary China as it strives to take its place on the twenty-first century world stage). Others point to global culture's diverse character and to the fact that, because of its technologized nature, it does not resemble anything that has previously moved around the world. Hannerz (1990), too, believes that it is 'marked by an organisation of diversity rather than by a replication of uniformity' (p. 237) and that 'many local settings are increasingly characterised by cultural diversity' (p. 49). The net result is that it is 'no longer so easy to conform to the ideal type of a local', given the '. . . influx of meanings as well as of people and goods . . . the increased inter-connectedness of various local cultures . . . the development of cultures without a clear anchorage in any one territory . . . and a global, inter-connected diversity' (p. 237). Moreover, a large number of people are now directly involved with more than one culture. Hannerz (1991; 1992) refers to this when he talks of 'cosmopolitans' and 'locals', examples of the former being transnational politicians, diplomats, bureaucrats, business people, journalists and international academics, although global media is rendering everyone something of a cosmopolitan.

Similarly, Cvetkovich and Kellner (1997, p. 9) also argue that contemporary Western consumer culture is marked by diversity, but diversity increasingly operating on a new global scale:

> global culture operated precisely through the multiplication of different products, services and spectacles targeted at specific audiences. Consumer and media industries are becoming more differentiated and are segmenting their customers and audiences into more categories. In many cases this involves the simulation of minor difference of fashion and style as significant, but it also involves a proliferation of more highly differentiated culture and society in terms of an ever-expanding variety and diversity of cultural artefacts, products and services.

If globalization is the distinguishing trend of the contemporary world, then the 'electronic reach' of Hollywood, McDonald's, Coca-Cola, Nike, Adidas, etc., is ensuring the spread of nothing less than a 'new world culture':

> the consumer society, with its panorama of goods and services; trans-national forms of architecture and design; and a wide range of products and social forms is traversing national boundaries and becoming part of a new world culture. (Cvetkovich and Kellner, op. cit., p. 7)

This new world culture is both brought into being and sustained by the media and entertainment industry, not just in terms of products, but as a desired Americanized lifestyle (Wark, 1994). With reference to the National Baseball Association, Andrews (1997) explores this idealized 'globally shared culture'. He presents the NBA as a 'global space' filled by new global community signs (Coca-Cola, McDonald's, Disney, Benetton, Bay Watch). These texts and practices are not only 'intrusive', they are also part of what he regards as an immensely seductive popular culture, allied to global marketing, entertainment and profit-generation and mediated world-wide.

Instantaneous transmission and volume are the reasons why many are less interested in the content of global culture and more in its consequences and possibilities. Hebdige (op. cit.), for example, argues that people world-wide can now, in ever-growing numbers, connect with like-minded others, perhaps less in shared class interests, but in terms of what he terms 'communities of affect'. Examples would include allegiance to Manchester United as a global football club (with fan clubs all over the UK, Europe, even North and South America); to a pop star (Madonna's global fan club); and the coming together in temporary, but nevertheless global, gatherings like the Live Aid, Sport Aid and Band Aid rock concerts of the recent past. He sees these emotion-based cultural gatherings as emblematical of our mass-mediated times. Americanized culture, in particular, pop music and what Williams (1994) terms 'sporting muzak' (the world-wide commodification of sport, especially football and basketball) together now constitute a shared, global culture that binds young people world-wide together in spite of their language or home background (or even their socio-economic circumstances). Its participants are akin to what Maffesoli (1988) terms 'neo-tribes', people dispersed world-wide but, nevertheless, sharing a common enthusiasm as an 'interest group'. Nostalgia can often be an important element (Robertson, op. cit., even talks of 'wilful nostalgia'): for example, the transnational popularity of 'line dancing' is based on a de-territorialized, nostalgic re-interpretation of the 'old American West'.

If Jameson (op. cit.) views such mobilizations as merely the predictable manifestations of late capitalism seeking out new arenas in which to operate, then Hebdige (op. cit.) is more inclined to take the longer-term potential more seriously and to depict them as holding out the promise of new, radical telecommunicated global politics. Indeed, the 'flattening out' of cultural difference, riding on the back of telecommunication technology is, Robertson (op. cit.) opines, resulting in a heightened 'global consciousness'. There is a strong interest in fictional global narratives (that is, events that will have an impact upon everyone on the planet: for example, X-File-like story-lines about human cloning; the coming of aliens; global extinction by a meteor; or shared global predicaments associated with the ecological crisis or the emergence of new viruses and diseases): indeed, as Appadurai (1990) makes clear, people world-wide are increasingly living 'fictional lives', based on media narratives and imagery.

We conclude our exploration of 'global culture' by focusing upon what many would regard as its two defining (and interrelated) characteristics, namely that it is consumerist and also (to a large extent) postmodernist.

3.2 GLOBAL CULTURE AS GLOBAL CONSUMERISM

For many commentators (for example, Sklair, 1991; Lury, 1996) the emergence of global culture is the direct outcome of late capitalist restructuring to shape desires, create needs and, thereby, open up new arenas for capital accumulation. Some view this as an abject surrender to commodification, commer-cialization and consumerism (Foster, 1985) and blatant cultural degradation by the media, advertising and communication industries in their drive to maximize profits. As Beck (2000) comments, contemporary cultural globalization is 'a promising route to the profit-paradise' (p. 43).

Lifestyle choices lie at the heart of consumerism as dreams are marketed over genuine needs. Thompson (op. cit.) points out, among those who could afford it, shopping has long been far more than just purchasing goods: rather, shoppers feel that through the act of shopping they are buying into (however modestly) a more exciting, sensual world. The opening up of new markets is driven by the mass media (in particular, advertising and television) as the major conveyor of fashion and lifestyle imaginings. Signifiers of health, happiness, beauty and sexiness have been commodified and chained by association to products which, advertising assures, will automatically endow the user with the desired attributes (Williamson, 1990; Cook, 1994). Global consumerism thrives on the promotion of brand names like Rolex, Porsche, Chanel, Dom Perignon (as symbols of material success); of Nike and Reebok (of 'sportiness'); and of Emporium Armani and Versace (of fashionability). Transnational, transcultural aspirational clusters, based on what people would like to be rather than what they are, come into existence as a result of commercial lifestyling and are more 'real' to people today than the surviving vestiges of class solidarity. Indeed, the two great traditional markers of collective identity, nation and class, are seen to be disintegrating under the onslaught of global media, which now has the power,

to move people not just to buy the products of the culture industries, but to buy into networks that offer forms of community and alliance which can transcend the (old) confines of class, gender, regional and national culture. (Hebdige, 1989, pp. 90–91)

3.3 GLOBAL CULTURE AND POSTMODERNISM AS 'NEW TIMES'

As we have already noted in Section 2.5 above, many commentators link globalization with postmodernity and the highly diverse and mobile cultural forms comprising postmodernism, which is founded on the production and consumption of symbols (a feature of which is their speed of transfer), not just material objects. For Waters (op. cit., p. 156) it is the 'continuous flow of ideas, information, commitment, values and tastes mediated through mobile individuals, symbolic tokens and electronic simulations.' Harvey (op. cit.) alerts us to the product diversity now riding on the back of the increased speed of commodity circulation:

> Improved systems of communication and information flow, coupled with rationalisation in the techniques of distribution (packaging, inventory control, containerisation, market feed-back, etc.) make it possible to circulate commodities through the market system with greater speed. (p. 285)

But opinions vary about the worth of postmodernism, the hallmarks of which are 'hyper-commodification' (Crook *et al.*, 1992) and what Baudrillard (1983) terms 'simulacra'. There are those who praise its vitality, originality and ingenuity: it is seen to shrug off the old elitism of high culture and be eclectic, playful, ironic and innovative in film, fashion, literature and architecture. Incompatible worlds can coexist in the same space: it is common practice now, for example, to use the emotive appeal of classical music to advertise and sell cars, or link an operatic aria to a globally televised sporting spectacular. Thompson (op. cit.), commenting on the dynamism of contemporary cultural forms, discerns cross-overs between 'producers of cultural artefacts and the general public: architecture, advertising, fashion, films, the staging of multi-media events, grand spectacles, political campaigns, as well as the ubiquitous television' (p. 266).

However, one of the most frequent charges levelled at postmodern culture is that it is 'depth-less', little more than glossy appearance, illusion, superficial filmic images (Jameson, op. cit.), an attachment to cleverly crafted surfaces and effects. It is often described in terms of *mélange*, collage and montage: only such descriptions, it claims, are capable of capturing the novel cross-overs in musical forms, imagery, clothing, food and lifestyles now evident world-wide. For example, Pieterse (1995, p. 58) refers to the emergence of a global *mélange* as cultures and styles collide and merge, '. . . cultural hybridization reflects the mixing of Asian, African, American and European cultures: hybridization is the making of global culture as a global *mélange*'. Postmodernism's technologized base certainly makes previously unthinkable linkages possible as part of what Perry (op. cit.) terms its mass-mediated spectacle, carefully crafted and imbued with high entertainment value. Similarly, Lull and Hinerman (1997) see its hallmark as an insatiable appetite for media spectacles and scandals globalized by television.

In the light of all this it is not surprising, therefore, that Robertson (op. cit.) describes contemporary cultural globalization as nothing less than a 'postmodern game', one in which people world-wide are increasingly implicated and in which new traditions are constantly being invented. Cvetkovich and Kellner (op. cit.) echo this view when they write that we are living amidst the 'funhouse of hyper-real media images and the play of floating signifiers in the postmodern carnival' (p. 11). Similarly, Andrews (op. cit.) writing about the US's National Basketball Association sees it as an example of a 'hyper-real circus . . . a phantasmagorical cast of simulated characters' (p. 76). The NBA is, he argues, like Disney, a 'theme park', filled by imagined personalities and a non-threatening black style, a simulated racial harmony articulated in terms of the Reaganite policy of avoiding race by rendering racial divisions invisible. Television ensured the hyper-real, reconstructed NBA became globally available not as basketball, but as '. . . a phantasmagorical world of commodity signals, narratives and identities, triumphs and tragedies, successes and failures, heroes and villains' (p. 78).

4 CULTURAL GLOBALIZATION

What are the dynamics behind the unprecedented globalization of culture and 'global culture's' ever-increasing movement (in volume, variety and speed) across geographical, political and linguistic borders? Issues raised in this section are amplified in Parts B1, B2 and C1.

4.1 WHAT IS CULTURAL GLOBALIZATION?

Cultural globalization can be viewed in different lights, whether progressive and liberating or threatening, impoverishing and destructive of local culture and business. Similarly, local culture is sometimes regarded as something worthy under threat, whereas in other discourses it is presented as backward and parochial. Held *et al.* (op. cit.) identify three broad responses to cultural globalization, namely those who forecast cultural homogenization as an outcome of the impact of Western media and consumerism ('hyperglobalizers'); those who regard the impact of global culture as being relatively superficial ('sceptics'); and those who predict the emergence of new, exciting global cultural networks and hybrids ('transformationists').

What is undeniable, however, is that under the influence of globalization Western consumer culture has spread out and reconstituted across geographical borders. Of course, cultural transfer of sorts has always gone on in one form or another, but now time-space compression (Massey, 1994) has greatly accelerated it. The centre can now 'travel' to the periphery more easily (thus introducing new ethnic identities to cultures on the periphery) and, alternatively, the periphery to the centre (for example, through economic migrants and the importation of 'exotic' goods). As Cvetkovitch and Kellner (op. cit.) justifiably claim, '. . . there are now few corners of the world immune from the viral forces of a global consumer and media culture' (p. 15).

Contemporary cultural globalization, then, is generally seen as different from anything that has superseded in that, for the first time ever, it is impos-

sible to be unaffected by it wherever one lives. Held *et al.* (op. cit.) conclude: '. . . there is no historical equivalent of the global reach and volume of cultural traffic through contemporary telecommunication, broadcasting and transport infrastructures . . . (p. 327) . . . no historical parallel exists for such intensive and extensive forms of cultural flows that are primarily forms of commercial enrichment and entertainment' (p. 368).

4.2 AGENTS OF CULTURAL GLOBALIZATION

Held *et al.* (op. cit.) distinguish between new media technologies (clearly the leading agents of cultural globalization) and the corporate infrastructure within which they operate:

- *New media technologies.* Western consumer culture rides on the back of a communicational revolution. Technological changes have transformed the speed, capacity and sophistication of telecommunication systems as one innovation has followed another in quick succession. The Internet is now advancing rapidly (and, through ADSL, linking with television) and there is now the prospect of a global mobile telephone network. A host of new cable and fibre optic telecommunicational technologies are being developed, along with the digitalization and networking of televisions, telephones and computers. Meanwhile, the volume, intensity, geographical extensity and speed of messages are all increasing, with the ownership and use of satellite technology still heavily skewed towards the West.
- *The global media corporation infrastructure.* It is not just the technology *per se*, but the globalization of the corporate infrastructure in which it is embedded that is crucial. The deepening of global markets for films, music, television and news has been accompanied by the development of multinational culture industries incorporating a variety of alliances and projects. A group of around twenty-five huge transnational corporations

dominate the global markets of television, news and entertainment. The vast majority are US-based and all are in OECD countries. Among them are household names like Walt Disney, Time-Warner, CBS and Viacom and the leading global television providers are WTN, CNN, News International, with news controlled by United Press International, Associated Press and Reuters. Most combine media with widening business portfolios.

Held *et al.* (op. cit.) go on to identify the principal agents of cultural globalization, namely pop music, television, cinema, television and tourism:

● *Pop Music.* Pop Music is, without doubt, one of (if not 'the') great 'globalizers'. Dependent on neither written or spoken language, and locking into the universal human need for rhythm and melody, pop music is now, literally, 'everywhere'. The market is dominated by American pop music, followed by British, and has been closely allied since the mid-1950s to youth subculture. Pop music is the archetypal product of Western capitalism and the search is always on for novel musical sounds, styles and promotable 'stars'. Black, ethnic music and street music is repackaged to appeal to a wider audience and 'world music' occupies only a small share of the market (Robinson *et al.*, 1991) compared to Western pop.

● *Television.* Television now has a genuinely global 'reach' (although most receivers are obviously found in richer Western countries) and the growth of terrestrial channels has increased demand for Western imports. Televised sport, in particular football, attracts huge audiences worldwide. A combination of satellite and cable has facilitated cross-border ownership, but overall control is predominantly vested in Anglo-American hands.

● *Cinema.* Perhaps the biggest step towards the emergence of a global culture as we conceive it today came with the mass-mediation of moving pictures and sound recording. Waters (op. cit.) regards these technologies as 'democratising' in

that they blurred the distinction between 'high' and 'low' cultures, a distinction which has became increasingly hard to draw. Cinema is a hugely multinational industry dominated by the US as a producer and distributor while itself remaining largely impervious to foreign films. Meanwhile, India and Hong Kong have become important centres for Indian and Asian film production. Both the US and Indian film industry are immensely strong on their own turf, but (because of the global presence of the English language) US film can enjoy a global profile.

● *Tourism.* More people are now moving around the world than ever before and the World Tourist Organization estimates that tourist movement alone will soon be in excess of a billion annually. Most come from North America, Western Europe and Japan and (as will be evident in Part B2) their impact on the economic and cultural character of locales can be transformatory.

Sustained interpersonal interaction is the most powerful agent of cultural transmission, but how much genuine cultural intermingling actually occurs in touristic settings is open to question. At the heart of cultural globalization lies the two-way dynamic between the global and the local, namely: (1) the global's penetration of local culture; (2) the local's penetration of global culture.

The latter, however, is less common than the former and, when it does occur, is likely to be an exploitation of the local by the infinitely more powerful global media and cultural agencies. It is to this that we now turn.

4.3 THE GLOBAL IMPACTING UPON THE LOCAL

Obvious examples of global cultural products and businesses impacting upon the local are easy to identify:

● McDonald's, Burger King, Pizza Hut, Pepsi and Coca-Cola.
● Levi-Strauss, Benetton, Nike and Reebok.

- The American film, television and music industries.
- Global advertising (for example, for American Express).

In spite of the fact that in the non-Western (especially in the developing) world what is deemed 'desirable' and prestigious is frequently presented by advertisers as coming 'from abroad' (Classen and Howes, 1996). Classen (1996) found there was evidence of the selective incorporation of global market products to safeguard a distinct local identity. Imported goods are 'indigenized', their meanings transformed in line with the values of the host culture. To use an analogy, world-wide Coca-Cola is mixed with other drinks! Similarly, non-Western cultures are greatly influenced by Western dress codes. Craik (op. cit.) provides us with two examples where Western influences are 'localized' in non-Western cultures:

- Female politicians in Korea have developed a dual system of dress in which Western and traditional clothing are mixed. They wear the traditional Korean skirt and dress jacket ('hanbok') to assert nationalism, but on other occasions they wear Western clothes to convey Western values of material success and careerism.
- Hagan dancers in the New Guinea Highlands make outrageous costumes to outshine each other. To do so, they often incorporate into their native apparel Western objects like empty meat and fish tins, combs, labels and clips.

4.4 THE LOCAL IMPACTING UPON THE GLOBAL

Examples of the local swept up into the global are:

- Local products marketed globally as conveying some national 'essence' such as Fosters lager ('essentially Australian'); malt whisky ('essentially Scottish'); or even the Irish pub, complete with a fake ancient bicycle chained outside ('essentially Irish'), etc.

- Local foods that have been globalized, like Italian pizza, Indian curry, Chinese and Cantonese cuisine, or French, Californian and Spanish wines.
- African percussion rhythms, or Indian sitar music, incorporated into Western pop.

Furthermore, global companies like Benetton often market clothes based on the allure of difference and exoticism as Western designers plunder Indian, African and Oriental styles in search for that lucrative 'seasonal look'. The influence of non-Western styles is conspicuously flaunted and percolates down to the cheap versions sold in the high streets. Notions of 'difference' and of 'foreign-ness' can win competitive advantage (Axford, 1995).

Of course, the full impact of globalization impacting on the local is far more than the local availability of media products and other goods. This is well illustrated by: first, Albrow (1996) and, in particular, his study of the London Borough of Wandsworth (which is reproduced in Part B1, extract 3); and, second, by other writers (for example, Alleyne-Dettmers, Eade, Fennell and O'Byrne) in the thought-provoking volume edited by Eade (1997). Indeed, there is undoubtedly a growing interest among cultural anthropologists and ethnographers in observing the ways in which global consumer culture interacts with local culture and the mixtures that emerge (Huntingdon, 1993; Barnet and Cavanagh, 1994). Cvetkovich and Kellner (op. cit., p. 13) point to the importance of these interactions between global and local, claiming that these '. . . constitute the economic, political, social, cultural and even personal matrixes within which individuals increasingly live and die, define themselves and experience the world today.' Classen (op. cit.), for example, looks at the impact of Western consumerism in North West Argentina and discovers a 'surreal consumerism . . . a surreal juxtaposition . . . a society awash with the products and images of the global market' (p. 40). She records, among other things, the 'peddling of Santa Claus in the summer' and street vendors selling not traditional local goods, but 'aspirins, cassettes, razors, artificial flowers and posters of foreign rock stars'. Meanwhile, 'the latest model cars share the roads with horse-drawn carts . . .' (p. 52).

While cultural locals are undoubtedly absorbing elements of mass-mediated global culture, it must be borne in mind that there is likewise an insatiable demand for new cultural products (Fiske, 1989). Global consumer capitalism appropriates aspects of the local with profit potential; repackages them in idealized, decontextualized forms; and then promotes them in terms of their novelty value (for example, 'genuinely' ethnic cuisine, holidays, fashion and music, etc.). The development of a location as a tourist centre often leads to a revival of highly stereotypical, dubiously 'traditional' arts and crafts, furnishings, wood and leather working in order to meet global tourists' expectations. Indeed, much of a global tourist's experience consists of disembedded ethnic motifs.

It is becoming clear that the distinction between 'the local' and 'the global' has, as new geo-political and geo-cultural maps have emerged, become less and less meaningful. Production and consumption patterns are no longer firmly anchored in the local, yet 'local difference' is incorporated and utilized on a global scale. 'African' cloth is now made in Holland and Germany, and a high proportion of the clothes sold in British high streets are not manufactured in the UK. Increasingly the global has control over the local so that a drop in the stock market in any of the world's major economies has an influence throughout the entire world. The local is increasingly a hybrid formed out of regional, national and global forces and today no local is untouched by the global (Mohammadi, 1997), so much so that Robertson (1992, p. 37) suggests we might as well consider 'the local as a "micro" manifestation of the global' in that locals everywhere can no longer escape the influence of global mass culture. Meanwhile, Beck (2000) talks of cultural 'de-location' and 're-location' and concludes that '. . . local cultures can no longer be justified, shaped and renewed in seclusion from the rest of the world . . . there is a compulsion to re-locate de-traditionalized traditions within a global context of exchange, dialogue and conflict' (p. 47).

For Enloe (1989), too, the local is more and more a global product and Friedman (1995, p. 72) argues that 'localizing strategies are themselves inherently global'. Clearly the local is shaped by global trade, investment, speculation and cultural transfer and Hannerz (op. cit.) expresses this by referring to a globe-wide discourse of locality, by which he is pointing to the growing interconnectedness of local cultures in the climate of the global. Although everyday experience is necessarily local, it is increasingly for people everywhere shaped by global processes. However, as yet there is still no coherent, widely shared concept by people world-wide of 'global identity'.

Finally, it is worth bearing in mind that contemporary cultural change is at its most intense in some non-Western cultures where, to quote Axtmann (op. cit.), extreme dialectical tensions exist, '. . . between modernization and cultural indigenization, between the universal and the particular, and the global and the local – in short, the dialectic between homogeneity and heterogeneity' (p. 41).

4.5 'GLOBAL LOCALIZATION' AND 'GLOCALIZATION'

The 'local' and 'global' constitute a crude dichotomy and there is a need for intermediate concepts to analyse cultural globalization. Cultural globalization is not just a top-down process, but involves a process of localization. It is in the interest of global capitalism to stimulate local market diversity and both Coca-Cola and Sony use the term 'global localization' to describe the process whereby their products are embedded and then promoted within the local culture.

One leading writer who has devised another useful intervening concept is Robertson (1995), who uses 'glocalization', originally a Japanese marketing term, to indicate the targeting of goods and services on a global scale, but aimed at local markets. Indeed, 'the glocal' is held by him to be at the heart of contemporary globalization. He defines it as 'the creation and incorporation of locality, processes which themselves largely shape, in turn, the compression of the world as a whole' (p. 40). Likewise, another commentator (Luke, 1995) points to the emergence of what he terms 'glocal communities':

> 'The local' and 'the global' are commingling in new 'glocal' modes of production across and outside of national boundaries . . . Borders today are highly porous and the preserve of global flows of goods and services are continuously eroding them ever more every day . . . The modelling of their behaviour in production and consumption is more glocal than national . . . The notion of 'national interest' has less and less meaning in these glocal webs of interdependence. (p. 101)

4.6 CULTURAL MOVEMENT

One highly original commentator who has attempted to theorize some of the processes underpinning the movement of culture is Appadurai (op. cit.) and whose cultural 'flow' model is examined later in Section 7.5. Another is Hannerz (1991) who, in emphasizing that today a large number of people are directly involved with more than one culture, refers to what he terms a highly mobile and dynamic 'global ecumene': 'Humankind has finally bid farewell to that world which could, with some credibility, be seen as a cultural mosaic of separate pieces with hard, well-defined edges. Because of the great increase in the traffic in culture, the large scale transfer of meaning systems and symbolic forms, the world is increasingly becoming one, not only in political and economic terms . . . but in terms of its cultural construction as well, a global ecumene of persistent cultural interaction and exchange' (p. 107).

He generates two concepts to describe this cultural movement:

- 'situational tendency', in which a peripheral people are pounded from a cultural centre and eventually assimilate the incoming meanings and, in time, become indistinguishable from that centre.
- 'maturational tendency', which is the process whereby global cultural forms are absorbed and reproduced in the local culture. They coexist alongside the local culture and, in time, become hybridized.

He focuses on the differential aspect of global cultural influences, with particular reference to cultural reproduction in the Third World. While some local cultures are self-sufficient and can resist global influences (for example, Japan), less developed (or long-colonized) countries may have weakened cultures and less economic power to resist global cultural influences.

Hannerz (op. cit.) provides us with two further highly useful concepts: first, 'peripheral corruption scenario'; and, second, 'local cultural entrepreneurs', which he defines as follows:

- 'peripheral corruption scenario' is where a centre offers high ideas which are adopted by the periphery and corrupted. An example might be the adoption of the British judicial system in Nigeria, a country internationally ostracized because of its abuse of human rights;
- 'local cultural entrepreneurs' are key players in the localization of global cultural messages. An example would be Friedman's (1990; 1997) study of cultural production and consumption in the construction of identity among peripheral peoples. He points to the way in which imported designer clothes are worn with their labels sewn externally in Brazzaville, capital of the People's Republic of the Congo. Here, in a city known as the 'Paris of the Congo' but firmly on the periphery, local cultural entrepreneurs recycle these global cultural icons to connote success and international 'cool'.

However, debates still revolve around two opposing tendencies in cultural globalization, namely 'cultural homogeneity' and 'cultural hybridization', and it is to these that we now turn.

5 CULTURAL HOMOGENIZATION AND HYBRIDIZATION

One of the great debates continues to be whether the globalization of Anglo-American popular culture is having a homogenizing effect or leading to the development of new hybrid cultural forms. A third position is that globalization simultaneously results in a degree of both homogeneity and hybridization. Issues raised in this section are amplified in Parts B1, B2 and C1.

5.1 CULTURAL HOMOGENIZATION

The proponents of cultural homogenization argue that accelerating globalization in the form of global media, information systems and huge multinational organizations is eroding local cultures and traditions. Beck (2000) captures this well:

> In the villages of Lower Bavaria, just as in Calcutta, Singapore or the 'favelas' of Rio de Janeiro, people watch Dallas on tv, wear blue jeans and smoke Marlboro as a sign of 'free, untouched nature'. (p. 42)

Later he refers to the 'single commodity world' where local identities are replaced with 'symbols from the publicity and image departments of multinational corporations . . . satellites make it possible to overcome all national and class boundaries and to plant the carefully devised glitter of white America in the hearts of people all around the world' (p. 43).

Because the icons of Western (specifically American) popular culture are everywhere, it is commonsensical to believe that eventually all cultural difference will be erased and cultural sameness superimposed, fuelled by the immensely powerful, transnational media corporations. Indeed, until recently this was the widely accepted view. Hamelink (1983) was among a host of early commentators who were concerned that cultural diversity world-wide is under threat as everywhere begins to look and feel the same, what Tomlinson (1991, p. 135) terms a

'broad process of (cultural) convergence . . . in the cultures of the world.' A few years earlier fears of US media domination lay behind the McBride Report (1980), which led UNESCO to call for a restructuring of global media along more egalitarian lines. The World Trade Organization and the International Telecommunications Satellite Organization (Intelsat) are among the prestigious international bodies that have attempted to establish guidelines for the regulation of global cultural flows. Moreover, a number of countries have taken the fears of American cultural imperialism very seriously. For example, France, and, to a lesser extent Spain and Italy, have attempted to control American imports, especially film, by imposing tariffs. Canada, too, has long regulated the degree to which the US can be a stakeholder in the Canadian media and telecommunications industry. For political reasons China, Burma and North Korea monitor and seek to control incoming Western images and goods, while a stringent ban on satellite dishes still operates in Iran.

One way of approaching global culture is in terms of Schiller's (op. cit.) influential macro-economic domination theory which holds that cultural imperialism (and the anticipated cultural homogenization arising from it) results from multinational capitalism and its insatiable drive for new markets and maximum profits. This imperialism is particularly associated with the hegemonic cultural, economic and political role of the US. The apparent desire for all things American leads Andrews (op. cit.) to ask, perceptively, 'whether the global consumer is obsessed by the trappings of America *per se*, or whether the global mass market is merely dominated by American commodity signs . . .' (p. 82). However, America means different things to different people at different times and in different places (Lash and Urry, op. cit.) and we should be wary of the easy assumption that 'Americanization' will ever result in the elimination of local culture and the emergence of a homogenized global culture.

It is undeniable that new communicational technologies are shrinking the world and, as Cvetkovich and Kellner (op. cit., p. 3) put it, there is a 'dramatic penetration of global forces into every realm of life in every region of the world'. The fear is that, world-wide, local cultural difference is being attacked and eroded by mass-produced Western goods (James, 1993). This 'Coca-colonization' (Hannerz, op. cit.) is interpreted by some as a recolonization of the non-Western world by fetishized Western goods carrying with them hugely invasive connotations of Western success and affluence. Since the world is run in ways that both protect and promote Western political, economic and cultural values (Huntington, 1993), this process is extremely difficult to arrest. Indeed, technological advance ensures it is growing, resulting in the ever-widening spread of consumerism. Western media images are depicted as cultural invaders, effectively eroding indigenous cultures and spreading a commodified Western one.

5.2 THE ATTACK ON CULTURAL 'AUTHENTICITY'

Perhaps more than anything else, the global spread of consumerist culture is attacked for destroying 'cultural authenticity'. That which is 'authentic' is being replaced by cultural forms and practices that are false and shallow. An example often used is the impact of tourism and the emergence of the heritage industry. For Crick (1989), for example, the commodification of tradition has spelt the end of cultural authenticity. As we have previously mentioned, ethnic tourism and cuisine have to gratify the expectations of tourists so images and products are created, not in response to local, traditional values, but to meet the desires of Western consumers with money to burn. This is felt by many to hinder indigenous development, forcing people to become more Western at the same time as internalizing the West's (false) image of them. There is always a danger that in time people will come to accept the West's pastiche of their culture as 'authentic' (Gewertz and Errington, 1991; Graburn, 1995).

Another way in which 'authentic' local goods seem to be under attack is the careful glocal marketing of global products by identifying with salient features of the local market. Global goods are advertised and promoted in local terms, sometimes with comic results (Solomon, 1994). Conversely,

Western manufacturers retail (often bizarre) versions of local products in the West.

In summary, the cultural homogeneity thesis boils down to a fear that everywhere is, at least culturally, becoming similar and that local and national cultures ('ethnies') are being subsumed by a shallow, inauthentic and synthetic global culture based on the economic domination of the West and the products of the gigantically powerful, transnational media operators like CNN, Sky, Time-Warner and the Sony Corporation: nowhere in the 'borderless world' (Ohmae, 1990) is now beyond the reach of their 'electronic arms'. These fears about cultural imperialism are passionately held, fuelled by the ready availability of ever-cheaper technologies (televisions, video recorders and camcorders, audio and video cassette 'Walkmans', etc.) pumping out what Western cultural critics dismiss as a globe-wide menu of cultural pap. Indeed, the most pessimistic version of cultural imperialism sees local culture being eradicated and surviving only in museums and heritage centres. Similar misgivings are even evident in a rich country like the UK, where there is considerable concern that the whole 'British way of life' is under attack not only from the other side of the Atlantic, but from the European Union and the move towards increased political and economic integration.

5.3 OBJECTIONS TO CULTURAL HOMOGENIZATION

At the outset it must be stressed that accurately measuring the actual degree of cultural change is notoriously difficult. No culture anywhere exists in a 'pure', pristine state: all cultures have changed over time and continue to change (although, clearly, the speed of change varies from one to another). Cultural anthropologists who focus on 'local arrangements' (or what Douglas and Isherwood, 1979, term 'assemblages') and the manner in which new meanings are locally attached to imported goods (for example, Wilk, 1996; Weismantel, 1989) throw a valuable light upon cultural globalization. Moreover, cultural globalization is uneven in its impact (for example, it is clearly greater in a 'global city' like London than in an isolated rural community in the Shetlands). There has undeniably been some degree of homogenization through the global flow of mass cultural consumption (especially among young people) and this has predominantly been 'from the West to the rest'. But many have questioned whether the homogenizing effect of Western culture (and US media in particular) has been as deep and enduring as is commonly assumed (for example, Sinclair *et al.*, 1996). Similarly, Held *et al.* (op. cit.) question whether the homogenization of consumption in the area of American film and television has been translated with the same vigour into other cultural arenas. They claim, too, that there is evidence that 'after many decades of US commercial domination in popular culture, local and national alternatives are reviving' (p. 373).

Others observers doubt, too, whether national cultures are, in fact, being destroyed and point out that they have long been hybridized (Bird *et al.*, 1993). It is difficult for example, to define, given its diversity, what 'British' or 'American' culture really is. Indeed, Pieterse (op. cit.) argues that 'continued accelerating globalization means the hybridization of (already) hybrid cultures' (p. 64). Neither can homogenization be assumed to be straightforward. Howes (1996) expresses this well when he argues that the assumption that goods, on entering another culture, will inevitably retain and communicate the values they are accorded by their culture of origin must be questioned. It is a grave mistake to treat people as passive receptacles of cultural products because reflexivity (in the form of people's perceptions) intervenes. How we react to cultural products (whether music, fashion, television) will vary and there is unlikely to be a uniform response (Miller, 1992; Thompson, op. cit.). The global is received in different ways in different locals and there is unlikely ever to be a homogeneous global television audience: for example, 'EastEnders' is 'received' and 'read' differently when watched in London, Rio or Madras. Similarly, McDonald's and Coca-Cola are vehicles for potential cultural globalization but, as Axford (op. cit.) points out: '. . . while these products are consumed around the world, their reception is "localised" and made sense of through local world views and cultural practices' (p. 160).

Held *et al.* (op. cit.) state this even more strongly: '. . . simple notions of homogenisation, ideological hegemony or imperialism fail to register properly the nature of these encounters and the interplay, interaction and cultural creativity they produce' (p. 374).

While national and local cultural identities cannot escape being influenced by global cultural flows, it does not then follow that they are necessarily reconstituted by them (Held *et al.*, op. cit.). Friedman (op. cit.) in his study of a small Hawaiian village notes that, although Miloli is intricately involved in the larger world, its inhabitants protect and 'localize' their culture. Similarly, Axtmann (op. cit.) argues that recipients of media texts inevitably bestow their own meanings upon them and interpret them in line with their own cultures, modifying cultural products in line with personal needs. Because of this, the very 'Western-ness' of the global cultural message undermines its capacity to create a global culture. The result, he maintains, is that 'political, economic and cultural aspects of globalization will result in the proliferation of cultural "particularisms", collective identities and the political creation of "otherness"' (p. 48). He has little sympathy with the view of an emerging cultural homogeneity, even less an economic one: the reverse, in fact, in that the forces of cultural and economic homogeneity are, paradoxically, likely to 'accentuate heterogeneity and fragmentation. Global capitalism is still best analysed as a system of structural inequality' (p. 34).

5.4 ALL-CONQUERING 'WESTERNIZATION'?

People appear to be able to slide between experiences of both the local and the global in their everyday lives, but the 'televised global' is seldom experienced as being as tangible as one's own, everyday, local life. Furthermore, advocates of cultural homogenization often forget the rate and magnitude of contemporary cultural change and the complexity of the interaction between the global and the local. Pop music and McDonald's may be everywhere but, clearly, they do not erase local culture. Indeed, people have the capacity to 'belong' to a number of cultures or sub-cultures simultaneously; inhabit a number of cultural arenas; and juggle multiple cultural affiliations. Indeed, Hannerz (op. cit.), in rebutting any hasty assumptions of cultural homogenization, argues that an openness to foreign cultural influences need not result in an impoverishment of local and national culture. On the contrary, it can provide people with technological and symbolic resources for managing their own culture in new ways. Far from the global swamping the local, it can stimulate a revival of local culture.

This view is echoed by Tomlinson (op. cit.) when he writes that 'cultural synchronisation could in some areas increase variety in cultural experience' (p. 113). Talk is often of all-conquering Westerniza-tion, yet he reminds us that this is perhaps a prema-ture assumption and poses a question: 'When Japanese exports to the US exceed American exports to Japan, is not the spectre of Western consumer imperialism an outdated myth?' (p. 188). Undoubt-edly the largest impact is that of Western, specifi-cally American, culture (widely criticized for being a 'civilization of the image'). However, Huntington (op. cit.) reminds us, as a counterweight to this, that we should not forget the de-Westernization and indi-genization currently occurring in many non-Western cultures. Axtmann (op. cit.) sees ethno-nationalism and religious fundamentalism as attempts to recon-struct traditions in the face of homogenizing cultural globalization, as 'a re-affirmation or re-invention of a particularistic collective identity' (p. 40). Similarly, many interpret the new social and religious move-ments as acts of resistance to Westernization. Held et al. (op. cit.), moreover, claim that there is evidence that cultural flows have begun to be reversed '. . . primarily through migration but also through other cultural forms shifting from South to North and East to West. Music, food, ideas, beliefs and literature from the South and East have been percolating into the cultures of the West, creating new lines of cultural inter-connectedness and fracture' (p. 369).

Cultural influence is often assumed to be solely a Westernization process even though the West con-sumes goods from outside the West from Japanese cars to Mexican food. Indeed, the world post-World War II seems to have been subjected to a dual process of Americanization and Japanization. However, the low prestige value associated with non-Western man-ufacturers means the origins of Eastern and Far Eastern goods are often obscured in order to make them more profitable. Their origins are disguised by the use of Western brand names and neologisms like Gold Star (Korea), Panasonic and Walkman (both Japan). This leads Classen and Howes (op. cit.) to conclude that: '. . . while Western cars may be adver-tised in Japan with Western actors, Japanese cars are not advertised in the West with Japanese actors, but in "typical" Western settings' (p. 185).

Likewise, non-Western products (for example, Eastern goods or Colombian coffee) are often adver-tised in the West by stressing the exoticism of 'the other'. A final irony is that many non-Western coun-tries, rather than passively succumbing to the deluge of Western goods, exploit their popularity and adapt them, as in the counterfeiting of expensive watches and perfume, capturing the image, not the quality.

Another charge levelled against those who deplore the damaging effects of cultural homogenization is that they are guilty of a 'particularly Western-centred concern'. Tomlinson (op. cit.) reminds us that the critique of homogenization may turn out to be a particularly Western-centred concern. What might be perceived as an example of cultural homogeniza-tion by the cultural tourist might not be interpreted in the same way by local people. He gives as an example a tribesman who is the proud owner of a stereo cassette player. Does he view this as a regret-table outcome of 'creeping capitalism'? If the tribesman was to adopt 'the privileged role of the cultural tourist would the sense of the homogeniza-tion of global capital have the same threatening aspect?' (p. 109).

It might be claimed that people's needs are similar everywhere and that cars and televisions cut across cultural divides. Tomlinson (op. cit.) asks why we should be concerned if everything becomes similar if it is the outcome of autonomous choices? Writers like Sola Pool (1979) defend the free market and see the development of a homogenized, globally shared culture. The crucial issue is whether the valorization of cultural difference includes acceptance of cannibalism, slavery, torture, female circumcision and state control.

Alternatively, the wider availability of quality health care, hygiene, food, along with tolerance and democracy – all aspects of culture – are highly laudable and beneficial. Tomlinson (op. cit.) asks are critics of homogeneity objecting to homogeneity *per se* or to a certain kind of homogeneity based on the spread of Western popular culture and comments that it is 'quite different to object to the spread of something bad than to object to the spread of uniformity itself' (p. 113). He comments:

> we can safely say that a substantial number of people in developing societies are willing recipients of 'imperialist media texts'. . . the temptation is strong for intellectuals who do feel cultural imperialism is a 'threat' to 'speak for' the culture by attributing a form of 'false consciousness' to the masses who don't. (p. 94)

He further argues that fears of homogenization are not compatible with the ways in which ordinary people live their lives:

> In everyday activities like working, eating or shopping, people are likely to be concerned with their immediate needs – their state of health, their family and personal relations, their finances and so on. In these circumstances the cultural significance of working for a multinational, eating lunch at McDonald's, shopping for Levis, is unlikely to be interpreted as a threat to national identity, but how these mesh with the meaningful realm of the private: McDonald's as convenient for the children's birthday party; jeans as a dress code for leisure-time activities . . .' (p. 87)

5.5 CULTURAL HYBRIDIZATION

Cultural 'hybridization' (sometimes termed 'creolization') is best defined as a process of recontextualization and meaning re-attribution: foreign cultural imports are assigned fresh meanings within the receiving culture. The focus is upon reception and the consumer's meaning-making as they are inserted into new cultural surroundings, but in which:

> there is no guarantee that the intention of the producer will be recognized, much less respected, by the consumer from another culture. . . . The potential, therefore, is for the emergence not of global cultural homogenization, but for a plethora of new local, hybrid forms and identities. (Howes, op. cit., pp. 6–8)

Globalization has indubitably increased opportunities for the movement of people, goods, businesses and services to operate in markets beyond national borders. Appadurai (op. cit., p. 303) aptly describes this de-territorialization as 'money, commodities and persons ceaselessly chasing each other around the world'. Meanwhile, transnational diaspora are producing conditions for new hybridized cultures and identities (Lash and Urry, 1994) and Waters (op. cit.) observe that globalization is resulting in a heightened and more mobile 'ethnic pluralism' also a 'greater connectedness and de-territorialization. The possibility arises, therefore, of an increased measure of ethnic pluralism, but in which ethnicities are not tied to any specific territory or polity' (p. 136).

The cultural upheaval occasioned by globalization is at its most intense in non-Western cultures (Axtmann, op. cit.), but world-wide there is increased intercultural communication and openness to new cultural influences; increasing numbers of people have become multicultural in that they are now actively involved in more than one culture; and there is a greater tolerance of other cultures. Ethnicity no longer resides in the narrowly local, as is witnessed in the proliferation of ethnic cuisine, ethnic fashion, ethnic holidays and ethnic music. All over the globe there has been an indigenization of music, art, architecture, film and food and what was feared by many (namely Western cultural domination) is becoming less likely. The strong version of cultural homogeneity is now widely rejected as simplistic in that it overlooks: (a) how global cultural products are assimilated within 'locals', and (b) how non-Western cultures impact upon the West (and upon each other).

Rather than the emergence of a homogenous global culture, we appear to be witnessing the birth of a greatly increased global cultural diversity:

> From world music to exotic holidays in Third World countries, ethnic television dinners, to Peruvian woolly hats, cultural difference sells. In the commodification of language and culture, objects and images are torn free of their original referents and their meanings have become a spectacle open to almost infinite translation. (Rutherford, 1990, p. 11)

However, Pieterse (op. cit., p. 60) points out that cultural hybridization will not necessarily weaken existing relations of power or in any way threaten Western cultural hegemony. Although the emerging global culture is held to be the product of inter-culturalism rather than multiculturalism, 'being modern' (wealthy and powerful) still largely equates with 'being Western'.

Cultural globalization is likely to produce both similarities and, at the same time, differences. It is for this reason that Archer (1988; 1990) sees cultural 'dis-integration' and 're-integration' simultaneously taking place on both state and international levels. Cultural flows are seen to produce degrees of both cultural homogeneity and heterogeneity, the product being transnational, hybridized 'third cultures', which cannot be understood merely as the product of bilateral exchanges just between nations. Rather, new global processes (based on the increased flow of images, knowledge, ideas, information, goods, services and people) are making available new cultural possibilities as the world becomes both a more culturally singular and, paradoxically, a more diverse place.

5.6 PROCESSES OF CULTURAL HYBRIDIZATION

Far from homogenizing, globalization is seen to occasion difference, what Waters (op. cit.) describes as a two-way process of 'de-classifying' and 'de-differentiating' culture. Howes (op. cit.), in particular, draws attention to the importance of the context of reception of global goods and the consumer's meaning-making. As a consequence, there is 'no guarantee that the intention of the producer will be recognized, much less respected, by the consumer from another culture'. (pp. 5–6). Subversions can take place between production and consumption as goods are 're-made on the street':

> The world as seen through the window of the corporate boardroom situated on the twentieth floor of some glass office tower may well look like a single place . . . but as we know from anthropology, there is rather more going on 'out there'. (Howes, op. cit., p. 7)

In cultural hybridization globalization is seen to be setting up a dialectic between the local and global, out of which are being born increased cultural options. A good example is that of 'global food' which 'has simultaneously encouraged the expression of sameness and difference . . . re-authenticating local identities in a "global context"' (James, 1996, p. 84). It purposely blends together culinary traditions and openly exploits heterogeneity in a *mélange* of East and West, often exploiting connotations of the exotic. It is not unusual to find foods from very different culinary traditions (for example, curried chips with a pasta dish or lasagne, etc.) on the same menu in international hotels and airports. Food globalization is also evident in the convenience foods on offer in giant UK superstores like Tesco and Sainsbury, where sauces spice up plain dishes with 'sexy' Italian, French or Cajun flavours.

6 MEDIA IMPERIALISM AND 'GLOBAL MEDIA'

Media (in particular television and film) is the crucial agency in cultural globalization. But are earlier fears about American media imperialism unfounded in the light of what we now know about media reception? Issues raised in this section are amplified in Parts C1 and C2 below.

6.1 MEDIA IMPERIALISM

Debates surrounding cultural imperialism focus upon the perceived threat of cultural domination posed by the economically powerful Western culture industries through their ownership of the means of production and transmission of cultural goods within the global capitalist market. In this perspective what is generally termed 'global culture' is held to be an ideological tool in the service of a revitalized, accelerated phase of global capitalism, characterized by Lash and Urry (op. cit.) as 'the end of organized capitalism'. Western control of the world economy and technological domination (especially of the media) is the bedrock upon which cultural hegemony is built. Writers like Mattelart (1979); Mattelart *et al.* (1984) and Schiller (op. cit.) have long placed media imperialism at the heart of this, but tend to assume that watching American television means that American values are assimilated. Others (for example, Kroker and Cook, 1988; Lull and Hinerman, 1997) also point to television as being seminally important, lending support to Tomlinson's (op. cit.) argument that we are living in a global society which is increasingly becoming a mirror of television.

However, advocates of media imperialism are surprisingly vague about how media messages are actually received in specific cultural contexts and tend to assume that imported media inevitably results in cultural subordination and cultural homogeneity. Many fail to locate media within local discourses and practices that inevitably shape its reception. Following on from Held *et al.*'s (op. cit.) threefold typology of responses to globalization,

Mackay (2000) examines the spread of global media, specifically television. He sees arguments falling into three categories, which he terms 'globalizers' (whether positive or pessimistic); 'traditionalists'; and 'transformationalists'. What does he mean by each?

- *Globalizers.* Positive globalizers view increasing media flows as opening up positive opportunities (the Internet, for example, as holding out the possibility of giving 'voice' and democratizing communication on a world-wide scale). Pessimistic globalizers, however, point to the increasing inequalities occasioned by the concentration of media ownership in the hands of the media global corporations led by Time-Warner, Disney, Bertelsmann, Viacom, Tele-Communications Incorporated, News Corporation and Sony who largely control the content, production and transmission of television globally (along with films, music, videos, news, cartoons and sports). Their media products join other American consumer products and, together, constitute a huge deluge of material threatening local cultures everywhere.
- *Traditionalists.* Traditionalists are less concerned about the long-term colonizing impact of 'global culture'. For example, CNN International carries a high proportion of American news and a low proportion of international news. Countering this is the fact that world-wide it is only available to a modest number of households. Also, global television imports are often use to fill less popular slots in viewing schedules and domestic television (local and regional) appears to have retained its popularity for viewers. To equate television volume with cultural impact is, therefore, problematical. UK domestic television, for example, shows a high proportion of imported programmes during the night, when it is watched by a relatively small viewing audience consisting of day workers, the unemployed and insomniacs! Traditionalists confidently point to the vitality of local cultures (as opposed to the shallowness of much imported media) and their ability to resist erosion by American media intrusion. Indeed, some commentators (notably Sparks, 1998) assert

that there is, in fact, no such thing (as yet) as 'global television'.

- *Transformationalists*. Transformationalists argue that transnational flows of television are more varied than either the globalizers or traditionalists acknowledge. They turn to research which demonstrates not passive consumption, but the active engagement of audiences when watching television (for example, Miller, 1987, and Liebes and Katz, 1993). Also, they question the picture of unidirectional television flows from America and point to countervailing flows (for example, Latin American television links with Spain and Portugal and Latin American television programmes exported to the US). Sinclair *et al*.'s (op. cit.) notion of 'geo-linguistic regions' (regions linked linguistically, culturally and historically) is seen to provide a more sensitive analysis of the multidirectional flows of television globe-wide, regionally and locally).

6.2 MEDIA RECEPTION

Notions of unidirectional cultural imperialism and electronic colonialism will always be problematic because, according to Bredin (1996):

> the cultural conditions under which electronic media and messages are received affect the uses to which technologies are put and the meanings produced. The persistence of cultural tradition is related to strategies of resistance and these often generate transformation in the dominant modes of mass communication. (p. 161)

Meanwhile, Tomlinson (op. cit.) asks how (since it is not cultural imposition by coercion as in colonial times) can cultural practices be imposed in a context which is no longer actually coercive? Is contemporary global culture simply a set of 'mediated images' or a more complex 'mediation of cultural experience'? (p. 35).

The charge that transnational corporations coerce Third World countries into buying goods that have no real use or meaning for them, and which play no

authentic role in their culture, may be justified. But what must not be assumed is 'passive consumption'. Rather, the ability of consumers to indigenize products to serve their own cultural interests must be stressed, along with the resistance strategies people employ against any easy take-over of their way of life. The evidence to date suggests that those most heavily subjected to a barrage of global consumerist goods are well aware of transnational cultural dumping as an aspect of environmental degradation. While some commentators accuse Third World countries of encouraging the proliferation of Western products and images and, thereby, 'colonising themselves', another point of view is that of Howes (op. cit.): 'Rather than let consumer goods colonize them, local peoples instead "colonize" consumer goods, imposing their own system(s) of values and practices on them and maintaining their cultural integrity' (p. 191).

Much of the research emphasis to date has been on global media institutions rather than on how audiences respond to imported media texts. Bredin (op. cit.) argues that global media must be viewed in terms of its local impact and it is a mistake to privilege the international over the interactional. In a revealing study she monitored the introduction of radio and television into aboriginal communities in northern Canada and reports little evidence that watching television caused viewers to reject traditional values. They consciously brought into play resistance strategies that owed much to their historical experience of colonialism and Bredin (op. cit., p. 163) concludes that they used radio and television as a 'means of cultural self-definition and translation' and that, generally, studies fail to take into account 'the historical processes of contact and change which (such) aborigine groups have previously negotiated' (p. 165).

Conversely, global media providers often adapt their outputs to cater for local tastes: MTV, for example, adapts to local audiences and cuts down on its American content, mixing it with local news in Europe, Asia and Latin America (Negus, op. cit.). Indeed, local broadcasting is often a *mélange* of locally produced and imported items. For example, BBC Radio Wales blends together local, Welsh regional, British and international items in its news programmes (as does the *Western Mail*, Wales' premier daily paper). The Welsh-language television channel S4C broadcasts live football from Spain and Italy in Welsh with English subtitles for non-Welsh-speaking viewers. In Los Angeles there is a Spanish radio station run by Spanish immigrants and broadcasting a mixture of English and Hispanic music while promoting Spanish identity and local links with Spain. Hybrid programmes incorporate elements of both Spanish and American culture and, in the process, aim to appeal both to Spanish and non-Hispanic American listeners.

6.3 'THE MOMENT OF CULTURAL IMPACT'

What happens at what Tomlinson (op. cit., p. 70) aptly terms the 'moment of cultural impact'? The mere availability of American commodities clearly must not be uncritically equated with the Americanization of local cultures (Barker, 1999). In fact, if Bredin (op. cit.) is to be believed then it can result in the converse, namely the reaffirmation of local and national cultural identities. In the past commentators have been too ready to depict 'the masses' as easily succumbing to and allowing themselves to be manipulated by global consumer culture. The fact is that while Western commodity signs are globally circulated, on reception they are often reworked and given new meanings. It is for this reason that Cvetkovich and Kellner (op. cit., p. 27) repeatedly call for a deeper exploration of 'the complex relations between local situations and their global contexts'.

Tomlinson (op. cit., p. 63), focusing on the reception of global television, argues that this is shaped by what is going on in people's lives and which is far more powerful than mere representations. He draws a distinction between 'culture-as-lived-experience' and 'culture-as-represented-in-media', but the problem remains that the nature of the 'effects' are still poorly substantiated and a great deal more work needs to be done on what Ang (1985) terms the

'interpersonal drama' of texts: that is, how media products are interpreted (even subverted) in different cultural contexts. Two decades ago Fejes (1981), for example, was attacking the unexamined assumptions about the manipulative effects of media products and calling for studies of their cultural impact and reception: to watch Western television programmes does not necessarily mean people 'become Western'. Furthermore, it is all too easy to underestimate the audience's sophistication and active engagement with imported texts (Katz and Liebes, 1985; Liebes and Katz, op. cit.). As Tomlinson (op. cit., p. 56) concludes, '. . . people are too active and complex in their responses to texts for the claims of widespread easy cultural manipulation to stand' and are 'less deceived than critical media theorists have supposed' (p. 57).

An early study by Dorfman and Mattelart (1975) of Donald Duck presents the comic strip as a hugely invasive and effective ideological tool which conceals the true, exploitative nature of Western capitalism. They assume its effects but, as Boyd-Barrett (1982) argues, this ignores the processes by which individuals interpret media imports. Cultural imperialism is too often viewed as an ideological property of the media text itself (big cars, rich men, beautiful and available women), rather than how it is received. Tomlinson (op. cit.) accordingly argues that: '. . . what the cultural critics overlook(ed) is the capacity of the audience to negotiate the possible contradictions between alien cultural values and the "pleasure of the text"' (p. 46).

He also introduces the useful term, the 'focus of meaning': if most people's focus of meaning is in the family and personal-sexual relations, then it is hardly surprising that the reception of programmes like Dallas is likely to be primarily shaped by these concerns. Dallas will be received differently in different places. Moreover, it has spawned a whole genre of local versions, as in the case of Mexican and Brazilian 'telenovelas'.

Contemporary research on media reception presents viewing not as passive assimilation, but as active transformation of images and in line with the receiver's cultural norms and values. Roth and

Valaskakis (1989) make clear that imported media can be appropriated to serve the needs of local audiences. For example, Harding (1995) shows how WBA imagery, as broadcast on Sky TV, has been appropriated by young British inner-city black youth as an affirmation of their own identity through a celebration of American blackness and an assertion of the 'cultural other' (Hall, 1991) within British society. Likewise, 'global stars' like Madonna are everywhere and are used in identity construction locally, but are articulated variously according to how they are received. Madonna, for example, is received differently by different constituencies world-wide, whether teenage girls, heterosexuals, gays, lesbians or ethnic audiences. Rather than being an actual person she is best regarded as a carefully crafted, polysemic 'text', composed of a set of signifiers to guarantee her appeal to a multi-segmented global audience (Henderson, 1993). Similarly, Valaskakis (1988) shows how a popular American television character of the recent past ('the Fonz' in the comedy 'Happy Days') was variously received in very different cultural locales.

It is hard not to disagree with Tomlinson (op. cit.) when he writes that: 'Extravagant claims for media power seem to arise where theorists come to see the media as determining rather than as mediating cultural experience: that is, at the centre of things rather than as related to other practices and experiences' (p. 63).

There is an accumulating body of research to justify the assertion that at least at the level of audiences 'it is inconceivable that there could be a global culture' (Lash and Urry, op. cit., p. 308). Furthermore, claims of media imperialism which assume the undiluted reception of images (that is, unaffected by the receiver's age, gender, ethnicity and geography), or which do not distinguish between the contexts of media production and media consumption, are ethnographically naïve.

7 KEY THEORISTS

The eminent commentators below mirror the earlier distinction made between:

- 'global culture-as-product' (particularly as an aspect of postmodernism, namely Harvey, Baudrillard and Virilio); and
- 'cultural globalization-as-process' (and the originators of the two leading models to theorize it, namely Robertson and Appadurai).

7.1 DAVID HARVEY

The overcoming of space (by increasing travel speed and, thereby, reducing travel time) has always been a way of ensuring profit. The spate of inventions in the last part of the nineteenth century and into the early twentieth century (for example, the steam train and ship, the internal combustion engine, aviation, the telegraph, telephone and wireless) 'reorganized space' to reduce time and 'reorganized time' to reduce space and were motivated by the lure of commercial advantage and, thereby, financial gain. Similarly, the two world wars drove ahead, as part and parcel of the war effort, spectacular advances in communications, jet propulsion and rocketry. Today (as mentioned previously) we are witnessing a blossoming of communicational and informational technologies linking the computer, television, telephone, satellite and cable. Space has been 'technologically eliminated'. The instantaneity of 'real time' coverage on global television means we can be both 'there' and 'here', an experience that is sure to grow with the development of virtual reality technologies about to come on stream. As these innovations develop, costs of both operation and equipment drop, as in the case of the advent of wide-bodied jets on long-haul journeys and international freight through the introduction of containers with greater capacity.

Harvey's 1989 study of postmodernism has already achieved the status of a classic. His account of the history of time-space compression advances the case that market forces have always been at its heart (encapsulated in the old adage that 'time costs money'). He identifies the economic depression that swept Britain and Europe in 1846–47 as a turning point in that thereafter, throughout the latter half of the nineteenth century, there was a radical readjustment in the sense of time-space in economic, political and cultural life. Europe had already reached such a degree of spatial integration in financial life that the whole continent was vulnerable to simultaneous crisis-formation. The result was that the old Enlightenment certainty of 'absolute space and place' collapsed in the face of insecurity of 'relative space and place' and in which events in one place impacted on several others. Indeed, he traces the development of modernism as a response to the crisis experienced after 1848 in the changed relationship between time and space; the gradual growth of globalism; and the speeding up of capital circulation. The question after the turbulence across Europe in 1848 was, 'What time are we in?' But why was this? He attributes it to a number of factors:

- The invention of new technologies of communication like the telegraph, telephone, wireless, the cinema and photography. It was at this time that the first radio signal was beamed around the world from the Eiffel Tower. Perhaps most remarkable of all was how quickly the telephone (especially in the US) became a popular business and domestic technology (Harvey points to the fact that in 1914 alone 38 billion telephone calls were made in the US).
- The development of new technologies of transportation like railways, balloons, steam ships, the bicycle, motor cars, aeroplanes, airships, tube trains and tube networks in cities like London.
- The emergence of new systems of credit, corporate organization, distribution, investment, foreign trade and production (for example, Ford's invention of the assembly line).
- Big advances in science, like the X-ray and, most influential of all, Einstein's theorizing (1905 and 1916).
- Imperial conquest and colonial de- and re-territorialization. As Harvey says, by the 1880s it was possible to read about yesterday's Imperial adventures in the morning paper. By the latter half of the nineteenth century the shrinkage of space was bringing previously autonomous communities into touch and there were already signs of what we now see in contemporary globalization, namely superficial homogeneity superimposed on underlying diversity.
- A succession of 'World Exhibitions' from 1851 onwards.
- Meanwhile, artists began to explore the nature and meaning of time in new ways and began to decompose the traditional space and format of painting (as in Manet and, later, Picasso and Braque) and writers to question the traditional meaning of space-time (as in Proust and Joyce). Artists abandoned homogeneous space and linear perspectives and photography (including aerial photography) and advances in printing made possible radically different perspectives on the earth's surface than had been previously available.

In view of the rapidity of these developments perhaps it is not surprising that by 1911 a progressive group in Germany was calling for the establishment of a 'world office' to organize human affairs more efficiently on a world scale, an ideal of fraternal co-operation in stark contrast to the first global conflict in 1914–18.

Taken together these developments were undoubtedly the 'nail in the coffin' for Enlightenment ideals of time-space relations as the 'truth of experience' no longer coincided with the place in which it occurred. With reference to postmodernity, Harvey (op. cit.) points to the immensely varied, consumer-driven product diversity now riding on the back of the increased speed of commodity circulation, all of which had its origins in the latter half of the nineteenth century:

Improved systems of communication and information flow, coupled with rationalisation in the techniques of distribution (packaging, inventory control, containerisation, market feed-back, etc.) now make it possible to circulate commodities through the market system in ever greater speed. (p. 285)

7.2 JEAN BAUDRILLARD

A key figure in debates exploring the link between postmodernism and globalization is undoubtedly Baudrillard (op. cit.). His argument is that reality has been joined (if not partially replaced) by a media-generated 'hyper-reality' which, in turn, has resulted in a 'decomposition of cultural meanings'. Time-space compression has exaggerated tendencies already present in modernism and Baudrillard attempts an analytical account of postmodernism in which consumption is now seen to play the critical role in defining people's identities and consciousness so that styles of consumption are held to have super-seded the old class-consciousness. Baudrillard provides us with a compelling theory of commodity culture in which the world is constructed out of 'simulacra' (or simulations) which have no founda-tion in any reality except their own. In Baudrillard's eyes mass media is not a means of communication since there is no dialogue or feedback. Rather, it is a carefully constructed entertainment and he appeals to us all not to take it seriously and, thereby, to refuse to play the 'media game'.

Baudrillard focuses upon the media's capacity to seduce us with its simulations, which can be more authentic than the original and undermine any contrast to the real by absorbing the real within itself (Poster, 1986). Examples might be the images of a country in a travel advertisement; or newly made, reproduction furniture which is even more 'authentic' than the genuine period pieces. Indeed, a simulation can fit the stereotype better than the original. As a consequence, in a televisual culture based on simulacra, it is becoming more and more difficult to distinguish the 'real' from the fake, the hyper-real, which is increasingly becoming even 'more real' than the original. It is no longer a matter of the false representation of reality, but that the real is no longer 'real' anywhere. Baudrillard's 1983 study of Disneyland illustrates how hyper-reality actually operates. Disneyland is a play of illusions, which encapsulates America's values in comic strip form and, in the process, conceals the contradictions in American society (Perry, op. cit.). Disneyland simu-lates a false, idealized reality by packaging what is understood as being the essence of a nation (and carefully excising from view anything that might contradict it, like rubbish on the roadway or vagrants in doorways).

Similarly, a soap opera may be fiction, but it is 'real' in its impact on its viewers. Media images do not merely represent reality: they are reality because their meaning derives from their position within a system of signs and not from reference to the 'real world' outside that system. Media uses rapidly changing montages of micro images etched in light which have no firm origin or referent, deriving their meaning not from reference to external reality, but from their relations with each other. Baudrillard argues that a multiplicity of constantly shifting cultural codes are at work and that there is no longer a fixed metacode against which they can be judged and to which they all relate.

Although a controversial figure, it is undeniable that Baudrillard's influence has been considerable and many have taken him, with varying degrees of enthusiasm, as the starting-point for their own analyses (Perry, op. cit., details some of these). An example of one such writer is Luke (op. cit.), who points to the virtual, hyper-real nature of what he depicts as the new 'global territories' which fuse the local and the global. This takes further Massey's (op. cit.) view that under globalization a new sense of place and culture has developed as opposed to the more closed, introverted sense of place and culture of the past. These new global territories are in-creasingly the venue for social, political, economic and cultural creolization. However, he sees '. . . the concrete reality of place . . . gradually being displaced by the tangible, imaginary flow (of) . . . networks of informational circulation' (p. 100).

Globalization is being accompanied by the emergence of a 'cybersphere', more specifically a 'telesphere', which is coextensive with, but distinct from, the natural biosphere and the industrial technosphere. It is composed of: '. . . artificial spaces created by streams of data, audio and video. In this third nature, there are innumerable new regions of action, developing their own agendas, interests and values beyond, behind and beneath the nation state' (p. 93).

In other words, globalization has spawned a 'placeless' sense of the real, one based on simulation. He comments:

> Simulation in the global flow goes beyond the old realist dimensions of space and time, sender and receiver, medium and message, expression and context as the world's complex webs of electronic media generate unbound areas of new hyperspace with 'no sense of place'. (p. 97)

We are currently witnessing the emergence of artificial 'neo-worlds' and 'techno-regions':

> transnational topographies and trans-cultural territories emerge in the flow from processes of international communication, travel, commerce and transportation. No longer grounded in one planetary place, one ethno-national location or one environmental site, these semi-imaginary, semi-concrete neo-worlds form their own diverse techno-regions of socio-economically re-engineered cultural space. Increasingly they are also becoming the most meaningful homelands of contemporary individuals and groups. They are simulations of territory, models for behaviour, circuits of operationalization that frame thought and action globally. (p. 103)

For Luke (op. cit.) the virtual spaces he terms 'neo-worlds' are now at the very heart of the global postmodern: 'The third nature of cyberspace exists in mappings, simulations, linkages, imageries and models that are beyond the containment of nation-states in the neo-worlds of postmodern time-space compression' (p. 106).

The notion of hyper-reality is, however, not just applicable to culture. The use of new communicational technologies in international financial transactions have given rise to a hyperspace of 'fast capitalism' as the global flow of capital, energy, goods and people speeds up to accompany the proliferation of images, simulations and symbols. These bypass geographical and political boundaries; are beyond the constraints of space and time; and, in this sense, are 'post-historical'.

7.3 PAUL VIRILIO

Virilio's (2000) argument is that what we commonsensically understand as the 'here and now' of territory is being redefined globally by the new technologies linking satellites to televisions, telephones and computers. The 'real time' of telecommunications ('action-at-a-distance') has superseded the 'real space' of immediate action. So much now 'happens' without the need to go anywhere and an 'instantaneous present' has been substituted for the old sovereignty of territory:

> The relationship between space and time has been changed by technology, so much so that there has emerged an instantaneous, interactive 'space-time' that has nothing in common with the topographical space of geographical or even simply geometrical distance. (p. 2)

Spatial distance is being transformed 'tele-topologically' (p. 4) as 'space-speed' gains dominance over 'space-time'. 'Electronic meteorology' is ensuring the electro-optical environment now replaces the classical ecological environment. The whole world is available to the gaze of orbiting satellites, so much so that we can now talk of a 'telepresent', or 'a real-time, tele-reality is supplanting the reality of the real-space presence of objects and places' (p. 7). 'Real-time' has won out over 'real-space' and the world is being reduced to 'one huge cathode shop window' (p. 4). Through the 'electronic window' of television the 'real-time of live television broadcasting prevails over the real space of a land actually crossed. . . .' (p. 10), so much so that we can now make journeys without actually moving. A 'teletopian reality' (or a 'tele-living present') is now indistinguishable from, and has become part of, 'real life'.

The relationship between time and space has been transformed to such an extent that 'the instant interface is being substituted for the longest journey times' (p. 21). What he terms 'polar inertia' is setting in that 'now everything arrives without any need to depart' (p. 21). Image transfer can take place on the spot: from now on 'the speed of light has the upper hand over sunshine or ordinary lighting'

(p. 58) '. . . we are witnessing . . . the progressive disappearance of the space of anthropological-geographic reference in favour of a more visual piloting . . .' (p. 76). He argues that technological globalization has made 'inertia' the defining condition of our time, dominated as it is by the 'electro-optical environment'. The outcome of all this is that we are really becoming 'tele-actors in a living cinema' (p. 23) '. . . inhabiting not so much the time of clocks and calendars as that truer-than-nature "real time" . . .' (p. 31). With the development of increasingly more sophisticated computer graphics we will soon have as 'reality' an interactive virtual environment and will end up: 'acting instantaneously in a geographical environment that has itself become virtual' (p. 85).

A parallel argument is that of Auge (1995), who sees us living in 'supermodernity' (even 'hyper-modernity'), which is the product of global technology and the 'global play of reflections dependent on the whim of the remote control button' (p. 109). He distinguishes between 'place' (which is encrusted with historical moments and social life) and 'non-place' (where individuals are connected in a uniform manner and where no organic social life is possible). It is a characteristic of supermodernity that we are in transit through these non-places for more and more of our time, examples of which are motorway and aircraft travel, shopping, hotels, airports, or sitting in front of computers or television, etc. These 'non-places' are like parenthesis through which daily lives in supermodernity move. They are defined by words and texts, by tickets, passes, visas and passports. He presents Disney as an example of the fictionality of the world, what he terms 'spectacularizing' and sees non-places having the capacity to fictionalize. He concludes that:

> one is never far from Disneyland in an airport or a big hotel and it is, moreover, very seldom that one does not come across some traces of its presence there on a poster or in a window display. Mickey's ears are listening all over the world. (p. 115)

Finally, in *War of Dreams* Auge (1999) turns his attention to the role of dreams, myth and fiction in the age of satellite television and the Internet. He argues that it is a defining feature of supermodernity that the border between reality and fiction is constantly blurred as reality is 'fictionalized' by the global mass media.

7.4 ROLAND ROBERTSON

Roland Robertson (op. cit.) has been the principal catalyst behind the development of the sociology of cultural globalization as the world witnesses the ever-developing cross-cultural, transnational production of meanings and the local becomes an aspect of the global. An extract from his important contribution to understanding globalization (in collaboration with J. A. Chirico) appears in Part B2(11). He argues that it is difficult to predict the outcome of globalization and rejects its depiction as no more than modernity (or late modernity) operating on a global scale (Giddens, op. cit.) since this underestimates the significance of the politics of global culture, including issues relating to ethnicity, race, nationalism and gender. Instead, he advances a model which, he claims, accounts for heterogeneity and distances himself from earlier ones like Wallerstein's (op. cit.) world systems theory in which capitalism was seen to operate globally but which he feels ignores the complexities and contradictions inherent in contemporary cultural globalization. Instead he stresses the increased interconnectedness between selves, humankind, national societies and the world system of societies.

He emphasizes the extent to which people are more and more aware of living in the world as one place. Life everywhere is increasingly shaped by global events, globalization always involves a process of localization. However, across the world there is growing consciousness of interdependence. He claims that 'globalization as a concept refers both to the compression of the world and the intensification of the world as a whole' (p. 8). Although it permeates the affairs of all societies across the world, it will never result in the emergence of a single, cohesive system. He points to the paradox that, while the concept of the homogeneous national society is breaking down, '. . . in an increasingly globalized world there is a heightening of civilizational, societal, ethnic, regional and, indeed, self-consciousness' (p. 27).

Robertson (op. cit.) depicts globalization as being driven by a two-way process, namely the 'universalization of particularism' and the 'particularization of universalism' (p. 100). Global capital, for example, is increasingly tied to world-wide, universalistic supply and particularistic demand, bringing culture and economy together in the 'tailoring of products to increasingly specialized regional, societal, ethnic, class and gender markets – so-called micro-marketing' (p. 100). This echoes earlier work by Archer (op. cit.), who contrasts localism (characterized by 'bounded cultures' and face-to-face relations) and cosmopolitanism (transnational cultural networks extended in space through new communicational technologies).

The interpenetration between 'the particular' and 'the universal' delineates a set of principles underlying contemporary globalization, including 'the interpenetrating processes of socialisation, individualisation, the consolidation of the international system of societies, and the concretization of the sense of humankind' (p. 104). People are influenced by the global, but this is interpreted locally and local transformations are as much a part of globalization as the lateral extension of social connections across time and space. It is for this reason that it is important not to see globalization as 'squeezing' locals, but as a dialectic, with people as intermediaries between the global and the local. Mass communication and travel bring the world to the individual and the individual to the world. Meanwhile, time-space compression means that people (certainly the technology and information rich) are living in a shrinking world of 'reflexive interlocutors'.

Universalism is rarely a straightforward 'top-down' imposition because, as Spybey (op. cit., p. 34) says, 'social institutions do not reproduce themselves, but have to be reproduced by human beings'. Similarly, Smith (1992, p. 66) writes about the reception of Western cultural products in the Third World: '. . . the audiences in Third World countries tend to interpret these products and experiences in ways that are specific to the perceptions and understanding of their own peoples.' Beck (op. cit., p. 45) echoes this in that 'globalization does not mean globalization automatically, unilaterally or one-dimensionally'.

Global culture is the product of a continuous interplay between its universalistic aspects and its particularistic reproduction. Its outcome is uncertain and is, as he puts it, 'up for grabs', pointing to the business and economic success of Japan as an example of universalistic particularism. The Japanese selectively incorporated ideas from other cultures so particularizing the universal and incorporated into their production methods the Confucian stress upon loyalty and routine, application and efficiency, along with the Samurai group tradition. Western production methods were imbued with East Asian traits. What has resulted is a unique Japanese particularism that has become widely accepted as Japanese production methods have now been influential world-wide.

The process of cultural globalization is not without its paradoxes. Robertson maintains that cultural difference is a key ingredient of late capitalism, along with the creation of transient micro-markets (whether national, gendered, ethnic/racial, social and stratificational, etc.). A number of commentators have noted that while the world has, indeed, become a 'smaller' and more unified place (in terms of economy, human rights and communication) it has simultaneously become culturally more diverse. We are, argues Waters (op. cit.), witnessing,

> a complex interweave of homogenizing with differentiating trends . . . the globalization of popular culture has apparently paradoxical, but actually consistent, effects in simultaneously homogenizing and differentiating. Certainly it can homogenize across the globe in that what is available at any locality can become available in all localities, but at any particular locality it can increase the range of cultural opportunity. (p. 40)

In conclusion, the Robertson model is a strong and confident rebuttal to those who interpret globalization as solely a macro-scale matter and who play down the individual dimension. It alerts us to the paradoxes of cultural globalization as a process based on both centralization and, at the same time, decentralization. It also highlights the fact that objective globalization (driven by the global economy and telecommunicational technology) is, simultaneously, subjective globalization, resulting in new, more complex identities in the face of increased polyethnicity, multiculturality, diasporations and the opening up of post-colonial spaces. His work has stimulated a developing sociology of globalization based on glocal cultural investigation as the products of the global are interpreted locally. Globalization, as Beck (2000) points out, '. . . can be grasped in the small and concrete, in the spatially particular, in one's own life, in cultural symbols that all bear the signature of the glocal' (p. 49).

7.5 ARJUN APPADURAI

Appadurai (op. cit.) is currently one of the most influential analysts of globalization and an extract from his work appears in Part B1(5) below. He insists from the outset that cultural globalization does not mean that the world is becoming more culturally homogeneous. In fact, it is a hugely unsettled one witnessing complex movements of people, ideas, images, finance, technology, labour and culture. His 'flow' model offers an original way of conceiving of this, dispensing with the notion of a dominant centre and a dependent periphery and, instead, presenting a more mobile, dynamic, process-based model. These 'flows' are carried on by a variety of agencies and are 'inflected by the historical, linguistic and political situatedness of different sorts of actors, whether nation states, multinationals, sub-national groups, and religious, political and economic movements, villages, neighbourhoods and families' (p. 296).

He identifies five 'flows', namely ethnoscapes, technoscapes, financescapes, mediascapes and ideoscapes (and Waters, op. cit., adds a sixth, an extension of ideoscapes, namely 'sacriscapes':

- *Ethnoscapes*. These refer to the movement of people, whether immigrants, exiles, refugees, guest workers or tourists. Today the movement of people is at an unprecedented level as people move further, faster and more frequently. Increasing numbers of people are on the move for different reasons (for pleasure, for work, for survival, etc.), but when they do so, so do ideas, goods and cultures. The established links between place, state and notions of nationhood are being disrupted more and more by the movement, resettlement and diaspora-creation.

- *Technoscapes*. Messages now move instantaneously and in greater volume across the planet. Geographical and political boundaries have been rendered 'porous' (for example, by the Internet). Technoscapes have resulted in 'increasingly complex relationships between money flows, political possibilities and the availability of both low and highly-skilled labour' (pp. 297–98).

- *Financescapes*. The speed and volume of global capital flows are both rapid and complex and national economies can no longer stand alone, but are linked through a global grid of capital transfer. Traditional indicators of national wealth (like a country's GNP) are increasingly less significant in the global economy. Currency markets, stock exchanges, commodity speculators and banks world-wide move capital around the globe in order to generate the highest rates of return. Given the sheer scale and speed of currency transfer it is not surprising that global fiscal crime is massively on the increase.

- *Mediascapes*. These are 'image-centred, narrative-based accounts of strips and bits of reality' (p. 299), interconnected repertoires of print, celluloid and electronic screens now disseminated globally. He indicates both the positive and negative aspects of mediascapes. Global media can expand 'the horizons of hope' (as they did in the case of both the eastern bloc countries and South Africa); be informative and emancipatory; aid progressive thinking and transnational links; and elevate small or marginalized 'voices' to the global stage. Mediascapes refer, however, not only to the messages and images, but also to the motives of the small number of gigantic corporations (mostly American) that largely control the production and transmission of global television.

- *Ideoscapes*. Ideoscapes are composed of the 'big' ideas, ideologies and counter-ideologies. Among these are: notions of citizenship, freedom, franchise, democracy and representation; welfare and human rights; equality of opportunity; the privacy of persons and of property; sovereignty and patriotism; individual and collective responsibility; and the value of rationality and of a rational mind. Ideoscapes do not just refer to capitalist principles, however, but also to those underpinning communism, socialism, liberalism and fascism. Waters (op. cit.) points to what he regards as an omission, namely what he terms 'sacriscapes', or religious ideas and their associated values.

He maintains that to understand contemporary globalization is to appreciate its complex, dynamic, interactive set of processes. Capital, labour, finance, technology and cultural artefacts now operate globally. Central to Appadurai's model is that the most significant global flows occur both in and through growing disjunctures between the flows. Furthermore, Appadurai (op. cit.) asserts that global media has the effect of blurring the division between the realistic and the fictional: 'an important fact of the world we live in today is that many persons on the globe live in "imagined worlds", and not just in imagined communities, and are thus able to contest, even subvert, the "imagined worlds" of the official mind and of the entrepreneurial mentality that surround them . . . These offer a series of elements (characters, plots and textual forms) out of which scripts can be formed of imagined lives, their own as well as those of others living in other places' (p. 299).

Beck (op. cit., 2000) picks up on Appadurai's notion of 'possible lives'. Personal identity is to be understood less in terms of geography, nation, ethnicity and culture, but in terms of how people dream:

'More people in more parts of the world dream of and consider a greater range of possible lives than they have ever done before . . . The spectacles through which people perceive and evaluate their lives, hopes, setbacks and present situations are made up of the prisms of possible lives which television constantly presents and celebrates. Increasing numbers of people world-wide are bombarded by the global imagination industries' version of glittering, enticing commodity forms of possible lives. (p. 54)

8 THE EXTRACTS

What is 'globalization'? How does it operate, particularly with reference to the globalization of culture? What are the outcomes? How does it affect people world-wide? What is the role of the 'local-global' nexus? Why is the twenty-first century already being labelled the 'global age'? What light do the social sciences (including media and cultural studies) throw upon globalization? What key concepts can be brought into play to analyse and theorize globalization?

These and many other questions were in our minds when writing the General Introduction, which is supplemented below by extracts from the works of leading commentators on globalization.

Part A sets out to define globalization. Part B focuses on globalization and culture. Part C has as its subject the primary role played by the media (especially television) and other communicational technologies in globalization, whilst Part D contextualizes the above in the new configurations emerging in the 'global political economy'.

PART A

GLOBALIZATION AND SOCIETY

The extracts in Part A raise a number of issues such as:

- How 'globalization' is defined by a number of leading commentators.
- The nature of globalization (in the eyes of Giddens and Robertson, including Albrow on the 'global age').
- Hirst and Thompson's controversial assertion that globalization is a myth.
- Debates concerning the impact of globalization (including Tomlinson's important contribution).
- Globalization and 'Late-' (or 'Post-') Modernity.
- The changing nature of 'global scale' and Massey on 'time–space' compression.
- Globalization and the corporate organization, including 'globality' as a form of management.
- The emergence of 'global civil society' and an accompanying sense of 'global citizenship'.
- Finally, the focus falls upon the hierarchy of 'global cities' that are now at the heart of the fast-developing 'global economy' and of the global 'information society'.

1 A SHRINKING WORLD

Nigel Thrift

That light overhead, the one gliding slowly through the night sky, is a telecommunications satellite. In miniature, it contains the three main themes of this chapter. Through it, millions of messages are being passed back and forth. Because of it, money capital seems to have become an elemental force, blowing backwards and forwards across the globe. As a result of innovations like it, the world is shrinking – many places seem closer together than they once did.

The satellite is itself a sign of a world whose economies, societies and cultures are becoming ever more closely intertwined – a process which usually goes under the name of globalization (Giddens, 1991). But what sense can we make of this process of globalization? Again, the satellite provides some clues. Those millions of messages signify a fundamental problem of representation. Simply put, the world is becoming so complexly interconnected that some have begun to doubt its very legibility. The swash of money capital registering in the circuits of the satellite comes to signify the 'hypermobility' of a new space of flows. In this space of flows, money capital has become like a hyperactive child, unable to keep still even for a second. Finally, the shrinking world that innovations like the satellite have helped to bring about is signified by time-space compression. Places are moving closer together in electronic space and, because of transport innovations, in physical space too. These three simple themes of legibility, the space of flows, and time-space compression can therefore be seen as 'barometers of modernity' (Descombes, 1993), big ideas about what makes our modern world 'modern' . . .

So how might we see barometers like illegibility, the space of flows and time-space compression? To begin with, we can recognize that a globalizing world offers new forms of legibility which in turn can produce new forms of illegibility. For example,

electronic telecommunications provide more and new kinds of information for firms and markets to work with but the sheer weight of information makes interpretation of this information an even more pressing and difficult task (Thrift, 1994). The space of flows is revealed as a partial and contingent affair, just like all other human enterprises, which is not abstract or abstracted but consists of social networks, often of a quite limited size even though they might span the globe. Finally, time-space compression is shown to be something that we have learned to live with and are constantly finding new ways of living with (for example, through new forms of subjectivity). It might be more accurately thought of as a part of a long history of immutable mobiles that we have learnt to live through and with. After all, each one of us is constructed by these 'props', visible and invisible, present and past, as much as we construct them.

From: A hyperactive world, by Nigel Thrift, in *Geographies of Global Change*, edited by R. J. Johnston, P. J. Taylor and M. J. Watts, Blackwell, 1995.

2 GLOBALIZATION

J. Lull

The term 'globalization' has been coined to describe the scope of current developments in communication and culture (Featherstone, 1990). But this term must be qualified. We do not live in a global village where a mythic, all-encompassing, technology-based super society replaces outdated and unwanted local social systems and cultures. Despite technology's awesome reach, we have not, and will not, become one people. It is true that potent homogenizing forces including military weaponry, advertising techniques, dominant languages, media formats, and fashion trends undeniably affect consciousness and culture in virtually every corner of the world. Such spheres of

From: *Media, Communication and Culture: A Global Approach*, by J. Lull, Polity Press, 1995.

influence introduce and reinforce certain standardizing values and practices. But these political–economic–cultural influences do not enter cultural contexts uniformly. They always interact with diverse local conditions. Put into practice on a global scale, homogenizing cultural forces encounter a wide variety of ideologies and traditions producing a range of 'heterogeneous dialogues' (Appadurai, 1990). Just as TV programs, films, and popular music don't turn individual consumers into passive dupes in any single society, the power to transmit information worldwide likewise does not stimulate automatic imitation or conformity at the national or cultural level.

Forces of modernity have no doubt changed the face of world cultures and altered political-economic relationships too. But the resulting pervasive globalization is 'more an organization of diversity than a replication of uniformity' (Hannerz, 1990). Local and regional influences do not disappear in the face of imported cultures. The very concept of culture presumes difference. As British sociologist Anthony D. Smith points out:

'If by "culture" is meant a collective mode of life, or a repertoire of beliefs, styles, values, and symbols, then we can only speak of cultures, never just culture; for a collective mode of life, or a repertoire of beliefs, etc., presupposes different modes and repertoires in a universe of modes and repertoires. Hence, the idea of a "global culture" is a practical impossibility' (1990, p. 171).

Even the nation-state, which by some accounts these days is declining in power as a necessary social structure, still demarcates important cultural differences. One need look no further than the effort to bring the 'European Community' together to see how difficult it is to unify and politicize cultural differences.

---

3 WHAT IS GLOBALIZATION?

C. Barker

Globalization is constituted by a set of processes which are intrinsic to the dynamism of modernity and as a concept refers both to the compression of the world and the intensification of consciousness of the world as a whole (Robertson, 1992), that is, the ever increasing abundance of global connections and our understanding of them. As I have already suggested, the 'compression of the world' can be understood in terms of the institutions of modernity and thus globalization can be grasped in terms of the world capitalist economy, the nation-state system, the world military order and the global information system (Giddens, 1984; 1985), whereas the reflexive 'intensification of consciousness of the world' can be profitably viewed through more postmodern lenses.

On one level globalization is an economic phenomenon. One half of the world's largest economic units are nations, the other half consists of transnational corporations. The top 200 transnationals, 89 of which are based in the US and 25 in Japan, produce between a third and a half of world output. In the sphere of car production 22 firms produce 90 per cent of global production (Giddens, 1989). Such productive activity has to be financed and to do so an Australian based company might consider Japanese loans arranged by a New York bank's London offices. These could be arranged at any time of the day or night with the aid of electronic communication. Globalization thus refers to economic activity on a global scale and is an aspect of time-space compression or the 'shrinking world' . . .

Economic globalization has been a process of creating a world economy, though one which has grown in an uneven way. Both 'world systems theory' (Wallerstein) and 'dependency theory' (Frank) in their protests against global inequality tend to obscure some of the differences between regions; we need to recognize degrees of incorporation into the world economic order and the various levels of econ-

---

From: *Global Television*, by C. Barker, Blackwell, 1997.

omic development. There are, for example, not only differences between the western capitalist zone and the former eastern bloc nations, but also between newly industrializing nations like Brazil, Mexico, Taiwan, South Korea, Hong Kong, Singapore and the seven poorest nations on earth: Chad, Bangladesh, Ethiopia, Nepal, Mali, Burma and Zaire (Worsley, 1990).

Globalization is also concerned with issues of cultural meaning, including issues of texts, representation and identity. This is an enormous field of concerns which I do not intend to explore fully here. At this stage I simply wish to raise some interrelated issues. For example, Walter Benjamin (1973) pointed out the way in which 'originals' associated with the rituals of specific places (art galleries, theatres) were being outstripped by art made specifically for reproduction so that 'originality', in the historical sense, becomes the luxury preserve of the wealthy. The contemporary implications of this are manifold, but include the idea that culture can span time and place, that culture in the age of electronic reproduction will come to us via the screen, video, radio, etc. rather than us going to it in a ritualized space. Cultural artefacts and meanings from different historical periods and geographical places can mix together and be juxtaposed.

The values and meanings attached to place remain significant, but the networks in which people are involved extend far beyond their physical locations. The combination of historical population migration with the world-wide circulation of images has created new global identities so that, for example, black people in Brixton, Johannesburg or New York may have forms of solidarity and sympathy with each other far stronger than any they have with their next-door neighbour. Democratic forces world-wide may show solidarity with the students of Tianenmen Square by employing fax machines, and Greenpeace can come to form a globally effective campaigning organization, not least through the strategic use of television images (Hebdige, 1990).

As Hebdige (1990) argues, cosmopolitanism is an aspect of day-to-day life. Diverse and remote cultures are becoming accessible today (as signs and commodities) via our televisions, radios, supermarkets and shopping centres. We may choose to eat 'Indian', dress 'Italian', watch 'American' and listen 'African'. However, such globalizing cultural tendencies need to be counterpoised to the re-emergence of the politics of place. Thus, attachment to place can be seen in the renewal of forms of Eastern European nationalism, neo-fascist politics and, to some degree, Islamic fundamentalism which, though itself having global aspirations, can be understood in part as a response to the spread and perceived threat of western modernity. All the examples above are to do with cultural difference and the creation of new alliances across national boundaries connected with those identities. Are we witnessing, then, the creation of regional or even global meanings shared by the majority of people? Is there in any sense a global culture? To the degree that there is, television is playing a significant role in international image and information flows.

What is 'global culture'?

If by 'global culture' we mean a unitary world culture, or a bounded culture connected to a world state, then we are a long way from such a scenario. As Smith (1990) has pointed out, cultures tend to be particular, time-bound and expressive of identities which historical circumstances have formed over long periods. Such cultural feelings and values refer to three components of shared experience: a sense of generational continuity, shared memories of specific events and people, and a common sense of destiny on the part of the collectivity. As yet, Smith argues, there is little in the way of shared world memories to underpin a global culture. On the other hand, we may be able to identify global cultural processes, of both cultural integration and disintegration, which are independent of inter-state relations. Some of these processes represent homogenization, particularly in the field of commodities and consumer culture, so that Coca-Cola, the Big Mac and Dallas are known world-wide, while others involve ethnic resilience, fragmentation and the re-emergence of powerful nationalistic sentiments associated with the myths, memories and symbols of local places rather than global spaces.

Clifford (1992), among others, has argued that culture and cultural identities can no longer be adequately understood in terms of place, but are better conceptualized in terms of travel. This includes peoples and cultures which travel and places/cultures as sites of criss-crossing travellers. In one sense this has always been the case; consider Britain as at various moments populated by Celts, Saxons, Vikings, Normans, Romans, Afro-Caribbeans, Asians, etc., so that the 'English' language is a hybrid of words from all over the world. Likewise, the US, home of native American Indians, English, French, Spanish, Africans, Mexicans, Irish, Poles and too many more to mention. However, the accelerated globalization of late-modernity has increased the relevance of the metaphor of travel because all locales are now subject to the influences of distant places. Such influences include electronic communication like television, so that we can all be travellers from the comfort of our front rooms.

Further, at any given moment, identity of place, that is, national identity, is only one competing subject position among many others. This is a stance underlined by Giddens (1985) when he argues that, for most people most of the time, national identity is not at the forefront of their minds. Identity and meaningful experience are much more likely to arise in the realms of the private spheres of family, friends and sexual relationships. Since day-to-day life is one geared to routine, national sentiments are not only distinct from them but tend to rise and fall according to circumstances.

While such processes are evident across the boundaries of nation states the continued resilience and significance of the state is also a feature of our times. What we are seeing is a set of economic and cultural processes dating from different historical periods and with different developmental rhythms being overlaid upon each other, creating global disjunctures as well as new global connections and similarities. For example, the expansion of capitalism, the globalization of financial flows, the movements of ethnic peoples, the development of technology, the spread of the media and the diffusion of ideologies are not set in any inevitable or fixed relationship to one another: rather the need is

to try and understand just exactly how they are related (Smith, 1990). The relationship between economic globalization and world cultural processes is, thus, not straightforward. Having said that, many of these issues are bound up with the economics of capitalism and consumer culture which represents a decisive – though not wholly determining – moment.

---

4 GLOBALIZATION AS GLOBAL AWARENESS

J. Friedman

In recent years there has developed a relatively large literature dealing with globalization. Much of this discussion has centred on what at first appeared to be an aspect of the hierarchical nature of imperialism, that is, the increasing hegemony of particular central cultures, the diffusion of American values, consumer goods and lifestyles. In some of the earliest discussions it was referred to as 'cultural imperialism' and there was great alarm concerning the obliteration of cultural differences in the world, not just in the official 'economic' periphery but in Western Europe where, in the late 1950s and 1960s, there was a genuine fear, at least among the cultural elites, of the 'defi americain' and the hegemony of Coca-Cola culture. Today this theme has been developed primarily in the work of cultural sociologists and, more recently, among anthropologists, into a more complex understanding of cultural processes that span large regions of the world. Robertson has recently formulated the question of globality as a duality of objective and subjective processes. 'Globalization refers both to the compression of the

From: Global system, globalization and the parameters of modernity, by J. Friedman, in *Global Modernities*, edited by M. Featherstone, S. Lash and R. Robertson, Sage, 1995.

world and to the intensification of the consciousness of the world as a whole' . . . (1992, p. 8).

In my own terms, globalization is very much about global awarenesses but, also, about the way in which they are established in definite periods of the history of already existing global systems. Globalization is about processes of attribution of meaning that are of a global nature. This should not be conflated with global processes of attribution that are local, such as nationalisms, ethnicities, Balkanizations, which are in fact localizations rather than globalizations. Robertson's universal religions establish transnational identities, but they can only do so if those who participate in them actually identify as such. Buddhism, for example, is very local in Sri Lanka, where it is strongly tied to the constitution of the state itself. Its more ecumenical versions in California and elsewhere, as global movements, have a very different focus. The fact that Nigerians watch Dallas might be a very localized phenomenon among actual viewers who, even while they are aware of the imported (that is, global) status of the programme, may use such status to define a set of local hierarchical relations that bear little resemblance to the society that produced the programme. But the cosmopolitan who chuckles at this fact is the true representative of globalization since the meaning that he attributes to the appearance of Dallas in Africa is global in nature, the meaning of the cosmopolitan, equivalent, I would argue, to the meaning of the modern. The formation of ethnicities and nations, while a global product, cannot be understood in terms of cultural diffusion. While Robertson apparently agrees with Wallerstein's characterization of nationalism as a global phenomenon, the latter sees it in terms of global forces and relations themselves and not the spread of an idea. Particularization is a product of the global system in particular phases of its 'development' and not a general characteristic, of the 'global field'. For example, the appearance of Fourth World movements for the re-establishment of cultural–political autonomy among indigenous peoples is a global process in social terms. It is a change in identification that has accompanied the decline of modernist identity in the hegemonic centres of the world

system. Yet the forum offered by the World Council of Indigenous Peoples, the large number of media reports, Hollywood films such as 'Dancing with Wolves' have all heightened the representability of Fourth World peoples as such. The latter phenomenon is globalization, but here too, its appearance now is a determinate product of the global system in a phase of decentralization and de-hegemonization . . .

---

5 GLOBALIZING THE WORLD
A. Mohammadi

Some communication scholars believe it important to examine the global development of international communications (Frederick, 1993; Hamelink, 1994; Stevenson, 1993; Schiller, 1996). By 'globalization' scholars refer to the way in which, under contemporary conditions especially, relations of power and communication are stretched across the globe, involving compressions of time and space and a recomposition of social relationships. Schiller (1989; 1996) and Hills (1986) have drawn our attention to rapid market changes as one consequence of deregulation and, furthermore, the emergence of not only new mega corporations, but also a new class of merchants of cultural commodities, entertainments and information technology. This class Bagdikian usefully names 'Lords of the Global Village' (Bagdikian, 1989) . . .

Other scholars believe that by globalizing the world through the electronic highway it is possible 'to govern' the world (Schiller, 1996). The rapid development of satellite communications is crucial here if the rest of even the Western world is to keep up with the US. By removing distance, satellite

From: Introduction, by A. Mohammadi, in *International Communication and Globalization*, edited by A. Mohammadi, Sage, 1997.

communication is a major factor in the globalization of the market. Similarly, computerization is a precondition of the information economy. Schiller suggests that one of the reasons why the US wanted to capture the control of international communication circuits from British cable interests was to build satellites 'to bypass the British Empire's monopoly in international communication' (Schiller, 1996, p. 93).

Today, one of the most significant functions of globalization is the so-called 'free flow of information'. If we consider CNN a global corporation, its major function is news and information, but this news service is constructed from a mainly US perspective. In a similar way, US cultural industries and media entertainment based on the doctrine of the free flow of information have had influence all over the whole world.

The present plan of constructing an information highway in the West means better access for US global firms to global markets. They are already in a dominating position. The information highway will be at the service of those countries that can afford to pay for the information. Building and owning the electronic highway will be especially beneficial to those firms that are mainly US-based. As history since World War II has shown, US companies always lead the global market. Schiller indicates that 37,000 companies 'currently occupy the command posts of the world commercial order, the largest 100 transnational companies, in 1990, had about $3.2 trillion in global assets, of which $1.2 trillion were outside of their own home countries' (Schiller, 1996, p. 94).

We should also note that Time-Warner, Bell Atlantic, AT&T, IBM and COMCAST are the largest players in cultural commodities, communication and information technology in the world today. In the face of the gigantic power of transnational corporations, it is not clear what will happen to the role of nation states. Many critics predict 'the end of the nation state'. Jean-Marie Guehenno (1995), for example, asks a very important question: without the nation, can democracy survive? It is hard to imagine a world which, in the twenty-first century, may be dominated by a few transnational compan-

ies. Will nations and states become manipulated and powerless?

The rapid growth of domestic markets is occurring in developing countries as well as in Western societies. The important dimension of the global market is a lack of equal competition. The US-based mega corporations will eventually fill the cultural space of the world market, in a situation in which there is a shortage of actual programmes for international television.

International communication also affects the cultural balances and boundaries of the world. Kenworthy (1996) divides the world into eight large cultural blocs: the Latin, Anglo-Saxon, Germanic-Scandinavian, Slavic, Muslim, African, Indian and Sinitic cultures. The Anglo-Saxon culture covers Britain, North America, Australia, New Zealand and South Africa. Since World War II the cultural influence of these regions has been growing very fast. Most of the mega cultural firms are based on the commodification of Anglophone culture. Most cultural traffic flows out of the Anglophone regions. Whether one agrees with Kenworthy's categories or not, it is critical to look at the globalization process in relation to cultural production and the shifting zones of cultural influence.

---

6 GIDDENS AND ROBERTSON ON GLOBALIZATION

J. Eade

Although Roland Robertson (1992) has noted the considerable disagreement over definitions of globalization, a prime concern among commentators has been the compression of both time and space. Anthony Giddens (1990), for example, analyses the

From: Introduction, by J. Eade, in *Living the Global City: globalization as local process*, edited by John Eade, Routledge, 1997.

ways in which space and time have become compressed in terms of two processes: 'distanciation' and 'disembedding'. Distanciation refers to 'the conditions under which time and space are organized so as to connect presence and absence' (Giddens, 1990, p. 14), while disembedding concerns the ways in which social relations are lifted out of their local contexts and restructured 'across indefinite spans of time-space' (ibid., p. 21). The significance of nation-state boundaries and institutions declines as global and local social relations interweave and world-wide social relations intensify. Globalization does not necessarily lead to increasing social homogenization according to Giddens because distanciated relations are frequently engaged in a dialectical transformation. For Giddens 'local transformation is as much a part of globalization as the lateral extension of social connections across time and space' (ibid., p. 64).

While the analysis of globalization provided by Giddens focuses on social relations, Roland Robertson chooses to emphasize 'the scope and depth of consciousness of the world as single place'. Globalization, therefore, involves not just 'the objectiveness of increasing connectedness' but also 'subjective and cultural matters'. Robertson draws attention to the growth of 'globe talk' – 'the discourse of globality' – which 'consists largely in the shifting and contested terms in which the world as a whole is defined' and which is 'a vital component of contemporary global culture' (Robertson 1992, p. 113).

The implications of globalization for notions of locality are developed by Robertson in a more recent discussion where he claims that globalization entails the reconstruction and 'the production of "home", "community" and "locality"' (Robertson 1995, p. 30). Rather than the local and the global constituting analytical opposites, locality 'can be regarded, with certain reservations, as an aspect of globalization' (ibid.). Through global compression localities are both brought together and invented (ibid., p. 35). While globalization is useful as an analytical concept referring to the 'simultaneity and the interpenetration of what are conventionally called the global and the local, or – in more abstract vein – the universal and the particular', Robertson

suggests that 'glocalization' might be a more accurate term to describe the global/local relationship. Glocalization refers, in the subjective and personal sphere, to the construction and invention of diverse localities through global flows of ideas and information.

Although Giddens and Robertson share a mutual interest in the interweaving of global and local processes, Robertson's discussion of globality leads him to criticize Giddens for failing to appreciate 'the significance of culture' (Robertson 1992, p. 144) and, therefore, being unable to theorize 'the issue of "other cultures"'). Giddens is further taken to task for not realizing that:

> The whole idea that one can sensibly interpret the contemporary world without addressing the issues that arise from current debates about the politics of culture, cultural capital, cultural difference, cultural homogeneity and heterogeneity, ethnicity, race and gender, and so on, is implausible. (p. 145).

Despite their differences in approach towards globalization, Giddens and Robertson have both emphasized the importance of reflexivity in their understanding of global/local relations. In the process they have drawn on a sociological heritage which includes such 'masters' as Weber, Simmel, Durkheim and Parsons. Against postmodern attempts to deconstruct the social their discussion of globalization presents a case for the continuing relevance of academic sociology and its intellectual heritage.

Albrow's 'global age'

Martin Albrow also rejects the postmodern deconstruction of the social but claims that globalization presents Sociology with a novel challenge. The coming of what he calls the 'global age' (cf. Albrow, 1996) requires a new sociological framework as sociology is itself globalized as individual sociologists enjoy the freedom of collaborating with their colleagues 'anywhere on the globe' and appreciate 'the world-wide processes within which and on which they work' (Albrow 1990, p. 7). He detects, therefore, the emergence of a 'universal discourse' which embraces 'multiple interlocutors based on different regions and cultures' (ibid., p. 8). An illustration of the way in which traditional sociological concepts can be reconstituted is provided (in Chapter 2 of this volume) where we explore community, culture and milieu. We suggest that globalization entails, for example, the deterritorialization of traditional concepts, their disaggregation and resynthesis, their extension 'to embrace new realities' and their global operationalization as well as 'the generalization of local concepts to the level of global relevance and their assimilation into a transnational discourse'.

7 GLOBALIZATION AND THE SOCIAL SCIENCES

J. N. Pieterse

Globalization, according to Albrow, 'refers to all those processes by which the peoples of the world are incorporated into a single world society, global society' (1990, p. 9). Since these processes are plural we may as well conceive of globalizations in the plural. Thus in Social Science there are as many conceptualizations of globalization as there are disciplines. In Economics, globalization refers to economic internationalization and the spread of capitalist market relations. 'The global economy is the system generated by globalizing production and global finance' (Cox, 1992, p. 30). In International Relations, the focus is on the increasing density of interstate relations and the development of global politics. In Sociology, the concern is with increasing world-wide social densities and the emer-

From: Globalization as hybridization, by J. N. Pieterse, in *Global Modernities*, edited by M. Featherstone, S. Lash and R. Robertson, Sage, 1995.

gence of 'world society'. In Cultural Studies, the focus is on global communications and world-wide cultural standardization, as in Coca-Colonization and McDonaldization, and on post-colonial culture. In history, the concern is with conceptualizing 'global history' (Mazlish and Buultjens, 1993).

All these approaches and themes are relevant if we view globalization as a multi-dimensional process which, like all significant social processes, unfolds in multiple realms of existence simultaneously. Accordingly, globalization may be understood in terms of an open-ended synthesis of several disciplinary approaches. This extends beyond Social Science, for instance to ecological concerns, technology (Henderson, 1989) and agricultural techniques (for example, green revolution).

Another way to conceive of globalizations plural is that there are as many modes of globalization as there are globalizing agents and dynamics or impulses. Historically these range from long-distance cross-cultural trade, religious organizations and knowledge networks to contemporary multinational corporations, transnational banks, international institutions, technological exchange and transnational networks of social movements. We can further differentiate between globalization as policy and project – as in the case of Amnesty International, which is concerned with internationalizing human rights standards – or as unintended consequence – as in the case of the 'globalizing panic' of AIDS. Globalism is the policy of furthering or managing (a particular mode of) globalization. In political economy it refers to policies furthering or accommodating economic internationalization (Petras and Brill, 1985); or to the corporate globalism of transnational enterprises (Gurtov, 1988); and in foreign affairs, to the global stance in US foreign policy, in its initial post-war posture (Ambrose, 1971) and its post Cold War stance.

These varied dimensions all point to the inherent fluidity, indeterminacy and open-endedness of globalizations. If this is the point of departure it becomes less obvious to think of globalizations in terms of standardization and less likely that globalizations can be one-directional processes, either structurally or culturally.

8 GLOBALIZATION AS MYTH

P. Hirst and G. Thompson

. . . our scepticism deepened until we became convinced that globalization, as conceived by the more extreme globalizers, is largely a myth. Thus we argue that:

> The present highly internationalized economy is not unprecedented: it is one of a number of distinct conjunctures or states of the international economy that have existed since an economy based on modern industrial technology began to be generalized from the 1860s. In some respects, the current international economy is less open and integrated than the regime that prevailed from 1870 to 1914.

> Genuinely transnational companies (TNCs) appear to be relatively rare. Most companies are nationally based and trade multinationally on the strength of a major national location of production and sales, and there seems to be no major tendency towards the growth of truly, international companies.

> Capital mobility is not producing a massive shift of investment and employment from the advanced to the developing countries. Rather, foreign direct investment (FDI) is highly concentrated among the advanced industrial economies and the Third World remains marginal in both investment and trade, a small minority of newly industrializing countries apart.

> As some of the extreme advocates of globalization recognize, the world economy is far from being genuinely 'global'. Rather, trade, investment and financial flows are concentrated in the triad of Europe, Japan and North America and this dominance seems set to continue.

> These major economic powers, the G3, thus have the capacity, especially if they co-ordinate policy, to exert powerful governance pressures over financial markets and other economic tendencies. Global markets are thus by no means beyond regulation and control, even though the current scope and objectives of economic governance are limited by the divergent interests of the great powers and the economic doctrines prevalent among their elites.

. . . We should emphasize that this book challenges the strong version of the thesis of economic globalization, because we believe that without the notion of a truly globalized economy many of the other consequences adduced in the domains of culture and politics would either cease to be sustainable or become less threatening. Hence most of the discussion here is centred on the international economy and the evidence for and against the process of globalization. We are well aware that there are a wide variety of views that use the term 'globalization'. Even among those analysts that confine themselves to strictly economic processes, some make far more radical claims about changes in the international economy than others. . . . Some less extreme and more nuanced analyses that employ the term 'globalization' are well established in the academic community and concentrate on the relative internationalization of major financial markets, of technology, and of certain important sectors of manufacturing and services, particularly since the 1970s. Emphasis is given in many of these analyses to the increasing constraints on national level governance that prevent ambitious macro-economic policies that diverge significantly from the norms acceptable to international financial markets. Indeed, both authors have over some time drawn attention to such phenomena in their own work.

Obviously, it is no part of our aim here to deny that such trends to increased internationalization have occurred or to ignore the constraints on certain types of national economic strategy. Our point in assessing the significance of such internationalization as has occurred is to argue that it is well short of dissolving distinct national economics in the major advanced industrial countries or of preventing the development of new forms of economic governance at the national and international levels. There are, however, very real dangers in not distinguishing clearly between certain trends toward internationalization and the strong version of the globalization

From: *Globalization in Question*, by P. Hirst and G. Thompson, Polity Press, 1996.

thesis. It is particularly unfortunate if the two become confused by using the same word, 'globalization', to describe both. Often we feel that evidence from cautious arguments is then used carelessly to bolster more extreme ones. . . . The strong version of the globalization thesis requires a new view of the international economy, as we shall shortly see, one that subsumes and subordinates national-level processes. Whereas tendencies toward internationalization can be accommodated within a modified view of the world economic system, that still gives a major role to national-level policies and actors. Undoubtedly, this implies some greater or lesser degree of change: firms, governments and international agencies are being forced to behave differently, but in the main they can use existing institutions and practices to do so. In this way we feel it makes more sense to consider the international economic system in a longer historical perspective, to recognize that current changes while significant and distinctive are not unprecedented and do not necessarily involve a move toward a new type of economic system.

9 PERSPECTIVES ON GLOBALIZATION

M. Miyoshi

The term 'globalization' is nearly as abused as 'postcoloniality'. If globalization means that the world is a seamless unity in which everyone equally participates in the economy, obviously globalization has not taken place. We do not live in an integrated economy, nor are we likely to in the foreseeable future. Similarly, if globalization means merely that parts of the world are inter-connected, then there is

From: Globalization, culture and the university, by M. Miyoshi, in *The Cultures of Globalization*, edited by F. Jameson and M. Miyoshi, Duke University Press, 1998.

nothing new about this so-called globalization: it began centuries ago, as Columbus sailed across the Atlantic, if not earlier. The only novelty is in the degrees of expansion in the trade and transfer of capital, labour, production, consumption, information, and technology, which might be enormous enough to amount to a qualitative change.

Capitalism has always been international and, thus, there are a number of analysts who deny the current idea of globalization altogether. Let me briefly mention just two cautious arguments on the subject among a great many. One is in an article by two British economists, Paul Hirst and Graham Thompson. They begin by defining the exact meaning of the word globalization by constructing an ideal model of global economy and then comparing it to current tendencies in international economy. The model is characterized by several features of a theoretically transnationalized economy. First, transnational corporations are totally unattached to any nation state. They point out, quite correctly, that there are very few real TNCs, most of the huge corporations being 'multinational' corporations, meaning having their headquarters in one country while operating semi-independently in many other countries – for example, General Motors, Honda, Coca-Cola, Nestlé and, by now, practically all other major, and many minor, corporations. Hirst and Thompson do not discuss, however, how 'multinationalism' relates to 'transnationalism'. Is one likely to evolve into the other, or is transnationalism to be precluded by immutable nationhood? Second, they argue that international trade is regional rather than global. By this they mean that the intra-OECD trade (Organization of Economic Co-operation and Development: the EU, US, and Japan) amounts to 80 per cent of world trade. This, too, is correct, except that no one disputes that wealth is inequitably distributed, and so in dollar figures, the North–South trade is obviously far smaller than the North–North trade. But this does not prove much. Globalization never meant global equality (in fact, its exact opposite is true: the gap between rich and poor is growing greater as time passes and that is precisely where this globalization discourse vitally connects with colonialism discourse). That is, the economic contributions of poorer countries and regions are bound to be small in absolute quantities and values, while at the same time these economies affect the economic and social structure of both themselves and industrialized countries by offering potential sites for outsourcing. Thus, the relative size in value terms of regional versus global trade means very little in discussing globalization. Third, Hirst and Thompson argue that international trading is a minor portion of the total economic activities of most countries except the European Union members. The figures they give are 25–30 per cent for European economies, and 10–15 per cent for the US and Japan. Wrong: the total trade/GDP ratios are: Canada, 46 per cent; Japan, 21 per cent; US, 20–25 per cent; and some NIES (newly industrialized economies), especially Taiwan, South Korea, Singapore, and Hong Kong, are even more active in global trade – Taiwan, 77 per cent, and South Korea, 62 per cent, for instance. Finally, they believe that the two most successful economies, Germany and Japan, are successful because they are 'nationalistic'. I think they are wrong again: first of all, I am not in the least sure that these two economies are so successful on their own; and to the extent, for example, that the Japanese economy has been stagnant and unsuccessful for the past several years after the real estate bubble burst, the reason most often offered for the failure is the excessive intervention by Japan's national bureaucracy that strangles the corporations with outmoded rules and regulations. If these two economists want to argue that globalization, complete integration, has yet to take place, of course they are right. It has not happened. But, if they want to say that regionally integrated economies (the triadic European Union, NAFTA, and the East Asia Co-Prosperity Sphere) are the future of the world economy, then I believe they are misreading the present and future of the world economy.

I prefer David Harvey's careful position offered in Chapter 11 of 'The Conditions of Postmodernity', entitled 'Flexible Accumulation – Solid Transformation or Temporary Fix?' To briefly summarize that chapter in this well-known book, it offers three views regarding the recent developments in the economy. The first is the 'globalists' (as represented here by Michael J. Piore and Charles E. Sabel), which sees a transformation that is so radical that in every dimension of social and political life 'none of the old ways of thinking and doing apply any more'. The contrasting 'conservative' position (by Anna Pollert, David Gordon and R. Andrew Sayer) is that 'there is nothing new in the capitalist search for increased flexibility or locational advantage', and that there is no solid evidence for any radical change in the way of capitalism – somewhat like Hirst and Thompson's position, discussed earlier. Against these two, Harvey takes a middle ground: he sees a transition from Fordism to flexible accumulation, a mix of 'highly efficient Fordist production (often nuanced by flexible technology and output)' in the US, Japan or South Korea, and more traditional production systems in other regions. Such a situation has changed 'the nature and composition of the global working class', as have 'the conditions of consciousness formation and political action. Unionization and traditional left politics become very hard to sustain'. 'Gender relations have similarly become much more complicated . . . as resort to a female labor force has become much more widespread. By the same token, the social basis for ideologies of entrepreneurialism, paternalism, and privatism has increased.'

I believe these three positions more or less suggest the range of views of world economy as it is being transnationalized at an extremely uneven pace in various regions of the planet. It is 'global' if we mean the plan and capability of market and labour penetration by industrialized economies. We need to recognize, as does Harvey, that industrial development is extremely uneven, and many parts of the world merely serve the benefits of industrial capital that is more and more restricted to fewer and fewer people.

10 DEBATES ABOUT THE NATURE OF GLOBALIZATION

R. Cohen

What is meant here by 'globalization', now such a powerful keyword in the social sciences? McCrew (1992) has produced an ambitious synthesis of the main propositions relating to globalization and the construction of a global society. He points to a set of intersecting elements which together signify that a global society is emerging. In particular, he submits:

- that the claims of the Enlightenment – proposing that human beings are essentially similar and have similar needs and aspirations – have now been embraced by most political leaders and by democratic movements in most countries;
- that there is world-wide financial, economic, technological and ecological interdependence;
- that there is a growing perception, aroused and confirmed by the satellite pictures from space, that 'planet Earth' is a single place;
- that with the collapse of the Soviet Union the bifurcation of the world no longer exists. The 'Third World' has also disappeared as a coherent category. There is, so to speak, only 'One World';
- that goods, capital, knowledge, images, communications, crime, culture, pollutants, drugs, fashions and beliefs all readily flow across territorial boundaries; and
- that we are 'on the rocky road' to 'the first global civilization' – a discrete world order with shared values, processes and structures.

Despite the surface power and appeal of this argument, we should not be overwhelmed by it. We need to bear in mind at least five major qualifications.

First, a number of writers on globalization slip uneasily between description and prediction. Many of the factors mentioned by those who engage in 'global babble' are of tendential, not actual, significance.

Second, there are some profound disagreements between the statements made by global theorists. For example, the cultural, postmodernist and voluntarist versions of globalization (Featherstone, 1994, Robertson, 1994) are in marked contrast to the still potent work of Wallerstein (1984), who proposes a leftist, 'hard' version of globalization, emphasizing the dominance and fateful impress of the capitalist world economy.

Third, there are two strongly divergent theses about the future of nation-states. The more radical view is that they are in the process of dissolution in the face of global pressures. The more conservative view, which is less well aired but may be correct, is that nation-states are adapting to the new pressures by changing their functions. For example, it can be argued that the nation-state no longer crystallizes and organizes domestic capital, but that it continues to police inward labour flows and seeks to galvanize, although with diminishing capacity, a single identity around a national leadership, common citizenship and social exclusion of outsiders.

Fourth, a number of the theorists of globalization are remarkably apolitical in describing how globalization occurs. Although a number of the writers concerned announce their left-wing credentials, they implicitly accept the 'invisible hand of the (global) market', ignoring the powerful hegemonizing forces at work. As Waters (1996, p. 3) reminds us, globalization is 'a consequence of the expansion of European culture across the planet via settlement, colonization and cultural mimesis'. Only the last involves some element of consent.

Finally, there are some clearly observable countertendencies to globalization. Whatever the future of the nation-state, there is no doubt that nationalism as a force and as an ideology is on the increase. National movements organize ethnicities and subethnicities and often seek to find for them an exclusive territorial expression? As with nationalism and ethnicity, so too with religious fundamentalism, racism, sexism and other forms of social exclusion, all of which also seem to be on the increase, despite globalization.

From: *Global Diasporas*, by R. Cohen, UCL Press, 1997.

Relevant aspects of globalization

Within the rich array of possible understandings of and counter tendencies to globalization, I would like to emphasize five aspects that have particular bearing on the study of diasporas. These five elements will form the basis of my subsequent discussion.

- A world economy with quicker and denser transactions between its subsectors due to better communications, cheaper transport, a new international division of labour, the activities of transnational corporations and the effects of liberal trade and capital-flow policies.
- Forms of international migration that emphasize contractual relationships, family visits, intermittent stays abroad and sojourning, as opposed to permanent settlement and the exclusive adoption of the citizenship of a destination country.
- The development of 'global cities' in response to the intensification of transactions and interactions between the different segments of the world economy and their concentration in certain cities whose significance resides more in their global, rather than in their national, roles.
- The creation of cosmopolitan and local cultures promoting or reacting to globalization.
- A deterritorialization of social identity challenging the hegemonizing nation-states' claim to make an exclusive citizenship a defining focus of allegiance and fidelity in favour of overlapping, permeable and multiple forms of identification.

Each of these aspects of globalization has, in different ways, opened up new opportunities for diasporas to emerge, to survive and to thrive.

11 FROM IMPERIALISM TO GLOBALIZATION

J. Tomlinson

Globalization may be distinguished from imperialism in that it is a far less coherent or culturally directed process. For all that it is ambiguous between economic and political senses, the idea of imperialism contains, at least, the notion of a purposeful project: the intended spread of a social system from one centre of power across the globe. The idea of 'globalization' suggests interconnection and interdependency of all global areas which happens in a far less purposeful way. It happens as the result of economic and cultural practices which do not, of themselves, aim at global integration, but which nonetheless produce it. More importantly, the effects of globalization are to weaken the cultural coherence of all individual nation-states, including the economically powerful ones – the 'imperialist powers' of a previous era. John Urry regards this process of globalization as a symptom of the 'end of organized capitalism':

There has been a 'globalization' of economic, social and political relationships which have undermined the coherence, wholeness and unity of individual societies. Such developments include the growth of multinational corporations whose annual turnover dwarfs the national income of many individual nation states . . . the growth of means of mass communication which can simultaneously link 20–30 per cent of the world's population in a shared cultural experience; the possibility of technological disasters that know no national boundaries.

To take up Urry's last point, the sense of globalization as a disorganized process is seen most clearly in the unintended consequences for a shared environment of 'late modern' production and consumption practices. It is becoming increasingly obvious that the Western political-economic principles of unfettered economic growth, the free market, and the sovereignty of the consumer are producing

From: *Cultural Imperialism*, by J. Tomlinson, Pinter Publishers, 1991.

awesome problems for the global environment. As Fred Steward says:

> Human capacity to affect the planetary environment appears to have reached a new level. . . . Consequences are expressed beyond both the workers in the industry and the direct consumers of its products. A local event like a nuclear plant melt-down has an impact across the world through the radiation released. Individual consumption decisions on the use of aerosols containing CFCs can affect planet-wide systems such as the ozone layer. Environmental impacts become increasingly cumulative and indirect. They are expressed over new and unpredictable time spans.

As Steward goes on to recognize, the political regulation of the environmental hazards attending capitalist mass production and consumption is now much more problematic. For these effects can no longer be contained within national boundaries, and yet no effective global, supranational political bodies exist with powers to control production and consumption. Environmental globalization occurs, as it were, beyond the political imagination of 'sovereign' nation-states.

The example of environmental globalization is just one, albeit the most dramatic, of a number of ways in which the old global order is breaking down. The incapacity of sovereign nation-states to deal with the material side-effects of their own and others' industrial and technological practices has its parallel in the complex and anarchic interdependence of the world money markets. Rumours about the US economy can produce activity on the Tokyo market which may have the effect of increasing interest rates, and thus mortgages, in the UK. The cultural experience of people caught up in these processes is likely to be one of confusion, uncertainty and the perception of powerlessness. For who is to blame? All that can be answered here is 'global market forces'. And this is not a satisfying answer, since it does not connect with any of the ways in which people understand their existence as members of a political community. There is simply no way in which the

legitimacy of these immensely powerful global economic forces can be established within the existing political framework of nation-states. We cannot vote in or out multinational corporations or the international market system, and yet these seem to have more influence on our lives than the national governments we do elect.

All this can be viewed in terms of a cultural experience of globalization which extends to all countries of the world. In the 'age of imperialism', the cultural experience of those in the 'core' countries was stabilized by the 'imagined community' of the nation-state. This represented, in David Held's words, 'a national community of fate' – a community which rightly governs itself and determines its own future'. The idea of cultural imperialism in this period drew on the image of relatively secure cultural communities exercising influence over other 'weaker' cultures. As national governments in late modernity are less and less able to act autonomously in the political economic sphere, all this changes. When people find their lives more and more controlled by forces beyond the influence of those national institutions which form a perception of their specific 'polity', their accompanying sense of belonging to a secure culture is eroded. The average European or North American probably no longer experiences the cultural security their national identity used to afford. So the implicit terms of reference of cultural imperialism seem to be altered in a world where the dominant areas of cultural production do not have a matching sense of cultural confidence.

The general cultural insecurity of globalization has been described in some of the more considered accounts of 'postmodernity'. Fredric Jameson, for example, speaks of 'the incapacity of our minds, at least at present, to map the great global multinational and decentred communicational network in which we find ourselves caught as individual subjects'.

What Jameson is trying to describe is what he calls a new 'cultural space': the 'as yet untheorized original space of some new "world system" of multinational or late capitalism'. This, he argues, is the space created by a third great expansion of capitalism, after the earlier expansions of, first, national markets and then the 'older imperialist system'. The latest expansion of capitalism produces a truly 'global' system, which can be seen not only in the complex networks of international finance and multinational capitalist production, but also in the spatial context of cultural experience that it produces. What Jameson suggests is that people's experiences are shaped by processes which operate on a global level – and this level is beyond our present powers of imagination. Attempts to articulate this experience can be seen in certain elements of contemporary popular culture. For example he points to the vogue in popular fiction for narratives of 'high-tech paranoia':

> . . . in which the circuits and networks of some putative global computer hook-up are narratively mobilized by labyrinthine conspiracies of autonomous but deadly interlocking and competing information agencies in a complexity often beyond the capacity of the normal reading mind. Yet conspiracy theory (and its garish narrative manifestations) must be seen as a degraded attempt – through the figuration of advanced technology – to think the impossible totality of the contemporary world system.

The reality of the networks of global technology which influence our lives (computers shifting capital around the globe in seconds) can be only dimly grasped in cultural terms. This is because we none of us actually 'live' in the global space where these processes occur: an information technology network is not really a human space. Our everyday experience is necessarily 'local' – and yet this experience is increasingly shaped by global processes.

---

12 GLOBALIZATION AND (LATE-/POST-) MODERNITY

A. Scott

The question of the relationship between alleged processes of globalization and more familiar accounts of modernity and modernization has been highly problematic. Anthony Giddens, for example, asserts simply that 'modernity is inherently globalizing' (1990, pp. 63 and 177). Roland Robertson is more cautious. While claiming that 'the problem of modernity has been expanded to – in a sense subsumed by – the problem of globality' (1992, p. 66), Robertson also warns that the 'present concern with globality and globalization cannot be comprehensively considered simply as an aspect or outcome of the Western project of modernity or, except in very broad terms, enlightenment' (1992, p. 27). These proclaimed differences become apparent when we examine the terms with which globalization might be thought to be associated but which its theorists say it is not, namely Americanization or cultural imperialism.

It has been a central contention of recent debate that it is no longer a specific societal model which is being exported or globalized (for example, 'the American way'). Even those whose analysis has emerged out of development theory and who are therefore sensitized to the exportation of Western models, stress that the relationship of globalization to Americanization is by no means a straightforward one. In this spirit Leslie Sklair notes: 'capitalist consumerism is mystified by reference to Americanization, while Americanization, the method of the most successfully productive society in human history, gives its imprimatur to capitalist consumerism' (1991, p. 134). Globalization is not, in other words, a polite way of saying Americanization.

It is thought to be characteristic of late modernity that highly diverse cultural practices and material (from world music to world religion) might provide the source of exportable commercialized culture.

From: Introduction, by A. Scott, in *The Limits of Globalization*, edited by A. Scott, Routledge, 1997.

Indeed commercialized culture can be sold all the more effectively where it can be tailored to the local context or, alternatively, where it has an 'exotic feel'. What is being sold in all cases is the idea of selling – of consumerism – itself; the idea that the world is a market of cultural artefacts and resources from whose vast range the consumer must choose. Sklair's notion of the 'culture-ideology of consumerism' is intended to draw attention to this aspect: 'The specific task of the global capitalist system in the Third World is to promote consumerism among people with no regard for their own ability to produce for themselves, and with only an indirect regard for their ability to pay for what they are consuming' (1991, p. 131).

Similarly, Lash and Urry argue that a globalized culture of consumption cannot be subsumed under any one dominant substantive ideology: '. . . contemporary developments do not produce straightforwardly dominant ideology, that is sets of ideas which in some way involve legitimization, dissimulation, unification, fragmentation and reunification' (1994, p. 306).

Thus, not only is globalization thought not to be tied to any substantive notion of the 'Good Society', it may, according to its critics, well preclude any discussion of what such a society might look like. As objects of consumption and transmission all social forms are equal. It is the individual as sovereign consumer who must decide on the basis of his/her own preferences what is good 'for them':

> Junk culture is the spoilt brat of affluence, but in its ceaseless acts of proliferation and unprincipled celebrations of novelty, it also denies the possibility of any debate on the Good Society predicates as that must be on enduring, if contested, principles and on rational discourse for their contestation. (Archer, 1990, p. 102)

Margaret Archer's observation here suggests that modernization and globalization are really quite distinct indeed. The ethnocentric assumptions of the modernizers have been replaced by the relativism of a market in which consumer preferences rather than any form of public discourse establish the criteria by which the 'good society' is to be judged. In Lash and Urry's terms, a postmodern 'network of communication and information' replaces an at least partially rational discourse of ideology. While the claims of modernizers could at least be challenged by holding up some alternative societal model, consumerism and technology claim neutrality and impartiality. They profess to be merely the most efficient mechanisms for placing bets on which societal forms are preferable, the outcome being determined by the aggregate of individual choices.

Of course, this difference may be more apparent than real because (as Sklair's comments on 'imprimatur' imply) it is the market itself, and the idea of the market as the appropriate medium for social interaction, which comes to embody (Archer might say 'usurp') a substantive conception of the Good Society. Globalization and modernization may not be so different after all. The notion of the consumer as an isolated individual with sets of preferences upon which basis choices are made can be held to embody quite specific values and assumptions. Later I shall suggest that sociological accounts of globalization have sometimes tended to take the claims of markets and of technology to neutrality vis-à-vis specific societal models at face value.

Globalization and/or fragmentation?

A second theme which has permeated recent discussions is the claim that processes of globalization and fragmentation are complementary. This, too, is thought to distinguish globalization from modernization. No longer is it claimed that the world is converging upon a consensus (cf. Kerr et al., 1960). Nor is it argued, in the style of modernization theory, that we are moving from particularism to universalism. Rather, globalization is held to be a complex interaction of globalizing and localizing tendencies (so-called 'glocalization'); a synthesis of particularistic and universalistic values. As Robertson notes, 'we are, in the late twentieth century, witnesses to – and participants in – a massive, twofold process involving the interpenetration of the universalization of particularization and the particularization of universalism' (1992, p. 100). Likewise, Ulf Hannerz argues that globalization is characterized by the 'organization of diversity rather than by a replication of uniformity' (1990, p. 237) while Jonathan Friedman claims that 'ethnic and cultural fragmentation and modernist homogenization are not two arguments, two opposing views of what is happening in the world today, but two constitutive trends of global reality' (1990, p. 311).

The point Hannerz and Friedman make about the heterogeneity of global culture has also been made about the global economy. Thus Anthony McGrew argues that 'globalization is highly uneven in its scope and highly differentiated in its consequences' (1992, p. 23), while Bob Jessop is even more explicit:

> Whereas Fordism could plausibly be interpreted in terms of the diffusion of the American model to other national economics, there is currently no single hegemonic growth model (Japanese, American and West German models are in competition) and even more extensive financial and industrial internationalization makes it even more important for most national economics to find distinctive niches in the world-wide division of labour. (1988, p. 160)

The suggestion here is that globalization is occurring in the absence of either a cultural or an economic 'hegemony' and that processes of standardization and diversification, and unification and fragmentation, are occurring simultaneously.

In the sphere of cultural analysis perhaps the most influential version of this argument is the one advanced by Arjun Appadurai (1990) through his now well-known distinctions between 'ethnoscapes', 'mediascapes', 'technoscapes', 'financescapes' and 'ideoscapes'. Appadurai's argument is that globalization is characterized precisely by the divergence of these aspects; by the fact that these 'scapes' 'follow increasingly non-isomorphic paths' (1990, p. 301). With these distinctions Appadurai theorizes the compatibility and simultaneity of convergence and fragmentation which is thought to distinguish both the recent debate from the earlier notions of simple convergence which characterized theories of modernization and the most recent from earlier phases of societal development.

---

13 CONQUEST OF THE GLOBAL SCALE

N. Smith

It might seem that the borders of the global scale are self-evidently given by the natural borders of the planet but, as with other scales, the global scale *per se* is socially produced. The world of the Roman Empire, to take an obvious example, covered only a small percentage of' the planet's surface, while conversely, the realities of space travel strongly suggest the imminent expansion of the 'global' scale. Indeed, hundreds of billions of dollars devoted to space travel have already had a significant effect on the world economy over the last four decades. With the capitalist mode of production, the global scale is primarily a construct of the circulation of capital.

The conquest of the global scale is difficult to discuss except historically. Sub-planetary global worlds – whether highly localized (as with the various peoples of Amazonia, Central Africa or Borneo who were periodically 'discovered' by nineteenth-century European explorers) or the larger empires such as Ming Dynasty China – were constructed by various mixes of political, cultural, economic and ideological power. The economic construction of a unified global scale came only with the globalization of the world market in the early

From: On globalization, by N. Smith, in *Mapping the Futures*, edited by J. Bird, B. Curtis, T. Putnam and L. Tickner, Routledge, 1993.

twentieth century. Since then, the global scale has been less demarcated by the political colonization of 'new' territories, previously outside the world market, by nationally based European capitals; rather, it is the internal dynamics of economically uneven development, structured according to the specific social and economic relations of capitalist society, that patterns the global scale. Accordingly, the global is divided not only according to the political divisions of the nation state, but according to the differential levels of development and under-development experienced and achieved by these states in the world market.

The conquest of the global scale may seem like an impossible idea or set of events to grasp, but it is very real. In class terms, the capitalist class came to rule through a series of more or less recognizable national revolutions between the seventeenth and twentieth centuries; some were violent political over-throws of previous ruling classes, others were quieter revolutions resulting from an accretion of power in the market. The important point is that they did not remain isolated in separate states but that through political as well as economic means the rising bourgeoisie actively coalesced different islands of national power into global hegemony. Integrally involved were not only projects of class domination but also those of oppression, especially but not exclusively on the basis of race and gender. These intertwined histories of conquest – enslavement, robbery, denial of property ownership, dis-enfranchisement – sought to contain incipient social struggles at a lower geographical scale, as struggles over the body or over nationalism for example, while asserting the global claims of capitalism.

---

14 TIME–SPACE COMPRESSION

D. Massey

Imagine for a moment that you are on a satellite, further out and beyond all actual satellites; you can see 'planet earth' from a distance and, unusually for someone with only peaceful intentions, you are equipped with the kind of technology which allows you to see the colours of people's eyes and the numbers on their number plates. You can see all the movement and tune in to all the communication that is going on. Furthest out are the satellites, then aeroplanes, the long haul between London and Tokyo and the hop from San Salvador to Guatemala City. Some of this is people moving, some of it is physical trade, some is media broadcasting. There are faxes, e-mail, film distribution networks, financial flows and transactions. Look in closer and there are ships and trains, steam trains slogging laboriously up hills somewhere in Asia. Look in closer still and there are lorries and cars and buses, and on down further, somewhere in sub-Saharan Africa, there's a woman – among many women – on foot, who still spends hours a day collecting water.

Now, I want to make one simple point here, and that is about what one might call the power geometry of it all; the power geometry of time-space compression. For different social groups, and different individuals, are placed in very distinct ways in relation to these flows and interconnections. This point concerns not merely the issue of who moves and who doesn't, although that is an important element of it; it is also about power in relation to the flows and the movement. Different social groups have distinct relationships to this anyway differentiated mobility: some people are more in charge of it than others; some initiate flows and movement, others don't; some are more on the receiving-end of it than others; some are effectively imprisoned by it.

In a sense at the end of all the spectra are those who are both doing the moving and the communicating and who are in some way in a position of

---

From: *Space, Place and Gender*, by D. Massey, Polity Press, 1994.

control in relation to it – the jet-setters, the ones sending and receiving the faxes and the e-mail, holding the international conference calls, the ones distributing the films, controlling the news, organizing the investments and the international currency transactions. These are the groups who are really in a sense in charge of time-space compression, who can really use it and turn it to advantage, whose power and influence it very definitely increases. On its more prosaic fringes this group probably includes a fair number of Western academics and journalists – those, in other words, who write most about it.

But there are also groups who are also doing a lot of physical moving, but who are not 'in charge' of the process in the same way at all. The refugees from El Salvador or Guatemala and the undocumented migrant workers from Michoacan in Mexico, crowding into Tijuana to make a perhaps fatal dash for it across the border into the US to grab a chance of a new life. Here the experience of movement, and indeed of a confusing plurality of cultures, is very different. And there are those from India, Pakistan, Bangladesh, the Caribbean, who come half way round the world only to get held up in an interrogation room at Heathrow.

Or (a different case again) there are those who are simply on the receiving end of time-space compression. The pensioner in a bed-sit in any inner city in this country, eating British working-class-style fish and chips from a Chinese take-away, watching a US film on a Japanese television; and not daring to go out after dark. And anyway the public transport's been cut.

Or (one final example to illustrate a different kind of complexity) there are the people who live in the 'favelas' of Rio, who know global football like the back of their hand, and have produced some of its players; who have contributed massively to global music, who gave us the samba and produced the lambada that everyone was dancing to last year in the clubs of Paris and London; and who have never, or hardly ever, been to downtown Rio. At one level they have been tremendous contributors to what we call time-space compression; and at another level they are imprisoned in it.

This is, in other words, a highly complex social differentiation. There are differences in the degree of movement and communication, but also in the degree of control and of initiation. The ways in which people are placed within 'time-space compression' are highly complicated and extremely varied. But this in turn immediately raises questions of politics. If time-space compression can be imagined in that more socially formed, socially evaluative and differentiated way, then there may be here the possibility of developing a politics of mobility and access. For it does seem that mobility, and control over mobility, both reflects and reinforces power. It is not simply a question of unequal distribution, that some people move more than others, and that some have more control than others. It is that the mobility and control of some groups can actively weaken other people. Differential mobility can weaken the leverage of the already weak. The time-space compression of some groups can undermine the power of others . . .

So, at this point in the argument, get back in your mind's eye on a satellite; go right out again and look back at the globe. This time, however, imagine not just all the physical movement, nor even all the often invisible communications, but also and especially all the social relations, all the links between people. Fill it in with all those different experiences of time-space compression. For what is happening is that the geography of social relations is changing. In many cases such relations are increasingly stretched out over space. Economic, political and cultural social relations, each full of power and with internal structures of domination and subordination, stretched out over the planet at every different level, from the household to the local area to the international.

It is from that perspective that it is possible to envisage an alternative interpretation of place. In this interpretation, what gives a place its specificity is not some long internalized history but the fact that it is constructed out of a particular constellation of social relations, meeting and weaving together at a particular locus. If one moves in from the satellite towards the globe, holding all those networks of social relations and movements and communications in one's head, then each 'place' can be seen as a particular, unique, point of their intersection. It is, indeed, a meeting place. Instead then, of thinking of places as areas with boundaries around, they can be imagined as articulated moments in networks of social relations and understandings, but where a large proportion of those relations, experiences and understandings are constructed on a far larger scale than what we happen to define for that moment as the place itself, whether that be a street, or a region or even a continent. And this in turn allows a sense of place which is extroverted, which includes a consciousness of its links with the wider world, which integrates in a positive way the global and the local.

This is not a question of making the ritualistic connections to 'the wider system' (the people in the local meeting who bring up international capitalism every time you try to have a discussion about rubbish-collection), the point is that there are real relations with real content – economic, political, cultural – between any local place and the wider world in which it is set. In economic geography the argument has long been accepted that it is not possible to understand the 'inner city', for instance its loss of jobs, the decline of manufacturing employment there, by looking only at the inner city. Any adequate explanation has to set the inner city in its wider geographical context. Perhaps it is appropriate to think how that kind of understanding could be extended to the notion of a sense of place.

A progressive concept of place

These arguments, then, highlight a number of ways in which a progressive concept of place might be developed. First of all, it is absolutely not static. If places can be conceptualized in terms of the social interactions which they tie together, then it is also the case that these interactions themselves are not motionless things, frozen in time. They are processes. One of the great one-liners in Marxist exchanges has for long been, 'Ah, but capital is not a thing, it's a process.' Perhaps this should be said also about places; that places are processes, too.

Second, places do not have to have boundaries in the sense of divisions which frame simple enclosures.

'Boundaries' may of course be necessary, for the purposes of certain types of studies for instance, but they are not necessary for the conceptualization of a place itself. Definition in this sense does not have to be through simple counterposition to the outside; it can come, in part, precisely through the particularity of linkage to that 'outside' which is therefore itself part of what constitutes the place. This helps get away from the common association between penetrability and vulnerability. For it is this kind of association which makes invasion by newcomers so threatening.

Third, clearly places do not have single, unique 'identities'; they are full of internal conflicts. just think, for instance, about London's Docklands, a place which is at the moment quite clearly defined by conflict: a conflict over what its past has been (the nature of its 'heritage'), conflict over what should be its present development, conflict over what could be its future.

Fourth, and finally, none of this denies place nor the importance of the uniqueness of place. The specificity of place is continually reproduced, but it is not a specificity which results from some long, internalized history. There are a number of sources of this specificity . . .

---

15 GLOBALIZATION AS A MODE OF ORGANIZATION

A. Mattelard

Levitt's (Director, *Harvard Business Review*) approach is based on four observations: the world is becoming a 'global village'; the market is no longer national, but world-wide, in scale; the urban way of life predominates; and certain major tendencies can be observed (the development of individualism, the

From: *Mapping World Communication*, by A. Mattelard, University of Minnesota Press, 1997.

Americanization of youth, the emancipation of senior citizens, and so forth). From these observations spring three hypotheses: the homogenization of needs under pressure of new technologies; price competition (consumers are ready to sacrifice their specific preferences to take advantage of cheap and reasonably good quality products); and economy of scale (the standardization made possible by the homogenization of world markets permits the reduction of costs). Levitt recommended that corporations create a single product for the whole world market, market it at a single price (the lowest possible), promote it in the same way in each country and use the same distribution circuits everywhere. In other words, roughly, he recommends that they imitate firms like Coca-Cola, one of the few that follow such a strategy. This theory of the homogenization of needs and markets and the standardization of products has been subjected to numerous criticisms by those who think that the world, on the contrary, is becoming more differentiated and who recommend a return to the original definition of the term 'marketing', which is to segment the market according to the differences that run through it.

Globalization is both an internal and an external affair. It is a way of organizing a firm and a way of relating to world space. To describe this new mode of organization, the economic literature calls on the metaphors of the hologram, the amoeba, and frequently the language of biology. The corporation and the world-as-market are treated through the prism of the living organism.

We must understand these metaphors as signifying an end to the rigidity of hierarchies within the corporation, the decline of forms of pyramidal authority inherited from the military conceptions of managers shaped by World War II, in which the retention of information was a source of knowledge-as-power and where everything functioned by sanction and penalty. By contrast, here is a model of management based on information and communication networks, in which personnel are implicated and made to feel responsible for fixing and realizing objectives, and in which positive criticism seeks the harmony of networks of interaction, tapping employees' informal and spontaneous creativity and

capacity to innovate. This model involves appropriating knowledge and skill and reinvesting them continually in the organization. . . . To Fordism's separation of tasks is opposed a new form: the capillarity of the managerial function, its diffusion within the body of the enterprise. And since the employee is a part of the whole, he or she is also a carrier of the whole.

Globality as a mode of management has no meaning unless it is linked to the corporation's mode of inserting the business into the world economy and world market. . . . Fed by an incessant flow of information, the network-corporation abandons its vertical and centralized structure and adopts fluctuating contours. Consider, for example, the more and more frequent call for sub-contracting (which may give rise to further sub-contracting). The network transforms and regenerates itself constantly.

This mode of organization places the corporation in the first rank of clients for integrated communication services (radio, television, visionphone, voice messaging, data transfer, telecopying, etc.), which open the way for the unification of systems across normalized networks such as ISDN (integrated services by digital network). A portable terminal allows each subscriber to receive polymorphous messages transmitted to him or her from any point on the planet connected to the network.

---

16 'GLOBAL SOCIETY'

M. Shaw

Global society, to put it at its strongest, is no more or less than the entire complex of social relations between human beings on a world scale. As such it

From: The theoretical challenge of global society, by M. Shaw, in *Media in Global Context*, edited by A. Sreberny-Mohammadi, D. Winseck, J. McKenna and O. Boyd-Barrett, Arnold, 1997.

is more complete and self-sufficient than just about any other society which has been or could be envisaged. It still represents a partial abstraction relative to the history of human societies, and relative to the natural and living world as a whole. It does not have to be seen as having needs (as in the original functionalist model), as being based on imperatives (such as capital accumulation in the Marxist account of capitalism) or as necessarily entailing a given set of functions and institutions. Its emergence and the social relations, systems and institutions within it can be described under the rubric of historical discontinuity and contingency rather than of functional or historical necessity.

While global society in this sense contains all social relations, not all relations are actually defined at a global level. Global society can also be seen, therefore, as the largest existing, and also the largest possible, framework or context of social relations, but not necessarily the immediately defining context of all social relations. As in all large-scale, complex societies there are many contexts in which relations can be defined, and most are not located in the largest or more general context. Crucial to understanding global society is to comprehend the changing contextualization of social relations, and one of the critical issues is to grasp the extent, forms and processes of globalization. Globalization, indeed, can be seen as the way in which social relations become defined by specifically global contexts.

Global society can be said to exist, in the sense that global relationships are sufficiently strong and established to be defined as the largest context of social relationships as a whole. In an equally if not more important sense, however, it can still be seen very much as an emergent reality.

If global society is still emergent, then this should increase our caution over ascribing to its forms which have characterized previous societies, and draw our attention to its historically specific features. A fundamental feature of global society is the exceptional complexities of its segmentation and differentiation, which subsumes and transforms the complexity of the pre-existing civilizations and national and tribal societies while producing many more from the processes of globalization themselves.

Global society is best understood, therefore, as a diverse social universe in which the unifying forces of modern production, markets, communications and cultural and political modernization interact with many global, regional, national and local segmentations and differentiations. Global society should be understood not as a social system but as a field of social relations in which many specific systems have formed – some of them genuinely global, others incipiently so, and others still restricted to national or local contexts.

Given the segmentation of global society (many of its institutions take a qualitatively different form from those of other societies) the most evident difference between global and national societies is the lack of a centralized state. The contrast here, is, however, a false one, since national societies in modern times exist only by virtue of three conditions: their dependence on particular states, these states' relationships with other states and the segmentation of wider social relations in line with state divisions. These fundamental, structuring facts are overlooked in any comparison which takes national societies as a baseline for global society.

Where national societies have states, global society has a state system. We are so used to thinking of the society-state relationship in a one-to-one sense, in which a single state constitutes the ultimate source of power and authority in a given society, that this concept of state power in global society may seem confusing. The familiar concept of one society, one state is, however, a historically specific one, and to generalize it, and expect any newly identified society to conform to it by definition, is to be guilty of illegitimate generalization.

Interestingly, international relations theorists have characterized the state system as an anarchic one, and in a well-known work Hedley Bull defined 'international society' as an 'anarchic society' comparable with 'primitive' stateless societies. There are problems with this concept of 'international' as opposed to 'global' society. In particular, the definition of it as a 'society' of states to be compared with societies composed of individual human beings raises severe methodological problems. Nevertheless, the idea that a society can be characterized by anarchic relations

– that is, by the absence of a clear central authority structure, and in particular of a central state – is clearly valid.

Global society as 'anarchy'?

Although we are used to the idea of a society in which economic relations are anarchic (the essence of a market-based economy), the idea of political anarchy is challenging. Yet global society is a society in which anarchy prevails at both these crucial levels of social organization. The economic system of global society is at root that of the global market, co-ordinating an enormously complex division of labour in the production and exchange of commodities. The political system of global society is basically that of the competitive international system of states, co-ordinating an equally complex diversity of national-state politics. The global cultural system is largely one of diverse, part-competing, part-overlapping, part-distinctive, part-integrated national and sub-national cultures organized around a wide range of principles.

The novel sense in which we talk of a global society at the end of the twentieth century depends, however, on something more than an awareness of these various forms of anarchy (which have characterized the emerging global society for decades, if not centuries). Nor is it merely that, as a result of the development of communications, we have a heightened awareness of the anarchic nature of our world. This is important, but what is most significant is that as a result of this heightened awareness we are beginning to experience transformations of systems, institutions and culture. Military, political, economic and cultural crises are increasingly defined as global crises; even relatively limited regional conflicts are seen as global issues. Global society is beginning to be more than the sum of its parts, or, to be more precise, more than a framework for the competition of its parts.

It is in this sense that we should view the development of specifically global institutions (as well as regional and other transnational institutions). The global economic system consists not merely of a global division of labour and global market exchanges, but increasingly also of a variety of global (and regional) economic institutions aiming to regulate these processes. Although such institutions – GATT, IMF, Group of 7, EC, etc. – are dominated by the major Western states, banks and other corporations, they are distinct from any specific state or private interests and operate effectively as global regulators.

The global political system, similarly, consists not merely of an ever-growing number of individual nation-states and alliances or groupings of states. Global (and regional) institutions (above all, with all its defects, the UN) play an increasingly critical role. No matter that such institutions are manipulated by the major Western powers, and that their actions – especially military intervention (as in the Gulf in 1990–91) or non-intervention (as in Bosnia in 1992–93) – depend largely on the interests and policies of these powers, and especially of the US. These are the developing global political institutions, and not surprisingly they reflect the current realities of global politics.

The global cultural system likewise can be characterized by the growth of global and regional elements. Although no one should doubt the tenacity of particularistic ideas and identities, as of particular economic and political interests, the growth of a common culture is still very striking. It is not just, of course, that means of communication have been transformed and that global communications systems have developed, dominated like most other economic fields by Western corporations with global reach. Nor is it merely that the standard cultural commodities – images, ideas, information – of Hollywood and CNN are globally diffused. More important, although less easily summarized, are the ways that through these processes, intermeshing with economic and political globalization, people are coming to see their lives in terms of common expectations, values and goals. These cultural norms include ideas of standard of living, lifestyle, entitlements to welfare, citizenship rights, democracy, ethnic and linguistic rights, nationhood, gender equality, environmental quality, etc. Many of them have originated in the West, but they are increasingly, despite huge differences in their meanings in different social contexts, parts of the ways of life and of political discourse across the world. In this sense, we can talk of the emergence of a global culture, and specifically of global political culture.

Global civil society?

A vital issue here is whether we can posit the growth of a global civil society. The concept of civil society forms a pairing with that of the state. In a weak and inclusive sense, civil society denotes society as distinct from the state; in this sense, clearly we can talk of a global civil society, based on the emerging global economy and culture. In a stronger sense, however, writers such as Gramsci have seen civil society in terms of the way in which society outside the state organizes and represents itself, forming both a source of pressure on and, in a certain sense, an extension of the state. Civil society in this sense is constituted by its institutions – classically churches, press, parties, trade unions, etc., but in modern terms also including a variety of communications media and new (no longer directly class-based) social movements and campaigns. The institutions of civil society have historically been national and constituted by the relationship to the nation-state; indeed they may be said to be essential components of the nation. Civil society has been, almost by definition, national.

It is clear that this situation, too, has begun to change in a fundamental way. As an increasing number of issues are being posed in global terms, the common threads weaving together civil societies in many countries have grown ever stronger. Between Western societies, the creation of a common military system during the east–west conflict, and with it of a common economic space, has encouraged the linking of civil societies. Within Western Europe, especially, the development of the European Union at a state level has brought forward – however contradictorily, since there is also societal resistance to European unity – a greater convergence of civil society. Across the former communist world, the collapse of the system revealed the weakness of civil society; while one result is a resurgence of nationalism, there is also an unprecedented opening of civil society to the West. In the rest of the world, there is also a decline of ideas of a Third World, and with it of the programme of national economic independence. There is a greater world-wide recognition of global interdependence, which has been strengthened since 1989.

Does the global linking of civil society amount to the development of global civil society? Clearly such a development must be in its early stages, and yet there are reasons for saying that it has well begun. Civil society has always been seen as symbiotically linked with the state. Global civil society is coming into existence in an interdependent relationship with the state system, and especially with the developing international state institutions. The development of global civil society can best be understood in terms of a contradictory relationship with the state system. Civil society represents social interests and principles which may well conflict with the dominant interests in the state system. Just as national civil societies may express ideologies which are in contradiction to state interests, so global civil society, in so far as it is constructed around ideas of human rights, for example, may express ideologies which are formally upheld within the state system, but whose consistent application is in contradiction with dominant state interests. Global civil society thus constitutes a source of constant pressures on the state system, although its development is in turn very much dependent on developments in the state system.

The development of global civil society raises the issue of how far global principles of identity are now becoming important. Clearly important groups in all parts of global society are beginning to see membership of this society as a key identifier, alongside nationality and other affiliations. In some parts of the world, other forms of transnational identity are becoming more important – Europeanism, for example, which fairly clearly has close links to globalism, and Islam, which although universal in form is (like most other traditional religions and political ideologies) potentially antithetical to globalism in practice. The strength of globalism and related transnational identifiers is a key sociological test of the emergence of global civil society.

17 WORLD CITIES

P. L. Knox

World cities, then, are nodal points that function as control centres for the interdependent skein of material, financial, and cultural flows which, together, support and sustain globalization. They also provide an interface between the global and the local, containing economic, socio-cultural and institutional settings that facilitate the articulation of regional and metropolitan resources and impulses into globalizing processes while, conversely, mediating the impulses of globalization to local political economies. As such, there are several functional components of world cities:

- They are the sites of most of the leading global markets for commodities, commodity futures, investment capital, foreign exchange, equities and bonds.
- They are the sites of clusters of specialized, high-order business services, especially those which are international in scope and which are attached to finance, accounting, advertising, property development and law.
- They are the sites of concentrations of corporate headquarters – not just of transnational corporations, but also of major national firms and of large foreign firms.
- They are the sites of concentrations of national and international headquarters of trade and professional associations.
- They are the sites of most of the leading NGOs (non-governmental organizations) and IGOs (inter-governmental organizations) that are international in scope (e.g. the World Health Organization, UNESCO, ILO (International Labour Organization), the Commonwealth Lawyers' Association, the International Federation of Agricultural Producers).
- They are the sites of the most powerful and internationally influential media organizations (including newspapers, magazines, book publishing, satellite television), news and information services (including newswires and on-line information services), and culture industries (including art and design, fashion, film, and television).

There is a great deal of synergy in these various functional components. A city like New York, for example, attracts transnational corporations because it is a centre of culture and communications. It attracts specialized business services because it is a centre of corporate headquarters and of global markets; and so on. At the same time, different cities fulfil different functions within the world-system, making for different emphases and combinations of functional attributes (that is, differences in the nature of 'world-city-ness'), as well as for differences in their absolute and relative localization (i.e. differences in the degree of world-city-ness).

Here are four (rather crude) criteria: the headquarters offices of major service corporations (banking, insurance, etc.), the headquarters offices of major industrial corporations, the headquarters offices of transnational GOs and IGOs, and cultural centrality (as reflected by the index of primacy relative to the city's national urban system). Based on these criteria, only London, New York, Paris, and Tokyo have both a full range of world-city functions and a high degree of localization of these functions. A number of cities – Chicago, Dusseldorf, Frankfurt, Los Angeles, Madrid, Montreal, Munich, Rome, Toronto, Washington, and Zurich – are 'rounded' world cities but with a significantly smaller share of each function. Osaka is a significant world city in business terms, but not in terms of cultural centrality or international affairs; Brussels and Stockholm, on the other hand, are distinctive for their importance as centres for international agencies and organizations. It is also worth noting that several metropoli that are often cited as world cities – including Hong Kong, Mexico City, Miami, São Paulo, Singapore, and Vancouver – are entirely absent. . . . This is simply because their scores on all four criteria used here are low.

These variations notwithstanding, world cities have come to be regarded as settings with distinctive

From: World cities and the organization of global space, by P. L. Knox, in *Geographies of Global Change*, edited by R. J. Johnston, P. J. Taylor and M. J. Watts, Blackwell, 1995.

attributes. John Friedmann (1986), writing largely in the context of the New International Division of Labour, hypothesized that world-city formation would result in metropolitan restructuring to accommodate not only the physical settings for concentrations of international activities and their supporting infrastructure, but also the new class factions and the spatial and class polarization that is consequent upon evolving local labor and housing markets. King (1990), Fujita (1991), Machimura (1992), and Sassen (1991), among others, have explored these restructuring processes and elaborated the attributes and characteristics of world-city labor markets, housing markets, and property markets.

The linkages between world cities, along with their relationships to processes of globalization, have been subject to rather less attention. World system theory tends to portray world cities as the 'cotter pins' that hold together the global hierarchy of core, semi-periphery, and periphery (Rodriguez and Feagin, 1986). This fits comfortably with the widespread notion of a global hierarchy of world cities, a hierarchy dominated by London, New York, and Tokyo, with a second tier of cities of regional transnational importance (that is, Amsterdam, Frankfurt, Los Angeles), a third tier of important international cities (for example, Madrid, Seoul, Sydney, Zurich), and a fourth tier of cities of national importance and with some transnational functions (for example, Houston, Milan, Munich, Osaka, and San Francisco – Friedmann, 1994). One might add a fifth tier that includes the likes of Atlanta, Georgia, Rochester NY, Columbus, Ohio, and Charlotte, NC, and the 19 Japanese 'technopolis' new towns: places where an imaginative and aggressive leadership has sought to carve out, distinctive niches in the global market place. Columbus, for example, with a substantial 'informational' infrastructure that includes CompuServe, Sterling Software/Ordernet, Chemical Abstracts, the Online Computer Library Centre, and the Ohio Supercomputer Centre, has managed to have itself designated as an 'Infoport' by the UN Conference on Trade and Development which is seeking to facilitate international trade through computer networks and electronic data interchange. In the Japanese 'technopolis' programme, collaboration between government, business, and the academic community is aimed at establishing new urban forms using fibre-optic systems, integrated digital network services, international teleports, local-area computer networks, and so on, as platforms for the next phase of neo-Fordist economic globalization. . . . (Gibson *et al.*, 1992; Rimmer 1993).

Global metropolitanism

Global metroplitanism is, of course, closely tied to the material culture promoted by transnational capitalism: designer products, services, and images targeted at transnational market niches, promoted through international advertising agencies, the motion picture industry, and television series. One common interpretation of this is that it represents the homogenization, universalization and 'Americanization' of global culture through the economic and political hegemony of the US and of US-based transnational corporations (Mattelart, 1979). But though the world may 'dream itself' to be American, this means different things to different people, depending on the ways in which American imagery is appropriated and, more often than not, subverted by the mere fact of becoming iconic (Olalquiaga, 1992). Furthermore, although American-based transnational capitalism and media may be the indisputable locus of pop-culture mythologies (Blonsky, 1992), it is clear that America has difficulty competing with Japanese cars, cameras, and hi-fi systems, Italian design, German engineering, French theory and British TV comedy shows. Meanwhile, it is now clear that the recourse to Orientalism – the Western world view that developed as a repository for all the exotic differences and otherness repressed or cast out by the West as it sought to construct a coherent identity (Said, 1978) – has had to yield to the plural histories, diverse modernities and alternative moral orders uncovered by globalization.

Rather than suggesting cultural homogenization, then, global metropolitanism invokes a differential and contingent reach, through world cities, that embodies tensions and oppositions rather than convergence and uniformity. McGrew (1992) characterizes these oppositions as follows:

Universalism v. Particularism – although globalization tends to universalize many spheres of social life (e.g. the iconography of materialistic consumerism, the idea of citizenship, the ideology of the nation state), it also provokes a sociospatial dialectic in which the social construction of difference and uniqueness results in particularism (e.g. the resurgence of regional and ethnic identities).

Homogenization v. Differentiation – just as globalization fosters similarity in material culture, institutions and lifestyles, the 'differential of contemporaneity' means that 'global' tendencies are articulated and imprinted differentially in response to varying local circumstances.

Integration v. Fragmentation – the functional integration of labour markets, consumer markets, political institutions and economic organizations that unites people across traditional political boundaries also gives rise to new cleavages. Labour, for example, has become fragmented along lines of race, gender, age and region.

Centralization v. Decentralization – another aspect of the sociospatial dialectic provoked by globalization involves new movements (e.g. localized environmental movements and the 'postmodernism of resistance' that seeks to deconstruct Modernism (Foster, 1985) in opposition to concentrations of power, information and knowledge.

Juxtaposition v. Syncretization – whereas time-space compression and global economic interdependence tend to juxtapose civilizations, lifestyles, and social practices, it can also fuel and reinforce sociocultural prejudices and sharpen sociospatial boundaries.

The global metropolitanism mediated and reproduced by world cities is thus complex, dynamic, and multi-dimensional. The most direct contribution of world cities to global metropolitanism stems from the critical mass of what Sklair (1991) calls the transnational producer-service class, with its 'transnational practices' of work and consumption. These are the people who hold international conference calls, who send and receive faxes and e-mail, who make decisions and transact investments that are transnational in scope, who edit the news, design and market the international products, and travel the world for business and pleasure. World cities not only represent their workplaces but are the proscenia for their materialistic, cosmopolitan lifestyles, the crucibles of their narratives, myths, and transnational sensibilities. These new sensibilities are, in turn, adopted by the mass-market consumers of the 'fast' world. The lingua franca of this populist dimension of global metropolitanism is the patois of soap operas and comedy series; its dress code and world view are taken from MTV and the sports page, its politics from cyberpunk magazines, and its lifestyle from promotional spots for Budweiser, Carlsberg, Levis, Pepsi, Reebok, Sony and Volvo.

Of course, the more this global pop culture draws from the hedonistic materialism of the transnational elite, the more the latter is driven toward innovative distinctiveness in its attitudes and material ensembles. The more self-consciously stylish the transnational bourgeoisie, the more 'tongue-in-chic' the wannabes and the cyberpunks. As this dialectic has unfolded (via global networks in television and advertising), more people have come to see their lives through the prisms of others' lives, as presented by mass media. Consequently, fantasy has become a social practice characteristic of global metropolitanism. But these fantasies, too, become caught in the sociospatial dialectic of the fast world, the result being the further confusion of spatial and temporal boundaries and the collapse of many of the conventions that formerly distinguished fantasy from reality. The cognitive space of world cities, emptied of traditional referential signifiers, thus comes to be filled with simulations: iconographies borrowed from other times, other peoples, and other places (Olalquiaga, 1992). Nowhere is this more apparent than in the large, set-piece developments that have come to characterize the built environment of world cities (and aspirant world cities): the 'variations on a theme park' (Sorkin, 1992) that constitute the landscapes of transnational power.

World cities and metro-centric global culture

Throughout the urban system represented by this hierarchy, the 'transnational practices' of the 'transnational producer-service class' necessary to globalization have begun to generate new cultural structures and processes which echo and reverberate through the daily practices and spatial organization of the rest of the 'fast' world. The global metropolitanism resulting from these transnational practices is not merely a state of interconnectedness and a shared, materialistic culture-ideology of consumerism (Sklair, 1991). It involves, at various levels, not only cultural homogenization and cultural synchronization, but also cultural proliferation and cultural fragmentation. It involves both the universalization of particularism (that is, dissolving the traditional boundaries of space and time, the relativism of postmodernity continuously propagating and redefining uniqueness, difference, and otherness) and the particularization of universalism (that is, crystallizing transnational practices around specific regional, class, gender, and ethnic groups. Robertson, 1991).

This global metropolitanism is closely tied to the compression of the world and the speeding up of production and consumption, of politics, and development. Yet globalization involves much more than the speeding up and spreading out of people's activities. While traditional links to family, neighborhood, region, and nationality are subverted by high-tech, high-speed networks and devices, quantitative changes – more decisions, more choices, more mobility, more interaction, more objects, more images – become qualitative – new lifestyles, new world views. . . .

18 GLOBAL CITIES

P. Sarre and J. Blunden

Gentrified dockland neighbourhoods, the desolate inner city, car-based commuter suburbs, out-of-town shopping centres, homeless persons in city-centre streets begging for 'spare change', asthma caused by vehicle emissions, clean water on tap from a privatized water company (for those who can pay): the pieces of the local urban mosaic form a wider, global picture. Another part of that picture is a new role for some cities in the affluent world, a role as global cities, the nodes that integrate the global financial structures through which world trade is conducted, the command points in the world economy and in chains of urbanism which link the environments of cities around the planet.

There is disagreement about which cities qualify as global cities, though the claims of London, New York and Tokyo (the three main world stock exchanges which between them, because of their time-zones, allow twenty-four hour trading) are unchallenged (see Hamnett, 1995). Sassen (1991) suggests that the more globalized economic life becomes, the more concentrated becomes its management in a few key centres. One of the influences in the restructuring of the world's financial system and its urban geography was the Third World debt crisis of 1982, which undermined the leading role of traditional transnational banks. The key factor, though, has been deregulation of national financial markets. The result, argues Sassen, has been to shift the centre of gravity of the financial industry away from large transnational banks and towards 'major centres of finance' (p. 19). King (1990) argues that:

> the world city is increasingly 'unhooked' from the state where it exists, its fortunes decided by forces over which it has little control. Increasingly the city becomes an arena for capital, the site for

From: *Environment, Population and Development*, by P. Sarre and J. Blunden, Hodder, 1996.

specialized operations of a global market. Forced to compete with its major international rivals, obstacles to that competition are, independent of state policies, progressively removed. It is here where the interests of local populations are directly in conflict with, and are sacrificed for, the interests of international capital . . . (which) require public sector spending on infrastructural facilities while simultaneously, they look for tax concessions to persuade them to stay. (King, 1990, pp. 145–8)

The concentration of financial institutions in the centres of the global cities creates a demand for space: for example, there are 350 foreign banks with offices in New York, and 2,500 other foreign financial companies. This demand is further fuelled by the need for offices for those who provide the services needed by banks and investment trusts – the lawyers, accountants and others in what is known as the producer services sector. The result is a skyline in which the towers of these financial giants vie for supremacy. The high wages paid to those working in these temples of capital lubricate the gentrification process. Manufacturing simply cannot compete in the market for land and so traditional sources of blue-collar employment are squeezed out, to be replaced by the restaurants, hotels and boutiques required to sustain the global city. These provide substantial employment opportunities, but the jobs are typically part-time, low paid and involve anti-social hours. Thus social polarization is a key feature of the global city. To the extent that ethnic minority migrant populations are likely to seek the kind of casualized low-paid jobs on offer, it is sometimes argued that the global city encompasses within it a Third World city.

At best we can try to manage such cities. The notion of planning them, in the sense that an ancient city like Chang'an was planned, no longer has real meaning. Is the global city a sustainable urban form? The crisis of the finance markets in 1987 certainly damaged the property industry in such cities, but the inertia and slow recovery means the cities' role has developed, not disappeared. Would a major collapse of the world monetary system signal the end of such cities? Is the real threat a social one, caused by the juxtaposition of wealth and poverty?

---

19 SHIFTING THE BOUNDARIES OF POVERTY IN THE GLOBAL CITY

L. Buffoni

Social phenomena and individuals' everyday lives undergo major change in globalized conditions. In this paper, I have looked at poverty experienced across a city, in order to provide illustrations of the way global processes can have an impact on individuals' lives at local level, and in particular at the way people respond to globalization itself, by changing their perceptions of their own and others' well-being.

Going back to my initial working definition – poverty as lack of material and cultural resources which restricts the ability to socialize – we can observe some transformations currently at work. For some respondents the possibility of maintaining social relations across the world and of knowing about poverty in the world transforms the perception of their own relative poverty. Denzel's insights are due to personal experience. John has constructed his 'awareness' through the media. And Joseph works actively for changing conditions of relative poverty in the world, both in his local environment and in the international setting.

The respondents' words imply that living in a global city can result in a variety of forms of social coping, in which individual strategies are played on an extended horizon. The opportunities offered by

From: Rethinking poverty in globalized conditions, by L. Buffoni, in *Living the Global City*, edited by J. Eade, Routledge, 1997.

the global city, in terms of technology, communications, cultural and social opportunities, can be transformed into relevant social resources ... if one has the necessary capabilities despite lacking material resources.

On the other hand, the dislocation of local communities brought about by globalization may be an element of additional disadvantage for those who are worse off and do not have access to 'global networking'. They experience further isolation and see their social resources decrease. A reduced set of capabilities due to age, material resources and technological illiteracy makes life in globalized conditions even more difficult. For elderly people who are confined to a limited area of society, since they are out of the working environment and have a reduced amount of friendships and marital relationships (Taucer, 1995, p. 156), technologies and access to communications are of little use, if they lack the necessary capabilities to make use of them. Additional capabilities in terms of socialization and ability of making new friends have to be recycled from the past in order to maintain and/or create relationships which are no longer available within the local community.

The image of the global city is one of complexity but not of duality: a place where isolation and destitution is a lived everyday phenomenon, but at the same time it is a place where opportunities are available even to the 'worse off'. A variety of forms of social coping and capabilities is built up, in a puzzled socioscape constituted by sociospheres of uneven access to resources. The various social worlds are not closed but draw resources, meanings and knowledge from the outer, global social setting, thus dissociating the boundaries of access and non-access. Poverty in a globalized setting results in a shifting reality, which in turn means that 'poverty' as a concept has to undergo constant rethinking.

20 GLOBAL HIERARCHY OF CITIES

S. Sassen

(Another) issue addressed ... is the question of urban hierarchies: how has the globalization of economic activity affected the whole notion of urban hierarchies, or urban systems, which the specialized literature typically sees as nationally based? Are New York, London, and Tokyo actually part of two distinct hierarchies, one nation-based and the other involving a global network of cities? Each of these three cities is the pre-eminent urban center in its country, though none quite to the extreme that London is in the UK. And unlike London and Tokyo, New York City is part of a tier of major cities that includes Los Angeles, Chicago, Boston, San Francisco and, because it is the national capital, Washington, DC Yet the evidence made it clear that New York City emerged over the last decade as the leading international financial and business center in the US, with Los Angeles a far second.

Through finance more than through other international flows, a global hierarchy of cities has emerged, with New York, London, and Tokyo not only the leading cities, but also the ones fulfilling co-ordinating roles and functioning as international marketplaces for the buying and selling of capital and expertise. Stock markets from a large number of countries are now linked with one another through New York, London, and Tokyo. In the era of global telecommunications, we have what is reminiscent of the role of an old-fashioned marketplace, which serves as a connecting and contact point for a wide diversity of often distant companies, brokers, and individuals.

Furthermore ... in many regards New York, London and Tokyo function as one trans-territorial marketplace. These three cities do not simply compete with each other for the same business. They also fulfil distinct roles and function as a triad. Briefly, in the 1980s Tokyo emerged as the main

From: *Global City*, by S. Sassen, Princeton University Press, 1991.

center for the export of capital; London as the main center for the processing of capital, largely through its vast international banking network linking London to most countries in the world and through the Euromarkets; and New York City as the main receiver of capital, the center for investment decisions and for the production of innovations that can maximize profitability. Beyond the often-mentioned need to cover the time zones, there is an operational aspect that suggests a distinct transterritorial economy for a specific set of functions. . . .

Urban form and the global city

The urban form that has developed in the last two decades associated with this spatial reorganization of economic activity has clearly been one of growing densities and extreme locational concentration of central functions and of the production of innovations. Are we reaching the limit of this urban form, notwithstanding the massive high-rise office complexes still under construction in London and Tokyo, with a few more planned for New York? Clearly the case of New York suggests that we may have reached the limits in the centralizing of functions, partly because of an increasingly disadvantageous trade-off between the benefits and costs of this agglomeration.

An important factor that needs to be considered is the massive infrastructural investments required by a telecommunications system. This effectively creates barriers to entry. While in principle any city could consider developing telecommunications capability of the first order and hence compete for a number of functions now concentrated in major cities, in practice entry costs are so high, in addition to the costs of continuous incorporation of the newest technology, that for the foreseeable future, major cities such as New York, London, and Tokyo have an almost absolute advantage. Arguably, a new phase of innovation in telecommunications technology might make the current infrastructure obsolete and lead to the equivalent of the earlier 'suburbanization' of large-scale manufacturing that resulted from the obsolescence of the physical structures that housed manufacturing in the large cities. At that point we

could, conceivably, enter a whole new phase in the development of urban economic systems. . . .

Immigrants in New York and London, in turn, have produced a low-cost equivalent of gentrification. Areas of New York once filled with shutup storefronts and abandoned buildings are now thriving commercial and residential neighborhoods. On a smaller scale, the same process has occurred in London. The growing size and complexity of immigrant communities has generated a demand and supply for a wide range of goods, services, and workers. In both cities, the residential and social separateness of the immigrant community becomes a vehicle to maximize the potential it contains. Small investments of money and direct labor in homes and shops by individuals become neighborhood upgrading because of the residential concentration of immigrants. This upgrading does not fit the conventional notions of upgrading, notions rooted in the middle-class experience. Its shapes, colors, and sounds are novel. They, like the cosmopolitan work culture of the new professionals, are yet another form of the internationalization of global cities. . . .

In this perspective, such developments as the growth of an informal economy and the casualization of the labour market – evident in all three cities – emerge not as anomalous or exogenous to these advanced urban economies, but as in fact part of them. A new class alignment is being shaped and global cities have emerged as one of the main arenas for this development: They contain both the most vigorous economic sectors and the sharpest income polarization. The concrete expression of this new class alignment in the structures of everyday life is well captured in the massive expansion of a new high-income stratum alongside growing urban poverty.

Global cities and the global economy

This book has examined the consequences for cities of a global economy. Beyond their sometimes long history as centers for world trade and finance, some cities now function as command points in the organization of the world economy, as sites for the production of innovations in finance and advanced services for firms, and as key marketplaces for capital. In the literature of both urbanism and political economy, there are important gaps in our knowledge of the regulation, management and servicing of spatially dispersed, but globally integrated, economic activities. This book sought to fill these gaps in current knowledge by showing how certain cities function in concert to fulfil such tasks.

These cities play, then, a strategic role in the new form of accumulation based on finance and on the globalization of manufacturing. The clearest representation, if one were to abstract a simplifying image from the complexity of this reality, is that the global city replaced the industrial/regional complex centered on the auto industry as the key engine for economic growth and social patterning. This is not to say that finance was unimportant then and manufacturing is unimportant today. Nor is it simply that the financial industry has replaced the auto industry as the leading economic force. It is to emphasize that a whole new arrangement has emerged for accumulation around the centrality of finance in economic growth. The sociopolitical forms through which this new economic regime is implemented and constituted amount to a new class alignment, a new norm of consumption where the provision of public goods and the welfare state are no longer as central as they were in the period dominated by mass manufacturing. A focus on the actual work processes involved in these various activities reveals that it has contributed to pronounced transformations in the social structure, directly through the work process in these industries – finance, producer services, and the range of industrial services they require and indirectly through the sphere of social reproduction, the maintenance of the high-income and low-income workers it employs. It is this combination of a new industrial complex that dominates economic growth and the sociopolitical forms through which it is constituted and reproduced that is centered in major cities and contains the elements of a new type of city, the global city.

21 THE INFORMATIONAL CITY

Manuel Castells

The spatial evolution of European cities is a historically specific expression of a broader structural transformation of urban forms and processes that expresses the major social trends that I have presented as characterizing our historical epoch: the rise of the Informational City. By this concept I do not refer to the urban form resulting from the direct impact of information technologies on space. The Informational City is the urban expression of the whole matrix of determinations of the Informational Society, as the Industrial City was the spatial expression of the Industrial Society. The processes constituting the form and dynamics of this new urban structure, the Informational City, will be better understood by referring to the actual social and economic trends that are restructuring the territory. Thus the new international and inter-regional division of labour ushered in by the informational society leads, at the world level, to three simultaneous processes:

The reinforcement of the metropolitan hierarchy exercised throughout the world by the main existing nodal centres, which use their informational potential and the new communication technologies to extend and deepen their global reach.

The decline of the old dominant industrial regions that were not able to make a successful transition to the informational economy. This does not imply, however, the all-traditional manufacturing cities are forced to decline: the examples of Dortmund or Barcelona show the possibility to rebound from the industrial past into an advanced producer-services economy and high technology manufacturing.

The emergence of new regions (such as the French Midi or Andalucia) or of new countries (for example, the Asian Pacific) as dynamic economic centres, attracting capital, people, and commodities, thus recreating a new economic geography.

From: European cities, the information society and the global economy, by Manuel Castells, in *Studying Culture*, edited by A. Gray and J. McGuigan, Arnold, 1993.

In the new economy, the productivity and competitiveness of regions and cities is determined by their ability to combine informational capacity, quality of life, and connectivity to the network of major metropolitan centres at the national and international levels ... By space of flows I refer to the system of exchanges of information capital, and power that structures the basic processes of societies, economies and states between different localities, regardless of localization. I call it 'space' because it does have a spatial materiality: the directional centre located in a few selected areas of a few selected localities; the telecommunication system, dependent upon telecommunication facilities and services that are unevenly distributed in the space, thus marking a telecommunicated space; the advanced transportation system, that makes such nodal points dependent on major airports and airlines services, on freeway systems, on high-speed trains; the security systems necessary to the protection of such directional spaces, surrounded by a potentially hostile world; and the symbolic marking of such spaces by the new monumentality of abstraction, making the locales of the space of flows meaningfully meaningless, both in their internal arrangement and in their architectural form. The space of flows, superseding the space of places, epitomizes the increasing differentiation between power and experience, the separation between meaning and function.

The Informational City is at the same time the Global City, as it articulates the directional functions of the global economy in a network of decision making and information-processing centres. Such globalization of urban forms and processes goes beyond the functional and the political, to influence consumption patterns, lifestyles, and formal symbolism.

Finally, the 'Informational City' is, also, the 'Dual City'. This is because the informational economy has a structural tendency to generate a polarized occupational structure, according to the informational capabilities of different social groups. Informational productivity at the top may incite structural unemployment at the bottom or downgrading of the social conditions of manual labour, particularly if the control of labour unions is weakened in the process

and if the institutions of the welfare state are undermined by the concerted assault of conservative politics and libertarian ideology.

The filling of downgraded jobs by immigrant workers tends to reinforce the dualization of the urban social structure. In a parallel movement, the age differential between an increasingly older native population in European cities and a younger population of newcomers and immigrants forms two extreme segments of citizens polarized simultaneously along lines of education, ethnicity, and age. There follows a potential surge of social tensions.

The necessary mixing of functions in the same metropolitan area leads to the attempt to preserve social segregation and functional differentiation through planning of the spatial layout of activities and residence, sometimes by public agencies, sometimes by the influence of real-estate prices. There follows a formation of cities made up of spatially coexisting, socially exclusive groups and functions, that live in an increasingly uneasy tension vis-à-vis each other. Defensive spaces emerge as a result of the tension.

This leads to the fundamental urban dualism of our time. It opposes the cosmopolitanism of the elite, living on a daily connection to the whole world (functionally, socially, culturally), to the tribalism of local communities, the macro-forces that shape their lives out of their reach. The fundamental dividing line in our cities is the inclusion of the cosmopolitans in the making of the new history while excluding the locals from the control of the global city to which ultimately their neighbourhoods belong.

Thus the Informational City, the Global City, and the Dual City are closely interrelated, forming the background of urban processes in Europe's major metropolitan centres. The fundamental issue at stake is the increasing lack of communication between the directional functions of the economy and the informational elite that performs such functions, on the one hand, and the locally-oriented population that experiences an ever deeper identity crisis, on the other. The separation between function and meaning, translated into the tension between the space of flows and the space of places, could become a major destabilizing force in European cities, potentially ushering in a new type of urban crisis.

Back to the future?

The most important challenge to be met in European cities, as well as in major cities throughout the world, is the articulation of the globally-oriented economic functions of the city with the locally-rooted society and culture. The separation between these two levels of our new reality leads to a structural urban schizophrenia that threatens our social equilibrium and our quality of life. Furthermore, the process of European integration forces a dramatic restructuring of political institutions, as national states see their functions gradually voided of relevance, pulled from the top toward supranational institutions and from the bottom toward increasing regional and local autonomy. Paradoxically, in an increasingly global economy and with the rise of the supranational state, local governments appear to be at the forefront of the process of management of the new urban contradictions and conflicts. National states are increasingly powerless to control the global economy, and at the same time they are not flexible enough to deal specifically with the problems generated in a given local society. Local governments seem to be equally powerless vis-à-vis the global trends but much more adaptable to the changing social, economic, and functional environment of cities.

22 GLOBAL CITIZENSHIP

P. Macnaghten and J. Urry

To the extent that a global citizenship may develop, it will be the product of often informed groups and associations seeking to escape the 'power-containers'

From: *Contested Natures*, by P. Macnaghten and J. Urry, Sage, 1998.

of both national and supranational states and corporations and energized by passionate opposition to those institutions. The UN has calculated that there are 50,000 such NGOs (Beck, 1996). But such a resistance does not produce agreement upon the causes and consequences of global disorder. Indeed such a resistant order especially to global institutions is highly fragmented and disparate. They embrace, according to Castells (1997), the Zapatistas in Mexico, the American militias or the Patriots more generally, Aum Shinrikyo in Japan, environmental NGOs – and, we may add, the women's movement, New Age-ists, religious fundamentalisms, and so on. They are all opposed to aspects of the new global order; and yet they all employ the technologies of that order, so much so that Castells (1997) terms the Zapatistas the 'first informational guerrillas' on account of their widespread use of computer-mediated communication and the establishment of a global electronic network of solidarity groups. Similar widespread use of the Internet is to be found among the American Patriots, who believe that the federal state is turning the US into a part of the global economy and destroying American sovereignty. They particularly oppose federal attempts to regulate the environment, as opposed to sustaining local customs and culture. Another sphere of resistance lies in the burgeoning consumer boycott movement, where large numbers of people boycott all sorts of consumer products for ethical reasons, ranging from all products French (due to nuclear testing in the South Pacific), to Faroese fish (because of their whaling practices), to W.H. Smith (targeted for selling soft porn). Indeed, as Beck (1996, p. 16) states, what brought Shell to its knees in the Brent Spar fiasco was not Greenpeace but a mass public boycott organized through global media networks.

So what may develop is a global citizenship which is endlessly resistant, forever opposing states and corporations, their 'we-know-best' world, and their often self-serving attempts to manage, regulate and order protest, what Beck (1996) terms 'globalization from below'. Our notion here is of a cosmopolitan civil society with no originating subject and no unnegotiated agreement on which objects are to be contested (see Held, 1995, on democracy as 'transnational'). One unintended and paradoxical outcome of such resistance, opposition and contestation, which employs all the global gadgetry of the hyper-modern world, is to produce the kinds of global dwellingness that escape from both the nation-state and market deregulation. It is such a cosmopolitan civil society which frees itself from the overarching structures of the contemporary world, an immensely heterogeneous and cosmopolitan civil society which the globe needs instantaneously, in order possibly to survive into glacial time.

Whether such intense globalizing processes will facilitate or impede a reasonable environment for 'in-humans' (such as cyborgs) and 'in-animals' (such as carnivorous cows) in the next century is a question of inestimable significance and awesome indeter-

minancy. What Adams (1996) terms 'Future Nature' and its wonderful wildness may have a short shelf-life. The instantaneous power of mega-corporations, the untrustworthiness of nation-states and the managerialism of supranational organizations may paradoxically generate a global resistance and cosmopolitan citizenship, albeit constituted by highly different and deeply antagonistic groupings. But such developments may also unleash a wildness of nature that takes its revenge upon human society and leaves nothing at all for future global citizens to sense as all contested natures come to an end.

GLOBALIZATION AND CULTURE

The extracts in Part B pick up on many of the issues relating to cultural globalization and 'global culture' outlined in the General Introduction. It is divided into two sections, B1 and B2.

Among the topics addressed in B1 are:

- cultural globalism, cultural identity and the composition of what is increasingly referred to as 'global culture'.
- the emergence of a 'placeless geography' of new electronic cultural spaces.
- cultural flows and cultural de-territorialization in the new global cultural economy.
- 'globalizing the local' and 'localizing the global'.
- cultural homogenization, hybridity and the creation of cultural '*mélanges*'.
- postmodernism and globalization.
- 'world music' and the importance of 'localism'.

The extracts in B2 are in three groups:

- the first addresses globalization and consumerism. Topics include how global branding and merchandising works; the impact of Western consumerism upon the Argentine North West; the response of Islam to Western consumerism; and the construction, projection and reception of two contemporary American global cultural icons, namely the NBA (National Basketball Association) and Madonna.
- the second features increasing global cosmopolitanism and the impact of tourism world-wide by reference to heritage tourism in the UK; sex tourism in Japan; and the advent of postmodern 'post-tourism'.
- the third focuses on identity in the global age, concluding with belief systems, in particular the rise of Fundamentalism and the resurgence of (new) religions across the globe.

PART B1

GLOBAL CULTURE

1 CULTURAL GLOBALISM

Peter Worsley

Even in the Amazon men own transistors as well as bows and arrows, and I have seen very poor agricultural labourers in villages in Brazil for whom renting a TV is among their highest domestic priorities and it is switched on all day long. The programmes, like the radio programmes the Amazonian Indians listen to, are often the same as those being listened to and watched by people in Los Angeles.

Yet it was not until 1991 that Leslie Sklair produced the first study that devotes as much cultural space to cultural (he calls it 'culture-ideology') as to economic and political globalism. Even so, he treats culture in the 'arts' sense and looks at it in largely economic terms as a consumer industry in which First World tastes and wants are exported to the Third World. The Third World merely receives these things.

The content of culture . . . receives little attention. Media institutions themselves simply log figures of programmes sold and transmitted and viewing audiences. A more dialectical and qualitative approach would show that although ownership is decisively concentrated in the hands of a few Western transnationals, so that the profits flow back to the 'North' (which includes Australia and Japan), the cultural traffic is not all one way. The great forms of popular music in the twentieth century, indeed, have been black, from jazz and calypso to reggae, rock and beyond. The cultural source of the world's modern popular music, then, has been the South. But its main market is the North, where it is consumed by mass audiences. Jazz itself incorporated white influences, such as Sankey and Moody harmonies. Today, there has been so much more cross-over of styles, including new syntheses of music from very diverse cultures of both the North and the South (Mali, Zaire, Bangladesh), that a special name has had to be coined to describe them: 'world music'.

From: *Knowledges: What Different Peoples Make of the World*, by Peter Worsley, Profile Books, 1997.

---

2 A 'PLACELESS' GEOGRAPHY OF IMAGE

D. Morley and K. Robins

The new merchants of universal culture aspire to a 'borderless world'. BSkyB beams out its products to a 'world without frontiers'; satellite footprints spill

From: *Spaces of Identity: Global Media, Electronic Landscapes and Cultural Boundaries*, by D. Morley and K. Robins, Routledge, 1995.

over the former integrity of national territories. With the globalization of culture, the link between culture and territory becomes significantly broken. A representative of Cable News Network (CNN) describes the phenomenon:

> There has been a cultural and social revolution as a consequence of the globalization of the economy. A blue-collar worker in America is affected as much as a party boss in Moscow or an executive in Tokyo. This means that what we do for America has validity outside America. Our news is global news. (quoted in Fraser, 1989)

What is being created is a new electronic cultural space, a 'placeless' geography of image and simulation. The formation of this global hyperspace is reflected in that strand of postmodernist thinking associated particularly with writers like Baudrillard and Virilio. Baudrillard, for example, invokes the vertigo, the disorientation, the delirium created by a world of flows and images and screens. This new global arena of culture is a world of instantaneous and depthless communication, a world in which space and time horizons have become compressed and collapsed.

The creators of this universal cultural space are the new global cultural corporations. In an environment of enormous opportunities and escalating costs, what is clearer than ever before is the relation between size and power. What we are seeing in the cultural industries is a recognition of the advantages of scale and in this sphere, too, it is giving rise to an explosion of mergers, acquisitions and strategic alliances. The most dynamic actors are rapidly restructuring to ensure strategic control of a range of cultural products across world markets. The most prominent example of conglomerate activity is, no doubt, Rupert Murdoch's News Corporation, which has rapidly moved from its base in newspapers into the audiovisual sector. Through the acquisition of Fox Broadcasting, 20th Century Fox and Sky Channel, Murdoch has striven to become involved at all levels of production and distribution. The most symbolic example of a global media conglomerate, however, is Sony. From its original involvement in consumer electronic hardware, Sony has diversified into cultural software through the acquisitions of CBS and Columbia Pictures. The Sony-Columbia-CBS combination creates a communications giant, a 'total entertainment business', whose long-term strategy is to use this control over both hardware and software industries to dominate markets for the next generation of audiovisual products (Aksoy and Robins, 1992). What is prefigurative about both News Corporation and Sony is not simply their scale and reach, but also the fact that they aspire to be stateless, 'headless', decentred corporations. These global cultural industries understand the importance of achieving a real equi-distance, or equi-presence, of perspective in relation to the whole world of their audiences and consumers.

If the origination of world-standardized cultural products is one key strategy, the process of globalization is more complex and diverse. In reality, it is not possible to eradicate or transcend difference. Here, too, the principle of equi-distance prevails: the resourceful global conglomerate exploits local difference and particularity. Cultural products are assembled from all over the world and turned into commodities for a new 'cosmopolitan' marketplace: world music and tourism; ethnic arts, fashion and cuisine; Third World writing and cinema. The local and 'exotic' are torn out of place and time to be repackaged for the world bazaar. So-called world culture may reflect a new valuation of difference and particularity, but it is also very much about making a profit from it. Theodore Levitt (1983, pp. 30–1) explains this globalization of ethnicity. The global growth of ethnic markets, he suggests, is an example of the global standardization of segments:

> 'Everywhere there is Chinese food, pitta bread, country and western music, pizza and jazz. The global pervasiveness of ethnic forms represents the cosmopolitanization of speciality. Again, globalization does not mean the end of segments. It means, instead, their expansion to world-wide proportions'.

Now it is the turn of African music, Thai cuisine, Aboriginal painting and so on, to be absorbed into the world market and to become cosmopolitan specialities.

---

3 GLOBALIZATION, CULTURE AND LOCALITY

M. Albrow

In the last thirty years transformations of industrial organization in the advanced societies, accompanied by the acceptance of the ideas of post-industrialism and postmodernity, mean that the problem-setting for community analysis has shifted. In the last decade globalization theory has brought issues of time, space and territorial organization into the centre of the frame of argument. We have to look again at the way social relations are tied to place and re-examine issues of locality and culture.

Our data about people in one small area suggest that locality has a much less absolute salience for individuals and social relations than older paradigms of research allow. They live in a global city, London, which has already been the focus for much globalization research. However, research has largely focused on links with international finance, on urban development and on the more emphatically international lifestyles of jet-setters and yuppies. Scant attention has been paid to everyday life. Thus Knight and Gappert's useful volume on cities in a global society contains twenty-three papers, but not one considers everyday life in the city. Yet the volume already implies quite different patterns of living for those caught up in global processes and takes us far

From: Travelling beyond local cultures, by M. Albrow, in *Living the Global City: globalization as a local process*, edited by J. Eade, Routledge, 1997.

outside notions of locality as the boundary for meaningful social relations.

Yet the theorization of everyday life under global conditions effectively introduces a range of considerations which takes us beyond ideas of postmodernity and post-industrialism. These ideas evolved out of earlier mass society concerns and the notion of the fragmentation of industrial society. To that extent postmodernity theory lent credence to the idea of a dissolution of concepts without effectively advocating an alternative frame. Indeed very often the claim was implicit that the search for an alternative was a doomed project from the beginning.

Globalization theory, on the other hand, does commit itself to propositions about the trajectory of social change which do not envisage a collapse into chaos or a meaningless juxtaposition of innumerable and incommensurable viewpoints. It puts on the agenda a recasting of the whole range of sociological concepts which were forged for the period of nation-state sociology.

We do not have to begin from scratch. For our purposes in this chapter we can draw on a number of core propositions about globalization based on earlier work. In exploring their relevance for local social relations we will find that we develop them further and discover the need to advance additional ones. Our starting points to which we will return are:

1. The values informing daily behaviour for many groups in contemporary society relate to real or imagined material states of the globe and its inhabitants ('globalism').
2. Images, information and commodities from any part of the earth may be available anywhere and anytime for ever-increasing numbers of people world-wide, while the consequences of world-wide forces and events impinge on local lives at any time ('globality').
3. Information and communication technology now make it possible to maintain social relationships on the basis of direct interaction over any distance across the globe ('time-space compression').
4. World-wide institutional arrangements now permit mobility of people across national boundaries

with the confidence that they can maintain their lifestyles and life routines wherever they are ('disembedding').

We could add to this list but for the moment it is sufficient to permit us to turn to our local studies and identify the patterns of social life which call out for new sociological conceptualizations. Before doing so we ought to add that while these propositions are associated with the general theory of globalization, the extent to which they necessarily implicate the globe as a whole, or require the unity of the world, is open to an argument which does not have to be resolved here in order to show their relevance for studies of local social relations.

Social and cultural spheres in an inner London locality

The transformations of the last sixty years now make it difficult to capture anything in London like the picture of locality you will find in a study such as Hoggart's. The paradigmatic equivalent of his account in empirical research was the work of Willmott and Young at the Institute of Community Studies in 1957. But they were capturing a world imminently dissolving. The variety of possibilities now evident extend our conceptual capacities to the extreme. They certainly burst the bounds of nation-state sociology.

Our research on locality and globalization is based in the inner London borough of Wandsworth, south of the river, west of centre, formed from the amalgamation of seven or eight nineteenth century villages, which give their names to the local areas within what is a largely continuous residential belt. In terms of race politics headlines Wandsworth has led a quiet life in comparison with neighbouring Lambeth. Its press image is mainly associated with the policies of the Conservative-controlled local council which has been known as the 'flagship' authority of the Thatcher years for its advocacy of low local taxation; contracting out of local services; and the sale of council houses.

This image of tranquil continuity through change is maintained even for the area of Tooting, which has a large Asian immigrant population. Yet even a cursory visit suggests that the concept of local culture is unlikely to fit new conditions. Given that the task of reconceptualization and documenting new realities is long term, I will not attempt to prejudge our findings by a premature characterization of Tooting. However, if we turn to our respondents in Tooting and, instead of seeking to fit them to pre-given sociological categories, listen to their own references to locality, culture and community, we already detect the possibility of new cultural configurations occupying the same territorial area.

Adopting an individualistic methodology as one strategy for penetrating the new social relations, we can identify a range of responses which take us beyond the notion of local culture and community without suggesting any corollary of anomie or social disorganization as the old conceptual frames tended to assume. At this stage we are not offering a holistic account of social relations in this area of London, but we can already say that globalization theory is going to allow us to interpret our respondents in a quite different way from older sociologies which focused on place rather than space.

True we can find old-established 'locals', benchmarks for analysis, but if we let them speak, the nuances of a new age come through. Take 73-year-old Grace Angel, who was born in Wandsworth and has lived in her house in Tooting for over fifty years, who met her husband when they carried stretchers for the injured during the air raids on London in the World War II. He is now disabled, but she benefits from the support of her own age group, mainly white women, who meet at a Day Centre three times a week. She engages in all the traditional activities of a settled life, visiting family, knitting and enjoying crafts. She rarely leaves Wandsworth: she enjoys the sense of community.

At the same time her life is not confined by the locality. She tells how she writes letters to France and the US She also wrote 'to Terry Waite all the time he was held hostage and to his wife. I actually got a letter from him, thanking me for my support'. Into her local frame enters a mass media symbol of the conflict between the West and militant Islam. We have to ask where that fits in with the concept of local culture, not simply an ephemeral image cast on a screen as diversion or even information, but a global figure who becomes a personal correspondent.

Mrs Angel would hardly recognize the image of Tooting another resident provides. True, Reginald Scrivens only moved to Tooting seventeen years ago, but he has lived in London for thirty-two years and works in a City bank. He reads the broadsheet Conservative newspapers, has a drink with his colleagues after work and watches television with his wife in the evening. They don't socialize locally and he doesn't enjoy living in Tooting any more:

It's very mixed these days, with the Asians and the blacks, and a lot of the area is quite run down. It's not a nice place to walk through. There isn't any real community either. I still know a few people along my street, but most of the people I used to know moved out, because Tooting got so bad . . . Families come and go. Neighbours don't care about each other any more. The foreigners all stick together though. I'll say this about them – they look after their own. That's more than you can say about most of our lot these days.

His wife goes to local shops. He goes to a local church. They are not going to move. It is an easy journey to work in Central London.

Mr Scrivens lives in Tooting but is alienated from it, or rather Tooting falls short of an image of community which he thinks it might have had or ought to have. Yet it still is convenient enough to remain there. Convenience, however, can also combine with indifference. Forty-four-year-old Ted North came to Tooting from Yorkshire ten years ago and has worked as a traffic warden ever since, feels settled, belongs to the local Conservative club, rarely goes out of the area, but doesn't really notice whether there is a community as such.

A Londoner, who moved to Tooting three years ago at the age of 22 and became a postman, Gary Upton, is even more detached: 'Locality isn't all that important to me, but I don't really feel affected by the rest of the world either. I have my life to lead and I'll lead it wherever I am.'

Even a much older man, Harry Carter, a 62-year-old taxi driver, who has lived in Tooting for twenty-two years, would move anywhere and feels community spirit has totally disappeared almost everywhere in London. For him globalization is 'common sense' and 'obviously happening'. And if you are a young unemployed man like Dean Garrett, born in Tooting the year Harry arrived, living with your girlfriend and her parents, you are used to the Asians because you were brought up with them but stick with your own. You stay in Tooting and use its library and shops but not because of community feeling.

This indifference to place, however, can be transvalued into a positive desire for constant mobility and into an estimation of locality as a consumer good. Keith Bennett is 25, works in a shop and came to Tooting six months ago. He has travelled through the US, his mother lives abroad, he has completed a degree, reckons travel has changed his life and would love to go all over the world. He has never had a sense of community but values Tooting: '. . . because it's got a mixed feel . . . it helps to make people aware of other people . . . it's close enough to fun places like Brixton and Streatham, and it's easy to get into town from here.'

He is white but lives with an Asian family and has an Asian friend. His Asian friends tell him 'that they have a good community feel among other Asians but not with the whites'. For an older widow living alone, like 77-year-old Agnes Cooper, the issues of culture and community cannot be transvalued into spectacle as they are with Keith. She responds directly to their messages. The Asians are close-knit 'with no room for outsiders' and she was plainly baffled by a Sikh who could not understand the meaning of 'hot cross buns' at Easter when she tried to explain them to him. She has lived for fourteen years in Tooting and her social network and activity are as local as Grace Angel's, but she notices a lack of true community feeling. She remarked on people buying properties in the area just for resale.

Eight white residents of Tooting, each one with a different orientation to the local area, easily generalized into a different type, potentially raising a series of conceptual distinctions which render the question of the presence or absence of local community simplistic. This question makes more sense in the case of our older respondents, but their answers are quite different. For Grace it is there; Agnes is not sure; for Reginald it has gone; and for Harry it went a long time ago everywhere in London. Ted is younger than them and came later. He does not know whether community is there and is unconcerned as he gets on with his local life.

Our three young men have different responses again. As with Ted 'community' has lost salience, and locality has become facility. Globalist Keith finds Tooting a useful point from which to enjoy the world; for Gary its generalizable qualities are what counts, it could be anywhere and that suits him, while for Dean it's a question of necessity rather than values. There is nowhere else to go.

At one time a sociologist might have held that these were all different perspectives on the same phenomenon, partial points of view which could be composited into the social reality of Tooting. Later these views would have been held to justify a sociological relativism – perspectives which simply coexisted without any way of reconciling them. A later postmodernist view would find in them a fragmented, dislocated reality.

There is another (at least one) alternative. The Deans co-exist with the Agneses, the Reginalds with the Keiths. If they do not meet each other at least they encounter many others who are similar. These people inhabit co-existing social spheres, coeval and overlapping in space, but with fundamentally different horizons and time-spans. The reality of Tooting is constituted by the intermeshing and interrelating of these spheres. Grace's community is no more the authentic, original Tooting than is Ted's.

There is an additional vital point. Apart from Grace these white Tooting residents are all immigrants, they all moved into the area, respectively seventeen, ten, three, twenty-two, a half and fourteen years ago. It is an area which is always on the move and in that sense in- and out-migration is normal. Yet this does not preclude a sense of the 'other' in Tooting, namely the Asians, often perceived as holding together, as constituting a community in the sense that the whites are not. To that extent we can see the Asian community acquires in the eyes of the whites the qualities which they consider them-

selves to have lost. Instead of seeking to assimilate the incoming ethnic group, which in any case has lived there longer than them, whites like Keith, with Asian friends and living in an Asian family, may seek to be assimilated themselves. We may then be tempted to apply the concept of local culture, not to the white residents, but to the Asians.

Our oldest Asian respondent, Naranjan, is 65 years old and has lived in Tooting for nineteen years. She came from Tanzania but met her husband in India and nearly all her family live there apart from sons who live just outside London. She is in constant touch with her family in India and a sister in New York, usually by letter, and returns to India every year. Yet she and her husband are fond of Germany and Switzerland and she enjoys travelling. Otherwise she is very busy locally, sings in her temple, attends the elderly day centre and has friends in all ethnic groups.

Here the point which comes through strongly is that Indian culture is as much a family culture as a local one. Religious occasions encourage the maintenance of family ties across space. The disembedding Giddens associates with modernity effectively sustains pre-modern kin relations and permits a form of reverse colonization.

The same is the case with a much younger Pakistani woman, Zubdha, aged 26, born in Bradford, who came to Tooting three years ago. She is married and works in a social agency, maintains constant touch by telephone with family in Pakistan and visited over 120 friends and relatives there earlier in the year. However, she likes Tooting as a place where she is comfortable with her ethnic culture, can buy 'halal' meat, has plenty of friends and no wish to leave.

For the white population, looking in from the outside, the Asians in Tooting appear to constitute a community. From the inside the orientations are varied. One thing is clear, racial segregation is apparent to both sides, but its meaning varies from person to person. In some cases it is a matter of feeling safer rather than any deep identification with an ethnic group. Such was the case with a 28-year-old shop owner, born in Birmingham, who moved to Tooting four years ago and who has no contact with aunts and uncles in India. His experience in both Birmingham and Tooting was that Asian youths stuck together for safety but he feels a sense of community in Tooting, too, which does not extend to cover blacks and whites. He thinks he will stay in Tooting so that his daughter can settle in somewhere. Settling seems a matter of contingent considerations rather than anything deeper.

A much more recent newcomer is Ajit, also 28 years old, who came to Tooting from Delhi three years ago and brought his wife, but has broken off relations with his family in India. He has set up a small business and his contacts are other businessmen. He notices no real community but has no intention of returning to India either. He sees signs of racial barriers breaking down for young people and considers this process as providing hope for the future.

These hopes might be borne out by the experience of 18-year-old Kuldeep, who helps in his parents' shop. He came to Britain from Bombay with them six years ago and says that he could not now return to India because he feels 'too English'. He considers most white people to be very open but his friends are almost all Asian and they spend a lot of time together out in clubs or playing football.

The same questioning of his Indian identity arises for a 35-year-old Asian pharmacist, Kishor, who was born in East Africa and has lived in Tooting for ten years. He finds no real community and strong racial segregation but he appreciates Tooting for its convenient location for work and his sports club. He has distant cousins in the US whom he occasionally calls and when he has a holiday he usually goes to Portugal.

In sum, our Asian respondents have orientations to community as varied as those of the whites. They all acknowledge the barriers between Asian and white but their orientations to other Asians are not as the whites imagine. For a start, the most intense felt identification with the Asian community comes from women and their local involvements are matched by the strength of their ties with the subcontinent. The men have a more instrumental relationship with other Asians, one of mutual protection and business opportunity, but not one which leads them to celebrate cultural difference.

Out of these interviews emerge both real differences in involvement in local culture and quite refined conscious distinctions about the nature of community. Most observant of all is possibly a Jamaican-born black community worker, Michael, who has lived with his parents in Tooting for eighteen years and works in Battersea, the other side of Wandsworth. For him nothing happens in Tooting which could be called community life. He contrasts it with Battersea, but even there what goes on he attributes to boredom rather than real involvement. His own friends are spread across London and everything he does revolves around the telephone. He calls Jamaica and the US every week, and has been back to Jamaica every year for the last ten years. He sees Britain as just another American state but does not believe that the world is becoming a smaller place. Somehow for him the very strength of his Caribbean ties and the barriers coming down between people also push other people away.

New concepts for local/global conditions

We have cited individual cases at some length, not to confirm a general picture, nor to find a common thread. Indeed it would be possible to construct a different general type of orientation to living in the global city for each of our respondents. Equally we are not concerned to identify where some are right and others wrong. Our initial hypothesis is that each may be right for his or her own circumstances and social network.

Grace Angel and Naranjan both find active lives in a local community, one white and the other Asian, and we have no reason to think that these are not reliable respondents. It is just that their worlds co-exist without impinging on each other.

Similarly the much-travelled Keith Bennett and Michael, the Jamaican community worker, agree that there is no community life in Tooting. Each finds it a convenient base for a London life and links with the rest of the world. But just because they agree there is no reason to take their view to be of more weight than anyone else's.

Let us suppose that this is not a matter of perspectives; rather, that our interviews represent different realities, linked by their co-existence in a locality but not, thereby, creating a local culture or community. If that were the case the local area of Tooting would be characterized by a co-present diversity of lifestyles and social configurations. This diversity would then constitute the reality, not some average, of a set of dispersed readings of the same phenomenon.

Yet this diversity would not represent chaos. Broadly there is no sense from our interviews of a collapsing world, even if there is regret for a world that is past. Each respondent makes sense of a situation, each relating in a different way to the local area. Certainly there is no sense of a Tooting community which comprises the population of the local area. Nor even is there a configuration in Ellas' sense, except in so far as there is substantial agreement on the importance of the ethnic divide between whites and Asians. Yet ethnicity provides only one of the conditions for the lives of our respondents and in no sense creates an overall framework in the way Elias and Scotson's 'established' and 'outsiders' model encapsulates and co-ordinates the lives of the inhabitants of Winston Parva.

In other words, our material is suggestive of a different order of things, which requires different conceptualizations from those available even only twenty years ago. Note the word 'suggestive': we are talking about empirical possibilities. Their realization is not yet demonstrated by these few interviews. Further research will need to adopt a variety of methodologies and take account of contextual factors, such as the possible effects of local state policies, before it can conclude that the 'globalized locality' exists in Tooting. Moreover, the impact of any future political mobilization can never be discounted. None the less, we have enough evidence to warrant the close examination of an alternative theoretical framework for future research.

We can make sense of these interviews by drawing on globalization theory. In particular by taking account of the different time horizons and spatial extent of our respondents' social networks we can specify the new elements of regularly constituted social relations in a locality in a global city. Let us now advance four new propositions about locality paralleling the four on globalization we set out above:

1. The locality can sustain as much globalist sentiment as there are sources of information for, and partners in, making sense of world-wide events.
2. A locality can exhibit the traces of world events (for example, the expulsion of East African Asians) which remove any feeling of separation from the wider world.
3. The networks of individuals in a locality can extend as far as their resources and will to use the communications at their disposal. Time-space compression allows the maintenance of kin relations with India or Jamaica, as much as with Birmingham or Brentford.
4. The resources and facilities of a locality may link it to globally institutionalized practices. It is convenient both to be there if you want to use the products of global culture and as good as anywhere else as a base from which to travel. As such both transients and permanent residents can equally make a life which is open to the world.

Let us now bring these four propositions about a globalized locality together. In sum they suggest the possibility that individuals with very different lifestyles and social networks can live in close proximity without untoward interference with each other. There is an old community for some, for others there is a new site for a community which draws its culture from India. For some Tooting is a setting for peer group leisure activity, for others it provides a place to sleep and access to London. It can be a spectacle for some, for others the anticipation of a better, more multicultural community. . . .

4 SCENARIOS FOR PERIPHERAL CULTURES

U. Hannerz

The twentieth century has been a unique period in world cultural history. Humankind has finally bid farewell to that world which could with some credibility be seen as a cultural mosaic, of separate pieces with hard, well-defined edges. Because of the great increase in the traffic in culture, the large-scale transfer of meaning systems and symbolic forms, the world is increasingly becoming one not only in political and economic terms, as in the climactic period of colonialism, but in terms of its cultural construction as well; a global ecumene of persistent cultural interaction and exchange. This, however, is no egalitarian global village. What we see now is quite firmly structured as an asymmetry of centre and periphery. With regard to cultural flow, the periphery, out there in a distant territory, is more the taker than the giver of meaning and meaningful form. Much as we feel called upon to make note of any examples of counterflow, it is difficult to avoid the conclusion that at least as things stand now, the relationship is lopsided. . . .

The shaping of world culture is an ongoing process, toward future and still uncertain states. But perhaps one conceivable outcome has come to dominate the imagery of the cultural future, as a master scenario against which every alternative scenario has to be measured. Let us call it a scenario of global homogenization of culture. The murderous threat of cultural imperialism is here rhetorically depicted as involving the high tech culture of the metropolis, with powerful organizational backing, facing a defenseless, small-scale folk culture. But 'cultural imperialism', it also becomes clear, has more to do with market than with empire. The alleged prime mover behind the pan-human replication of uniformity is late Western capitalism, luring forever more communities into dependency on the fringes of an expanding world-wide consumer society. Homogenization results mainly from the centre-to-periphery flow of commoditized culture. Consequently, the coming homogeneous world culture according to this view will by and large be a version of contemporary Western culture, and the loss of local culture would show itself most distinctively at the periphery.

This master scenario has several things going for it. A quick look at the world today affords it a certain intrinsic plausibility; it may seem like a mere continuation of present trends. It has, of course, the great advantage of simplicity. And it is dramatic. There is the sense of fatefulness, the prediction of the irreversible loss of large parts of the combined heritage of humanity. As much of the diversity of its behavioral repertoire is wiped out, Homo Sapiens becomes more like other species – in large part making its own environment, in contrast with them, but at the same time adapting to it in a single, however complex way.

There is also another scenario for global cultural process, although more subterranean; thus not so often coming out to compete openly with the global homogenization scenario. We may call it the 'peripheral corruption scenario', for what it portrays as a recurrent sequence is one where the centre offers its high ideals and its best knowledge, given some institutional form, and where the periphery first adopts them and then soon corrupts them. The scenario shows elected heads of state becoming presidents for life, then bizarre, merciless emperors. It shows Westminster and Oxbridge models being swallowed by the bush. The centre, in the end, cannot win; not at the periphery.

Biases

The peripheral corruption scenario is there for the people of the centre to draw on when they are pessimistic about their own role in improving the world, and doubtful and/or cynical about the periphery. It is deeply ethnocentric, in that it posits a very uneven distribution of virtue, and in that it denies the validity and worth of any transformations at the periphery of what was originally drawn from the centre. There is little question of cultural difference here, but rather of a difference between culture

From: Scenarios for peripheral cultures, by U. Hannerz, in *Culture, Globalization and the World System*, edited by A. D. King, State University of New York, 1991.

and non-culture, between civilization and savagery
. . .

It is a more general familiarity with, as well as specific research experiences in, West African urban life that have done most to provoke my interest in the centre–periphery relationships of world culture and to shape my gut reactions to the scenarios I have pointed to.

In a Nigerian Town

Let me, therefore, say just something about the modest middle Nigerian town which I know best, its people and the settings in which meaning flows there. Some sixty years ago this town was just coming into existence, at a new junction of the railroad built by the British colonial government. It is a community, then, which has known no existence outside the present world system. The inhabitants are railroad workers, taxi drivers, bank clerks, doctors and nurses, petty traders, tailors, shoe shiners, teachers and school children, policemen, preachers and prostitutes, bar owners and truck pushers, praise singers and peasant women who come in for the day to sell produce in the market place. Apart from attending to work, townspeople spend their time in their rooms and yards, managing household affairs; going up and down the streets to greet one another; shopping; arguing and drinking in the beer and palmwine bars; or, especially if they are young men, taking in a show at the open-air movie theatre. Since about fifteen years ago, when electricity finally came to town at a time when the Nigerian oil economy was booming, they might watch TV – all of a sudden there were a great many antennae over the rusting zinc roofs. People had battery-operated record players long before and there were several record stores, but a number of them have since closed down. The listeners now prefer cassettes and there are hawkers selling them, mostly pirate editions, from the backs of their bicycles. People also go to their churches or mosques. (A couple of years ago, actually, a visiting preacher chose his words unwisely, and Christians and Muslims in the town proceeded to burn down a number of each other's houses of worship.)

Where Meaning Flows: Market, State, Form of Life and Movement

Now let me take a round of collective human existence such as this apart to see how culture is arranged within it. Culture goes on everywhere in social life, organized as a flow of meanings, by way of meaningful forms, between people. But it does so along rather different principles in different contexts. For a comprehensive accounting of cultural flow, it is useful, I think, to distinguish some small number of typical social frameworks in which it occurs; frameworks which in part because of globalization recur in contemporary life north and south, east and west; in an African town as well as in Europe or America. The frameworks are recurrent, that is, even as their cultural contents are different. The totality of cultural process, then, can be seen within these frameworks and in their interrelations. To begin with, one may look at these frameworks in synchronic terms. But time can be made to enter in and we can then return to the problem of scenarios, as a matter of the cumulative consequences of cultural process. All this, obviously, I can only hope to sketch roughly here.

I see primarily four of these typical frameworks of cultural process. Whatever culture flows outside these four, I would claim, amounts to rather little. The global homogenization scenario, as I have described it, is preoccupied with only one of these, that of the market, so if anything significant at all goes on in the other three, that scenario would obviously have to be marked 'incomplete'. But let us begin there. In the market framework, cultural commodities are moved. All commodities presumably carry some meaning, but in some cases intellectual, esthetic or emotional appeal is all there is to a commodity, or a very large part of it, and these are what we would primarily have in mind as we speak of cultural commodities. In the market framework, meanings and meaningful forms are thus produced and disseminated by specialists in exchange for material compensation, setting up asymmetrical, more or less centring relationships between producers and consumers. The market also attempts expansively to bring more and more of culture as a whole into its framework, its agents are in competition with one another, and they also keep innovating to foster new demand. There is, in other words, a built-in tendency toward instability in this framework.

The second framework of cultural process is that of the state, not as a bounded physical area but as organizational form. The state is engaged in the management of meaning in various ways. To gain legitimate authority state apparatuses nowadays tend to reach out with different degrees of credibility and success toward their subjects to foster the idea that the state is a nation, and to construct them culturally as citizens. This involves a degree of homogenization as a goal of cultural engineering. On the other hand, the state also takes an interest in shaping such differences among people as are desirable for the purpose of fitting categories of individuals into different slots in the structure of production and reproduction. Beyond such involvements in cultural process, some states more than others engage in what one may describe as cultural welfare, trying to provide their citizenry with 'good culture'; that is, meanings and meaningful forms held to meet certifiable intellectual and esthetic standards. Not least would this cultural welfare provide the instruments people may use in developing constructive reflexive stances toward themselves and their world.

The state framework for cultural process again involves a significant asymmetry between state apparatus and people. It concentrates resources at the centre for long-term cultural work, and the flow of meaning is mostly from the centre outward. In at least one current of the cultural flow which the state sets in motion the tendency may be toward a stability of meaning – the idea of the nation is usually tied to conceptions of history and tradition. But then, again, we should know by now that such conceptions may, in fact, be spurious and quite contestable.

The third framework of cultural process I will identify, for lack of a more precise term, as that of 'form of life'. It is surely a framework of major importance, in that it involves the everyday practicalities of production and reproduction, activities going on in work places, domestic settings, neighbourhoods, and some variety of other places. What

characterizes cultural process here is that from doing the same things over and over again, and seeing and hearing others doing the same things and saying the same things over and over again, a great deal of redundancy results. Experiences and interests coalesce into habitual perspectives and dispositions. Within this framework, too, people's mere going about things entails a free and reciprocal cultural flow. In contrast with the market and state frameworks, there are no specialists in the production and dissemination of meaning as such who are to be materially compensated for cultural work. While every form of life includes some people and excludes a great many others, there are not necessarily well-defined boundaries between them, and people may develop some conception of each other's forms of life through much the same kind of everyday looking and listening, although probably with less precision. As a whole, encompassing the variety of particular forms of life, this framework involves cultural processes which are diffuse, uncentred. The 'commanding heights' of culture, as it were, are not here. As the everyday activities are practically adapted to material circumstances, there is not much reason to bring about alterations in culture here, as long as the circumstances do not change. In the form of life framework, consequently, there is a tendency toward stability in cultural process.

In contemporary complex societies, the division of labour is the dominant factor in shaping forms of life, providing material bases as well as central experiences. But as the reciprocity and redundancy of the flow of meaning between people involved with one another at work, in domesticity and in sociability seem similar enough, I think of this as a single framework.

Looking now at my Nigerian town, or at peripheral societies generally, one can see that the variety of forms of life are drawn into the world system in somewhat different ways, as the local division of labour is entangled with the international division of labour. There are still people, fairly self-sufficient agriculturalists in the vicinity of the town, who seem only rather incompletely integrated into the world system in material terms and who just barely make it into the periphery. On the other hand, there are people like the railroad employees whose mode of existence is based on the fact that the desire arose, some time early in this century, to carry tin and groundnuts from inland Nigeria to the world.

But then, also, some forms of life more than others become defined, with precision and overall, in terms of culture which has flown and continues to flow from centre to periphery. It is true that through their livelihoods at least, the peasant women who come to market in the Nigerian town, or the praise singer who performs for local notables, are not very much involved with metropolitan meaning systems: the railroader, the bank clerk and the doctor are rather more. Yet there is no one-to-one relationship either between the specificity of such cultural definition and degree of world system material involvement. In many places on the periphery, there are forms of life owing their material existence, such as it may be, very immediately to the world system – forms of life revolving around oil wells, copper mines, coffee plantations. And yet the plantation worker may earn his living with a relative minimum of particular technological or organizational skills originating at the centre.

To the extent that forms of life, or segments of the daily round which they encompass, are not subjected to any higher degree of cultural definition from the centre, by way of the international division of labour or otherwise, there is room for more cultural autonomy. And of course, the strength of the culture existing in such reserves may be such that it also reaches back to penetrate into segments more directly and more extensively defined by the centre. This is putting things very briefly: we come back to the implications.

For the fourth and final framework of cultural process in contemporary life I would nominate that of movements, more intermittently part of the cultural totality than the other three, although it can hardly be gainsaid that especially in the last quarter-century or so, they have had a major influence – examples of this being the women's movement, the environmental movement, and the peace movement. In the present context of considering centre-periphery links of culture, I will say less about the movement framework, however, and mention it here

mostly for the sake of completeness. It is undoubtedly true, as Roland Robertson notes, that globalization often forms an important part of the background for the rise of contemporary movements. Yet it seems to me that the great transnational movements of recent times have not in themselves seemed to become fully organized in a reach all the way between centre and periphery. Some rather combine centre and semi-periphery, others parts of the periphery.

Market, state, form of life and movement can be rather commonsensically distinguished, but we see that they differ in their centring and decentring tendencies, in their politics of culture and in their cultural economies. They also have their own tendencies with respect to the temporal dimension of culture. At the same time, it is true that much of what goes on in culture has to do with their interrelations. States, markets and movements are ultimately only successful if they can get forms of life to open up to them. States sometimes compete in markets; nationalist movements have been known to transform themselves into states; some movements create internal markets, and they can be newsworthy and, thus, commoditizable in the market; forms of life can be selectively commoditized as life style news; and so on, indefinitely. These entanglements, involving often mutually contradictory tendencies, keep the totality alive, shifting, continuously unstable.

I propose that it may be useful to identify two tendencies in the longer-term reconstruction of peripheral cultures within the global ecumene. One might think of each (although I prefer not to) as a distinctive scenario of future cultural history, and in these terms they would bear some resemblance to the global homogenization scenario and the peripheral corruption scenarios respectively.

I will call one the 'saturation tendency' and the other the 'maturation tendency'. The saturation tendency is that which may be seen as a version of the global homogenization scenario, with some more detailed interest in historical sequence. It would suggest that as the transnational cultural influences (of whatever sort but, in large part, certainly market organized, and operating in a continuously open structure) unendingly pound on the sensibilities of the people of the periphery, peripheral culture will step by step assimilate more and more of the imported meanings and forms, becoming gradually indistinguishable from the centre. At any one time, what is considered local culture is a little more penetrated by transnational forms than what went before it as local culture, although at any one time, until the end point is reached, the contrast between local and transnational may still be drawn, and still be regarded as significant. The cultural differences celebrated and recommended for safeguarding now may only be a pale reflection of what once existed, and sooner or later they will be gone as well.

What is suggested here is that the centre, through the frameworks of cultural process within which the transnational flow passes most readily, and among which the market framework is certainly conspicuous, cumulatively colonizes the minds of the periphery, with a corresponding institutionalization of its forms, getting the periphery so 'hooked' that soon enough there is no real opportunity for choice. The mere fact that these forms originate in the centre makes them even more attractive, a peculiar but undeniable aspect of commodity esthetics in the periphery. This colonization is understood to proceed through relentless cultural bombardment, through the redundancy of its seductive messages. As the market framework interpenetrates with that of forms of life, the latter becomes reconstructed around their dependence on what was initially alien, using it for their practical adaptations, seeing themselves wholly or at least partially through it. . . .

The inherent cultural power of the form of life framework could perhaps also be such that it colonizes the market framework, rather than vice versa. This is more in line with what I see as the maturation tendency; a notion which has its affinities with the peripheral corruption scenario, although probably with other evaluative overtones. The periphery, it is understood here, takes its time reshaping metropolitan culture to its own specifications. It is in phase one, so to speak, that the metropolitan forms in the periphery are most marked by their purity; but on closer scrutiny they turn out to stand there fairly ineffective, perhaps vulnerable, in their relative isola-

tion. In a phase two, and in innumerable phases thereafter, as they are made to interact with whatever else exists in their new setting, there may be a mutual influence, but the metropolitan forms are somehow no longer so easily recognizable – they become hybridized. In these later phases, the terms of the cultural market for one thing are in a reasonable measure set from within the peripheral forms of life, as these have come to be constituted, highly variable of course in the degree to which they are themselves culturally defined in the terms drawn from the centre.

Obviously the creativity of popular culture in much of the third world, and not least in West Africa, fits in here. Local cultural entrepreneurs have gradually mastered the alien cultural forms which reach them through the transnational commodity flow and in other ways, taking them apart, tampering and tinkering with them in such a way that the resulting new forms are more responsive to, and at the same time in part outgrowths of, local everyday life

This, then, is the local scene which is already in place to meet the transnational culture industries of the twentieth century. It is not a scene where the peripheral culture is utterly defenseless, but rather one where locally evolving alternatives to imports are available, and where there are people at hand to keep performing innovative acts of cultural brokerage.

The Periphery in Creolization

I should begin to pull things together. It is probably evident that I place some emphasis on the theme of maturation and that I continue to resist the idea of saturation, at least in its unqualified form, which is that of global homogenization. In fact, in that form, it has suspiciously much in common with that 1940s or 1950s imagery of mass culture within the metropole which showed a faceless, undifferentiated crowd drowning in a flood of mediocre and mass-produced cultural commodities. Since then, metropolitan scholarship at home has mostly moved away from that imagery, toward much more subtle conceptions of the differentiation of publics, and the contextualized reception of culture industry products. Exporting the older, rather worn out and compromised notion to the periphery, consequently, looks suspiciously like another case of 'cultural dumping'.

It is, no doubt, a trifle unfortunate that there seems to be no single scenario to put in the place of that of global homogenization, with similarly strong – but more credible – claims to predictive power. But then prediction is not something the Human Sciences have been very good at, and in the case of the global ordering of culture, what I have said may, at least, contribute to some understanding of why this is so. The diversity of interlocking principles for the organization of cultural process involves too many uncertainties to allow us to say much that is very definite with regard to the aggregate outcome. . . .

If there is any term which has many of the right associations by which to describe the ongoing, historically cumulative cultural interrelatedness between centre and periphery, it is, I think, 'creolization', a borrowing from particular social and cultural histories by way of a more generalized linguistics. I will not dwell on the potential of a creolization scenario for peripheral cultures very long here, and it may be that what I take from a rather volatile field of linguistic thought is little more than a rough metaphor. Yet it has a number of components which are appropriate enough. I like it because it suggests that cultures, like languages, can be intrinsically of mixed origin, rather than historically pure and homogeneous. It clashes conspicuously, that is to say, with received assumptions about culture coming out of nineteenth-century European nationalism. And the similarities between 'creole' and 'create' are not fortuitous. We have a sharper sense than usual that creole cultures result as people actively engage in making their own syntheses. With regard to the entire cultural inventory of humanity, creolization may involve losing some, but certainly gaining some, too. There is also in the creolization scenario the notion of a more or less open continuum, a gradation of living syntheses which can be seen to match the cultural distance between centre and periphery. And just as it is understood to involve a political economy of language, so the creolization continuum can be seen in its organization of diversity to entail a political economy of culture.

Furthermore, there is the dimension of time. Looking backward, the creolist point of view recognizes history. Creole cultures are not instant products of the present but have had some time to develop and draw themselves together to at least some degree of coherence; generations have already been born into them, but have also kept working on them. Looking forward, the creolization scenario is open-ended. This is perhaps an intellectual cop-out, but again, probably an inevitable one. It suggests that the saturation and maturation tendencies are not necessarily alternatives, but can appear in real life interwoven with one another. When the peripheral culture absorbs the influx of meanings and symbolic forms from the centre and transforms them to make them in some considerable degree their own, they may at the same time so increase the cultural affinities between the centre and the periphery that the passage of more cultural imports is facilitated. What the end state of all this will be is impossible to say, but it is possible that there is none. . . .

---

5 DISJUNCTURE AND DIFFERENCE IN THE GLOBAL CULTURAL ECONOMY

A. Appadurai

It takes only the merest acquaintance with the facts of the modern world to note that it is now an interactive system in a sense that is strikingly new. Historians and sociologists, especially those concerned with trans-local processes and the world systems associated with capitalism, have long been aware that the world has been a congeries of large-scale interactions for many centuries. Yet today's world involves interactions of a new order and

From: Disjuncture and difference in the global cultural economy, by A. Appadurai, in *Public Culture*, Vol. 2:2, Spring, 1990.

intensity. Cultural transactions between social groups in the past have generally been restricted, sometimes by the facts of geography and ecology, and at other times by active resistance to interactions with 'the other' (as in China for much of its history and in Japan before the Meiji Restoration). Where there have been sustained cultural transactions across large parts of the globe, they have usually involved the long-distance journey of commodities (and of the merchants most concerned with them) and of travellers and explorers of every type. The two main forces for sustained cultural interaction before the twentieth century have been warfare (and the large-scale political systems sometimes generated by it) and religions of conversion, which have sometimes, as in the case of Islam, taken warfare as one of the legitimate instruments of their expansion. Thus, between travellers and merchants, pilgrims and conquerors, the world has seen much long distance (and long-term) cultural traffic. This much seems self-evident.

But few will deny that given the problems of time, distance, and limited technologies for the command of resources across vast spaces, cultural dealings between socially and spatially separated groups have, until the past few centuries, been bridged at great cost and sustained over time only with great effort. The forces of cultural gravity seemed always to pull away from the formation of large-scale ecumenes, whether religious, commercial, or political, toward smaller-scale accretions of intimacy and interest.

Sometime in the past few centuries, the nature of this gravitational field seems to have changed. Partly because of the spirit of the expansion of Western maritime interests after 1500 and, partly, because of the relatively autonomous developments of large and aggressive social formations in the Americas (such as the Aztecs and the Incas); in Eurasia (such as the Mongols and their descendants, the Mughals and Ottomans); in island Southeast Asia (such as the Buginese), and in the kingdoms of pre-colonial Africa (such as Dahomey), an overlapping set of ecumenes began to emerge, in which congeries of money, commerce, conquest, and migration began to create durable cross-societal bonds. This process was accelerated by the technology transfers and innovations of the late eighteenth and nineteenth centuries, which created complex colonial orders centred on European capitals and spread throughout the non-European world. This intricate and overlapping set of Eurocolonial worlds (first Spanish and Portuguese, later principally English, French, and Dutch) set the basis for a permanent traffic in ideas of peoplehood and selfhood, which created the 'imagined communities' of recent nationalisms throughout the world.

With what Benedict Anderson has called 'print capitalism', a new power was unleashed in the world, the power of mass literacy and its attendant large-scale production of projects of ethnic affinity that were remarkably free of the need for face-to-face communication or, even, of indirect communication between persons and groups. The act of reading things together set the stage for movements based on a paradox – the paradox of constructed primordialism. There is, of course, a great deal else that is involved in the story of colonialism and its dialectically generated nationalisms, but the issue of constructed ethnicities is surely a crucial strand in this tale.

But the revolution of print capitalism and the cultural affinities and dialogues unleashed by it were only modest precursors to the world we live in now. For in the past century, there has been a technological explosion, largely in the domain of transportation and information, that makes the interactions of a print-dominated world seem as hard-won and as easily erased as the print revolution made earlier forms of cultural traffic appear. For with the advent of the steamship, the automobile, the airplane, the camera, the computer, and the telephone, we have entered into an altogether new condition of neighbourliness, even with those most distant from ourselves. Marshall McLuhan, among others, sought to theorize about this world as a 'global village', but theories such as McLuhan's appear to have overestimated the communitarian implications of the new media order. We are now aware that with media, each time we are tempted to speak of the global village, we must be reminded that media create communities with 'no sense of place'. The world we live in now seems rhizomic, even schizophrenic, calling for theories of rootlessness, alienation, and psychological distance between individuals and groups on the one hand, and fantasies (or nightmares) of electronic propinquity on the other. Here, we are close to the central problematic of cultural processes in today's world.

Thus, the curiosity that drove Pico Iyer to Asia (in 1988) is in some ways the product of a confusion between some ineffable McDonaldization of the world and the much subtler play of indigenous trajectories of desire and fear with global flows of people and things. Indeed, Iyer's own impressions are testimony to the fact that, if a global cultural system is emerging, it is filled with ironies and resistances, sometimes camouflaged as passivity and a bottomless appetite in the Asian world for 'things Western'.

Iyer's own account of the uncanny Philippine affinity for American popular music is rich testimony to the global culture of the hyper-real, for somehow Philippine renditions of American popular songs are both more widespread in the Philippines, and more disturbingly faithful to their originals, than they are in the US today. An entire nation seems to have learned to mimic Kenny Rogers and the Lennon sisters, like a vast Asian Motown chorus. But Americanization is certainly a pallid term to apply to such a situation, for not only are there more Filipinos singing perfect renditions of some American songs (often from the American past) than there are Americans doing so, there is also, of course, the fact that the rest of their lives is not in complete synchrony with the referential world that first gave birth to these songs.

In a further globalizing twist on what Fredric Jameson has called 'nostalgia for the present', these Filipinos look back to a world they have never lost. This is one of the central ironies of the politics of global cultural flows, especially in the arena of entertainment and leisure. . . .

The central problem of today's global interactions is the tension between cultural homogenization and cultural heterogenization. A vast array of empirical facts could be brought to bear on the side of the homogenization argument, and much of it has come from the Left end of the spectrum of Media studies, and some from other perspectives. Most often, the homogenization argument subspeciates into either an argument about Americanization or an argument about commoditization, and very often the two arguments are closely linked. What these arguments fail to consider is that at least as rapidly as forces from various metropolises are brought into new societies, they tend to become indigenized in one or another way: this is true of music and housing styles as much as it is true of Science and terrorism, spectacles and constitutions. The dynamics of such indigenization have just begun to be explored systemically, and much more needs to be done. But it is worth noticing that for the people of Irian Jaya, Indonesianization may be more worrisome than Americanization, as Japanization may be for Koreans, Indianization for Sri Lankans, Vietnamization for the Cambodians, and Russianization for the people of Soviet Armenia and the Baltic Republics. Such a list of alternative fears to Americanization could be greatly expanded, but it is not a shapeless inventory: for politics of smaller scale, there is always a fear of cultural absorption by polities of larger scale, especially those that are nearby. One man's 'imagined community' is another man's political prison.

This scalar dynamic, which has widespread global manifestations, is also tied to the relationship between nations and states. For the moment let us note that the simplification of these many forces (and fears) of homogenization can also be exploited by nation-states in relation to their own minorities, by posing global commoditization (or capitalism, or some other such external enemy) as more real than the threat of its own hegemonic strategies.

The new global cultural economy has to be seen as a complex, overlapping, disjunctive order that cannot any longer be understood in terms of existing centre-periphery models (even those that might account for multiple centres and peripheries). Nor is it susceptible to simple models of push and pull (in terms of migration theory), or of surpluses and deficits (as in traditional models of balance of trade), or of consumers and producers (as in most neo-Marxist theories of development). Even the most complex and flexible theories of global development that have come out of the Marxist tradition are inadequately quirky and have failed to come to terms with what Scott Lash and John Urry have called 'disorganized capitalism'. The complexity of the current global economy has to do with certain fundamental disjunctures between economy, culture, and polities that we have only begun to theorize.

I propose that an elementary framework for exploring such disjunctures is to look at the relationship among five dimensions of global cultural flows that can be termed (a) ethnoscapes, (b) mediascapes, (c) technoscapes, (d) financescapes, and (c) ideoscapes. The suffix -scape allows us to point to the fluid, irregular shapes of these landscapes, shapes that characterize international capital as deeply as they do international clothing styles. These terms with the common suffix -scape also indicate that these are not objectively given relations that look the same from every angle of vision but, rather, that they are deeply perspectival constructs, inflected by the historical, linguistic and political situatedness of different sorts of actors: nation states, multinationals, diasporic communities, as well as sub-national groupings and movements (whether religious, political, or economic), and even intimate face-to-face groups, such as villages, neighbourhoods and families. Indeed, the individual actor is the last locus of this perspectival set of landscapes, for these landscapes are eventually navigated by agents who both experience and constitute larger formations, in part from their own sense of what these landscapes offer.

These landscapes thus are the building blocks of what (extending Benedict Anderson) I would like to call 'imagined worlds', that is, the multiple worlds that are constituted by the historically situated imaginations of persons and groups spread around the globe. An important fact of the world we live in today is that many persons on the globe live in such imagined worlds (and not just in imagined communities) and thus are able to contest, and sometimes even subvert, the imagined worlds of the official mind and of the entrepreneurial mentality that surround them.

By ethnoscape, I mean the landscape of persons who constitute the shifting world in which we live: tourists, immigrants, refugees, exiles, guest workers, and other moving groups and individuals constitute an essential feature of the world and appear to affect the politics of (and between) nations to a hitherto unprecedented degree. This is not to say that there are no relatively stable communities and networks of kinship, friendship, work, and leisure, as well as of birth, residence, and other filial forms. But it is to say that the warp of these stabilities is everywhere shot through with the woof of human motion, as more persons and groups deal with the realities of having to move or the fantasies of wanting to move. What is more, both these realities and fantasies now function on larger scales, as men and women from villages in India think not just of moving to Poona or Madras, but of moving to Dubai and Houston, and refugees from Sri Lanka find themselves in South India as well as in Switzerland, just as the Hmong are driven to London as well as to Philadelphia. And as international capital shifts its needs, as production and technology generate different needs, as nation-states shift their policies on refugee populations, these moving groups can never afford to let their imaginations rest too long, even if they wish to.

By technoscape, I mean the global configuration, also ever fluid, of technology and the fact that technology, both high and low, both mechanical and informational, now moves at high speeds across various kinds of previously impervious boundaries. Many countries now are the roots of multinational enterprise: a huge steel complex in Libya may involve interests from India, China, Russia and Japan, providing different components of new technological configurations. The odd distribution of technologies, and thus the peculiarities of these technoscapes, are increasingly driven not by any obvious economies of scale, of political control, or of market rationality but by increasingly complex relationships among money flows, political possibilities and the availability of both un- and highly-skilled labour. So, while India exports waiters and chauffeurs to Dubai and Sharjah, it also exports software engineers to the US – indentured briefly to Tata-Burroughs or the World Bank, then laundered through the State Department to become wealthy resident aliens, who are in turn objects of seductive messages to invest their money and know-how in federal and state projects in India. . . .

It is useful to speak as well of financescapes, as the disposition of global capital is now a more mysterious, rapid, and difficult landscape to follow than ever before, as currency markets, national stock exchanges, and commodity speculations move 'mega-monies' through national turnstiles at blinding speed, with vast, absolute implications for small differences in percentage points and time units. But the critical point is that the global relationship among ethnoscapes, technoscapes and financescapes is deeply disjunctive and profoundly unpredictable because each of these landscapes is subject to its own constraints and incentives (some political, some informational, and some techno-environmental), at the same time as each acts as a constraint and a para-meter for movements in the others. Thus, even an elementary model of global political economy must take into account the deeply disjunctive relationships among human movement, technological flow and financial transfers.

Further refracting these disjunctures (which hardly form a simple, mechanical global infrastruc-ture in any case) are what I call mediascapes and ideoscapes, which are closely related landscapes of images. Mediascapes refer both to the distribution of the electronic capabilities to produce and dissem-inate information (newspapers, magazines, television stations and film-production studios), which are now available to a growing number of private and public interests throughout the world, and to the images of the world created by these media. These images involve many complicated inflections, depending on their mode (documentary or entertainment), their hardware (electronic or pre-electronic), their audiences (local, national or transnational), and the interests of those who own and control them. What is most important about these mediascapes is that they provide (especially in their television, film, and cassette forms) large and complex repertoires of images, narratives and ethnoscapes to viewers throughout the world, in which the world of commodities and the world of news and politics are profoundly mixed. What this means is that many audiences around the world experience the media

themselves as a complicated and interconnected repertoire of print, celluloid, electronic screens and billboards. The lines between the realistic and the fictional landscapes they see are blurred, so that the farther away these audiences are from the direct experiences of metropolitan life, the more likely they are to construct imagined worlds that are chimerical, aesthetic, even fantastic objects, particularly if assessed by the criteria of some other perspective, some other imagined world. . . .

Ideoscapes are also concatenations of images, but they are often directly political and frequently have to do with the ideologies of states and the counter-ideologies of movements explicitly oriented to cap-turing state power or a piece of it. These ideoscapes are composed of elements of the Enlightenment worldview, which consists of a chain of ideas, terms, and images, including freedom, welfare, rights, sovereignty, representation and the master term, democracy. The master narrative of the Enlighten-ment (and its many variants in Britain, France, and the US) was constructed with a certain internal logic and presupposed a certain relationship between reading, representation and the public sphere. But the diaspora of these terms and images across the world, especially since the nineteenth century, has loosened the internal coherence that held them together in a Euro-American master narrative and provided, instead, a loosely structured synopticon of politics, in which different nation-states, as part of their evolution, have organized their political cultures around different keywords. . . .

This globally variable synaesthesia has hardly even been noted, but it demands urgent analysis. Thus democracy has clearly become a master term, with powerful echoes from Haiti and Poland to the former Soviet Union and China, but it sits at the centre of a variety of ideoscapes, composed of distinctive pragmatic configurations of rough trans-lations of other central terms from the vocabulary of the Enlightenment. This creates ever new termino-logical kaleidoscopes, as states (and the groups that seek to capture them) seek to pacify populations whose own ethnoscapes are in motion and whose mediascapes may create severe problems for the ideoscapes with which they are presented. The fluidity of ideoscapes is complicated in particular by the growing diasporas (both voluntary and involuntary) of intellectuals who continuously inject new meaning-streams into the discourse of democracy in different parts of the world.

This extended terminological discussion of the five terms I have coined sets the basis for a tentative formulation about the conditions under which current global flows occur: they occur in and through the growing disjunctures among ethnoscapes, technoscapes, financescapes, mediascapes and ideoscapes. This formulation, the core of my model of global cultural flow, needs some explanation. First, people, machinery, money, images, and ideas now follow increasingly non-isomorphic paths; of course, at all periods in human history there have been some disjunctures in the flows of these things, but the sheer speed, scale, and volume of each of these flows are now so great that the disjunctures have become central to the politics of global culture. The Japanese are notoriously hospitable to ideas and are stereotyped as inclined to export (all) and import (some) goods, but they are also notoriously closed to immigration, like the Swiss, the Swedes and the Saudis. Yet the Swiss and the Saudis accept populations of guest workers, thus creating labour diasporas of Turks, Italians and other circum-Mediterranean groups. Some such guest-worker groups maintain continuous contact with their home nations, like the Turks, but others, like high-level South Asian migrants, tend to desire lives in their new homes, raising anew the problem of reproduction in a deterritorialized context.

Deterritorialization, in general, is one of the central forces of the modern world because it brings labouring populations into the lower-class sectors and spaces of relatively wealthy societies, while sometimes creating exaggerated and intensified senses of criticism or attachment to politics in the home state. Deterritorialization, whether of Hindus, Sikhs, Palestinians, or Ukrainians is now at the core of a variety of global fundamentalisms, including Islamic and Hindu fundamentalism. In the Hindu case, for example, it is clear that the overseas movement of Indians has been exploited by a variety of interests both within and outside India to create a compli-

cated network of finances and religious identifications, by which the problem of cultural reproduction for Hindus abroad has become tied to the politics of Hindu fundamentalism at home.

At the same time, deterritorialization creates new markets for film companies, art impresarios, and travel agencies, which thrive on the need of the deterritorialized population for contact with its homeland. Naturally, these invented homelands, which constitute the mediascapes of deterritorialized groups, can often become sufficiently fantastic and one-sided that they provide the material for new ideoscapes in which ethnic conflicts can begin to erupt. The creation of Khalistan, an invented homeland of the deterritorialized Sikh population of England, Canada, and the US, is one example of the bloody potential in such mediascapes as they interact with the internal colonialisms of the nation-state. The West Bank, Namibia, and Eritrea are other theatres for the enactment of the bloody negotiation between existing nation-states and various deterritorialized groupings.

It is in the fertile ground of deterritorialization, in which money, commodities and persons are involved in ceaselessly chasing each other around the world, that the mediascapes and ideoscapes of the modern world find their fractured and fragmented counterpart. For the ideas and images produced by mass media often are only partial guides to the goods and experiences that deterritorialized populations transfer to one another. In Mira Nair's brilliant film India Cabaret, we see the multiple loops of this fractured deterritorialization as young women, barely competent in Bombay's metropolitan glitz, come to seek their fortunes as cabaret dancers and prostitutes in Bombay, entertaining men in clubs with dance formats derived wholly from the prurient dance sequences of Hindi films. These scenes in turn cater to ideas about Western and foreign women and their looseness, while they provide tawdry career alibis for these women. Some of these women come from Kerala, where cabaret clubs and the pornographic film industry have blossomed, partly in response to the purses and tastes of Keralites returned from the Middle East, where their diasporic lives away from women distort their very sense of what the relations between men and women might be. These tragedies of displacement could certainly be replayed in a more detailed analysis of the relations between the Japanese and German sex tours to Thailand and the tragedies of the sex trade in Bangkok, and in other similar loops that tie together fantasies about 'the other', the conveniences and seductions of travel, the economics of global trade and the brutal mobility fantasies that dominate gender politics in many parts of Asia and the world at large. . . .

One important new feature of global cultural politics, tied to the disjunctive relationships among the various landscapes discussed earlier, is that state and nation are at each other's throats, and the hyphen that links them is now less an icon of conjuncture than an index of disjuncture. This disjunctive relationship between nation and state has two levels: at the level of any given nation-state, it means that there is a battle of the imagination, with state and nation seeking to cannibalize one another. Here is the seedbed of brutal separatisms – 'majoritarianisms' that seem to have appeared from nowhere and micro-identities that have become political projects within the nation-state. At another level, this disjunctive relationship is deeply entangled with various global disjunctures: ideas of nationhood appear to be steadily increasing in scale and regularly crossing existing state boundaries, sometimes, as with the Kurds, because previous identities stretched across vast national spaces or, as with the Tamils in Sri Lanka, the dormant threads of a transnational diaspora have been activated to ignite the micropolitics of a nation-state. . . .

States find themselves pressed to stay open by the forces of media, technology and travel that have fuelled consumerism throughout the world and have increased the craving, even in the non-Western world, for new commodities and spectacles. On the other hand, these very cravings can become caught up in new ethnoscapes, mediascapes, and, eventually, ideoscapes, such as democracy in China, that the state cannot tolerate as threats to its own control over ideas of nationhood and peoplehood. States throughout the world are under siege, especially where contests over the ideoscapes of democracy are

fierce and fundamental, and where there are radical disjunctures between ideoscapes and technoscapes (as in the case of very small countries that lack contemporary technologies of production and information); or between ideoscapes and financescapes (as in countries such as Mexico or Brazil, where international lending influences national politics to a very large degree); or between ideoscapes and ethnoscapes (as in Beirut, where diasporic, local, and trans-local filiations are suicidally at battle); or between ideoscapes and mediascapes (as in many countries in the Middle East and Asia) where the lifestyles represented on both national and international TV and cinema completely overwhelm and undermine the rhetoric of national politics. In the Indian case, the myth of the lawbreaking hero has emerged to mediate this naked struggle between the pieties and realities of Indian politics, which has grown increasingly brutalized and corrupt.

The transnational movement of the martial arts, particularly through Asia, as mediated by the Hollywood and Hong Kong film industries is a rich illustration of the ways in which long-standing martial arts traditions, reformulated to meet the fantasies of contemporary (sometimes lumpen) youth populations, create new cultures of masculinity and violence, which are in turn the fuel for increased violence in national and international politics. Such violence is, in turn, the spur to an increasingly rapid and amoral arms trade that penetrates the entire world. The world-wide spread of the AK-47 and the Uzi, in films, in corporate and state security, in terror, and in police and military activity, is a reminder that apparently simple technical uniformities often conceal an increasingly complex set of loops, linking images of violence to aspirations for community in some imagined world.

Returning then to the ethnoscapes with which I began, the central paradox of ethnic politics in today's world is that primordia (whether of language or skin colour or neighbourhood or kinship) have become globalized. That is, sentiments, whose greatest force is in their ability to ignite intimacy into a political state and turn locality into a staging ground for identity, have become spread over vast and irregular spaces as groups move yet stay linked to one another through sophisticated media capabilities. This is not to deny that such primordia are often the product of invented traditions or retrospective affiliations, but to emphasize that because of the disjunctive and unstable interplay of commerce, media, national policies and consumer fantasies, ethnicity, once a genie contained in the bottle of some sort of locality (however large), has now become a global force, forever slipping in and through the cracks between states and borders.

But the relationship between the cultural and economic levels of this new set of global disjunctures is not a simple one-way street in which the terms of global cultural politics are set wholly by, or confined wholly within, the vicissitudes of international flows of technology, labour and finance, demanding only a modest modification of existing neo-Marxist models of uneven development and state formation. There is a deeper change, itself driven by the disjunctures among all the landscapes I have discussed and constituted by their continuously fluid and uncertain interplay, that concerns the relationship between production and consumption in today's global economy. Here, I begin with Marx's famous (and often mined) view of the fetishism of the commodity and suggest that this fetishism has been replaced in the world at large (now seeing the world as one large, interactive system, composed of many complex subsystems) by two mutually supportive descendants, the first of which I call production fetishism and the second, the fetishism of the consumer.

By production fetishism I mean an illusion created by contemporary transnational production loci that masks trans-local capital, transnational earning flows, global management and often faraway workers (engaged in various kinds of high tech putting-out operations) in the idiom and spectacle of local (sometimes even worker) control, national productivity and territorial sovereignty. To the extent that various kinds of free-trade zones have become the models for production at large, especially of high-tech commodities, production has itself become a fetish, obscuring not social relations as such but the relations of production, which are increasingly transnational. The locality (both in the sense of the local factory or site of production and in the

extended sense of the nation-state) becomes a fetish that disguises the globally dispersed forces that actually drive the production process. This generates alienation (in Marx's sense) twice intensified, for its social sense is now compounded by a complicated spatial dynamic that is increasingly global.

As for the fetishism of the consumer, I mean to indicate here that the consumer has been transformed through commodity flows (and the mediascapes, especially of advertising, that accompany them) into a sign, both in Baudrillard's sense of a simulacrum that only asymptotically approaches the form of a real social agent and in the sense of a mask for the real seat of agency, which is not the consumer but the producer and the many forces that constitute production. Global advertising is the key technology for the world-wide dissemination of a plethora of creative and culturally well-chosen ideas of consumer agency. These images of agency are increasingly distortions of a world of merchandising so subtle that the consumer is consistently helped to believe that he or she is an actor, where in fact he or she is at best a chooser.

The globalization of culture is not the same as its homogenization, but globalization involves the use of a variety of instruments of homogenization (armaments, advertising techniques, language hegemonies and clothing styles) that are absorbed into local political and cultural economies, only to be repatriated as heterogeneous dialogues of national sovereignty, free enterprise and fundamentalism in which the state plays an increasingly delicate role: too much openness to global flows and the nation-state is threatened by revolt, as in the China syndrome; too little, and the state exits the international stage, as Burma, Albania, and North Korea in various ways have done. In general, the state has become the arbitrageur of this repatriation of difference (in the form of goods, signs, slogans and styles). But this repatriation or export of the designs and commodities of difference continuously exacerbates the internal politics of majoritarianism and homogenization, which is most frequently played out in debates over heritage.

Thus the central feature of global culture today is the politics of the mutual effort of sameness and difference to cannibalize one another and, thereby, proclaim their successful hijacking of the twin Enlightenment ideas of the triumphantly universal and the resiliently particular. This mutual cannibalization shows its ugly face in riots, refugee flows, state-sponsored torture, and ethnocide (with or without state support). Its brighter side is in the expansion of many individual horizons of hope and fantasy, in the global spread of oral re-hydration therapy and other low tech instruments of well-being, in the susceptibility even of South Africa to the force of global opinion, in the inability of the Polish state to repress its own working classes, and in the growth of a wide range of progressive, transnational alliances. Examples of both sorts could be multiplied. The critical point is that both sides of the coin of global cultural process today are products of the infinitely varied mutual contest of sameness and difference on a stage characterized by radical disjunctures between different sorts of global flows and the uncertain landscapes created in and through these disjunctures.

6 ONE WORLD

M. Featherstone

It has become a cliche that we live in one world. Here we think of a variety of images: the photographs of the planet Earth taken in space by the returning Apollo astronauts after setting foot on the moon; the sense of impending global disaster through the greenhouse effect, or some other man-made catastrophe; the ecumenical visions of various traditional and new religious movements to unite humanity; or the commercial use of this ecumenical

From: Global and local cultures, by M. Featherstone, in *Mapping the Futures: Local Culture, Global Change*, edited by J. Bird, B. Curtis, T. Putnam, G. Robertson and L. Tickner, Routledge, 1993.

sentiment which we find in the Coca-Cola advertisement which featured images of legions of bright-eyed young people from the nations of the world singing together 'We are the world'. Such images heighten the sense that we are interdependent; that the flows of information, knowledge, money, commodities, people and images have intensified to the extent that the sense of spatial distance which separated and insulated people from the need to take into account all the other people which make up what has become known as humanity has become eroded. In effect, we are all in each other's backyard. Hence one paradoxical consequence of the process of globalization, the awareness of the finitude and boundedness of the planet and humanity, is not to produce homogeneity but to familiarize us with greater diversity, the extensive range of local cultures.

The globalization of culture

That the process of globalization leads to an increasing sensitivity to differences is by no means pre-ordained. The possibility that we view the world through this particular lens, or form, must be placed alongside other historical possibilities. One perspective on the process of globalization which was accorded a good deal of credibility until recently was that of Americanization. Here a global culture was seen as being formed through the economic and political domination of the US which thrust its hegemonic culture into all parts of the world. From this perspective the American way of life with its rapacious individualism and confident belief in progress, whether manifest in Hollywood film characters such as Donald Duck, Superman and Rambo or embodied in the lives of stars such as John Wayne, was regarded as a corrosive homogenizing force, as a threat to the integrity of all particularities. The assumption that all particularities, local cultures, would eventually give way under the relentless modernizing force of American cultural imperialism, implied that all particularities were linked together in a symbolic hierarchy. Modernization theory set the model into motion, with the assumption that as each non-Western nation eventually became modernized it would move up the hierarchy and duplicate or absorb American culture, to the extent that ultimately every locality would display the cultural ideals, images and material artefacts of the American way of life. That people in a wide range of countries around the world were watching Dallas or Sesame Street and that Coca-Cola cans and ring-pulls were to be found all around the world, was taken as evidence of this process.

If one of the characteristics associated with post-modernism is the loss of a sense of a common historical past and the flattening and spatialization out of long-established symbolic hierarchies (see Featherstone, 1991), then the process of globaliza-tion, the emergence of the sense that the world is a single place, may have directly contributed to this perspective through bringing about a greater inter change and clashing of different images of global order and historical narratives. The perception of history as an unending linear process of the unifica-tion of the world with Europe at the centre in the nineteenth century and the US at the centre in the twentieth century, has become harder to sustain with the beginnings of a shift in the global balance of power away from the West. . . .

The ways in which different nations have been drawn together into a tighter figuration through closer financial and trade ties, through the increasing development of technology to produce more effi-cient and rapid means of communication (mass media, transport, telephone, tax, etc.), and through warfare has produced a higher density of inter-changes. There has been an increase in a wide variety of cultural flows which increase transnational encounters. Appadurai (1990), for example, refers to the increasing flows of people (immigrants, workers, refugees, tourists, exiles), technology (machinery, plant, electronics), financial information (money, shares), media images and information (from tele-vision, film, radio, newspapers, magazines) and ide-ologies and world views. While some might wish to see the motor force for these changes as the relentless progress of the capitalist economy towards a world system (Wallerstein 1974; 1980) or the movement towards a new, disorganized or 'post-Fordist' capital-ism (Lash and Urry, 1987), for Appadurai there is a disjuncture between the cultural flows. On the

practical level, the intensification of flows results in the need to handle problems of intercultural com-munication. In some cases this leads to the develop-ment of 'third cultures' which have a mediating function, as in the case of legal disputes between people from different national cultures (Gessner and Schade, 1990). In addition, there is the further new category of professionals (lawyers, management con-sultants, financial advisers, etc.) who have come into prominence with the deregulation and globalization of financial markets with 24-hour stock market trading, plus the expanding numbers of 'design pro-fessionals' (specialists who work in the film, video, television, music, fashion, advertising and consumer culture industries: King, 1990). All these specialists have to become familiar with a number of national cultures as well as developing, and in some cases living in, third cultures. The majority of these third cultures will draw upon the culture of the parent country from which the organization originated. It is, therefore, evident that the cultures which are devel-oping in many of the global financial firms have been dominated by American practices. The same situa-tion applies with regard to many culture industries, such as television, film and advertising. Yet these third cultures do not simply reflect American values, their relative autonomy and global frame of reference necessitates that they take into account the particu-larities of local cultures and adopt organizational cult-ural practices and modes of orientation which are flexible enough to facilitate this. Hence the practical problems of dealing with cultural flows between nations leads to the formation of a variety of third cultures which operate with relative independence from nation states.

Furthermore, this is not to imply that the increased cultural flows will necessarily produce a greater tolerance and cosmopolitanism. An increasing familiarity with 'the other', be it in face-to-face relations, or through images, or the repre-sentation of the other's world view or ideology, may equally lead to a disturbing sense of engulfment and immersion. This may lead to a retreat from the threat of cultural disorder into the security of ethnicity, traditionalism or fundamentalism, or the active assertion of the integrity of the national culture in global cultural prestige contests (e.g. the Olympic Games). To talk about a global culture is equally to include these forms of cultural contestation. The current phase of globalization is one in which nation states in the West have had to learn to tolerate greater diversity within their boundaries which is manifest in greater multiculturalism and polyethnicity. This is also in part a consequence of their inability to channel and manipulate global cultural flows successfully, especially those of people, information and images, which increases the demand for equal participation, citizenship rights and increased autonomy on the part of regional, ethnic and other minorities. Those who talk about such issues within nation states are also increasingly aware that they are talking to others outside the nation state.

7 CULTURAL GLOBALIZATION IN ZANZIBAR

A. Gurnah

So, where does all this talk about Zanzibar, cultural games, binary opposites and recovery get us? I believe it takes us a long way from many of the current discussions; if I may list a few:

Culture is globalized and it is not entirely or even mainly a negative experience. When Zanzibaris sing rock and roll or South Americans laugh at a Chaplin film we should be glad, particularly when we notice also English people are eating curries and reading African and Indian writers. This connotes a widening of human experiences and wisdom.

The existence of group and individual cultural modalities ensures the confirmed existence and the workings of 'family cultural resemblances' and individual choices. It helps to explain the internal struggles and accommodations within cultures (e.g. the

From: Elvis in Zanzibar, by A. Gurnah, in *The Limits of Globalization*, edited by A. Scott, Routledge, 1997.

old folk in Zanzibar and the young people). It also explains the meaning of 'organic' culture, not as a collection of ossified traditions, but what a group or individuals come to construct and recognize as theirs and as life enhancing.

Through this discussion I have in any case gained a greater understanding of how culture is shared and spread essentially not even mainly through brutality and mindless copying, but for positive reasons connected with human curiosity and the desire to improve and enrich our lives; it is the super highway for life-sustaining social knowledge and change.

Cultural imperialism is often shorthand for identification of other struggles rather than clear explanation of cultural slavery. The cultural process is far too complex to be viewed in such a limited fashion. In cultural exchange both sides are affected for better or worse in the short term. Almost all imperializing nations end up civilizing and culturally broadening their own people through their attempts to occupy others.

Imperialism of culture is a real enough experience, but not one which either lasts long or has a lasting harmful impact. For example the imposition of the English language on African people and Americanism on the Japanese both show the diabolical taking of liberties by imperialists. However, the people whose liberties were so grossly violated soon learnt to find ways to benefit from both.

The point is, a better understanding of cultural processes should pave the way for more intelligent cultural action and allow the processes of culture-complex to provide an efficient interrogation of cultural exchanges for greater knowledge and for obviating and keeping at bay mystifying immoralities.

As much as culture–complexes work between nations, they do so between classes, community groups and gender groups in the same nation. The working class and women are not passive receivers of ruling-class or high culture domination. They do not, any more than do 'immigrant' workers in European countries, merely fight and resist such cultural imperialism, but also play an important role in shaping and reshaping the dominant culture around them, and create new syntheses.

8 THE MYTH OF GLOBALIZATION

J. Street

There are many critiques offered of globalization. My own concern is with the way in which the rhetoric of global culture has become detached from the material and institutional conditions that underlie the appearance of globalization.

'Global culture'

The term 'global culture' itself suggests, as we have seen, two visions of the product. Either a multiplicity of forms of expression, values and experiences, deriving from across the world and with no one set taking precedence over the others. Or it refers to a single culture which is specific to no one group – an interpretation of 'We are the World', in which 'we' refers to everyone who inhabits the planet. Both these pictures of the global culture, though, are attacked by critics (see Murphy, 1983; Featherstone, 1990; McGrew and Lewis, 1992). The culture being touted across the globe often emerges from one bit of the world – America – and carries with it American experiences and perspectives.

While it is true that Anglo-American products are modified to appeal to their international audience, the product itself still retains the hallmarks of its origins. There may be concessions, ways of 'tailoring' an original design, to suit certain markets, but these are small compromises within the main framework. It is not just that English is the language of much popular culture; it is also that the images and concerns of the Anglo–American region are most prevalent. The film Black Rain may have been shot in Japan and used Japanese actors to star alongside the American Michael Douglas, but it was fear of Japanese economic success that fuelled the plot.

A similar criticism can be directed at 'global multiculturalism'. The diverse cultures do not just emerge into the global airwaves. They are selected.

From: 'Across the Universe': the limits of global popular culture, by J. Street, in *The Limits of Globalization*, edited by A. Scott, Routledge, 1997.

Tour operators choose particular resorts because of what their wealthy clients expect. 'World music' is defined by Anglo–American record companies according to marketing strategies that particular audiences represent or require (Frith, 1989; Redhead and Street, 1989).

So the first challenge to the notion of global culture is that no such culture exists, either in its unitary or its multicultural form. This is not to deny that the world is increasingly connected up, that there is greater interaction between cultures, only that the net effect is not a plurality of equal cultures, or a harmonious synthesis of them in one global culture. Cultures form part of a struggle for power, in which resources (both cultural and financial) are not evenly distributed (Jayaweera, 1987).

Another line of criticism is less concerned with the product itself, and more with the use to which it is put, the way it is interpreted. Even if there is a global culture, it would be wrong to see it as meaning the same to everyone. This is amply demonstrated by the way jazz was used and abused in the Soviet Union. At one time it was banned as a product of capitalist decadence; at another it was feted as the authentic voice of an oppressed people (Starr, 1983), and both readings of jazz are at odds with its interpretation elsewhere. Culture does not simply impose itself upon peoples. While, as Ferguson notes, Canada imports 90 per cent of its Anglophone TV Drama, 'there is considerable evidence that Canada continues to maintain a value system and way of life distinctive from the US' (Ferguson, 1992, p. 81). Writers about Britain also warn of the danger of seeing American culture as a synonym for 'Americanization' (Webster, 1988; Strinati, 1992). The myth of America takes on different meanings in different contexts. In other words, the argument that there is a global culture may also be less vulnerable to the argument that there is not a global process of cultural interpretation. The same artefact does not elicit the same response wherever it is seen or heard. In popular culture, context is vital. 'We may all hear each other's sounds these days', writes Frith, 'but we still read them differently' (1991, p. 281). This is not just a theoretical point about how culture is understood, it is one about the organization of culture and about relations of power.

If the 'global culture' is in fact the culture of a particular part of the globe, then we may be suspicious of the claim that we are now dealing with global industries. Rather, we are dealing with multinational corporations who need to expand their market or their product base. This means discovering, or organizing, new audiences; it also means finding 'new' products. The phenomenon of 'global' companies can, in fact, be a mistaken description of 'corporate transnationalization at a higher level of magnitude' (Ferguson, 1992, p. 75). The appearance of global companies may disguise a reality in which corporate structure is forced to change to adapt to new markets or technologies.

Furthermore, the picture of global industry operating unconstrained also omits the possibility of national and local mediating interests. It is important to notice that the actual delivery of popular culture depends on the processes which are peculiar to particular national (and sub-national) structures. This process is most apparent in the organization of broadcasting, and is clearly exemplified in the contrast between Britain and the US. The degree of regulation both of the airwaves and of the organizations allowed to inhabit them have an impact upon what can be heard/seen (Malm and Willis 1993; McQuail and Siune, 1986). The same can be claimed for popular music (Street, 1993).

The dominant political ideology of the 1980s, the voice of the market liberal, held that culture was best managed by the market – that culture was, in fact, or ought in principle to be, free from political interference. The empirical claim that underpinned this argument, has, however, to be treated with some scepticism. On a number of fronts, political actors have considerable influence over the form and content of popular culture. It is only necessary to preview the work of Reporters Sans Frontieres (1993), on the censorship and regulation of national systems of communications, to realize the extent of the national political management of culture.

'Global culture' is also subject to the effects of other agencies besides the broadcasters. Government – at various levels – can have and impact on what is available and what access is allowed to it. Writing of the interaction of Government and the music

industry, Malm and Willis observe: 'Laws can be made, taxes can be introduced and exempted, cultural and media policies can be formulated, subsidies can be constructed and aimed at increasing the music industry's activities with national and local music, as opposed to national imports' (1993, p. 26). It does not follow from this, of course, that national governments succeed in their ambitions. It is a long path from policy intent to policy implementation. None the less, the way nation states organize culture involves a process of negotiation and struggle. And what Malm and Willis reveal, with a series of detailed case studies, is that there are many different results to these relationships, results that can be measured by the music making and consuming that any one country enjoys. Much, too, may depend on the structure of interests within the nation state. Governments may be able to regulate some aspects of broadcasting better that others. In Tanzania, the radio carries a high proportion of nationally produced music. Television cannot match this because there is no national film industry to supply videos. Thus, the TV stations make use of imported videos, courtesy of MTV. In other words, there is no unitary process of globalization and the extent of it is dependent upon political structures and forces which are specific to national and local states.

But it is not just that states differ between themselves in the ways in which they try to manage culture. Within each state, the forms of infrastructure has an effect upon what is being consumed and how. Though there is a pervasive impression that the world has been 'wired up', it is not altogether accurate. While it is true that in Britain and America there is a high penetration of radio and television (in 1989, 98 per cent of households had at least one TV set (PSI, 1992: 2)), other nations have much lower levels of access, and in Britain, the cable network has developed more slowly that in other European countries (Dyson and Humphreys, 1986). Furthermore, the access and use of communications technology is not uniformly spread. British Asian and Afro-Caribbean groups are more likely to have a satellite dish than other groups; they also show greater willingness to subscribe to cable (PSI, 1993: 3 and 19).

9 THE IDEA OF 'GLOBAL CULTURE'

B. Axford

Culture is better seen as an interpretative framework or context, as a source of identity, or a means, Lash and Urry say, of 'telling people who they are' (1994, p. 129). Applied to a global context, this usage requires evidence of the ways in which local subjects are constituted through global relations (Friedman, 1993, p. 4). However, exactly what is meant by 'global culture' is still a matter of some dispute, despite the growing fascination with the idea (Featherstone, 1990).

'Is there a global culture?' asks Featherstone (1990, p. 1), while Immanuel Wallerstein, with a different agenda in mind, queries 'can there be a such a thing as world culture?' (1991, p. 184). On the face of it these may seem strange questions given the apparent weight of evidence available. As Featherstone points out, even in the absence of the cultural homogeneity and integration which might be afforded by a world state, it would seem that global cultures exist, carried through networks which are not tied to any particular jurisdiction or national cultural milieu. It is also clear that not all global phenomena are world-integrative, even if they are world-wide: witness the deconstructive effects of Ethan-nationalism. By contrast, the spread of universal or cosmopolitan cultures – through consumerist ideologies, global marketing strategies and, most significantly, through the potential of 'tele-comedia' to change the way in which people live and think – presages a global future in which meaning and identities are not tied to place or limited in chronological time.

The sort of products available through global flows can be highly individuated, ranging from digital newspapers to interactive television drama, and they are 'localized' largely through the tailoring of products and services to fit market niches. Locality as visceral identity is replaced by locality as part of

a map of variable tastes. 'Global' consumer products and cultures, for example the concept of the Ford Mondeo as a 'world car', rely on the ability of designers and marketeers to produce a standard overall design with sufficient flexibility to allow for local variation on the common denominators of taste. In this version the characteristics of global culture are that it is 'universal, timeless and technical' (Smith, 1990, p. 7). Previous 'universal' cultures – here Smith mentions the Greek and Roman cultures of the ancient world, and the Islamic and Christian cultures of the Middle Ages – were diffused from particular places and were heavy with history. By contrast, the putative global culture of today is 'bereft of roots' and 'situated in panoramic space' (p. 7). Because of these qualities, runs his argument, it is thin and inauthentic, and whole identities cannot be rooted in such poor soil.

Maybe so, but this argument seems to miss the key point about the significance of global culture or, more to the point, global processes, which is that they are likely to produce ambivalence rather than coherence of identity, or to spawn multiple identities: local, national or European; gay, black or Cherokee. Thus do they serve to 'weaken the seams of old orders' (Friedman, 1993, p. 212). Moreover, the claim that global culture is inauthentic when set against the 'real' identity space of the nation-state, and the 'culturally thicker' identities of localities and communities of affect, would not of itself negate the potential force of global processes in the destruction of these identities, especially where it can be seen that globalization does contribute to the creation of a vertiginous, rootless and, in Smith's sense, 'culture-less' space. In fact, the normative burden of Smith's argument is precisely that global cultures encourage agents to 'forget history' in the sense written of by Ardener (1989) and to construct identities that are stripped of previous meanings in a world now dominated by Baudrillardian 'hypertechnology' (Baudrillard, 1983). Although Smith does not draw this parallel, similar kinds of argument are made about the 'presentism' that informs postmodernist constructions of social life.

Leaving aside normative judgements for the moment, it must be an empirical matter as to what

From: *The Global System: Economics, Politics and Culture*, by B. Axford, Polity Press, 1995.

sort of institutions and processes help to anchor and to change identities, not one that can be argued a priori (Schlesinger, 1991). Consequently, I want to oppose the idea that a contextless and 'free-wheeling cosmopolitanism' is turning national and local cultures into shallow and homogenized cultural spaces (Smith, 1990). This rather simplistic interpretation of the effects of global cultures and cultural products fails to see beyond their 'mediatized' forms to the ways in which the 'signs and flows' of the global cultural economy are providing opportunities for the creation of those 'third cultures' . . . (Featherstone, 1990, p. 1). It is highly unlikely that these flows and signs, whether in mass communications or in tourism, will produce 'a' global culture, given the diversity in their reception and use by local audiences. However, because they permit forms of social inter-action not tied to place or limited in time, it is proper to see them as contexts or frames of reference within which new identities may be formed, and new understandings of the world fashioned.

Furthermore, we do not have to dismiss the identity-generative power of global cultures to see that local cultures caught up in the processes of globalization can and do resist transformation, or otherwise retain their vitality. There is a wealth of evidence, not all of it anecdotal, to dispute the claim that the world is being homogenized culturally . . . (Harvey, 1989; Pred and Watts, 1992). Likewise the argument that cultural identities are increasingly negotiable in these confused times rings hollow in the face of the robustness of social and cultural forms and 'codes and practices which resist and play back systemicity' (Featherstone, 1990, p. 2). Of course, it is sometimes tempting to treat these forms romantically, as the residues of inure palpable 'communities' which once existed, but we should be wary of both nostalgia and colourful metaphors for the apocalypse. Pred and Watts (1992) describe the present global condition as a 'totality of fragments', and this is a useful encapsulation of a world connected but not unified economically and culturally, and in which the globalization of production and consumption has yet to produce globalized meaning. It is entirely appropriate that Pred and

Watts's description can be read either in approbation of these developments, or as a lament. . . .

Global culture and postmodernity

Thompson's (1993) discussion of Habermas's concept of the public sphere conveys the modernist slant of much thinking about culture, which is ambivalent and guilty about its own universalist pretensions. Modernity destroys traditional cultures and replaces them with cultures built on reflexivity, but while traditional cultures are still viewed either with a certain amount of nostalgia as the residues of authentic communities or, more romantic still, as the home of atavistic and savage identities, postmodern transformations are generally anathema. Such at any rate is the claim of Frederick Jameson (1991) in his critique of the cultural hyperspaces of postmodernity, which draws upon a Marxist cultural problematic to examine the creation of what he calls the 'postmodern hyperspace'. Jameson has very little truck with the authentic-inauthentic divide referred to above; in the postmodern hyperspace what you see is what you get, there are no deeper meanings. For Jameson, hyperspace is the space physical or discursive as well as epistemological – in which 'the truth of experience no longer coincides with the place in which it takes place' (p. 44). Instead there are economic and cultural flows and communication networks in which individuals are caught up in and in which, through processes of aesthetic invention and re-invention, they are able to establish new self-identities of a more or less ephemeral nature (Lash and Urry, 1994).

The cultural politics of postmodernity is thus much more fluid than that dominated by the grand narratives of earlier phases of capitalism, principally the narrative of social class, which bred a one-dimensional politics of 'left' versus 'right'. Because of changes in the character of capitalist societies and the collapse of the state-socialist alternative there is greater room for the expression of previously non-thematized interests, notably feminism and the environmental movement, but also ethnic identities and forms of communitarianism. Jameson laments these changes, not because he objects to the formation of new identities and interests, but because he sees in them one more twist in the successful restructuration of capitalist hegemony and not its transcendence. But his pessimism over the demise of modernist narratives contrasts sharply with what Kenneth Thompson (1992, pp. 240–3) calls the 'constructive postmodernism' of writers like Dick Hebdige (1989).

In a significant contribution to the sociology of these 'new times', Hebdige (1989) also deconstructs the narrative of social class, but sees in the fragments a new politics and a more complex social and cultural division of labour, based on the shifting wants and aspirations of groups that form around any number of themes, issues and desires. In these new milieus identities are constructed from popular culture, from the mass media and in the fall-out from the once 'real' politics of class, which is replaced by a 'lifestyle' politics fed on aspiration marketing. Significantly, the changes are seen as generally emancipatory, offering new imaginaries and providing new possibilities for agents to realize their potential and to upset the course of usual politics. To be sure, restructuring in this way is unlikely to produce the pristine public realm of the bourgeois imagination (Habermas, 1994), but the point is that there are quite different ways of looking at these 'new realities' (Drucker, 1989). . . .

10 POSTMODERN POPULAR CULTURE

C. Barker

For Baudrillard and Jameson, consumerism is implicated in a 'depthless culture' of signs without referents. From a different perspective writers like Chambers (1987; 1990), Collins (1989) and Hebdige (1988) have discussed the ways in which

From: *Global Television*, by C. Barker, Blackwell, 1997.

commodities form the basis for multiple identity construction, particularly in relation to youth and popular culture, emphasizing the active meaning production of consumers so that they become 'bricoleurs' selecting and arranging elements of material commodities and meaningful signs. Indeed, Paul Willis (1990) argues that because the construction of meaning occurs through actual usage rather than being inherent in the commodity, it is possible for a creative 'common culture' to be formed through the consuming practices of young people.

These more positive versions of consumption are tied in with the construction of a variety of life-styles in postmodern culture through the purchase and consumption of consumer goods, reflecting particular tastes and preferences. The postmodern can thus be read as the democratization of culture and of new individual and political possibilities. It can be argued that:

> Postmodernism, whatever form its own intellectualizing might take, has been fundamentally anticipated in the metropolitan cultures of the last twenty years: among the electronic signifiers of cinema, television and video, in recording studios and record players, in fashion and youth styles, in all those sounds, images and diverse histories that are daily mixed, recycled and 'scratched' together on that giant screen which is the contemporary city. (Chambers, 1987, p. 7)

The democratic possibilities of postmodern popular culture lie in the legitimacy being accorded to it, since though it is a statement of the obvious, popular culture is popular and can represent a more democratic cultural movement than traditional high culture. Further, the creative play through which such cultural forms are produced and consumed offers democratizing possibilities because, while the production of popular music, film, television and fashion is in the hands of transnational capitalist corporations, the meanings are produced, altered and managed at the level of consumption by people who are active producers of meaning. This is particularly significant in an environment of semiotic excess whereby the widespread circulation of signs with multiple meanings makes it harder for any dominant auditing to stick; the possibility is opened up for people to create their own meanings and styles from a range of signs and sites of activity. People range across a series of terrains, sites of meaning, that are not of their own making but from which they can actively produce sense so that the 'bricolage' of film, TV and architecture is echoed in the patchwork of self-constructed postmodern identities:

> The 'making' in question is a production, a poiesis – but a hidden one, because it is shattered over areas defined and occupied by systems of 'production' (television, urban development, commerce, etc.) and because the steadily increasing expansion of those systems no longer leaves 'consumers' any place in which they can indicate what they make or do with the products of these systems. To a rationalized, expansionist and at the same time centralized, clamorous and spectacular production corresponds another production, called 'consumption'. The latter is devious, it is dispersed, but it insinuates itself everywhere, silently and almost invisibly, because it does not manifest itself through its own products, but rather through its ways of using the products imposed by a dominant economic order. (de Certeau, 1984, pp. 12–13)

That the circumstances of postmodern culture both constitute and are constituted by fresh possibilities can be seen in the emergence of new voices, of the 'other' of modernity, in new social movements and in new forms of struggles in and through popular culture. This has taken a number of forms: the emergence of feminism and of black politics, the appearance of 'life politics', of ecology and peace movements, the voices from non-Western cultures, the challenges to notions of progress and development by new-age travellers, the demands for free movement and public space implicit in 'rave', the 'declaration of independence, of otherness, of alien intent, a refusal of anonymity, of subordinate status' (Hebdige, 1988, p. 35), of certain sub-cultures and the possibility of the creation of a radical plural democracy based on diversity and difference argued

for by Laclau and Mouffe (1985). There are no guarantees, no universal foundations, for such a project and it remains only a possibility inherent in postmodern culture.

These are contradictory times. We face increased social control and surveillance, poverty and powerlessness, transnational corporations and mass-produced culture yet we are also learning to value diversity, difference, popular culture and popular meaning construction, the decline of a dominant culture and the potential for new forms of solidarity. Within urban geography one finds the metaphors of the landscape and the vernacular where the former is the wider terrain erected by multinational urban re-developers and the latter represents the re-shaping of the space on the ground by popular sentiment and practices. This is an apt metaphor for the possibilities of a global postmodern culture and, while the landscape continues to be shaped by multinational power in its various manifestations, the vernacular still holds the potential to be shaped by the power of the popular. It is a hope, a possibility, perhaps a utopia.

Postmodernism and the globalization of television

The development of global television as a fundamentally commercial form has placed advertising in the visible forefront of its activities. Television remains the central vehicle for international advertising both in its multi-local and global branding forms; television's organizational forms and programming strategies are heavily structured by the advertising industry. Though global branding remains a limited phenomenon, television is central to the production and reproduction of a postmodern 'promo-culture' centred on the use of visual imagery to create value-added brands or commodity-signs. While the excitement and brashness of consumer culture has an undoubted appeal, the concern is that it is eroding a public sphere based on the ideal of rational debate. While consumers may be critical decoders of adverts, the terrain is shaped by multinational corporations who are not subject to any kind of democratic control and whose prime concern is profit.

The globalization of television both constitutes and is constituted by the postmodern flow of images from different times and places. That is to say, television is postmodern in part because it draws from the ever increasing sources offered to it by the wider processes of globalization, which in turn globalize a postmodern form whose origins lie in the West. Such a postmodern culture is a reflexive and contradictory culture. On the one hand, the institutional terrain and the production of culture is increasingly commodified and controlled by transnational corporations, Western culture is almost completely a commercial one, while on the other, we are all increasingly reflexive about ourselves, our culture, and the history, conditions and techniques of cultural production. The tensions between a centrally – and commercially – produced culture and an active, knowledgeable audience is at the centre of an understanding of global television and of cultural conditions in general, whether that be in New York, Bombay or Mexico City.

11 POSTMODERNISM

F. J. Schuurman

Postmodernists react against the modernity discourse. Thus Lyotard (1984; 1985) believes that Auschwitz and Stalin heralded the ultimate fiasco of the modernity project. Science is not employed to emancipate humanity, but enlisted by capital and subjugated to efficiency rather than truth. There is no one single truth, as depicted by modern philosophy; rather there is a plurality of perspectives, each with its own language, its own rules and myths.

From: Postmodernism, by F. J. Schuurman, in *Beyond the Impasse: development theory in the 1990s*, edited by F. J. Schuurman, Zed Books, 1993.

French post-structuralists such as Derrida (1973; 1976), Deleuze and Guattari (1983; 1987) developed the thesis that language consists of a set of 'signifiers' which do not give access to reality, and where the existence of one reality is moreover doubted. Symbols become more important than the message they must convey. There is no longer a distinction between truth and lie, between reason and rhetoric, between essence and semblance, between science and ideology. An apparent reality is created by mass media through an endless circulation of symbols. Production no longer sets the tone in society, consumption of symbols replaces it. Universal values do not exist and meta-theories (both Marxism and modernization theories) which take universal values as given and see society as 'makeable' are suspect and merely contribute to an apparent reality. The Enlightenment ideal of the emancipation of humanity has not been achieved, nor can it be achieved.

There are three currents which fall under the term postmodernism, originating respectively from art, from literature and language philosophy (the post-structuralists), and from social sciences (the post-industrialists). The oldest claims to the title postmodernism lie with the arts, which, in the 1950s, reacted against the abstract in paintings and the International Style in architecture.

Of particular importance here is the philosophy of post-industrialism. The basic idea is that Western countries entered a post-industrial phase whereby the concentration on production of goods was replaced by production of technical knowledge (Bell, 1973; Touraine, 1974). Post-industrial society is a 'knowledge' society in which a growing part of the labour force is used for the production of technical knowhow. Basically, the argument goes as follows. Fordism reached a crisis in the 1970s, heralding a late-Fordist phase for capitalism, which exhibited the following features:

- increasing internationalization of capital, especially through the spread of assembly activities;
- a decrease in importance of the nation-state, and an absolute and relative decrease of the traditional core of the working class;

- a marked increase in the service class through the increased role of management, research and financial transactions;
- increasing unemployment and a growing distinction between skilled and unskilled labourers;
- an increasing difference in consumer patterns;
- a larger role of mass media in the process of socialization.

According to the post-industrialists, late Fordism displayed such distinct contours during the 1980s that it is legitimate to talk of a post-Fordist period. Here, the development of micro-electronics provides the industrial sector with an even more flexible organization, with a hard core of well-paid labourers in the areas of research and development and in management. The role of the state is reduced to keeping the whole internationally competitive. The individualization of society increases (e.g. the increase in single-person or childless households). Consumption is characterized by stressing constant renewal of the products on offer. This consumer hedonism leads to 'disposable life-styles' (Berman, 1982). The functionalistic aesthetic of Fordist use values, which were related to the norms of rigid Taylorist mass production, belongs permanently to the past.

12 GLOBALIZATION AND THE POSTMODERNIZATION OF CULTURE

B. S. Turner

I have also taken the view in this collection of essays that globalization is one of the social causes of the postmodernization of culture. Globalization brings about increasing diversification and complexity of

From: The self and reflexive modernity, in *Theories of Modernity and Postmodernity*, by B. S. Turner, Sage, 1990.

culture and complexity of cultures by interposing a variety of traditions within a community. Cultural globalization, therefore, forces upon modern societies, and upon intellectuals in particular, a new reflexivity about the authenticity of cultures, their social status and the nature of cultural hierarchy. Although human societies have always been faced with the issue of alien cultures and foreign intervention, globalization is producing a completely new level of multiculturalism and cultural diversity. This cultural diversity cannot be simply ignored and my argument, therefore, is that globalization requires a new cultural reflexivity, which in turn gives a special role to the intellectual as passing a judgement on the nature of national cultures. The old anthropological problematic of alien cultures becomes a persistent theme of modern intellectual enquiry as such, because nation-states are forced to enquire into the character of their national cultural identities. Globalization raises the possibility that all cultural systems are local cultures, because it is difficult to sustain the idea, for example, that British culture is a global culture. Reflexivity and cultural propinquity in a global context also produces a new focus on the self in postmodernity, because the relation between individual and national identity becomes highly unstable and uncertain.

Postmodernity is typically analysed as an effect of new technical means of communication and new patterns of information storage. In popular culture, the impact of radio, television, film and video on attitudes and practice has been enormous. The experiential impact of virtual reality is to suggest in a relatively direct way that the simulation of reality is technically feasible. Cultural postmodernism is also seen by sociologists to be a broad social response to rational modernism, particularly in architecture and domestic design. My intention is not to reject these theories of the social causes of the process of postmodernization; the point of my argument is to draw attention to the special role of globalization in the social production of postmodernity. Within this scenario, cultural tourism is a particularly potent force in the postmodern diversification of cultural experience. Global tourism increases intercultural exchange and forces cultural elites to come to terms with the heritage industry. Tourist fantasy permits the self to assume diverse social roles in exotic settings; tourism invents and demands empathy to play out short-term fantasy roles. Tourism tends to make cultures into museums, as cultural phenomena which can be viewed as quaint, peculiar and local. Tourism paradoxically is a quest for authentic local cultures, but the tourist industry, by creating an illusion of authenticity, in fact reinforces the experience of social and cultural simulation. The very existence of tourism rules out the possibility of authentic cultural experience. More importantly, ethnic or national cultures become local or folk cultures which are available to the tourist gaze.

As an illustration of this argument we could take Jean Baudrillard's account of America (1988). We can treat Baudrillard's study as, in fact, an intellectual tourist commentary on American postmodern culture. In particular, the style of Baudrillard's work creates the illusion of a car journey across the American landscape. A postmodern style of reading involves channel-hopping, random grazing and depthless scanning rather like a tourist pursuing culture through an ad hoc sample process (Rojek and Turner, 1993). The implication of postmodernism, therefore, is that in the postmodern world we are all tourists or, to use a term which is full of sociological significance, strangers in our own society. Thus the global diversity of cultures creates an alien environment in which all cultures appear strange. The counterpart, of course, for postmodern cultural alienation is nostalgia; that is, the nostalgic quest for real communities, real experience and real culture. Postmodernization produces a profound sense of the artificial and constructed nature of both social arrangements and cultural forms. All cultural artefacts appear, therefore, to be mere artefacts. It is important to recognize that the process of postmodernization is also in many respects a process of secularization, because it is difficult for religions to protect themselves from the critique of postmodern culture which regards all religious accounts of the world as merely 'grand narratives'. Secularization is an essential ingredient to the idea of the reflexive self and most traditional theories of the self, individualism and individuality have assumed a profound

process of social disenchantment of belief. Pluralistic belief, random commitment and religious experimentation would be compatible with a postmodern lifestyle; that is, with the idea of secularization as cultural pluralism. Postmodernism makes commitment to a single grand narrative unlikely. However, I do not want to suggest that the secularization of the faith takes place at this merely cognitive or intellectual level. It is not the case that people stop believing in God merely as a consequence of rational criticism; rather they stop believing in God when religious belief is eroded by transformations of everyday life which make belief either irrelevant or impossible. The postmodernization of culture in creating an experience of artificiality also brings religion into question at this everyday level. The multiplication of religious faiths in a multicultural society has in this everyday world a profoundly relativizing effect. This relativism is not of the old atheistic type about which Ernest Gellner has written in his 'Postmodernism, Reason and Religion' (1992). The relativism of postmodern cultures is more to do with the daily experience of consumerism in a context of global diversity and difference; in short, we have to see experiential secularity as the product of globalization. While Gellner has attempted to treat postmodernism as simply philosophical relativism, my argument has attempted to examine the impact of consumerism and postmodern cultural diversity on everyday experience and practice. In turn, fundamentalism should be regarded as a religious response to globalization, multiculturalism and postmodern pluralism. Western consumerism erodes the foundation of traditional lifestyles and therefore corrodes traditional religious practices not at the level of consciousness, but at the level of what Pierre Bourdieu has called the habitus.

If postmodernism is a challenge to religion, it is also a challenge to the traditional role of intellectuals. As we have seen, one of the significant social functions of the intellectual has been the guardianship of high culture and the protection of high culture from popular debasement. Postmodernism mixes high and low culture in a new system of kitsch culture and through the mode of parody and irony, and in so doing it undermines and questions traditional hierarchical patterns of high and low culture. At the same time, the consequences of globalization are to mix up local and global culture in a new melting pot of multiculturalism. Since high culture cannot be local culture, this effect of globalization has important consequences for the very possibility of the intellectual as a social role. Of course, postmodernism at the same time opens up new possibilities for the intellectual as an interpreter of the postmodern condition.

In this discussion I have self-consciously treated postmodernism and postmodernity as real states of affairs. I have restricted the notion of postmodernism to theories about postmodernization; that is, I have treated postmodernism as an intellectual movement in social thought and as a cultural criticism of modernism. By postmodernity, therefore, I refer to the social condition of modern societies which are going through a process of postmodernization. Postmodernity involves cultural differentiation and complexity, the loss of the authority of high culture, the growth of urban multiculturalism as a consequence of processes of globalization, and the prevalence of certain stylistic devices in culture, such as simulation, parody and irony. Postmodernization produces the experience of the artificial and constructed nature of culture and cultural experiences. In taking this view of postmodernism I am also self-consciously distinguishing this position from arguments presented by Anthony Giddens and Ulrich Beck. As we have seen, Beck and Giddens prefer to define modern societies in terms of either risk society or high modernity or reflexive modernity. They have specifically rejected the notion that postmodernization is a valid account of the transformation of modern culture. Their account of high modernity and risk society depends heavily on a particular view which they develop of the modern self, namely of the self as a project. The reflexive self is a core feature of the general progress of de-traditionalization in high modernity.

13 POSTMODERNISM AND CONSUMER CULTURE

M. Featherstone

A number of commentators have linked the rise of postmodernism to consumer culture (Bell, 1976; Jameson, 1984; Featherstone, 1991). Both terms give a central emphasis to culture. Here there seems to have been two displacements. The term consumer society marked a shift from considering consumption as a mere reflex of production, to conceiving consumption as central to social reproduction. The term consumer culture points not only to the increasing production and salience of cultural goods as commodities but also to the way in which the majority of cultural activities and signifying practices become mediated through consumption, and consumption progressively involves the consumption of signs and images. Hence the term consumer culture points to the ways in which consumption ceases to be a simple appropriation of utilities, or use values, to become a consumption of signs and images in which the emphasis upon the capacity to endlessly reshape the cultural or symbolic aspect of the commodity makes it more appropriate to speak of commodity-signs. The culture of the consumer society is, therefore, held to be a vast floating complex of fragmentary signs and images, which produces an endless sign play which destabilize long-held symbolic meanings and cultural order (Baudrillard, 1983; 1993; and Jameson, 1984, develop this argument).

This key feature of consumer culture (the fragmentation and over-production of culture) is often regarded as the central feature of postmodernism, something which was taken up by artists, intellectuals and academics in various ways as a problem to be expressed and theorized. Hence we often get references to the fragmentation of time into a series of perpetual presents and the loss or end of a sense of history (Vattimo, 1988). The inability to order the fragmented culture is also held to lead to an aesthet-

From: *Undoing Culture: Globalization, Postmodernism and Identity*, by M. Featherstone, Sage, 1995.

icization of everyday life through the inability to chain together signs and images into a meaningful narrative. Instead, the constant flow and bizarre juxtapositions of images and signs, as found for example in MTV, is regarded as producing isolated, intense affect-charged experiences (Jameson, 1994). The thematization of this fragmented, depthless culture in the 1960s within art and intellectual life underwent a further shift away from the high cultural stance of distanced moral indignation and condemnation of the impoverished mass culture towards embracing and celebrating the popular and mass culture aesthetic. Not only do we find that the mass cultural techniques of advertising and the media were copied and celebrated, as in pop art, but that the long-held doctrines of artistic originality and genius were rejected. In addition, this artistic movement criticized the high modernism system of artistic production and reproduction in which key artefacts and texts were canonized and institutionalized in the gallery, museum and the academy. Now art was seen and proclaimed to be everywhere in the city street, in the detritus of mass culture. Art was in advertising, advertising was in art.

We can make a number of points about the relationship between postmodernism and consumer culture which suggest that many of the modes of signification and experiences labelled as postmodern cannot simply be regarded as the product of a new epoch. 'postmodernity', or the cultural changes accompanying the post-war shift to a 'late capitalist' economy.

It is common in depictions of postmodern experiences to find references to: the disorientating melee of signs and images, stylistic eclecticism, sign-play, the mixing of codes, depthlessness, pastiche, simulations, hyper-reality, immediacy, a *mélange* of fiction and strange values, intense affect-charged experiences, the collapse of the boundaries between art and everyday life, an emphasis upon images over words, the playful immersion in unconscious processes as opposed to detached conscious appreciation, the loss of a sense of the reality of history and tradition; the decentring of the subject (see Jameson, 1984; Chambers, 1987; Lash, 1988; Baudrillard, 1983; 1993; Hebdige, 1988). The first point to note is that

these experiences are generally held to take place within the context of consumer culture leisure. The locations most frequently mentioned are theme parks and tourist sites (Disneyland being the exemplar), shopping centres, out-of-town malls, contemporary museums, gentrified inner city areas and docklands. Television is often referred to, with the emphasis given to the fragmented distracted mode of viewing with the channel-hopper or MTV viewer being the paradigmatic form. The most influential figure cited here is Baudrillard (1983; 1993), who suggests that television has produced the end of the social to the extent that social encounters become simulations with an 'as if it has already happened' hyper-real quality; at the same time television provides an overload of information which leads to an implosion of meaning (for examples of those who have sought to build on Baudrillard's work, see Kroker and Cook, 1988; Kaplan, 1987; Mellencamp, 1990).

The first thing we can note is that, with the exception of television, these experiences seem confined to specific locations and practices which are themselves not new in the sense that there is a long history within consumer culture of shopping centres, department stores, tourist sites which have produced simulations, sign-play and amazing spaces which encourage a childlike sense of wonder and controlled decontrol of the emotions. We find references to this in the depictions of the nineteenth-century modern city in the writings of Benjamin (1973) and Simmel (1990; 1991). Indeed it can be argued that this experience can be traced back to the carnivals and fairs of the Middle Ages (see Featherstone, 1991, Ch. 5). Yet the techniques for producing consumer culture illusion and spectacles have become more refined. There is a good deal of difference in technical capacity between the simulation of a trans-Siberian railway journey in which one sits in a carriage and looks through the window at a canvas of the landscape unfolding at the 1990 Paris Exposition and the latest Disney World simulator 'rides' in the sophistication of the detail achieved (through animatronics, sound, film, holograms, smell, etc.) and the capacity to achieve a complete sense of immersion in the experience. Virtual reality is the latest stage in this process (see Featherstone, 1995; Featherstone and

Burrows, 1995). Yet it is hard to argue that for the respective audiences we can necessarily assume that there is a greater suspension of disbelief today when one considers the sense of wonder on the faces of participants at earlier spectacles. What there may be is a greater capacity within consumer culture to be able rapidly to switch codes and participate in an 'as if' manner, to participate in the experience and then to switch to the examination of the techniques whereby the illusion is achieved, with little sense of nostalgic loss. The 'as if' world is of course heightened by the experience of television and the ways in which it can collapse time and space. The experiences, people, places and emotional tone captured on television and film give a particularly strong sense of instanciation and immediacy which can help to de-realize reality. Yet it is all too easy to assume that there is a complete socio-semantic loss through these postmodern tendencies in television. The meaning of television programmes and advertisements is neither a programmed manipulated one in line with the intentions of the programme makers, nor is it completely an open postmodern sign-play.

At the same time Disney World is not yet the world and the postmodern experiences usually take place in carefully circumscribed settings within consumer culture and leisure activities. When people leave these enclaved moments they have to return to the routinized everyday and work worlds in which they are enmeshed in a dense network of interdependencies and power balances. Here the dominant practical orientation makes it necessary to read other people's appearance and presentation of self with care, for clues of intentionality, albeit in commonsense taken-for-granted ways. It may be possible to switch codes to forms of play and parody, yet the imperatives of adhering to practical routines and getting the business done obviates too much signplay, emotional decontrol and swings between aesthetic detachment and immersion.

The collapse of the distinction between high and mass culture, the breaking down of academic categories, chimes closely with the perceived breaking down of the categories in everyday consumer culture. The various blends of poststructuralism, deconstructionism and anti-foundationalism evident in the

writings of Baudrillard, Lyotard, Derrida and Foucault were often lumped together (not without resistance from those so labelled) as postmodern theory. In their different ways they criticized the universalist claims of the metanarratives of the Western Enlightenment and argued for a greater appreciation of local knowledge, 'otherness', and the syncretism and multicoding of culture. In particular these theories offered a sharp critique of attempts to provide a unitary general explanation of society and history, be they founded on sociological, economic or Marxist premises. Yet it is a paradox that some of those who have been most centrally concerned in the popularization of the term postmodernism in the academic sphere have attempted to do just this: to neutralize the anti-foundational critical potential of postmodern theories by explaining them from the security of a meta-site.

---

14 CULTURAL DE-TERRITORIALIZATION

J. Lull

The first step in the formation of new cultural territories is de-territorialization. This concept, in Garcia Canclini's words, refers to 'the loss of the "natural" relation between culture with geographic and social territory (including) relocalizations of new and old forms of symbolic production' (1989, p. 288). Two other scholars of Latin American culture, William Rowe and Vivian Schelling, call it 'the release of cultural signs from fixed locations in space and time' (1991, p. 231). De-territorialization is the (partial) disintegration of human and symbolic constellations and patterns. It is the tearing apart of cultural structures, relationships, settings and representations. De-territorialization is a consequence of the cultural

From: *Media, Communication, Culture: A Global Approach*, by J. Lull, Polity Press, 1995.

disjunctures we have just discussed. It is one indication of the cultural change that the disjunctures stimulate. . . . Cultural de-territorialization (therefore) is
a profoundly human matter. The concept 'ought not
to be reduced to the movement of ideas or cultural
codes', as typical postmodernist discussions might
do, but should focus squarely on social, economic
and political problems and competitions (Garcia
Canclini, 1989, p. 305). . . .

Trans-culturation refers to a process in which cultural forms literally move through time and space
where they interact with other cultural forms, influence each other, and produce new forms. As we have
seen, these cultural syntheses often result from the
physical movement of peoples from one geographic
location to another. But many cultural crossings are
made possible by the mass media and culture industries. Modern technology reconstructs the essential
axes of cultural distance – space and time. This is the
case most obviously in terms of physical space. We
have already discussed at length how the transmission
and reception of information and entertainment
from one part of the world to another inspire new
cultural syntheses. But communications technology
also constructs new perceptions and uses of cultural
time. Film, still photography, kinescope, audio tape,
video tape, and today's digital audio and video information storage and retrieval systems give ready access
to cultural histories. The electronic media preserve
culture in ways print media can never do. People
today can re-interpret and use cultural symbolism in
new temporal contiguities, greatly expanding the
range of personal meanings and social uses. Mixing
the traditional with the modern is fully reasonable
and practical in the range of contemporary cultural
possibilities. It may even be necessary. As Martin-
Barbero points out, '[people] first filter and re-organize what comes from the hegemonic culture and then
integrate and fuse this with what comes from their
own historical memory', a process enhanced by
media (1993, p. 74; see, also, Rowe and Schelling,
1991). The cultural memory of symbolic forms and
communications technology is thus a basic resource
for exercises of cultural programming and power.

Trans-culturation synthesizes new cultural genres
while it breaks down traditional cultural categories.

Modern communications technology facilitates the
creative process. As Garcia Canclini observes,

> technologies of reproduction allow everyone to
> equip their home with a repertoire of discs and
> cassettes that combine high culture with the
> popular, including those who have already synth-
> esized many sources in the production of their
> works: Piazzola who mixes the tango with jazz
> and classical music; Caetano Veloso and Chico
> Buarque who have appropriated at the same time
> poetry of Afro-Brazilian traditions with post-
> Weberian experimental music. (1989, p. 283)

The information highway travels through
contexts of both cultural production and reception
as it simultaneously moves many directions in space
and time.

Transculturation produces cultural hybrids – the
fusing of cultural forms. Hybrid forms and genres
are popular almost by definition. Consider, for
example, the global flow of rap music in the 1990s.
Originating in America's inner-city ghettos, rap
music and hip-hop culture has travelled all over the
world where it has encountered and influenced many
kinds of local pop music. Some of the biggest selling
Latin American pop music artists fuse rap with pop,
salsa, tropical, and reggae. Mainland Chinese pop
singers have rap songs in their repertoires. Christian
rap is here.

The third concept, indigenization, is part of
hybridization. Indigenization means that imported
cultural forms take on local features. Continuing
with our example, consider what happens when rap
music is exported to a place like Indonesia. The unfamiliar, imported cadence and attitude of rap is
appropriated by Indonesian musicians. But the
sounds become indigenized at the same time.
Indonesian rap is sung in local languages with lyrics
that refer to local personalities, conditions, and
situations. The musical hybrid is an amalgam of
American black culture and Indonesian culture. But,
of course, hybrids such as this never develop from
'pure' cultural forms in the first place. American black
culture has already been strongly influenced by
African cultures and by European–American cul-

tures, while Indonesian culture reflects a history of Indian subcontinental and South-East Asian influences. They were hybrids themselves long before they met each other. Cultural indigenization takes place within national boundaries too. The spectacular Brazilian cultural tradition, Carnaval, is telecast throughout the country on the national TV system, Globo. But rather than imitate the famous Rio version of Carnaval, people throughout Brazil modify the 'TV stimulus' (not only of Carnaval, but of national TV fare generally) by diffusing it in ways that integrate local preferences and traditions (Kottak, 1990, p. 174). Furthermore, the Brazilian audience, especially lower middle class, working class, and lower class viewers, definitely prefer Brazilian programmes over imported television shows. This is the case in other Latin American countries too (Straubhaar, 1989). Imported television programmes that succeed anywhere in the world usually resonate harmoniously with local cultural orientations or represent universal genres such as melodrama and action.

Although transculturation, hybridization, and indigenization may indeed bring about 'the mutual transformation of cultures' (Rowe and Schelling, 1991, p. 18), the transformations often entail unequal economic power relations between the interacting cultures. The McDonald's hamburger franchise in Rio de Janeiro, for instance, promotes meal specials with titles such as 'McCarnaval' and 'Lanche Carioca' (the Rio resident's lunch). McDonald's, the external cultural form, has been indigenized. But to whose advantage? From McDonald's point of view, the idea is to sell more hamburgers by tapping into local culture. The Rio McDonald's may have a slightly Brazilian edge to its personality, but the local workers still scurry about for a minimum wage and most of the profits end up in San Diego. The market influences the Music Industry this way too. When the Australian rock band Midnight Oil's videos were exported to the US for airplay on MTV, for instance, background scenes were changed to look less Australian, more New York. We must always ask, therefore, on whose terms and for what purposes do cultural hybrids develop?

15 RESPONSES TO CULTURAL GLOBALISM

M. Featherstone

It should by now be apparent that the notions of global and local cultures are relational. It is possible to refer to a range of different responses to the process of globalism, which could be heightened or diminished depending upon specific historical phases within the globalization process.

First, we can point to the attitude of immersion in a local culture. This could take the form of remaining in a long-established locality by resisting being drawn into wider collectivities and erecting barriers to cultural flows. This, however, is difficult to achieve without military and economic power, which are essential if one is to avoid being drawn into broader regional interdependencies and conflicts. Hence there is the problem of being left alone, of remaining undiscovered, or of controlling and regulating the flow of interchanges even when geographical reasons (for example, the case of Japan) facilitate isolation. On a more mundane level, from the point of view of some tribes, this may come down to the question of the best strategies which can be used to resist or ignore those tourists who quest after some last authentic, untouched remnant of 'real culture' such as those who go to New Guinea on cannibal tours. This can be related to the problems faced by those in the West who in this context develop a sense of protective responsibility and seek to devise strategies to conserve what they take to be a genuine local culture without placing it in a protective reservation in which it becomes a simulation of itself.

Second, such communities, which are increasingly becoming drawn into the global figuration, will also have to cope periodically with the refugees from modernization, those members of ethnic groups who are romantically attracted to the perceived authenticity of a simpler life and sense of 'home'. Here we think of the disparaging descriptions of them by

From: *Undoing Culture: Globalization, Postmodernism and Identity*, M. Featherstone, Sage, 1995.

their host groups which display doubts about these people's capacity to acquire permanent membership with depictions such as 'red apples' (returning first nation North Americans, who are held to be red on the outside and white on the inside), and 'coconuts' (returning Hawaiians seen as brown on the outside and white inside: Friedman, 1990). While such groups can be seen as searching to live out their version of an 'imagined community', the caution on the part of the locals shows that a crucial dimension of the relationship between them can be understood in terms of established outsider struggles.

Third, variants of the refurbished imagined community also exist in the rediscovery of ethnicity and regional cultures within the current phase of a number of Western nation states which seek to allow a greater recognition of regional and local diversity and multiculturalism. Within certain contexts it may be appropriate to wear the mask of local affiliation, as when dealing with tourists or confronting local rivals (for example, Scotsmen on meeting Englishmen). This can entail varying degrees of seriousness and playfulness. This capacity to move backwards and forwards between various elements of national cultures, which are manifest in everyday public and work situations and the local affiliation, may take the form of regular ritual re-enactments of the imagined community. This is clearly the case in societies which have been settled by Europeans, such as the US, Canada, Australia and New Zealand, in which various indigenous local affiliations as well as the maintenance of imagined communities on the part of immigrant groups, has pushed the questions of multiculturalism and respect for local cultures firmly onto the agenda.

Fourth, those locals who travel, such as expatriates, usually take their local cultures with them (Hannerz, 1990). This is also the case with many tourists (especially those from the working class) whose expectation from the encounter with another culture is to remain on the level of sun, sea, sand plus 'Viva Espana'-style stereotypes. In effect they seek 'home plus' and will do all they can to take comforting aspects of their local culture with them and limit the dangers of intercultural encounters to 'reservation style' experiences (Bauman, 1990).

Fifth, there are those whose local affiliation is limited, whose geographical mobility and professional culture is such that they display a cosmopolitan orientation. Here we have those who work and live in 'third cultures' who are happy to move between a variety of local cultures with which they develop a practical, working acquaintance and the bridging third culture which enables them to communicate with like persons from around the world.

Sixth, there are cosmopolitan intellectuals and cultural intermediaries, especially those from the post-World War II generation, who do not seek to judge local cultures in terms of their progress towards some ideal derived from modernity, but are content to interpret them for growing audiences of those who have been through higher education within the new middle class and wider audiences within consumer culture. They are skilled at packaging and representing the exotica of other cultures and 'amazing places' and different traditions to audiences eager for experience. They are able to work and live within third cultures, as well as seemingly able to present other local cultures from within, and 'tell it from the native's point of view'. This group can be regarded as post-nostalgic, and can relate to growing audiences in the middle classes who wish to experiment with cultural play, who have forgone the pursuit of the ultimate authentic and real, who are content to be 'post-tourists' and enjoy both the reproduction of the effect of the real, the immersion in it in controlled or playful ways, and the examination of the backstage areas on which it draws (Fiefer, 1985).

16 MULTINATIONAL CAPITALISM AND CULTURAL HOMOGENIZATION

J. Tomlinson

... critics of multinational capitalism frequently do complain of its tendency towards cultural convergence and homogenization. This is the major criticism made in the discourse of cultural imperialism which takes capitalism as its target. A good example is Cees Hamelink's book, 'Cultural Autonomy in Global Communications'. Hamelink, who acknowledges the co-operation of both Schiller and Salinas, laces the issues of cultural autonomy and cultural homogenization – or what he refers to as 'cultural synchronization'- at the centre of his analysis. He is broadly correct in identifying the processes of 'cultural synchronization' (or homogenization) as unprecedented in historical terms and in seeing these processes as closely connected to the spread of global capitalism. But he fails to show why cultural synchronization should be objected to and, specifically, he fails to show that it should be objected to on the grounds of cultural autonomy.

In his opening chapter Hamelink lists a number of personal 'experiences of the international scene' to illustrate his thesis. For example:

In a Mexican village the traditional ritual dance precedes a soccer match, but the performance features a gigantic Coca-Cola bottle.

In Singapore, a band dressed in traditional Malay costume offers a heart-breaking imitation of Fats Domino.

In Saudi Arabia, the television station performs only one local cultural function – the call for the Moslem prayer. Five times a day, North American cops and robbers yield to the traditional muezzin.

In its gigantic advertising campaign, IBM assures Navajo Indians that their cultural identity can be

From: *Cultural Imperialism*, by J. Tomlinson, Pinter Publishers, 1991.

effectively protected if they use IBM typewriters equipped with the Navajo alphabet.

The first thing to note about these examples is precisely their significance as personal observations – and this is not to make any trivial point about their 'subjective' nature. Hamelink expresses the cultural standpoint of the concerned Westerner confronting a perplexing set of global phenomena. We have to accept, at the level of the personal, the sincerity of his concern and also the validity of this personal discourse: it is valid for individuals to express their reaction to global tendencies. But we need to acknowledge that this globe-trotting instancing of cultural imperialism shapes the discourse in a particular way: to say 'here is the sameness that capitalism brings – and here – and here ...' is to assume, however liberal, radical or critical the intention, the role of the 'tourist': the problem of homogenization is likely to present itself to the Western intellectual who has a sense of the diversity and 'richness' of global culture as a particular threat. For the people involved in each discrete instance Hamelink presents, the experience of Western capitalist culture will probably have quite different significance. Only if they can adopt the (privileged) role of the cultural tourist will the sense of the homogenization of global culture have the same threatening aspect. The Kazakhstan tribesman who has no knowledge of (and, perhaps, no interest in) America or Europe is unlikely to see his cassette player as emblematic of creeping capitalist domination. And we cannot, without irony, argue that the Western intellectual's (informed?) concern is more valid: again much hangs on the question, 'who speaks?'.

This said, Hamelink does draw from these instances an empirical conclusion which is, I think, fairly uncontroversial: 'One conclusion still seems unanimously shared: the impressive variety of the world's cultural systems is waning due to a process of "cultural synchronization" that is without historic precedent.'

For those in a position to view the world as a cultural totality, it cannot be denied that certain processes of cultural convergence are under way, and that these are new processes. This last is an important point, for Hamelink is careful to acknowledge that cultures have always influenced one another and that this influence has often enriched the interacting communities – 'the richest cultural traditions emerged at the actual meeting point of markedly different cultures, such as Sudan, Athens, the Indus Valley, and Mexico'. Even where cultural interaction has been in the context of political and economic domination, Hamelink argues, there has been, in most cases a 'two-way exchange' or, at least, a tolerance of cultural diversity. There is a sharp difference for him between these patterns and modern 'cultural synchronization': 'In the second half of the twentieth century, a destructive process that differs significantly from the historical examples given above threatens the diversity of cultural systems. Never before has the synchronization with one particular cultural pattern been of such global dimensions and so comprehensive.'

Let us be clear about what we are agreeing. It seems to me that Hamelink is right, broadly speaking, to identify cultural synchronization as an unprecedented feature of global modernity. The evaluative implications of his use of the word 'destructive', however, raises larger problems. It is one thing to say that cultural diversity is being destroyed, quite another to lament the fact. The latter position demands reasons which Hamelink cannot convincingly supply. The quotation continues in a way that raises part of the problem: 'Never before has the process of cultural influence proceeded so subtly, without any blood being shed and with the receiving culture thinking it had sought such cultural influence.' With his last phrase Hamelink slides towards the problematic of false consciousness. As we have seen more than once before, any critique which bases itself in the idea that cultural domination is taking place 'behind people's backs' is heading for trouble. To acknowledge that a cultural community might have thought it had sought cultural influence is to acknowledge that such influence has at least prima facie attractions.

This thought could lead us to ask if the process of cultural homogenization itself might not have its attractions. It is not difficult to think of examples of cultural practices which would probably attract a consensus in favour of their universal application: health care; food hygiene; educational provision; various 'liberal' cultural attitudes towards honesty, toleration, compassion and so on; democratic public processes, etc. This is not to say that any of these are indisputable 'goods' under any description whatever, nor that they are all the 'gifts' of an expanding capitalist modernity. We shall have cause, in the next chapter, to question both these issues. But it is to say that there are plenty of aspects of 'culture', broadly defined, that the severest critic of cultural homogenization might wish to find the same in any area of the globe. Critics of cultural homogenization are selective in the things they object to, and there is nothing wrong in this so long as we realize that it undermines the notion that homogenization is a bad thing in itself. But then we enter a quite separate set of arguments – not about the uniformity of capitalist culture, but about the spread of its pernicious features – which require quite different criteria of judgement.

Engaging with the potentially attractive features of homogenization brings us to see, pretty swiftly, the problems in its use as a critical concept. But there are other ways of approaching the issue, and one of Hamelink's arguments seems on the surface to avoid these problems. He argues that cultural synchronization is to be deplored on the grounds that it is a threat to cultural autonomy. I have argued against both the notion of autonomy as applied to a 'culture' in the holistic sense and against any logical connection between the concept of autonomy and any particular outcome of cultural practices. Autonomy, as I understand it, refers to the free and uncoerced choices and actions of agents. But Hamelink uses the notion of autonomy in what strikes me as a curious way, to suggest a feature of cultural practices which is necessary, indeed 'critical', for the actual survival of a cultural community.

Hamelink's reasoning appears to be based on the idea that the cultural system of any society is an adaptive mechanism which enables the society to exist in its 'environment', by which he seems to mean the physical and material features of its global location: 'Different climatic conditions, for example, demand different ways of adapting to them (that is, different types of food, shelter and clothing). Again, there is nothing particularly controversial about this, except in the obvious sense that we might want to argue that many of the cultural practices of modernity are rather more 'distanced' from the function of survival than those of more 'primitive' systems. But from this point he argues that the 'autonomous' development of cultural systems – the freedom from the processes of 'cultural synchronization' – are necessary to the 'survival' of societies. Why should this be so? Because the adequacy of the cultural system can best be decided upon by the members of the society who face directly the problems of survival and adaptation'.

There are a number of difficulties arising from this sort of argument. First, what does Hamelink mean by the 'survival' of a society? In his reference to very basic adaptations to environmental conditions he seems to trade on the idea that a culture allows for the actual physical survival of its members. At times he explicitly refers to the physical survival of people. For example, he claims that the intensive promotion of milk-powder baby food in the Third World by companies like Nestlé and Cow & Gate is a practice that can have life-threatening consequences:

> Replacing breast-feeding by bottle feeding has had disastrous effects in many Third World countries. An effective, adequate, and cheap method has been exchanged for an expensive, inadequate and dangerous product. . . . Many illiterate mothers, unable to prepare the milk powder correctly, have not only used it improperly but have also inadvertently transformed the baby food into a lethal product by using it in unhygienic conditions.

There are important issues having to do with the 'combined and unequal development' produced by the spread of capitalism of which this is a good example. . . . But the incidence of illness and death Hamelink refers to here, deplorable though it is, will obviously not carry the weight of his argument about cultural synchronization affecting the physical survival of whole populations in the Third World.

He cannot, plausibly, claim that cultural synchronization with capitalist modernity carries this direct threat. It is probably true that capitalist production has long-term consequences for the global environment, thus for physical survival on a global scale, but this is a separate argument.

At any rate, Hamelink's notion of survival seems to slide from that of physical survival to the survival of the culture itself. But this is a very different proposition, which cannot be sustained by the functional view of culture he takes as his premise. For the failure of a culture to 'survive' in an 'original' form may be taken itself as a process of adaptation to a new 'environment' – that of capitalist industrial modernity. A certain circularity is therefore introduced into the argument. Hamelink claims that unique cultures arise as adaptive mechanisms to environments, so he deplores heteronomy since it threatens such adaptation. But what could cultural synchronization mean if not an 'adaptation' to the demands of the social environment of capitalism?

The incoherence of this account arises, I believe, from the attempt to circumvent the problems of autonomy in cultural terms by referring the holistic view to a functional logic of adaptation. As I argued in the last chapter, autonomy can only apply to agents, and cultures are not agents. Hamelink seeks to bypass these problems with an argument that reduces the ethical-political content of 'autonomy' to make it a mere indicator of social efficiency – the guarantor of the 'best' form of social organization in a particular environment. His argument is incoherent precisely because autonomy cannot be so reduced: in cultural terms, 'best' is not to be measured against a simple index of physical survival. Things are far more complicated than this. Cultural autonomy must address the autonomous choices of agents who make up a cultural community; there is no escaping this set of problems by appeal to functionality. Hamelink gives the game away in his reference, cited earlier, to a form of cultural 'false consciousness' and elsewhere where he speaks of cultural synchronization as cultural practices being 'persuasively communicated to the receiving countries'.

I do not believe the appeal to autonomy grounds Hamelink's critique of cultural synchronization.

Even if it did, this would be an objection to the inhibition of independence by manipulation, not to the resulting 'sameness' of global culture. But Hamelink does want to object to 'sameness': this is implicit in his constant references to the 'rich diversity' of cultures under threat. What are the grounds for such an objection?

Adaptation to physical environments has, historically, produced a diversity in cultural practices across the globe. However the preservation of this diversity – which is what Hamelink wants – seems to draw its justification from the idea that cultural diversity is a good thing in itself. But this depends on the position from which you speak. If the attractions of a uniform capitalist modernity outweigh the charms of diversity, as they well may for those from the outside looking in, it is difficult to insist on the priority of preserving differences. Indeed, the appeal to variety might well be turned back on the critic of capitalism. For it might be argued that individual cultures making up the rich mosaic that Hamelink surveys are lacking in a variety of cultural experience, being tied, as Marx observed, to the narrow demands of the struggle with nature for survival. Cultural synchronization could in some cases increase variety in cultural experience.

It must be said immediately that arguments exist that the nature of such experience in capitalist modernity is in some sense deficient – shallow, 'one-dimensional', 'commodified', and so on. But this is not a criticism of homogenization or synchronization as such: it is a criticism of the sort of culture that synchronization brings. It is quite different to object to the spread of something bad – uniform badness – than to object to the spread of uniformity itself. This demands quite separate arguments about capitalism as a culture, and it is to these that we will now turn. It is worth making explicit the connection Hamelink sees between the processes of cultural synchronization and the spread of capitalism. As with Schiller, it is the transnational corporations who are the major players: 'The principal agents of cultural synchronization today are the transnational corporations, largely based in the US, which are developing a global investment and marketing strategy.'

Transnational firms are enormously significant in the organization of capitalism world-wide. This significance in terms of economic domination is not to be contested. But what are the cultural implications of multinational capitalism?

---

17 GLOBALIZATION AND CULTURAL IDENTITY

M. Featherstone

If globalization refers to the process whereby the world increasingly becomes 'one place' and the ways in which we are made conscious of this process (Robertson, 1992), then the cultural changes thematized under the banner of the postmodern seem to point in the opposite direction by directing us to consider the local. Yet this is to misunderstand the nature of the process of globalization. It should not be taken to imply that there is, or will be, a unified world society or culture – something akin to the social structure, only writ large. Such an outcome may have been the ambition of particular nation-states at various points of their history, and the possibility of a renewed world state formation process cannot be discounted in the future. In the present phase it is possible to refer to the development of a global culture in a less totalistic sense by referring to two aspects of the process of globalization.

First, we can point to the existence of a global culture in the restricted sense of 'third cultures': sets of practices, bodies of knowledge, conventions and lifestyles that have developed in ways which have become increasingly independent of nation states. In effect there are a number of trans-societal institutions, cultures and cultural producers who cannot be understood as merely agents and representatives of their nation-states. Second, we can talk

From: *Undoing Culture: Globalization, Postmodernism and Identity*, by M. Featherstone, Sage, 1995.

about a global culture in the Simmelian sense of a cultural form: the sense that the globe is a finite, knowable bounded space, a field into which all nation-states and collectivities will inevitably be drawn. Here the globe, the planet Earth, acts both as a limit and as the common bounded space on which our encounters and practices are inevitably grounded. In this second sense the result of the growing intensity of contact and communication between nation states and other agencies is to produce a clashing of cultures, which can lead to heightened attempts to draw the boundaries between the self and others. From this perspective the changes which are taking place as a result of the current phase of intensified globalization can be understood as provoking reactions that seek to rediscover particularity, localism and difference which generate a sense of the limits of the culturally unifying, ordering and integrating projects associated with Western modernity. So in one sense it can be argued that globalization produces Postmodernism. . . .

Such theories share with theories of mass culture a strong view of the manipulability of mass audiences by a monolithic system and an assumption of the negative cultural effects of the media as self-evident, with little empirical evidence about how goods and information are adapted and used in everyday practices (Tomlinson, 1991). Of course it is possible to point to the availability of Western consumer goods, especially major brands of food, drink, cigarettes and clothing, following the business and tourist trails to the remotest part of the world. It is also clear that certain images – the tough guy hero fighting against innumerable odds – have a strong appeal in many cultures. Hence we find Rambo movies played throughout southern and eastern Asia so that 'remote villagers in rural Burma could now applaud Rambo's larger-than-life heroics only days after they hit the screens of Wisconsin' (Iyer, 1989, p. 12). To take a second example, one of the major contemporary travel writers, Paul Theroux (1992, p. 178), in his book *The Happy Islands of Oceania* recounts how in the remotest parts of the Pacific Islands he found men coming up to him to tell him about the latest developments in the Gulf War they had heard on the radio. In addition

he found that in the tiny island of Savo in the Solomons Islands group, Rambo was a big folk hero. The one generator on the island had no use except as a source of power for showing videos. One can surmise that it may not be too long before Savo has its satellite TV receiver or personal computers which link it into the world-wide 'net'. Such accounts are by now legion, yet how are we to read them?

One possibility is to attempt to outline some of the absorption/assimilation/resistance strategies which peripheral cultures can adopt towards the mass and consumer culture images and goods originating from metropolitan centres (Hannerz, 1991).

---

18 'WORLD MUSIC'
K. Negus

Jeremy Tunstall (1977) makes the point that the characteristics of 'traditional' or 'indigenous' cultures are often assumed with very little research. He argues that it is often the elites and highly educated members of many poor countries who are the most active consumers of media products, while the poor rural dwellers who are short of land, food, literacy, income and life expectation are the main consumers of 'traditional culture'. This argument is borne out by statistical figures which show that the distribution of radios, televisions, telephones and musical equipment tends to correspond to existing patterns of social and economic inequality across the world (Golding, 1994). In many parts of the globe, people are simply not listening to recorded music or viewing music videos. Such a situation might invalidate claims about the direct 'effect' of cultural imperialism (Tunstall, 1977), but these circumstances also indicate how the domination of communication networks and media systems by major companies,

From: *Popular Music in Theory*, by K. Negus, Polity Press, 1996.

which target markets that are viable in terms of profitability and ignore those which are not, is contributing to significant world-wide 'information imbalances' (Hamelink, 1995). The 'effects' of imperialism on culture are numerous and need not be thought of in terms of stimulus–response models of behaviour (the absence of certain technologies and cultural products in some places is as much a consequence of imperialist patterns of domination as is their presence in other locations).

A number of writers have also pointed out that many so-called indigenous or traditional musical cultures, which are often revered for their purity or authenticity, are actually 'hybrid' forms that have been created from continual interactions between Western and Third World, dominant and subordinate nations, or between centre and periphery – the terminology varies: the point is that neat distinctions become blurred at the level of cultural practices (Goodwin and Gore, 1990; Reeves, 1993). One of the implications of this argument is that it is not only difficult to identify what the dominant and subordinate culture might be; these are then becoming mixed up in a way that is leading to new forms of 'global culture'.

Such an argument has been made about 'world music', a term first introduced as a marketing category by record companies (in the UK, France, North America, Japan and Australia) to lump together a vast amount of music that had previously been categorized as 'traditional', 'ethnic' or 'roots' music, particularly music from Africa, South America and Asia. The category world music (or sometimes 'world beat') has also been used to refer to the music of various artists who have tried to synthesize different types of music (whether Paul Simon, David Byrne, Peter Gabriel, Youssou n'dour or Cheb Khaled).

Judgements about this category of music have often been divided between those who celebrate it as an indication of new forms of 'global culture' and those who argue that this is yet more of the same imperialist exploitation. For Rick Glanvill (1989), world music involves exploitation and builds on a long practice whereby the music industries of Europe and North America have been 'revitalizing artistic forms' (Reeves, 1993) by drawing on musicians and

styles from the Third World. Not only has music been appropriated, removed from its context and packaged in a way that will make the most money, it has often been taken from musicians who have little copyright protection and who frequently receive no financial recompense. Glanvill (1989) has drawn an analogy between the production of world music and colonial trade patterns, arguing that the music of South America, Africa and Asia has been mined as a 'raw material' and then appropriated, used, re-packaged and sold back.

As Andrew Goodwin and Joe Gore (1990) have pointed out, it is misleading to view music as a 'raw material' that is simply mined. Glanvill neglects the processes of mediation, the way in which music is always being transformed as it is made and travels among musicians and between audiences. Some writers have taken up this point and suggested extending models of Anglo-American active audiences onto a more global stage, that this is an example of the 'margins' or 'periphery' fighting back against the 'centre' or global 'mainstream' (Chambers, 1994; Garofalo, 1993; Wallis and Malm, 1992). According to one version of this argument, the use of explicitly African elements does not involve the mining of source resources or exploitation, but a 'reuniting of rock with its roots' . . . it has been argued that new types of global culture are being made as new cosmopolitan, hybrid and multicultural forms which are contributing to both diverse and converging patterns of cultural practice across the world (Chambers, 1994; Lipsitz, 1994).

This is an important point because it again highlights that cultural activities in any one place cannot simply be interpreted as a response to or 'reflection' of the practices of imperial nations or corporations. There is no simple correspondence between the international movements of musical commodities in production and the way cultural forms are circulated through practices of consumption (Negus, 1996).

Drawing on the theories of Anthony Giddens (1990), John Tomlinson has argued that globalization can be distinguished from imperialism due to the way in which it is a 'far less coherent or culturally directed process . . . globalization suggests the interconnection and interdependency of all global areas which happens in a far less purposeful way' (1991, p. 175). As an explanation of the movement of cultural forms and musical commodities across the planet, globalization is a more benign theory. No one is really responsible. Power relations cannot be identified so easily, if at all. Change just seems to be happening as 'modernity' trundles like a 'juggernaut' across the world (Giddens, 1990).

Such an argument can then lead to a type of universalism – for example, that the thousands of people listening to Madonna and Michael Jackson, dancing to their music and reaching out their hands towards them at concerts are sharing in a universal musical language which touches a common chord across humanity and which transcends cultural differences. According to Michael Tracey, in his argument against cultural imperialism, the 'genius of American popular culture [is] to bind together better than anything else common humanity' (1985, p. 40). For Tracey, US culture is not offering exploitation, but a 'service'. Garofalo comes very close to implying the same thing when speculating about the world-wide popularity of Michael Jackson, suggesting that the 25 million people outside of the US who purchased Jackson's *Thriller* album were not 'unwitting dupes of imperialist power', but responding to an album that 'resonated with the cultural sensibilities of a broad international audience' (1993, p. 25).

The people who have bought Michael Jackson albums may not feel that they have been duped, and US music clearly contains many different elements from 'non-Western traditions' (Goodwin and Gore, 1990). However, this type of argument tends to assume that a cultural form is universal because it appears to be universally popular. It does not connect the widespread appeal of the artist with the systems of production and distribution that have put a Madonna or a Michael Jackson in the position to be universal in the first place. There may be many cultures around the world that have produced cultural forms that could be universally enjoyed. But some are more likely to get to a position to be enjoyed than others.

A question that needs to be asked here, and one which requires more research to answer, is how and through what processes did Michael Jackson become a 'dominant particular'? What are the historical-geographical dynamics of his success? While part of the answer would concern the qualities and characteristics of Michael Jackson's apparently universal appeal (that is, what his music means for various audiences), there is a further question here about who has access to the technologies and techniques of cultural production and distribution. This leads me back to Lenin's point about the international dynamics of capitalist imperialism: apparently universal forms of human behaviour have frequently become popular through relations of power and domination. Cultural imperialism does not need to imply that audiences are dancing to Madonna because they have rather passively absorbed cultural values from elsewhere. As I discussed (in Chapter 1), audiences can make their own meanings, develop their own uses and gratifications and use cultural products in a variety of ways. But, making meanings, actively using technologies and interpreting texts is not the same as having the power and influence to distribute cultural forms.

Although crude versions of cultural imperialism have been criticized for positing a rather passive, gullible and easily manipulated audience absorbing values from outside (Laing, 1986; Garofalo, 1993; Tomlinson, 1991), it seems to me that there is still much more to be written about imperialism before the world can be characterized as post-imperial. On this point it is important to bear in mind that processes of cultural imperialism have not simply and straightforwardly come about as a direct result of the culture industries or modern mass media technologies. The introduction of modern media forms was facilitated by patterns of domination and relationships of dependency that were established under colonial administrations. As Mohammadi (1995) has argued, when the colonial powers packed their bags and removed their national people from administrative positions and from running governments directly, it was not the end of their influence. They left behind many European values and attitudes. These were encoded within religious practices (taken by missionaries, for example), styles of politics, forms of education and professional training, as well as clothing styles and habits that did not exist before colonial domination. On this point, Annabelle Sreberny-Mohammadi (1996) has suggested that the dynamics of 'cultural imperialism' should be understood in relation to the way this has been facilitated by the 'cultures of imperialism', a dynamic that has a longer historical trajectory than the appearance of electronically recorded and transmitted media in the twentieth century.

---

19 THE DIMENSIONS OF 'MCDONALDIZATION'

G. Ritzer

Why has the McDonald's model proven so irresistible? Four alluring dimensions lie at the heart of the success of this model and, more generally, of McDonaldization. In short, McDonald's has succeeded because it offers consumers, workers, and managers efficiency, calculability, predictability, and control.

First, McDonald's offers efficiency, or the optimum method for getting from one point to another. For consumers, this means that McDonald's offers the best available way to get from being hungry to being full. . . . Other institutions, fashioned on the McDonald's model, offer similar efficiency in losing weight, lubricating cars, getting new glasses or contacts, or completing income-tax forms. In a society where both parents are likely to work, or where there may be only a single parent, efficiently satisfying the hunger and many other needs of people is very attractive. In a society where people rush, usually by car, from one spot to another, the efficiency of a fast-food meal, perhaps even without leaving their cars by wending their way along the drive-through lane, often proves impossible to resist.

From: *The McDonaldization of Society*, by G. Ritzer, Pine Forge Press, 1996.

The fast-food model offers people, or at least appears to offer them, an efficient method for satisfying many needs.

Like their customers, workers in McDonaldized systems function efficiently. They are trained to work this way by managers, who watch over them closely to make sure they do. Organizational rules and regulations also help ensure highly efficient work.

Second, McDonald's offers calculability, or an emphasis on the quantitative aspects of products sold (portion size, cost) and service offered (the time it takes to get the product). Quantity has become equivalent to quality; a lot of something, or the quick delivery of it, means it must be good. As two observers of contemporary American culture put it, 'As a culture, we tend to believe deeply that in general "bigger is better".' Thus, people order the Quarter-Pounder, the Big Mac, the large fries. More recently, there is the lure of the 'double this' (for instance, Burger King's 'Double Whopper With Cheese') and the 'triple that'. People can quantify these things and feel that they are getting a lot of food for what appears to be a nominal sum of money. This calculation does not take into account an important point: the extraordinary profitability of fast-food outlets and other chains, which indicates that the owners, not the consumers, get the best deal.

People also tend to calculate how much time it will take to drive to McDonald's, be served the food, eat it, and return home; then, they compare that interval to the time required to prepare food at home. They often conclude, rightly or wrongly, that a trip to the fast-food restaurant will take less time than eating at home. This sort of calculation particularly supports home-delivery franchises such as Domino's, as well as other chains that emphasize time saving. A notable example of time saving in another sort of chain is Lens Crafters, which promises people, 'Glasses fast, glasses in one hour'.

Some McDonaldized institutions combine the emphasis on time and money. Domino's promised pizza delivery in half an hour, or the pizza is free. Pizza hut will serve a personal pan pizza in five minutes, or it, too, will be free.

Workers at McDonaldized systems also tend to emphasize the quantitative rather than qualitative aspects of their work. Since the quality of the work is allowed to vary, workers focus on such things as how quickly tasks can be accomplished. In a situation analogous to that of the customer, workers are expected to do a lot of work, very quickly, for low pay.

Third, McDonalds offers predictability, the assurance that their products and services will be the same over time and in all locales. The Egg McMuffin in New York will be, for all intents and purposes, identical to those in Chicago and Los Angeles. Also, those eaten next week or next year will be identical to those eaten today. There is great comfort in knowing that McDonald's offers no surprises. People know that the next Egg McMuffin they eat will taste about the same as the others they have eaten; it will not be awful, but it will not be exceptionally delicious, either. The success of the McDonald's model suggests that many people have come to prefer a world in which there are few surprises.

The workers in McDonaldized systems also behave in predictable ways. They follow corporate rules as well as the dictates of their managers. In many cases, not only what they do, but also what they say, is highly predictable. McDonaldized organizations often have scripts that employees are supposed to memorize and follow whenever the occasion arises. This scripted behaviour helps create highly predictable interactions between workers and customers. While customers do not follow scripts, they tend to develop simple recipes for dealing with the employees of McDonaldized systems. As Robin Leidner argues,

> McDonald's pioneered the routinization of interactive service work and remains an exemplar of extreme standardization. Innovation is not discouraged ... at least among managers and franchisees. Ironically, though, 'the object is to look for new, innovative ways to create an experience that is exactly the same no matter what McDonalds you walk into, no matter where it is in the world.'

Fourth, control, especially through the substitution of non-human for human technology, is exerted over the people who enter the world of McDonald's. A human technology (a screwdriver, for example) is controlled by people; a non-human technology (the assembly fine, for instance) controls people. The people who eat in fast-food restaurants are controlled, albeit (usually) subtly. Lines, limited menus, few options, and uncomfortable seats all lead diners to do what management wishes them to do – eat quickly and leave. Further, the drive-through (in some cases walk-through) window leads diners to leave before they eat. In the Domino's model, customers never come in the first place.

The people who work in McDonaldized organizations are also controlled to a high degree, usually more blatantly and directly than customers. They are trained to do a limited number of things in precisely the way they are told to do them. The technologies used and the way the organization is set up reinforce this control. Managers and inspectors make sure that workers toe the line.

McDonald's also controls employees by threatening to use, and ultimately using, non-human technology to replace human workers. No matter how well they are programmed and controlled, workers can foul up the system's operation. A slow worker can make the preparation and delivery of a Big Mac inefficient. A worker who refuses to follow the rules might leave the pickles or special sauce off a hamburger, thereby making for unpredictability. And a distracted worker can put too few fries in the box, making an order of large fries seem skimpy. For these and other reasons, McDonald's has felt compelled to steadily replace human beings with non-human technologies, such as the soft-drink dispenser that shuts itself off when the glass is full, the french-fry machine that rings and lifts itself out of the oil when the fries are crisp, the pre-programmed cash register that eliminates the need for the cashier to calculate prices and amounts, and, perhaps at some future time, the robot capable of making hamburgers. This technology increases the corporation's control over workers. Thus, McDonald's can assure customers that their employees and service will be consistent.

20 GLOBAL–LOCAL INTERACTIONS

B. Axford

Friedman's (1993) account of the 'la sape' phenomenon offers a further example of the complexity of global–local interaction. Young men from the Congo and Zaire somehow acquire designer clothing, sojourn in Paris and then return home to parade their status as sophisticated consumers with cosmopolitan tastes. In Friedman's view this phenomenon is an obvious example of globalization, where this refers to the consumption of globalized commodities, or the willingness to 'buy into' a globally sanctioned version of high fashion. But it is not a sell-out of native culture in the crude sense of black Africans becoming thoroughly 'Westernized', or even a process which produces a 'hybrid' identity in the sense suggested by Hall (1992). Instead, the individuals involved are 'engaged in a specific practice of the accumulation of life-force' that 'assimilates the Western good to the particular expression of a process that is entirely African' (Friedman, 1993, p. 2). The Western artefact is encompassed by the local practice of 'la sape', but at the same time the particular form of the phenomenon is only imaginable when set in a global context. Much the same thing can be said of the millenarian cargo cults of Melanesia which, unless seen as the outcome of agents actively engaged in social practice, are liable to be interpreted either as the hybridized products of an unhealthy exposure to Western commercialism, or as some bizarre form of cultural resistance (Worsley, 1970).

Similarly, the adoption of black youth fashions and musical forms (hip-hop and rap) by some young, white, middle-class males and females in America, to become 'wiggers', does not ethnicize whites, although where it is politicized in opposition to racism it may be more than a passing 'style' revolt. More interesting to the present discussion is the phenomenon of young whites adopting the cultural products of a racially defined minority, whose 'native'

culture is already transformed through its exposure to the dominant culture that they (the whites, that is) are choosing to reject (Usborne, 1993).

It is possible to take this line of reasoning further. The idea of cultural reciprocity (Howell, 1993; Flannerz, 1992) also underlines the complexity of global–local interactions. Recent work in Social Anthropology has challenged the assumption that the flow of influence, power and cultural products in the global system is all in one direction, that is from core to periphery. Although there continues to be unequal cultural exchange (Hall, 1992, p. 305) there are greater areas of reciprocity than over-romanticized views of the 'corrupted innocence' of the non-Western world might suggest. Hall points to the relativizing of both core and periphery under the impact of globalizing forces and prefers an interpretation of the relationships between local and global in which local identities may be confirmed and even intensified by global processes. Howell (1993) cites the instance of the islanders of South Ryukyus, Japan, who adopted the Coca-Cola bottle as a convenient and cheap representation of the torso of a pregnant woman for use in religious ceremonies, and not as an icon of Western culture. Friedman (1993) also points to the production and marketing of cloth of tribal design by European (not African) textile companies as confirming how global production and consumption relations support local differences.

The contacts between local and global, the West and the rest, produce ambivalent identities; and the prosaic truth is that national and local identities often incorporate 'foreign' concepts into their culture, stripped of their origins and their local meanings, in order to fill perceived needs or gaps in local knowledge (Howell, 1993). The translation of the Japanese work ethic into Western systems of production has seen it reduced to a range of disparate techniques; New Age religions purporting to 'Easternize' spirituality are often a potpourri of quite different (and, in their local contexts, incompatible) traditions, sieved through sophisticated marketing techniques; and multiculturalism becomes a kind of designer chic, apparent even in such 'genesis environments' (Stark, 1992) as the new

From: *The Global System: Economics, Politics and Culture*, by B. Axford, Polity Press, 1995.

South Africa. Here 'Afritude' means going ethnic in casual dress, the purchase of native art, or perhaps achieving some fluency in one or more ethnic languages (Silber, 1994).

Many national societies and all metropolitan ones have become multicultural through large-scale labour migration, mostly from the periphery to the core of the world economy. This movement has not produced cultural uniformity and in fact the opposite is common, with the increasing celebration of 'otherness' sanctioned in official discourse and public policy in receiving societies. The proximity of 'alien' cultures to 'dominant' national ones need not produce cultural homogeneity because when one culture 'borrows' from another, what often happens is a de-contextualization of the borrowed culture: witness the 'wigger' phenomenon and, pace Hall (1992), the deracination of Chinese and Indian restaurants in the UK to become part of mainstream 'British' culture.

As Howell (1993) says, the appropriation of an alien cultural tradition involves the take-up of the novel or exotic but then its gradual 'conventionalization' and sometimes its rejection. These processes are not confined to the Western appropriation of non-Western 'cultural knowledge' but, with due variation introduced by the inequalities of power involved, are integral to the way in which new cultural scripts become institutionalized. Overall, the process seems as likely to sustain diversity as it is to produce uniformity. However, it would not do to underestimate the problems facing the reproduction of locality in a globalizing world. According to Appadurai (1993), three critical forces bear upon local reproduction: the nation-state and nationalism, diasporic flows and electronic communication. The starkest message of those who see globalization as swamping difference is that, increasingly, people 'want Sony, not soil' (Ohmac, 1993) and that ties of 'blood and belonging' (Ignatieff, 1994) will count for less and less in a world networked by fibre optics and hooked on television soaps.

21 GLOBALIZATION AND 'LOCALISM'

D. Morley and K. Robins

Globalization is about the compression of time and space horizons and the creation of a world of instantaneity and depthlessness. Global space is a space of flows, an electronic space, a decentred space, a space in which frontiers and boundaries have become permeable. Within this global arena, economies and cultures are thrown into intense and immediate contact with each other – with each 'other' (an 'other' that is no longer simply 'out there', but also within).

We have argued that this is the force shaping our times. Many commentators, however, suggest that something quite different is happening: that the new geographies are, in fact, about the renaissance of locality and region (compare the work of the GLC in London and other metropolitan authorities in Britain in the mid-1980s, and similar strategies adopted to 'regenerate' the economies of many American cities). There has been a great surge of interest recently in local economies and local economic strategies. The case for the local or regional economy as the key unit of production has been forcefully made by the 'flexible specialisation' thesis. Basing its arguments on the economic success of the 'Third Italy' . . . this perspective stresses the central and prefigurative importance of localized production complexes. Crucial to their success, it is suggested, are strong local institutions and infrastructures: relations of trust based on face-to-face contact; a 'productive community' historically rooted in a particular place; a strong sense of local pride and attachment.

In the cultural sphere, too, localism has come to play an important role. The 'struggle for place' is at the heart of much of the contemporary concern with urban regeneration and the built environment. Prince Charles' crusade on behalf of community

From: *Spaces of Identity: Global Media, Electronic Landscapes and Cultural Boundaries*, by D. Morley and K. Robins, Routledge, 1995.

architecture and classical revivalism is the most prominent and influential example. There is a strong sense that modernist planning was associated with universalizing and abstract tendencies, while postmodernism is about drawing upon the sense of place, about revalidating and revitalizing the local and the particular. A neo-Romantic fascination with traditional and vernacular motifs is supposedly about the re-enchantment of the city. This cultural localism reflects, in turn, deeper feelings about the inscription of human lives and identities in space and time. There is a growing interest in the embeddedness of life histories within the boundaries of place, and with the continuities of identity and community through local memory and heritage. Witness the enormous popularity of the Catherine Cookson heritage trail in South Tyneside, of 'a whole day of nostalgia' at Beamish in County Durham, or of Wigan Pier's evocation of 'the way we were'. If modernity created an abstract and universal sense of self, then postmodernity will be about a sense of identity rooted in the particularity of place: 'it contains the possibility of a revived and creative human geography built around a newly informed synthesis of people and place' (Ley, 1989, p. 60).

While globalization may be the prevailing force of our times, this does not mean that localism is without significance. If we have emphasized processes of de-localization, associated especially with the development of new information and communications networks, this should not be seen as an absolute tendency. The particularity of place and culture can never be done away with, can never be absolutely transcended. Globalization is, in fact, also associated with new dynamics of re-localization. It is about the achievement of a new global–local nexus, about new and intricate relations between global space and local space. Globalization is like putting together a jigsaw puzzle: it is a matter of inserting a multiplicity of localities into the overall picture of a new global system.

We should not idealize the local, however. We should not invest our hopes for the future in the redemptive qualities of local economies, local cultures, local identities. It is important to see the local as a relational, and relative, concept. If once it

was significant in relation to the national sphere, now its meaning is being recast in the context of globalization. For the global corporation, the global–local nexus is of key and strategic importance. According to Olivetti's Carlo de Benedetti,

> in the face of ever higher development costs, globalization is the only possible answer.

Marketers, he continues,

> must sell the latest product everywhere at once – and that means producing locally. (quoted in Scobie 1988)

Similarly, the mighty Sony describes its operational strategy as 'global localization'. NBC's vice-president, J. B. Holston III, is also resolutely 'for localism', and recognizes that globalization is 'not just about putting factories into countries, it's being part of that culture too' (quoted in Brown, 1989).

What is being acknowledged is that globalization entails a corporate presence in, and understanding of, the 'local' arena. But the 'local' in this sense does not correspond to any specific territorial configuration. The global–local nexus is about the relation between globalizing and particularizing dynamics in the strategy of the global corporation, and the 'local' should be seen as a fluid and relational space, constituted only in and through its relation to the global. For the global corporation, the local might, in fact, correspond to a regional, national or even pan-regional sphere of activity.

This is to say that the 'local' should not be mistaken for the 'locality'. It is to emphasize that the global–local nexus does not create a privileged new role for the locality in the world economic arena. Of course local economies continue to matter. That is not the issue. We should, however, treat claims about new capacities for local autonomy and 'proactivity' with scepticism. If it is indeed the case that localities do now increasingly by-pass the national state to deal directly with global corporations, world bodies or foreign governments, they do not do so on equal terms. Whether it is to attract a new car factory or the Olympic Games, they go as suppliants. And, even as supplicants, they go in competition with one another: cities and localities are now fiercely struggling against each other to attract footloose and predatory investors to their particular patch. Of course, some localities are able successfully to 'switch' themselves in to the global networks, but others will remain 'unswitched' or even 'unplugged'. In a world characterized by the increasing mobility of capital and the rapid recycling of space, even those that manage to become connected in to the global system are always vulnerable to the abrupt withdrawal of investment and to disconnection from the global system.

What is more, the global–local nexus is not straightforwardly about a renaissance of local cultures. There are those who argue that the old and rigid hegemony of national cultures is now being eroded from below by burgeoning local and regional cultures. Modern times are characterized, it is suggested, by a process of cultural decentralization and by the sudden resurgence of place-bound traditions, languages and ways of life. It is important not to devalue the perceived and felt vitality of local cultures and identities.

But again, their significance can only be understood in the context of a broader and encompassing process. Local cultures are overshadowed by an emerging 'world culture' – and still, of course, by resilient national and nationalist cultures.

It may well be that, in some cases, the new global context is recreating sense of place and sense of community in very positive ways, giving rise to an energetic cosmopolitanism in certain localities. In others, however, local fragmentation may inspire a nostalgic, introverted and parochial sense of local attachment and identity. If globalization recontextualizes and reinterprets cultural localism, it does so in ways that are equivocal and ambiguous.

It is in the context of this global–local nexus that we can begin to understand the nature and significance of the enterprise and heritage cultures that have been developing in Britain over the past decade or so. We want now to explore two particular aspects of contemporary cultural transformation (each in its different way centred around the relationship between tradition and translation).

22 THE GLOBAL–LOCAL NEXUS

P. J. Taylor, J. Watts and R. J. Johnston

Recent concern for geographical scale has concentrated on the global and the local as opposite ends of the range of social-space possibilities. But even these two seemingly straightforward concepts are by no means unproblematic (Smith, 1993). The global implies a world-wide universalism, whereas the reality is that the processes of globalization are quite uneven. In the communications revolution, for example, the majority of humanity is 'out of the loop' and there is little prospect of large swaths of the 'South' being hooked into the system in the foreseeable future (Castells, 1993). Similarly we can ask how local is local? If local implies community then only small neighborhoods and villages can be 'true' communities based upon face-to-face interactions. Most studies treat localities as the local scale which is defined in terms of a town or city and its dependent region. This involves many definitional problems, but there is an underlying notion of local economy and society in a symbiotic relationship facing the outside world (Cooke, 1989). However, despite these problems the chapters have been able to uncover a global–local nexus bridging a wide range of social practices. By nexus we mean that a complex connectivity exists between the two limiting geographical-scale possibilities. Five such examples can be easily identified from the chapters above.

Localities are often portrayed as 'economic victims' of global forces, where investment decisions made thousands of miles away can make or break communities. This is sometimes known as the regional dilemma in a new market-led world. But life is never that simple. Localities are not inert population aggregates, they are constituted of people and their social networks that can, and do, devise practices to attract, retain, boost, and otherwise ameliorate forces that seem to be beyond control. This

From: Re-mapping the World: What Sort of Map? What Sort of World?, by P. J. Taylor, J. Watts and R. J. Johnston, in *Geographies of Global Change: Remapping the World in the Twentieth Century*, edited by P. J. Taylor et al., Blackwell, 1995.

global–local nexus is, of course, enormously complex both economically and politically. This complexity is often related to a second nexus concerning the recent rise of multiple ethnic rebellions, religious revivals, and nationalisms. Each can be interpreted in part as local resistances to the homogenizing global political forces that favour larger and larger political spaces to counter economic globalization. These movements attempt to generate a politics sensitive to local needs, in reaction to the destructive and destabilizing impact of economic restructuring. A third nexus is a broader formulation to what lies behind ethnic revivals. The postmodern celebration of diversity in all its forms – gender, race, sexuality, physical ability, as well as religion and ethnicity – derives from a critique of the meta-narratives of modernity as a sort of intellectual globalization. The global implied by modernized space is countered by the local identified through diversity in places. But diversity is not universally accepted and intolerance has created a fourth 'new world disorder' nexus wherein global changes are translated into numerous local conflicts. Sometimes surrogate wars for outside powers, the contemporary world is ablaze with political 'flash points', civil wars that destroy local-ities, creating millions of refugees. These are the places we gasp at in horror on our television screens in the comfortable world. The fifth nexus treats the broader notion of destruction, the overloading of ecosystems locally to the point of producing un-inhabitable localities, which can culminate in the destruction of the earth as a living system.

The key point about these interlocking global–local nexuses is that they each represent real tensions between activities and consequences that are sepa-rated by geographical scale. The conundrum is that there is no easy way to overcome such problems of remoteness. No sooner is a solution found to one particularly onerous and dangerous situation than the world has moved on, spawning another series of related problems. For instance, many people looked forward to the end of the Cold War as a means of solving some very crucial problems, notably the threat of nuclear war. The Cold War is over but the problems have not disappeared; worries about nuclear proliferation, and many more problems, have

arisen. All we can say is that the world is now different, not necessarily better. And so we must return to the one unchanging fact of our world – that it is forever changing.

---

23 'ACTING LOCALLY, ACTING GLOBALLY'

P. Macnaghten and J. Urry

The environmental movement has employed the culturally illuminating motto: 'Think Global, Act Local'. What does this mean? What kind of reworking of the global–local nexus is involved in order that nature can be appropriately governed? Minimally, the motto indicates two processes. First, many environmental problems at the local and regional level do, in fact, have transnational origins in different parts of the globe and hence need inter-national agreements for states and other actors to propose measures to remedy them and to improve each locality (such as acid rain generated by cars and nationally based power station emissions imported to affect lakes and forests in other nation-states). And second, many large-scale problems require for their solution localized, decentralized actions from vast numbers of people, many of whom will not person-ally benefit from such a change since they will be spatially or temporally distant from the benefits of such a change (such as reducing the use of carbon fuels). We consider these in turn . . .

But the 'local' in 'acting locally' is more complex than this (see Dickens, 1996, pp. 189–90). First, the commitment to the 'local' may in fact make it hard to 'govern' nature appropriately. The local as promoted in national or international environmental policies may not resonate with and mobilize people's local concerns and interests. Chapter 7 showed the

From: *Contested Natures*, by P. Macnaghten and J. Urry, Sage, 1998.

mismatch between the rational and instrumental spaces of the local in official policy (such as saving energy, recycling bottles or using public transport) as compared with more moral and historically symbolic spaces of the local informing everyday concerns (such as protecting local spaces of the countryside, the right to hunt, concerns over dog mess, or anxieties about dirty beaches). Moreover, such local concerns are themselves being transformed and remade by many of the global processes outlined above. For example, increasing levels of commuting, migration, exile and tourism patterns all contribute to local communities being less based upon geographical propinquity. Indeed the 'local environment' is often most protected by those having little connection with it on a day-to-day basis of dwellingness. Recent research in Britain, moreover, suggests that it is the village and neighbourhood that more people identify with, rather than a broader district or county. In other words, people appear to feel attached to a unit that almost certainly has little power of influence to make much impact with regard to most globally relevant environmental issues (Gosschalk and Hatter, 1996).

Such clashes present considerable difficulties for policies aimed at mobilizing local action, especially when they are conceived of in national or international fora. Even more problematically, new rhetoric and social practices are emerging which contest conceptions of the local which have been historically based in the North Atlantic Rim and which rely upon the structures of the nation-state (see Eade, 1997, for various studies of 'globalization as local process'). National states are thus confronted by intense contestation over the local, on the one hand, and by delegitimization and the power of the global, on the other (see Lash and Urry, 1994: Chapter 11; and Harvey, 1996). And even if local responses and policies are developed, there is no simple way of ensuring that there is appropriate global co-ordination between the hundreds of thousands of local communities throughout the world.

But while acting locally may on occasions impede or produce outcomes opposed to thinking globally, there are other instances where acting for the globe may improve the local environment of particular places. An example of this would be a local campaign to reduce the use of cars within a rural area. This not only benefits future generations living elsewhere, providing of course that car drivers do not just transfer their driving onto other roads, but may also benefit local residents, whose air quality and aural environment will be improved. In such cases local-global co-ordination may be effected . . .

---

24 GLOBALIZING THE LOCAL AND LOCALIZING THE GLOBAL

M. Tehranian and K. K. Tehranian

A dual process of globalization of the local, and localization of the global, has thus made isolationism and dissociation virtually impossible for any nation – even those that devoutly attempted it for a while such as China, Saudi Arabia, Burma and Iran. While globalization is fundamentally a topdown process, localization is bottom-up. The agents of transnationalization consist of the global hard and soft networks primarily facilitated by the non-state actors. The hard networks consist of transportation, telecommunication and tourism (TTT) facilities spun around the globe connecting the core in network of communication. The soft networks provide the programmes that negotiate and integrate the competing interests and values of global players. These include global broadcasting, advertising, education and exchanges of information. In the meantime, the localization processes are working through their own hard and soft networks, at times employing the core networks and at other times developing their own independent periphery systems. The agents of localization and tribalization

From: *Taming Modernity: towards a new paradigm*, by M. Tehranian and K. K. Tehranian, in *International Communication and Globalization*, edited by A. Mohammadi, Sage, 1997.

consist of the nationalist, religious and culturalist movements and leaders voicing peripheries' interests and views. In contrast to the 'big media' of the core, they often employ the low-cost, accessible and elusive 'small media' such as low-powered radios, audio-cassettes, portaback videos, copying machines, and personal computer networking. Their software consists of the rich heritage of primordial myths and identities embedded in the traditional religious, nationalist, tribal and localist ideologies.

Transnational networks

However, the infrastructure of a global consciousness is fast growing by the media events and a pop culture orchestrated by such transnational networks as CNN, BBC, World TV, Star TV, MTV, the Internet and non-governmental organizations (NGOs). While the first five are largely-one way, topdown channels, the last two provide interactive, bottom-up, international and communication channels. The media events (Dayan and Katz, 1992) of the last few decades (the landing on the moon, the Sadat visit to Jerusalem, the Tiananmen Square incident, the Gulf War, and the signing of the peace accords between Yitzhak Rabin and Yasser Arafat) have brought about a new global consciousness of the common human destiny.

Since 1985, the steady growth of CNN into the world's first global news network has provided the elites in most parts of the world with a stream of live broadcasts in English, Spanish, Japanese, Polish, and soon French and German. In 1987, to counter the Western bias of its news, CNN started airing the CNN World Report, providing uncensored and unedited news reports from local broadcasters all over the world. 'By 1992, 10,000 local news items had been aired on the World Report, originating from a total 185 news organizations representing 130 countries. CNN's internationally-distributed satellite signal is within reach of 98 per cent of the world's population' (Pai, 1993; see also McPhail, 1993; Flourney, 1992). CNN has thus become more than a news medium. It is also serving as a channel for public diplomacy, working often faster than the private channels of traditional diplomacy. Many heads of state and responsible officials watch the CNN during crises in order to assess directly the events abroad while gauging the impact of those events on the domestic and international public opinion. Fidel Castro is reported to have been one regularly to watch the CNN service. During the Gulf Crisis, President Bush indicated at a press conference that he would call up President Ozal of Turkey while the latter was watching the CNN's live coverage; the telephone call came through a few minutes later while President Ozal was waiting for it. Peter Arnett's reporting from Baghdad during the Gulf War filled some of the communication gaps between Saddam Hussein and the rest of the world.

CNN, however, provides a global picture primarily through an American prism. Britain is trying to emulate the CNN success story through the BBC World Service Television, while Japan has considered the establishment of an NHK-led Global News Network, GNN (Lee, 1993). Star Television, acquired by Rupert Murdoch's News Corporation in 1993, covers most of Asia through direct broadcast satellite (DBS).

Similarly, MTV is exporting youthful, whimsical, irreverent, postmodernist, American cultural values into Europe, Asia, Africa and Latin America. Although possessing universal appeal, MTV is following a localization strategy wherever it goes. Stimulated by the example of a popular programme that is promotional in selling the music it plays, local record companies have been quick to take up the challenge. India's Megasound spent only US $5,000 to produce a video featuring India's first Hindi rap tune by the local artist Baba Segal . . . MTV is thus contributing to the creation of an intended or un-intended global, postmodernist sub-culture with far-reaching consequences.

25 THE INTERSECTION OF THE LOCAL AND THE GLOBAL

A. Cvetkovich and D. Kellner

The confluence of global culture with local and national culture is appraised quite differently. For some, a global media culture provides new sources for pleasures and identities that redefine gender, new role models and fantasies, and new cultural experiences. These lead to the fragmentation of old identities and subjectivities, and the constructions of new identities out of the multifarious and sometimes conflicting configurations of traditional, local, national, and now global forces of the present time. From this perspective, the intersection of the global and the local is producing new matrixes to legitimize the production of hybrid identities, thus expanding the realm of self-definition. And so although global forces can be oppressive and erode cultural traditions and identities, they can also provide new material to rework one's identity and can empower people to revolt against traditional forms and styles to create new, more emancipatory ones.

For some theorists this allegedly postmodern heterogeneity is positive, but for others it makes it easier to manipulate fragmented selves into consumer identities, synthetic models produced by the culture industries. From this perspective, the fragmentation and even dissolution of traditional identities result in superficial changes of fashion and style that reconceive identity in terms of looks and attitudes as opposed to fundamental commitments, choices and action. New postmodern selves who go from moment to moment without making fundamental choices or commitments live on the surface, lost in the funhouse of hyperreal media images and the play of floating signifiers, themselves becoming mere images and signifiers in the postmodern carnival.

Most of the new global populars that produce resources for identity come from North American media industries, thus from this perspective globalization becomes a form of Americanization. Figures of the global popular such as Rambo, Madonna, Beavis and Butt-Head, gangsta rippers, and other figures from US culture produce seductive models for new identities that find their adherents all over the world. But precisely such global figures can be appropriated locally to provide new hybridized models of identity. Global culture is indeed disseminating throughout the world; new fashion, style, sexuality and images are appropriated in many ways by individuals in specific local situations. But global models are confronted by national, regional and traditional models in many parts of the world.

In Asian countries, such as Japan, Korea, Taiwan, Hong Kong and Singapore, there are intense clashes among traditional, national, and global models of identity. Traditional culture and religion continue to play an important role in everyday life and compromises and syntheses are often constructed between traditional and modernizing global forces. Likewise, on the level of culture, young musicians often combine traditional musical forms with contemporary transnational ones or produce specific forms like Chinese rap or Japanese heavy metal. And on the level of sports, countries like Japan play baseball but in ways that reinforce traditional Japanese values and structures. Such a synthesis and hybridization is highly uneven, however. Singapore uses authoritarian state measures to protect traditional culture; Japan uses more paternalistic measures to privilege national culture; and Hong Kong and Taiwan are more open and laissez-faire.

In Europe, Asia, and Latin America, for example, MTV is adapted to local conditions and produces new hybrid forms. Indeed, the defining characteristics of global media culture are the contradictory forces of identity and difference, homogeneity and heterogeneity, the global and the local impinging on each other, clashing, or simply peacefully coexisting, or producing new symbioses as in the motto of MTV Latino that combines English and Spanish: 'Chequenos!' – meaning 'Check us out!' Yet globalization by and large means the hegemony of transnational cultural industries, largely American. In Canada, for instance, about 95 per cent of films

From: Introduction, by A. Cvetkovich and D. Kellner, in *Articulating the Global and the Local*, edited by A. Cvetkovich and D. Kellner, Westview Press, 1997.

in movie theaters are American; US television dominates Canadian television; seven American firms control distribution of sound recordings in Canada; and 80 per cent of the magazines on newsstands are non-Canadian. In Latin America and Europe the situation is similar: American media culture, commodities, fast food and malls are creating a new global culture that is remarkably similar on all continents.

Today, under the pressure of the dialectics of the global and the local, identity has global, national, regional and local components, as well as the specificities of gender, race, class and sexuality. Identity construction is thus heavily over-determined and the dialectics of the global and the local are producing new conflicts in which choices must be made concerning what features will define national and individual identity. This situation is highly contradictory with reassertions of traditional modes of identity in response to globalization and a contradictory *mélange* of hybrid identities – and no doubt significant identity crises – all over the world. From this perspective, celebrations of or attacks against allegedly postmodern selves miss the dynamics of the conflicts between the global and the local, which problematize selfhood, create the need for new choices and commitments, and produce new possibilities for the creation of identities that could be empowering.

Indeed, seeing identity as a construct rather than as a given, as something to be made and created rather than as an essential bedrock of personality, can empower people to increase their range of choices and can challenge individuals to choose to create their own unique selves and communities. The problematic of the global and the local can thus produce new insights into the construction of identity and show how identity today is more complex. Not only is there a proliferation of postmodern reconstructions of identity through image, but once again, tradition, religion, and nationalism must be confronted as forces that remain fundamental to the contemporary world and that continue to play important roles in national and personal life. Expanded modernization and globalization also create, as Anthony Giddens and others argue, increased capacities for reflexivity

that put in question both traditional and novel forms, sorting out positive or negative features – terms that will obviously be different for different individuals.

Rethinking identity requires openness to new forms of global identity or citizenship. If democracy is to play a genuinely progressive role globally, nationally, and locally, new ways must be created for citizens to participate in the different levels and dimensions that constitute their lives. In response to proliferating globalization, societies and individuals must rethink the problematics of democratization and the site and scope of democracy. Modern societies were predicated on the basis of a nation-state that would govern the area within its boundaries. Modern democratic theory gave citizens rights within their polis and, in theory at least, sovereignty over their common affairs – although there have been centuries of struggles over those rights and citizenship. But the space of both the nation-state and the power of its citizens are potentially undermined or are, at least, redefined in a new era of transnational corporations; a global information and media economy; supranational political and financial institutions; and the rapid penetration of national and regional boundaries by a cornucopia of products, services, and images from a global culture. Consequently, new modes of rethinking politics and democracy are necessary to respond to the new configurations of the global and the local.

---

26 THE GLOBAL IN THE LOCAL
A. Dirlik

. . . the transnationalization of production calls into question earlier divisions of the world into First, Second, and Third Worlds. The Second World, the

From: The global in the local, by A. Dirlik, in *Global–Local: Cultural Production and the Transnational Imaginary*, edited by R. Wilson and W. Dissanayake, Duke University Press, 1996.

world of socialism, is for all practical purposes, of the past. But the new global configuration also calls into question the distinctions between the First and Third Worlds. Parts of the earlier Third World are today on the pathways of transnational capital and belong in the 'developed' sector of the world economy. Likewise, parts of the First World marginalized in the new global economy are hardly distinguishable in way of life from what used to be viewed as the Third World. It may not be fortuitous that the north–south distinction has gradually taken over from the earlier division of the globe into the three worlds – so long as we remember that the references of north and south are not merely to concrete geographic locations, but metaphorical references: north denoting the pathways of transnational capital; and, south, the marginalized populations of the world, regardless of their actual location.

Ideologues of global capital have described this condition as 'global regionalism' or 'global localism', adding quickly, however, that 'global localism' is 70 per cent global and only 30 per cent local. They have also appropriated for capital the radical ecological slogan, 'Think globally, act locally'. The terms capture cogently the simultaneous homogenization and fragmentation that is at work in the world economy. Production and economic activity (hence, 'economic development') becomes localized in regions below the nation, while its management requires supranational supervision and co-ordination. In other words, the new pathways for the development of capital cut across national boundaries and intrude on national economic sovereignty, which renders irrelevant the notion of a national market or a national economic unit and undermines national sovereignty from within by fragmenting the national economy. Similarly, the necessity of supranational co-ordination transforms the functions of the nation-state from without, incorporating it within larger regional or global economic units.

The situation created by global capitalism helps explain certain phenomena that have become apparent over the last two to three decades, but especially since the 1980s: global motions of peoples (and, therefore, cultures); the weakening of boundaries (among societies, as well as among social categories); the replication in societies internally of inequalities and discrepancies once associated with colonial differences; simultaneous homogenization and fragmentation within and across societies; the interpenetration of the global and the local (which shows culturally in a simultaneous cosmopolitanism and localism of which the most cogent expression may be 'multiculturalism'); and the disorganization of a world conceived in terms of 'three worlds' or nation states.

27 THE LOCAL AND THE IMPORTANCE OF PLACE

K. Negus

Jocelyne Guilbault (1993) has observed that, as writers have begun to identify various 'world' and 'global' musics, so defining the 'local' has become a preoccupation in many parts of the world. In the 'traditionally dominant cultures', defining the characteristics of local culture has increasingly become a focus for debates about national distinctiveness and difference, while for 'small and industrially developing countries' discussions of local culture have often emerged as a reaction to the fear of losing cultural identity in the face of globalization, conceived as either global homogenization or cultural imperialism or both (Guilbault, 1993).

Debates about local distinctiveness, in contrast to the idea of emergent transcultural global forms, rest on the assumption that there is a connection between an actual place and the characteristics of the cultural forms that are produced there. The idea that certain musical sounds are associated with particular geographical places is a familiar one that has been used by the music industry in marketing campaigns and by audiences and artists when establishing a sense of identity for their music. Music has been constantly

From: *Pop Music in Theory*, K. Negus, Polity Press, 1996.

'placed' as it has been produced, promoted and listened to, whether as the sound of Strauss's Vienna, Elgar's England, Satie's Paris, the Mersey sound, the Manchester sound, the house sound of Chicago, the Delta Blues, the sound of merengue from the Dominican Republic or grunge from Seattle.

Many cities in the US have been associated with distinct musical sounds. At different moments the map has resonated with the sounds of Miami, Nashville, New Orleans, Philadelphia, San Francisco and Austin. This has sometimes been ephemeral when a city has become identified with a particular style for a short length of time (Seattle with grunge in the late 1980s and early 1990s, or flower power with San Francisco in the 1960s), or it may be more long term – for example, the way that Nashville has become a metonym that stands for country music (Curtis and Rose, 1983).

While such everyday connections between musical sound and geographical place are frequently taken for granted, they raise a number of intriguing but often theoretically vague questions about how the meaning of a place might be created, constructed and conveyed. Where, for example, is the 'Seattleness' of grunge or the Frenchness of Satie, and how do we recognize it when we hear it? Do you have to come from Chicago to produce a 'Chicago sound'? Such questions raise similar issues to those that were addressed (in Chapter 4) in discussions of identity (for example, concerning the gayness of gay disco music or the blackness of black music). Here I will try to build on what I have written (in the previous chapter) by indicating how this sense of locality might inform music making and be produced through musical practices.

Music and the sense of the local

For a number of writers who have been concerned with this issue (Wallis and Malm, 1984; 1992; Robinson, Buck and Cuthbert, 1991) there has frequently been an assumption that 'local' music has something valuable that connects it to a particular place – something that 'global' or 'international' music does not have. However, it is often very unclear what this might be. In Roger Wallis and Krister Malm's work, for example, the local is central to their study yet seems to be a particularly elusive and also very malleable concept. At one point they offer a definition of the local as a term that is used to denominate the level of music activity of the common man in society' (Wallis and Malm, 1992, p. 22). Apart from the sexism of such a definition, this vague category is then used with very little precision to refer to various types of music. Although formulated as a concept for music 'below the national level' (a household, village, town or county), the local soon becomes a synonym for a range of 'national' musics identified as Jamaican, Kenyan, Canadian, Swedish and Welsh (1992, pp. 236–52).

Robinson, Buck and Cuthbert also use the concept of 'local music' in a very malleable way, offering the following definition: 'By local we refer to a country or community, whichever represents the salient culture of a particular musician. In terms of individuals, we call all musicians who live and work within a specific place "local musicians" for that place; Michael Jackson is a local musician in New York City' (1991, p. 30).

Such a definition begs many questions. Would Michael Jackson also be a 'local' musician if he was recording in Tokyo or Berlin? Can a country and community represent the 'salient culture' of a musician in the same way? In what actual sense is such a culture 'local'? Such a definition also sits uncomfortably alongside the authors' reference to 'international popular music' as 'mass culture' and 'local music' as 'folk culture'. The dichotomy here is between a global and homogenous mass culture characterized by formulas, sameness and standardization and local, diverse, pluralistic varieties of music (more innocent, pure and immediate). A similar approach can be found in the writings of Wallis and Malm (1984; 1992), who frequently imply that local music comes from a place, whereas 'international pop music' seems to come from no place.

The point I am perhaps labouring here in this semantic nit-picking is that attempts to 'define' the local can lead to many ambiguities and contradictions. The concept is very loose and malleable and is frequently used in a confusing way over and sometimes against existing concepts (such as nation, community, town). Just as no sound, cultural form or corporation can be 'global' in anything but a partial way, so the characteristics of 'local music' (a country, a community, the sound of a star in a city) are so varied and lead to a rather confusing array of potential 'global–local' musical relationships. The 'local' seems to become as elusive, vague and all embracing as the 'global'.

In contrast to this approach, it might be more useful to adopt more precise terminology and, instead of trying to define the local, to ask how the local is given meaning in specific circumstances. In short, how is a sense of physical place (nation, town, room) represented, conveyed and experienced? . . .

While the imagination is an important element in many musical experiences, this type of anthropo-existential approach to place leads Stokes to suggest that by playing a private collection of CDs an individual can transcend the limitations of his or her own place on the planet and engage in a kind of musical tele-transportation. Although many people may often feel that music can transport them, the actual conditions of that experience are somewhat more mediated and grounded in very particular social circumstances. As Richard Barnet and John Cavanagh observed when referring to similar 'global dreams' to those evoked by Stokes: 'A pop song can carry an anxious 12 year old from the slum streets of Rio to a fantasy world of luxury and thrills . . . you can lie on a straw mat on the dirt floor of a Bangkok shanty town listening to Michael Jackson and imagine yourself living another life' (1994, pp. 36–7). The point being, of course, that the straw mat is still there while the music is playing. It is simply a fantasy and, as Tony Mitchell has pointed out, the practices of music consumption which include a feeling of moving across space are complex and contradictory and are just as likely to involve the listener in an 'imagined exotic adventure' (1993, p. 313) as they are to entail a sympathetic and more constructive engagement with 'other' places. . . .

My point here is that understanding how music comes to be connected to a particular place involves more than applying a concept of the 'local' or conceptualizing places in an ungrounded way, which confuses quite tangible 'real' things and the imagin-

ings of a listener. To avoid such confusions, it would be useful to analyse how that imagined place and sense of space is produced as a cultural construction and what its relationship to any real existing place might be. This is something that Sara Cohen has attempted to do in her work on the 'Liverpool sound'.

---

28 CULTURAL HYBRIDITY
G. Kapur

Globalization, which has a great deal to do with selling commodities, including units of the culture industry (exemplified by how hard the US fights for the export advantage of Hollywood and the American TV networks), comes with the theory that people around the globe negotiate at every turn and recycle and re-functionalize the foreign inputs anyway, to arrive at a hybrid fecundity.

Hybridity for Bhabha, let us remember, is the historical effect of colonialism, and it is to be used as a discursive device to decode the condition of postcolonialism. There is, along with this, a more functional form of hybridity. Therefore, a distinction has to be maintained between hybridity as a long-term cultural process involving materials, language, and difficult choices of discourse; hybridity as practice leading to a certain virtuosity learned against the risk of extinction in colonized cultures; and hybridity as a matter primarily of quick ingenuity required to ride current market demands, where an indigenous form and artisanal life adapts itself to the national-global market in whatsoever manner is most readily available. Nestor Garcia Canclini's trenchant argument along this track holds good for the survival, in Mexico, of indigenous traditions. They survive in

From: Globalization and culture: navigating the void, by G. Kapur, in *The Cultures of Globalization*, edited by F. Jameson and M. Miyoshi, Duke University Press, 1998.

their plurality by means that have a good deal to do with urbanism, innovation and a simultaneously closed and open identitarian politics of the post-modern age when the artefact has a new exchange value and prospers as a sign for reified communities in the globalized market. This can also serve as a success story for Indian crafts and for the evolving forms of popular art that capture the national and international imagination, not least the great Indian film industry.

We can go on from here to very briefly designate the more lively aspects of global culture as it transforms indigenous and national cultural formations. There have been cultural scenarios set up (as, for example, in Mexico and other Latin American societies) to prise open superposed cultures in an appropriate masquerade of representations. There are formal recodings of cultures, altering the terms devised in the great metropolis of the Western world (as happened in Japan after the World War II). There have been probings by historically deprived identities of a radically reconstituted otherness (as, for example, among the black vanguard in literature, in art, in performance). There are fantasies of plenitude proffered as resumed orientalist desire in contemporary Chinese films. And there is, finally, the reflexive option set up by each one of these intertwined possibilities that contribute to establishing a utopian realm of the other that is best reclaimed by that other. This is proved by the avant-garde now sweeping through the South, including Asia.

In India, at present, the national formation is disintegrating. There is an uncomfortable relationship between the public and the private, the state and commerce, the national and the global. With the new links between the Indian and the global markets, international ramifications are surfacing across the board in the culture industry (in the electronic media, film, advertising and art), and this cannot but have a certain emancipatory result – even if in the form of unbottled genii and quick innovation. Moreover, globalization allows for the first time a freedom from the national/collective/communitarian straitjacket; freedom also from the heavily paternalistic patronage system of the state. It allows freedom from a rigid anti-imperialist position in

which postcolonial artists find themselves locked; and the freedom to include in postcolonial realities other discourses of opposition such as those of gender and the minorities – discourses that question the ethics of the nation-state itself.

It is possible, then, that in India, as in various parts of Asia (Thailand, Indonesia, Hong Kong, Korea, the Philippines, China) the positively postcolonial avant-garde in film and in art will come now: a reflexivity posed as some form or other of counter-modernity made possible by the changed norms of cultural hospitality in the postmodern age. The initiative to hold international film festivals and biennials with a Third World, southern or regional focus is but a symptom of more substantial change in the actual political conditions building up to a breakthrough in the contemporary arts. With the older institutional structure built up during the nationalist or revolutionary phase in flux, with the not-so-hospitable economic realities of the postmodern age, the naked expropriation of the south by the trade and labour laws of the north, and with growing disparities mocking the unity of the nation itself, a new battleground for cultural action opens up. If it seems that this avant-garde will be a postmodern affair, it will not be without a serious challenge to the terms of that phenomenon precisely where those become baldly global.

---

29 GLOBAL MELANGE
M. Featherstone, S. Lash and R. Robertson

How do we come to terms with phenomena such as Thai boxing by Moroccan girls in Amsterdam, Asian rap in London, Irish bagels, Chinese tacos and Mardi Gras Indians in the US, or 'Mexican schoolgirls dressed in Greek togas dancing in the style of Isadora

From: *Global Modernities*, edited by M. Featherstone, S. Lash and R. Robertson, Sage, 1995.

Duncan' (Rowe and Schelling, 1991, p. 161)? How do we interpret Peter Brook directing the Mahabharata, or Ariane Manouchkine staging a Shakespeare play in Japanese Kabuki style for a Paris audience in the Theatre Soleil? Cultural experiences, past or present, have not been simply moving in the direction of cultural uniformity and standardization. This is not to say that the notion of global cultural synchronization (Hamelink, 1983; Schiller, 1989) is irrelevant – on the contrary – but it is fundamentally incomplete. It overlooks the counter-currents – the impact non-Western cultures have been making on the West. It downplays the ambivalence of the globalizing momentum and ignores the role of local reception of Western culture – for example the indigenization of Western elements. It fails to see the influence non-Western cultures have been exercising on one another. It has no room for crossover culture – as in the development of 'third cultures' such as world music. It overrates the homogeneity of Western culture and overlooks the fact that many of the standards exported by the West and its cultural industries themselves turn out to be of culturally mixed character if we examine their cultural lineages. Centuries of south–north cultural osmosis have resulted in an intercontinental crossover culture. European and Western culture are part of this global *mélange*. This is an obvious case if we reckon that Europe until the fourteenth century was invariably the recipient of cultural influences from 'the Orient'. The hegemony of the West dates only from very recent times, from around 1800, and, arguably, from industrialization.

One of the terms offered to describe this interplay is the creolization of global culture (Friedman, 1990; Hannerz, 1987). This approach is derived from creole languages and linguistics. 'Creolization' itself is an odd, hybrid term. In the Caribbean and North America it stands for the mixture of African and European (the Creole cuisine of New Orleans, etc), while in Hispanic America 'criollo' originally denotes those of European descent born in the continent. 'Creolization' means a Caribbean window on the world. . . . The Latin American term 'mestizaje' also refers to boundary-crossing mixture. . . . Another terminology is the 'orientalization of the world', which has been referred to as 'a distinct global process' (Featherstone, 1990). In Duke Ellington's words, 'We are all becoming a little Oriental' (quoted in Fischer, 1992, p. 32). It is reminiscent of the theme of 'East wind prevailing over West wind', which runs through Sultan Galiev, Mao and Abdel-Malek. In the setting of the 'Japanese challenge' and the development model of east Asian newly industrialized countries, it evokes the pacific century and the twenty-first century as the 'Asian Century' (Park, 1985).

Each of these terms ('creolization', 'mestizaje', 'orientalization') opens a different window on the global *mélange*. In the US 'crossover culture' denotes the adoption of black cultural characteristics by European Americans and of white elements by African-Americans. As a general notion, this may aptly describe global intercultural osmosis and interplay. Global 'cross-over culture' may be an appropriate characterization of the long-term global North-South *mélange*. Still, what is not clarified are the terms under which cultural interplay and crossover take place. Likewise in terms such as 'global *mélange*', what is missing is acknowledgement of the actual unevenness, asymmetry and inequality in global relations.

PART B2

GLOBAL CONSUMERISM, TOURISM AND IDENTITY

1 GLOBAL BRANDS AND GLOBAL BRANDING

M. de Mooij

In most categories, companies do not compete with products but with brands, augmented products that are differentiated and well positioned versus other brands in the category. In order to dominate, a global brand must be a leadership brand in all important markets in the world. Coca-Cola is now sold in 195 countries with 5.2 billion people. Landor Associates in 1990 compiled a list of the Top 10 most powerful brands world-wide: Coca-Cola was number one. In 1994, Young & Rubicam repeated the study, and again Coca-Cola was the number one brand world-wide. On a similar list by Interbrand, another consultancy that specializes in branding, Coca-Cola also took the number one position in 1990. In 1996, however, that place was held by McDonald's. Most brands vary widely on the criteria for comparing brands, such as a brand's market share, the variety of people (for example, age and nationality) the brand appeals to world-wide, and the loyalty of its consumers. Over the years, brands tend to shift position. Examples are Kellogg's, which was number two on the 1990 Interbrand list and disappeared from the list in 1996. Disney, on the other hand, not on the 1990 list, appeared on the 1996 list. Eight of the top 10 brands are American, one is Japanese (Sony), and one is European (Mercedes-Benz).

In global branding, the facets of the brands referred to are usually the formal brand identity (logo, symbol, trademark, brand name, colors, shapes), its positioning, its marketing mix, distribution, strategic principles, and advertising. The assumption is that the above facets should all be identical. Yet the classic examples of global brands are rarely fully globally standardized. If a global brand is defined as a brand of which all elements are standardized (identical brand name, package, and advertising world-wide), there are hardly any global brands — even Coca-Cola. What constitutes a global brand can be described as follows.

A global brand is one which shares the same strategic principles, positioning and marketing in every market throughout the world, although the marketing mix can vary. It carries the same brand name or logo. Its values are identical in all countries and it has a substantial market share in all countries and comparable brand loyalty. The distribution channels are similar.

Marlboro is the quintessential global brand. It is positioned around the world as an urban brand appealing to the universal desire for freedom and physical space, something that urban dwellers typically lack and that are symbolized by the 'Marlboro man' and 'Marlboro Country'. Also, everywhere, Marlboro is a premium brand. Its advertising

From: *Global Marketing and Advertising: Understanding Cultural Paradoxes*, by M. de Mooij, Sage, 1998.

concept is uniformly used world-wide, with only small allowances in the execution.

A global brand is positioned the same way in every market. If the brand is a premium-priced brand, it is premium-priced around the world. If it is positioned vis-à-vis an age segment of the market, the positioning must be similar in every market. This is an ideal that cannot always come true, as the competitive environment of markets may vary, causing the need for adaptations in positioning. Yet real leadership brands must aspire to being leadership brands in all markets.

For most global brands, the product mix will vary to meet local consumer needs and competitive requirements. For example, both Coca-Cola and Pepsi Cola increased the sweetness of their drink in the Middle East, where consumers prefer a sweeter drink. The issue is not exact uniformity, but rather whether it is essentially the same product that is offered. Other elements of the marketing mix, such as price, promotion, appeal, media, distribution channels and tactics, may also vary. There are marked differences in the added values imputed to Coca-Cola by US and non-US consumers. In the US, Coke is part of the social fabric of Americana, much like McDonald's. Outside the US, Coke exemplifies the idea of 'American-ness' in its own way. Non-American consumers drinking Coca-Cola outside the US are quenching their thirst, too, but they are drinking in a little bit of Americana as well. In non-Western societies, especially, the brand helps make aspirational American lifestyles a little more approachable. Procter & Gamble's Pampers brand was introduced in the US in the late 1960s. Pampers created a disposable diaper market by providing a product that was more convenient than a cloth diaper. Pampers is now one of P&G's largest brands and is sold through a similar marketing strategy world-wide.

A global brand is available in most countries in the world. McDonald's, in 1995, offered its services via more than 18,000 distribution points in 89 countries. In January, 1996, McDonald's made it known that they intended to open another 2,500 to 3,200 outlets annually from 1996 onward. Two thirds of those will be outside the US. The company has standard specifications for its technology, product, client service, hygiene, and operational systems, but its communications are localized.

The majority of brands with global availability are of US origin. In 1992, few European Union companies used domination strategies. In 1992, of 46 major EU-based food companies, half were present in only one or two countries, 24 per cent in two or three countries, 17 per cent in three or four countries, and only 9 per cent in five or more countries. One of the reasons given for the lag in developing strong brands in Europe is the lack of opportunities in branding compared with the US. Television commercials have been an important ingredient in the success of, for example, P&G brands, and the US television networks have provided an opportunity to reach the whole country with the same message. Not only was commercial television introduced much later in Europe, but more important language and cultural differences have prevented this from happening in Europe.

A global brand usually originates in a particular country. In many cases, in spite of being global, it is associated with that nation. This can be beneficial if the image of the country remains constant. In case of change, both upgrading (Japan from 'shoddy' to 'high quality') and downgrading ('American values' have become ambiguous; for some they are positive, for others negative) will influence the brand's image and acceptance. Japanese electronics companies currently gain from the label 'Made in Japan', and Marlboro has gained a great deal by being American.

A global brand may be a product that is not standardized at all. An example is Knorr soups and sauces: The package with brand name and logo as found in supermarkets around the world provides the global brand image, yet the contents follow local tastes. Examples are goulash soup in Hungary and chicken noodle soup in Singapore. The logo and packages are similar world-wide, however, and can be recognized easily among competitive brands world-wide.

There are many brands that have all the characteristics of a global brand, yet they do not carry the same brand name everywhere. Sometimes the brand identity is global, but the names or symbols vary from one country to another, often for historical reasons. Examples are the different brand names of Unilever ice cream, many of which represent the names of the original companies Unilever acquired. Yet the combination with the same logo makes them recognizable world-wide. Examples of names are: Ola in the Netherlands, Ol-a in Portugal, Frigo in Spain, Langnese in Germany and Russia, Eskimo in Hungary, Algida in Greece and Bulgaria, Eldorado in Italy, Good Humor in the US, Wall's in Singapore and Malaysia, and Streets in Australia.

Many detergent brands carry different names in different countries, although the brand identity and positioning are similar. Names of Unilever's detergents are Surf and Wisk in the US, Omo in the Netherlands and France, Skip in Spain, Persil in the UK, and Pollena in Poland. Reasons for using different names in different countries or regions may be legal, political, historical, or cultural, or due to language differences. The most important reason may well be to keep and leverage the brand names of an acquired company after having acquired it for its well-known local brand names. Companies buy other companies because of the brand name in which that company has invested years building an association network in the minds of consumers. Change would include loss of investment in the consumers' minds.

---

2 EL SPORTSMAN DRUGSTORE

C. Classen

Walking through the downtown streets of Tucuman and other Northwestern cities, one is struck by the number of English words used in store front displays.

From: Sugar cane, Coca-Cola and hypermarkets: consumption and Surrealism in the Argentine Northwest, by C. Classen, in *Cross-Cultural Consumption: Global Markets, Local Realities*, edited by D. Howes, Routledge, 1996.

Even products made in Argentina, particularly clothing, will occasionally be advertised with English names and slogans. Given that the number of English-speaking visitors to Northwestern Argentina is minimal, these English slogans are all directed towards Spanish speakers. Their purpose is evidently not to communicate a literal message, for which Spanish would be the logical medium, but to convey an image. They carry notions of trendiness and prestige associated with the English-speaking US. They signal that the products they refer to transcend the bounds of Argentine culture and participate in the global market-place, where English is the lingua franca.

The fact that this use of English in advertising is symbolic, rather than literal, leads to some rather interesting appropriations of English, or pseudo English terms. A brand of artificial sweetener is named 'Slap'. A range of soft drinks is called 'Spill'. In Buenos Aires one finds boutiques with names such as 'The World's Number 1 Cigarette Racing Team' and 'Stress'. The latter accompanies its name with a picture of a coat of arms, as though indicating that suffering from stress is a desirable sign of upper-class status in the postmodern world. One shoe and clothing store in downtown Tucuman (with a branch in the Paseo Shopping) is named 'El Sportsman Drugstore'.

The less elitist store owners will sometimes choose combinations of Spanish and English for their advertising, trying to combine down-home familiarity with American allure. One of the most popular of such linguistic hybrids is store names ending in 'landia' such as 'Radiolandia' or 'Todolandia' – the land of everything. . . . Among the kiosks and cafes with saints' names such as San Ramon and San Antonio in the poorer quarters of the cities, you can sometimes find a sign with the name of that non-canonical saint – San Guich – a Spanish variant of the English 'sandwich'.

3 THE NATIONAL BASKETBALL ASSOCIATION

D. L. Andrews

Although the NBA's popularity among the black populations of both the US and Britain can largely be attributed to the relative dearth of alternative representations of successful, charismatic, and exciting people of colour in the popular media as a whole, the scenarios differ when it comes to the dominant articulations of the game.

As previously outlined, in the US the NBA has been strategically promoted in such a way as to downplay and overlook the vast over-representation of African-Americans in terms of player personnel, so the NBA appeals also to the white hegemony in the American marketplace. In stark contrast, within a British context the game has been promoted as a celebration of American blackness, which has in its various manifestations provided a significant touchstone for British youth culture over the past forty years, through solemn adoption, ironic appropriation, or outright rejection. In his populist account of the rise of British 'hoop fever', Sven Harding places the NBA within the latest, inter-textually fabricated phase in the British importation of American blackness:

> Ask British sport fans their opinion of basketball a few months ago, and they would probably have told you that it was a stupid 'Yank' game, played by a bunch of ridiculously lanky guys in vests, running about a school gym trying to throw a bouncy rubber ball into an old wastepaper basket nailed to a notice board. Now, thanks in no small part to the hip, street-cred link between rap and basketball culture, vibrant gangster-action-packed, basketball-themed movies like 'Above the Rim' and 'White Men Can't Jump',

From: The (Trans) National Basketball Association: American commodity – sign culture and global–local conjuncturalism, by D. I. Andrews, in *Articulating the Global and Local: Globalization and Cultural Studies*, edited by A. Cvetkovich and D. Kellner, Westview Press, 1997.

and the fact that in some inner cities it is (understandably) cooler to wear a Chicago Bulls cap than a Manchester United shirt, it looks like the blinkers are finally coming off. And there's a new school of moneyed entrepreneurs, visionary coaches and fiercely ambitious players poised to cash in with their souped up, music-heavy, MTV-influenced version of the game. (1995, p. 50)

Evidently, in Britain the NBA is being promoted to appeal to a particular market segment – the ever-style-conscious youth population – as a marker of cultural and racial difference. Again this provides a glaring contrast when positioned against the racial avoidance, displacement, caricaturing, and stigmatization that distinguishes stimulated popular appeal of the NBA in the US. Through the concerted linkage of basketball with other manifestations of black American culture, and indeed with pertinent representatives of black British culture such as the reggae star Maxi Priest and the Arsenal and England football player Ian Wright – who, for a Nike endorser, displays refreshing candour when tackled on sensitive issues (see Liston, 1994, p. 17; Williams 1994, p. 392) – it could be argued that, however unwittingly, the popular presence of the NBA is contributing to Stuart Hall's (1991) goal of rediscovering the 'postcolonial other' within British society, a cultural and racial other that has for so long been silenced by the lingering racism of British imperial discourse. Although it would be foolhardy to acclaim uncritically one facet of what is after all a highly exploitative post-industrial capitalist system while condemning another, it does seem that the conjunctural articulation of the NBA in Britain provides a better chance for developing more progressive, complex, diverse and politically appropriate popular representations of black masculinity than those that currently proliferate in the US.

As well as representing fruitful avenues for further inquiry, the contrast between the localized articulation of the NBA in the US and Britain exhibits the inherent variety and dynamism of (global) popular cultural production and consumption. Immersing Tony Bennett's (1986) instructive definition of popular culture within a more global context, it is thus possible to identify the global popular as representing those forms and practices that vary in content and signification from one historical period to another and from one national cultural context to another. Keeping with Bennett's theorizing, the global popular 'constitutes the terrain on which dominant, subordinate and oppositional cultural values and ideologies meet and intermingle, in different mixes and permutations, vying with one another in their attempts to secure the spaces within which they can become influential in framing and organizing popular experience and consciousness' (1986, p. 19). By developing an understanding of the global popular as a context that potentially provides opportunities for the establishment of both progressive and reactionary practices and regimes of signification, one can see the importance of a globally oriented Cultural Studies. This critical pedagogy would attempt to provide a more adequate knowledge and understanding of the global popular. It is hoped that understanding the global cultural economy and its processes would inform popular practice in such a way as to allow people to formulate their own strategies of resistance against the exclusionary practices that continue to infect contemporary societies both from global and local contingencies (see Hall, 1990). Hence, if the expanding domain of critical Cultural Studies is to be true to its political roots and is to continue to respond to 'new historical articulations, new cultural events, changes in the tempo and texture of social life, new structures of social relationships and new subjectivities', (Grossberg 1989, p. 415), a thorough interrogation of the global popular would appear somewhat overdue.

4 ISLAM AND CONSUMERISM

B. S. Turner

In sum, the development of a global mass culture has now begun to shape and condition the lifestyles of the Third World, developing societies and post-Soviet states. These developments in mass culture have also made a major impact on the world of Islam, representing for Islamic religious leaders a new form of indirect colonial penetration, a form of internal cultural invasion. Many of these cultural changes in everyday life, which are the unanticipated consequences of mass media usage, were anticipated in Lerner's *The Passing of Traditional Society* (1958).

These developments of global mass consumerism can be seen as a further extension of westernization and symbolic penetration, providing a problematic mixture of localist cultures and mass universalism (Stauth and Zubaida, 1987). In the case of Sadat's open door policy in Egypt, critics of Sadat's regime argued that this economic policy involved not only complete capitulation to Western economics, but also involved the further undermining of Egyptian values, or more precisely Islamic values, by the spread of consumerism and western lifestyles. The critical evaluation of this situation suggested that at the level of peasant life, American consumerism stood for a further erosion of traditional values:

> As the peasant sits in the evening with his family to watch the TV that his son has purchased from the fruits of his labour in Saudi Arabia, the intrigues of J. R. Ewing and Sue Ellen in Dallas strip him of what is left of his legitimacy as a culture bearer in his own culture. Between programmes, he is told in English that he should be drinking Schweppes or in dubbed Arabic that he should use deodorant, and that all his problems are caused by having too many children – a total package of imported ideas. (El Guindi, 1982, p. 21)

From: *Orientalism, Postmodernism and Globalism*, by B. S. Turner, Routledge, 1994.

Of course, the symbolic meaning and functions of consumer items are complex and unstable. For example, during the Iranian revolution against the Shah, the wearing of the veil by women signified opposition to the regime, adherence to Islam, and political commitment to Shi'ism. The veil, however, also had a practical function, since it was difficult to identify women individually on the part of the secret service while they were veiled. In the aftermath of the revolution, on a global scale, the veil has come to signify a general commitment to Islamic fundamentalism. However, in Egypt poor and economically deprived university students often found veiling to be the most practical solution for avoiding sexual harassment, since the veil signifies purity, but also these students are unable to buy the very expensive Western clothes which the upper classes of the Egyptian society buy to demonstrate their own personal distinction. In recent years there has also developed a more fashionable upper middle class form of veil and associated dress which has become fashionable in some areas of Cairo. Again on a global perspective, it is possible to refer to these strata as 'an Islamic bourgeoisie' (Abaza, 1987). Even within Islamic fundamentalism, the multiplicity of the meanings of symbolic cultures can never be entirely contained.

Conclusion: Islamization and anti-consumerism

Following Jameson (1984), we can associate the emergence of a postmodernist culture with the development of consumerism and post-industrialism. While Islam responded to modernization through the development of an ascetic ethic of hard work and discipline, contemporary Islam has responded to postmodernity through a fundamentalist politics of global community and through an anti-consumerist ethic of moral purity based upon classical Islamic doctrine. These processes involve an apparent paradox: the emergence of a global system of communication made a global Islam possible, while also exposing the everyday world of Islam to the complication of pluralistic consumption and the pluralization of lifeworlds. While the Abrahamic faiths successfully survived modernization, there are profound problems for religious absolutism in the area of postmodernity. In epistemological terms Postmodernism threatens to deconstruct all theological accounts of reality into mere fairy tales or mythical grand narratives which disguise the metaphoricality of their commentaries by claims to (a false) authorship. These threats of deconstruction emerge out of the pluralization of lifestyles and life-worlds making perspectivism into a concrete everyday reality. Postmodernization of culture is a significant issue at the level of consumption and everyday lifestyle, and it is for this reason . . . that Gellner fails to see the real importance of Postmodernism in his 'Postmodernism, Reason and Religion' (1992).

There are various solutions to Postmodernism. In terms of the Weberian model, one solution to Postmodernism is a nostalgic quest for holism through fundamentalist traditionalism, whereby the village is opposed to the global market place. Another solution is nationalism, which involves an associational, but closed, relationship in which the nation-state is opposed to the egalitarian abstraction of globalist citizenship. Within this second model, ecumenicalism is a market place of beliefs which is more compatible with globalism, but which still attempts to retain some credibility in terms of truth by acknowledging that there may be variations on truth in the theological market place.

Islamization is an attempt to create at the global level a new 'Gemeinschaft', a new version of the traditional household which would close off the threat of postmodernity by re-establishing a communal ideology. Islamization is a political movement to combat westernization using the methods of western culture, namely a form of Protestantism within Islam itself. Islamization equals political radicalism plus cultural anti-modernism. Within this perspective, Islamic fundamentalism is a defense of modernization against Postmodernism. The outlook for global ecumenicalism does not appear to be a realistic option since, for example, the Abrahamic faiths in their fundamentalist mood claim an absolute truth. The problem is that the Islamic Household must view alternative global households as threatening and dangerous and, therefore, Islam constantly finds itself forced up against 'lands of war'. It is difficult to imagine how one can have several universalistic, global, evangelical, religions within the same world political space. How can one have mutually exclusive households within the same world cultural system?

5 SIMULATION AND THE QUEST FOR AUTHENTICITY

E. D. Pribram

The distinction between appearance and representation, in Baudrillard's view, is that representation refers to an original, a 'real', while appearance does not (Baudrillard, 1988, p. 170). Now, in our culture of information and the mass media, we are inundated with an over-abundance of images and signs that no longer have referential value but, instead, interact solely with other signs. This marks the advent of simulation. Rather than the previous vertical connection, if you will, between sign and meaning, there is, instead, the horizontal relationship of sign to sign.

> All the great humanist criteria of value, all the values of a civilization of moral, aesthetic and practical judgement, vanish in our system of images and signs. Everything becomes undecideable. (Baudrillard 1988, p. 128)

Moreover, everything becomes exchangeable, one sign for another. There is an uncertainty of meaning, free floating and indeterminate, rather than the stability of a referent tied to meaning.

From: Seduction, control and the search for authenticity: Madonna's 'Truth or Dare', by E. D. Pribram, in *The Madonna Connection: Representational Politics, Subcultural Identities and Cultural Theory*, edited by C. Schwichtenberg, Westview Press, 1997.

The process of simulation, the evolution from representation to appearance, is the result of implosion. Rather than the explosion of capitalism and commodification in the modern era, postmodernism is marked by an implosion, a collapsing inward of traditional boundaries and binary distinctions such as elite and popular culture, appearance and reality, and so on (Kellner, 1989, p. 68). Implosion, according to Baudrillard (1988, p. 210), is caused not by a lack but by an excess of information. Here, we arrive at the source of Baudrillard's definition of the obscene as explicit or fully visible. No longer that which is hidden in the sense of 'deep structures' of meaning (Baudrillard 1988, p. 164), the obscene marks the surface confusions of the postmodern information communication culture: that which is excessively available and made too evident.

'Truth or Dare' raises the question of the 'real' – which is public persona and which private individual? – but refuses to answer it. Or it does answer it by saying that the question itself is absurd and irrelevant. Madonna, this chameleon of appearances who refuses all fixed meanings, may be viewed as simulation in the context of Baudrillard's theories. If one sees her in this way, she can then be received at surface value, confusions and contradictions intact. That is, there is no definitive 'real', no authentic Madonna, beyond the person(a) we already know through her various incarnations, guises and forms. Following Baudrillard, if there is no authentic, then the appearances themselves, by displacing the authentic, become the real (or, to use his term, the 'hyper-real').

To attempt to distinguish between appearance and reality is, in Madonna's case, misleading. No ground and no means exist to 'prove' she is one way in (any) public and different in a separate, private existence. There is no hidden real that she keeps from us like a dark secret, no lie or deception. Ultimately, no distinction exists between her public self and some other concealed self, between the on-stage and off-stage aspects of her persona.

It is important to distinguish simulation from the 'illusion' portion of the reality-versus-illusion construct. In fact, simulation displaces the entire reality-versus-illusion equation. Simulation is the map that precedes and displaces the territory it once was intended to describe (Baudrillard, 1988, p. 166). It is of the order of an alternate reality, the hyper-real. As Baudrillard explains (1988, pp. 167–168):

To dissimulate is to feign not to have what one has. To simulate is to feign to have what one hasn't. One implies a presence, the other an absence. But the matter is more complicated, since to simulate is not simply to feign: 'Someone who feigns an illness can simply go to bed and pretend he is ill. Someone who simulates an illness produces in himself some of the symptoms' (Littre). Thus, feigning or dissimulating leaves the reality principle intact: the difference is always clear, it is only masked; whereas simulation threatens the difference between 'true' and 'false,' between 'real' and 'imaginary'.

To say something or someone is a simulation model does not imply feigning, pretending or mis-leading, measured against that which is not feigned, actual, or true. It is, rather, to say that in the post-modern world, simulacra are actualized, self-contained entities, without any measurement against a referent that would then render them representative. Therefore, simulacra displace or threaten the entire dichotomy of true versus false, or of reality and its opposite, illusion. Feigning or dissimulation replace only the false or illusory portion of the dichotomy, leaving the idea of the equation unharmed.

Madonna's various appearances – her form of seduction – divert others from their path (in the literal sense of seduction) precisely because they search for her authenticity. In both her performances and her comments during interviews, she discloses an awareness, a self-consciousness, that the game is about 'revealing' her 'true' self. The way to play the game to win is by constant renewal. And so, she keeps re-inventing herself, sometimes (as in her interviews) from moment to moment. And along the way, she dispenses clues and devises contradictions to keep us guessing. Indeed, her stock in trade (exchange value) depends on never being definitively placed. Once pinned down, fixed, made 'real', her persona as it is

currently formulated would cease to exist (for, of course, there are many aspects of her life she could easily clarify were she to choose to do so).

---

6 GLOBAL TOURISM
J. Urry

With the tendencies to globalization . . . different countries have come to specialize in different sectors of the holiday market for overseas visitors: Spain for cheaper packaged holidays, Thailand for 'exotic' holidays, Switzerland for skiing and mountaineering holidays, and so on. Britain has come to specialize in holidays that emphasize the historical and the quaint (North Americans often refer to Britain as that 'quaint country' or that 'old country'). This emphasis can be seen in the way that overseas visitors tend to remain inland in Britain, rarely visiting either the coast or much of the countryside. Such visitors cannot know about more than a handful of sights worth visiting and, apart from London, these will normally include Oxford, Cambridge, Stratford, York, Edinburgh and increasingly some of the sites of industrial tourism mentioned above (see Urry, 1988). This location within the global division of tourism has further reinforced the particular strength of the heritage phenomenon in Britain.

The preservation of heritage has been particularly marked in Britain because of the mostly unattractive character of the modern architecture produced in the UK. The characteristic modern buildings of the post-war period have been undistinguished office blocks and public housing towers, many with concrete as the most visible building material. Such buildings have proved to be remarkably disliked by most of the population, which has seen modern architecture as 'American'. Yet the contrast with the often striking and elegant North American skyscrapers located in

From: *The Tourist Gaze*, by J. Urry, Sage, 1990.

the downstream areas is particularly noticeable. In addition Britain had a very large stock of pre-1914 houses and public buildings suitable for conservation, once the fashion for the modern had begun to dissolve in the early 1970s. An interesting example of this can be seen in the changing attitude towards conservation, particularly of the Regency facades in Cheltenham, which is now one of the prime townscapes being strenuously preserved even though much of it had been scheduled for 'redevelopment' (Cowen, 1990).

So for a number of reasons heritage is playing a particularly important role in British tourism, and it is somehow more central to the gaze in Britain than in many other countries. But what is meant by heritage, particularly in relationship to notions of history and authenticity (see Uzzell, 1989, on the recent professional literature on heritage). A lively public debate has been raging in Britain concerned with evaluating the causes and consequences of heritage.

This debate was stimulated by Hewison's book on the heritage industry, which was subtitled *Britain in a Climate of Decline* (1987). He begins with the provocative comment that increasingly, instead of manufacturing goods, Britain is manufacturing heritage. This has come about because of the perception that Britain is in some kind of terminal decline. And the development of heritage not only involves the re-assertion of values which are anti-democratic, but the heightening of decline through a stifling of the culture of the present. A critical culture based on the understanding of history is what is needed, not a set of heritage fantasies.

Hewison is concerned with analysing the conditions in which nostalgia is generated. He argues that it is felt most strongly at a time of discontent, anxiety or disappointment. And yet the times for which we feel most nostalgia were themselves periods of considerable disturbance. Furthermore, nostalgic memory is quite different from total recall: it is a socially organized construction. The question is not whether we should or should not preserve the past, but what kind of past we have chosen to preserve. . . . The protection of the past conceals the destruction of the present. There is an absolute distinction between 'authentic history' (continuing and there-

fore dangerous) and 'heritage' (past, dead and safe). The latter, in short, conceals social and spatial inequalities; masks a shallow commercialism and consumerism; and may in part at least destroy elements of the buildings or artefacts supposedly being conserved. Hewison argues that: 'If we really are interested in our history, then we may have to preserve it from the conservationists' (1987, p. 98). Heritage is bogus history. . . .

What does need to be emphasized is that heritage history is distorted because of the predominant emphasis on visualization, on presenting visitors with an array of artefacts, including buildings (either 'real' or 'manufactured'), and then trying to visualize the patterns of life that would have emerged around them. This is an essentially 'artefactual' history, in which a whole variety of social experiences are necessarily ignored or trivialized, such as war, exploitation, hunger, disease, the law, and so on (see Jordanova, 1989).

---

7 PROMOTING PROSTITUTION TOURISM

H. Muroi and N. Sasaki

In Asian countries, tourism is an important means of earning foreign currency. In Korea, the government's plan to develop Chejudo, an island near to Japan, as a tourist resort aimed to attract 0.6 million tourists with the construction of hotels, casinos and kisaeng (prostitution) houses (Yamaguchi, 1980). In the case of the Philippines, from 1973 to 1980 tourists to the country increased by about 26 per cent and total foreign income from tourism reached $320 million in 1980. During this period, the government received large loans from

From: Tourism and prostitution in Japan, by H. Muroi and N. Sasaki, in *Gender, Work and Tourism*, edited by M. T. Sinclair, Routledge, 1997.

such international organizations as the World Bank and Asian Development Bank for the construction of its tourism-related infrastructure, including luxury hotels and paved roads in sightseeing areas. One of the important advantages of tourism is that it creates jobs. However, as Wood (1981, p. 7) has pointed out, 'There is some evidence that hotels run by multinational corporations tend to generate less employment than locally-managed hotels', whereas 'the largest single such "spin-off" occupation is often left politely unmentioned: prostitution. It has been estimated that tourism has helped create 100,000 prostitutes in Manila alone.'

Matsui (1993) claims that the governments of the South-East Asian countries increased their promotion of tourism to compensate for a decrease in exports in the late 1980s since, even in the first half of the decade, earnings from tourism sometimes exceeded those from the staple commodity, rice. The tourism campaigns of 'Visit Thailand Year' in 1987 stimulated a large increase in foreign tourists visiting the country. The number of Japanese travellers to the country rose from 108,500 in 1985 to 162,000 in 1987, a 49 per cent increase. Prostitution tourism in South-East Asian countries had, however, developed long before the 1980s. It is argued that prostitution spread over South East Asia to provide the US army with relaxation and recreation after the Vietnam War broke out in the 1960s. O'Grady (1992) argues that the end of the Vietnam War, in 1975, left a huge prostitution industry in these countries, and describes how two types of prostitution occurred in Thailand: first, cheap prostitution for local people and, second, large-scale prostitution tourism. O'Grady (1981) also pointed out that many of the five star hotels in Manila, which were built according to the Presidential Decree to promote tourism, were occupied by Japanese male tourists.

In the late 1970s and 1980s, many governments failed to act against sex tours because of the large amounts of profit generated by them. For example, even when Thailand was referred to as the 'brothel of Asia', high government officials introduced legislation which underpinned prostitution tourism (Mingmongkol, 1981). More recently, some high ranking officials have begun to question the promotion of tourism. Mechai Viravaidhya, Minister of Industry in Thailand, was the 'first minister to look not only at the financial benefits of tourism but also at its impact on the environment and society' (Kelly, 1991, p. 44) and proposed a 'Women Visit Thailand Year' campaign. Public statements by representatives of government and business have changed in the context of the many protests and criticisms which have been levelled at prostitution tours and in view of the spread of AIDS.

---

8 THE OBJECTS OF TRAVEL
C. Lury

. . . an understanding of the travels of objects, as well as those of people, needs to be developed to understand specific formations of tourism. What this brief consideration of global cosmopolitanism as a specific set of object-people practices suggests is that a new space is being created for tourism: in this space, tourists travel in a 'world where the only frontiers are in your mind', in which 'being there' is a combination of selective subjects and partial objects. It is a space of the in-between, in which dwelling and travelling are rendered indistinguishable, a space in which the combination of place and culture is a matter of technological knowhow or user-friendliness and open-mindeness. It is a space of artefacts and flows.

However, by describing this form of discrepant cosmopolitanism as global I am not implying that these relations of travelling-in-dwelling and dwelling-in-travelling are evenly dispersed across the world. I am not suggesting that 'we' seek simplicity and informality; nor do I mean to suggest that the (unevenly distributed) participants – objects and

From: The objects of travel, by C. Lury, in *Touring Culture: Transformations of Travel and Theory*, edited by C. Rojek and J. Urry, Routledge, 1997.

people – are equal partners in this set of practices. Flows do not flow all ways: while they create a 'world where the only frontiers are in your mind', it is also a world in which the very question 'Where do you want to go today?' has been claimed as a trademark for the computer firm Microsoft Corporation. Moreover, global cosmopolitanism is a form of cosmopolitanism in which the in-between-ness of both people and objects requires the ability and desire to move into and out of relations of open- and closed-ness, and this is not a propensity that is pre-given in either people or objects. Rather, it is a propensity that has to be created.

Indeed, Hannerz says of all cosmopolitanisms that they are:

> a matter of competence, and competence of both a generalized and a more specialized kind. There is the aspect of a state of readiness, a personal ability to make one's way into other cultures, through listening, looking, intuiting and reflecting. And there is cultural competence in the stricter sense of the term, a built-up skill in manoeuvring more or less expertly with a particular system of meanings and meaningful forms. (Hannerz, 1990, p. 239)

Hannerz further suggests cosmopolitans have what he describes as 'decontextualized cultural capital' that can be 'quickly and shiftingly recontextualized in a series of different settings' (1990, p. 246). More specifically, as a propensity of people, the openness to objects which has been described here as characteristic of global cosmopolitanism has been described by Featherstone (1991) as part of the lifestyle of the new middle classes. As such, it is an individualized capacity for 'calculated de-control' and 'de-distanciation' in which the (middle-class) person is enabled to move backwards and forwards between immersion in and distance from objects through the acquisition of a specific set of cultural competencies. It is a propensity of people that is both selective and exclusionary, ordering distinctions of taste in which other (people's) relations to objects are valued negatively.

In addition, however, what the examples above suggest is that the unevennesses and inequalities of

global cosmopolitanism – its discrepancies – are not simply a consequence of the propensity of (some groups of) individuals or people, but simultaneously a capacity produced in (some groups of) objects in specific relations of travelling and dwelling, namely flows. These objects do not require the travelling/dwelling relations of contextualization (as do both traveller – and tripper-objects) in order to achieve integrity as objects; they move as a consequence of their own effects, carrying within themselves their own contexts of use or environment as user-friendliness. As the outcome of specific technical practices in which culture operates as a construct, this is an enhancement which is accorded to some objects and not to others. In this way, global cosmopolitanism contributes to the formation of new hierarchies and transforms the terms of object-people practices in tourism.

What both sides of the argument suggest, then, is that the in-between open and closedness of objects and people in global cosmopolitanism should not be equated with dis-interestedness; rather, this form of cosmopolitanism represents a specific set of interests and investments: it is a combination of selected subjects and partial objects in a technologically-mediated space of flows. It is tainted. Nevertheless, despite this selectivity (of people) and partiality (of objects), I have chosen to describe this form of cosmopolitanism as global because it helps constitute an episteme in which the boundaries between things – between people, places and cultures – are being transgressed and then redrawn. In this way, it can be linked to the wider project of globalization as a play of forces and forms that Deleuze (1986, quoted in Rabinow, 1992, p. 234) has called 'fini-illimite', the creation of diversity by the endless combination of bits and pieces. The attention paid to the travelling/dwelling of objects here may help to highlight other aspects of this project. In particular, it suggests that the project of globalization is one in which the abstract, cartographically ordered space of some other kinds of travelling cultures (including some kinds of tourism) is called into doubt, put into flux, and re-figured through the movement of people and objects in flows. It is a shift from a cartographical ordering of space in terms of plural places or contexts of culture to a figuring of space as post-plural environments or constructs of culture (Strathern, 1991).

This is a space of flows in which time-space compression occurs, in which objects and people are dissected by the cut'n'mix of boundary crossing and return, in which culture as technology refers back into and outside itself, creating environments by design, and objects come to take on new capacities. It is a space which is not homogenous, but its heterogeneity is not unplanned; rather it is a space in which subjects and objects do not come face to face but interface. The possibilities for tourism of this new space of flows are only just beginning to be explored, but they have the potential both to expand the kind of journeys possible – through the incorporation of time-space compression and the multiplication of perspectives – and to provide the basis for new kinds of hierarchy among both travelling people and objects. . . .

9 POSTMODERNISM AND TOURISM

G. Ritzer and A. Liska

Postmodernism is a popular theoretical perspective and it is often and easily applied to tourism. The problem with most such analyses, indeed with most applications of postmodern social theory, is their reliance on a general characterization of that theory. The fact is that there are profound differences among the major practitioners of postmodern social theory, Baudrillard, Foucault, Lyotard, Jameson, Virilio and so on (and Ritzer, forthcoming). There are even important differences within the bodies of works of many of these thinkers. Thus, one must always be

From: 'McDisneyization' and 'post-tourism', by G. Ritzer and A. Liska, in *Touring Cultures*, edited by C. Rojek and J. Urry, Routledge, 1997.

wary of general statements about postmodern social theory.

The place to begin this discussion is with the more specific and concrete idea of the 'post-tourist'. Feifer is most often linked to this idea and its major elements (1985). First, the post-tourist finds it less and less necessary to leave home; the technologies discussed previously – television, videos, CD-ROM, the Internet and virtual reality allow people to 'gaze' on tourist sites without leaving home. Second, tourism has become highly eclectic; a pastiche of different interests – visits to sacred, informative, broadening, beautiful, uplifting, or simply different sites. The postmodern tourist simply has a lot more choices; for example, one can take a pleasure voyage on one of the huge cruise ships or choose a much smaller, but still comfortable, ship and take an expedition cruise to more remote locales (Houser, 1994). Then, there is the growth of eco-tourism (Hill, 1995) as well as lifestyle cruises (and other kinds of vacations) such as those for seniors, as well as for gays and lesbians (Tazzioli, 1995). Third, post-tourists are seen as realistically simply playing a series of games; they play at and with touring; they recognize that there is no 'authentic' tourist experience (MacCannell, 1989).

Rojek has also analyzed post-tourism in terms of three basic, albeit different, characteristics (1993). First, the post-tourist accepts the commodification of tourism; it and the products hawked along the way are all manifestations of consumerism. Second, tourism is seen as an end in itself, and not a means to some loftier goal. Third, post-tourists are drawn to the signs, especially the more spectacular signs, associated with tourism. Munt (1994) discusses 'other', middle class, post-tourists who seek to distance themselves from crasser post-tourists.

Bryman sees Disney as fitting reasonably well with the idea of the post-tourist, indeed Disney 'may well have played a prominent role in stimulating the attitude of the post-tourist' (Bryman, 1995, p. 177). In fact, Bryman adds additional weight to the idea of post-tourism by, for example, discussing the simulacra, the fakes that are more real than real, associated with post-tourism in general, and more specifically with Disney.

The obvious questions seem to be: Are we in fact in the age of the post-tourist? Have we left the era of the modern tourist? These may be the obvious questions, but once again they are really the wrong questions. As before, they imply the kind of periodization and grand narrative rejected by most postmodernists. The real question is: Do these postmodern ideas cast new and interesting light on tourism? Bryman makes the point that what Disney has to offer in this realm is not so new; its precursors had characteristics that could be described as postmodern.

The idea that there is a close linkage between commodification, consumerism and tourism is worthwhile and worth exploring. postmodernism has long been linked with the consumer society (Featherstone, 1991; Baudrillard, 1993). Clearly, tourism has become a commodity to be advertised, marketed and sold much like every other commodity (Urry, 1990). However, what is not emphasized enough is the degree to which tourism can become little more than a means to sell lots of other commodities. Again, Disney offers a wonderful example of this. A trip to Disney World is a desirable goal in itself as far as the Disney Corporation is concerned, but perhaps more importantly it is the gateway to the sale of lots of other Disney products. The process begins on entering the theme park, which can be viewed as a thinly disguised shopping mall set up to sell primarily a wide array of Disney products. It ends with the Disney Village Marketplace which is open late for those who want to shop after they have visited the park. Indeed, it is increasingly difficult to differentiate between shopping malls like Mall of America and theme parks such as Disney World (Barber, 1995). The former is a mall with an amusement park, the latter an amusement park with a mall. We will have more to say about this kind of 'implosion' later ... but other examples are the way that Las Vegas is currently being transformed into 'the world's largest theme park' (Grochowski, 1995), and the coming of Segaworld, the world's first interactive entertainment theme park, to London, combining the theme park with virtual reality (May, 1995). The only real difference between contemporary mega-malls and amusement parks is in the relative mix of shops and amusements.

There is a broader kind of implosion taking place involving various corporate purchases and mergers (such as Disney and broadcasting giant Capital Cities/ABC). These are designed to increase the horizontal and vertical integration of organizations involved in consumption in general, as well as in tourism in particular. Barber describes not only malls, but commercial strips and chain eateries, as theme parks (1995, p. 128). More specifically, there is a sense in which McDonald's is a theme park: a food chain featuring its own Mickey Mouse (Ronald McDonald), its miniature non-mechanical rides in the 'playlands' outside, its commercial tie ins with celebrities and with hit films, and its pervasive claim on American lifestyle. While McDonald's might not be the kind of tourist destination that malls have become, they are an integral part of such malls and many other tourist sites.

The growing popularity of outlet malls, often adjacent to resorts, also reflects this kind of implosion of shopping and amusement. According to one industry insider: 'Shopping has more and more become recreation. ... You can combine your vacation or weekend away with outlet shopping' (McEnery, 1995).

And some outlet malls, like Potomac Mills outside Washington DC, have become tourist destinations in their own right. Similarly, more Canadian package tours now go to the West Edmonton Mall than to Niagara Falls (Davidson, 1995). Timothy and Butler examined cross-border shopping between the US and Canada, and concluded: 'There are strong indications that under some conditions shopping is the primary motive, if not the only significant one, in the decision to make such a trip' (1994, p. 17) ...

The issue of authenticity is central to the literature on tourism (MacCannell, 1989). Authenticity is also of concern to postmodernism in general, and post-tourism in particular, specifically under the heading of simulacra. A postmodernist such as Baudrillard would argue that we live in a simulated world and that is nowhere more true than in the realm of tourism (Baudrillard, 1983). MacCannell (1989) argues that tourists are searching, not always successfully, for authentic experiences. The logic of postmodernism, with a society increasingly dominated by simulations, would lead us to believe, if we assume that MacCannell is correct, that tourists are increasingly doomed to failure in their search for authenticity.

We have already offered an overview of Ossi Park, the planned simulation of life in the old German Democratic Republic. Among the other examples are 'Fort Clatsop', in Astoria, Oregon, where tourists can find a 'full-scale replica of Lewis and Clark's winter camp' (Houser, 1994). There is also an example used by Baudrillard, the caves of Lascaux in France. A tourist who journeys to the authentic site will find that the caves have been closed and an exact replica, a simulation, of the caves has been opened to the public. While these are extreme cases, most 'authentic' tourist destinations have been turned into at least partial simulations. Not all such efforts are successful. A notable failed attempt was Disney's plan for a Civil War theme park outside Washington DC 'with fake Indian villages, a replica farm, mock Civil War battles and a faux fair. As with the caves of' Lascaux, this simulation was to be constructed 'within hailing distance of real Indian trails, actual farms, a county fairground and a town that was sacked and burned by Union troops' (cited in Barber, 1995, p. 135). Incidentally, the coming of virtual reality will mean a vast increase in the scope of such simulations. There is already, for example, a virtual tour of the tomb of the Egyptian Queen Nefertiti (Stille, 1995). And this says nothing about the increasingly popular, totally simulated, tourist destinations such as Disney World.

But we will develop a difficult argument here ... that is, rather than seeking authenticity as MacCannell suggests, it could be argued that people raised and living in a postmodern world dominated by simulations increasingly come to want, nay to insist on, simulations when they tour. For one thing, it is increasingly difficult to differentiate between the simulated and the real; indeed, Baudrillard argues that the real has disappeared, imploding into the world of simulations. In such a world, the tourist would not know an 'authentic' experience even if one could be found. For another, living on a day-

to-day basis with simulations leads to a desire for them when one becomes a tourist. Accustomed to the simulated dining experience at McDonald's, the tourist is generally not apt to want to scrabble for food at the campfire, or to survive on nuts and berries picked on a walk through the woods. The latter may be 'authentic', but they are awfully difficult, uncomfortable and unpredictable in comparison to a meal at a local fast-food restaurant or in the dining room of a hotel that is part of an international chain. Most products of a postmodern world might be willing to eat at the campfire, as long as it is a simulated one on the lawn of the hotel.

Thus, we would argue, in contrast to MacCannell, that many tourists today are in search of inauthenticity. The enormous popularity of the tourist destinations focused on in this essay – Disney World, Las Vegas, cruises, shopping malls and fast food restaurants – all speak to the relentless search for inauthenticity. Blissfully contented with our simulated lives, why should we search for anything but inauthenticity in our leisure-time activities?

Baudrillard makes this point about Disneyland, 'a perfect model of all the entangled orders of simulation' (1983, p. 23). Take, for example, the simulated submarine ride to which people flock in order to see simulated undersea life. Strikingly, many go there rather than the more 'genuine' aquarium (itself, however, a simulation of the sea) just down the road. How many actually go to the sea to view (say, by snorkelling) undersea life? And for those few who do, has not the sea itself been altered (simulated) to accommodate the tourist? In fact, it has, at least in one setting:

> For the snorkelling enthusiast, the place to head is Folkestone National Marine Reserve, Park and Marine Museum at Holetown [Barbados]. A taxi there costs about $12 from the ship. The government has built an area where the novice can swim and follow a series of underwater markers that picture what fish are likely to be seen. (Newbern and Fletcher, 1995)

But all is not entirely lost, since the McDonald's built on Barbados was forced to close after only six months!

Certainly, there are those tourists who continue to search out authentic settings and they can, at least to some degree, still find them. However, visits to them tend to be more expensive than to inauthentic locales. More importantly, it is likely to grow increasingly difficult to find the authentic. Authentic tourist sites are likely to go the way of the caves at Lascaux. That is, they are apt to be shut down and to have exact replicas built nearby. Failing that, they are likely to be so altered by the demands of catering to large numbers of tourists that they are apt to become simulated versions of their original pristine forms.

Let us use another example from Baudrillard's work. Suppose we wanted to spend our vacation among the people of a primitive tribe, the Tasaday. This sounds like an authentic experience. However, Baudrillard regards the Tasaday at least as it exists today, as a simulation, since the tribe has been 'frozen, cryogenized, sterilized, protected to death' (Baudrillard, 1983, p. 15). It may at one time have been a 'real' primitive tribe, but today what exists is nothing more than a simulation of what the tribe once was. And now we are beginning to see simulations of simulations. For example, the new Sega theme park in London will offer simulated (via virtual reality) rides of an already simulated ride in, say, Disney World (May, 1995). We move ever more deeply in Baudrillardian 'hyper-reality'. Even if we accepted the idea that people know the difference between a simulacra and the authentic, and we assume that at least some people set out in search of the authentic, Baudrillard would argue that their efforts will be thwarted by the fact that these are all simulacra.

This section has been devoted to postmodern ideas that have previously been applied to tourism. We close with the mention of a concept, 'ecstasy', that as far as we can tell has yet to be applied to tourism. By ecstasy, Baudrillard means unconditional metamorphosis, escalation for escalation's sake, a continuing process of spinning off out of' control until all senses are lost (Baudrillard, 1990). Ultimately, this out-of-control system reveals its emptiness and meaninglessness; it 'shines forth in its pure and empty form' (Baudrillard, 1990, p. 9).

It could be argued that tourism is becoming such an ecstatic form. Given the implosion discussed above, the de-differentiation that is affecting tourism in many different ways (Urry, 1994), anything and everything is coming to be defined as tourism. This is well illustrated by bus tours to shopping centres and even better by the proposed Ossi Park in Germany. With everything defined as tourism, it becomes a meaningless form. Yet, it is escalating dramatically. Baudrillard uses fashion to illustrate the ecstasy of the (post-)modern world, but increasingly tourism is just as good an illustration. It is increasingly obese and cancerous, that is, it is increasingly hypertelic. There is no end to tourism other than limitless increase. There is no end for the tourist than to visit as many sites as possible, if only on the Internet. This is obviously not intended as an exhaustive application of the idea of ecstasy, but to illustrate that there are many more conceptual resources within postmodern social theory that the student of tourism might find useful.

---

10 GLOBAL FUNDAMENTALISM

F. J. Lechner

Fundamentalism is fashionable – as a problem for social analysis more than as a form of religious faith and activism. To be sure, the re-emergence of a certain kind of religious traditionalism in the public arenas of some countries was sufficiently surprising to justify a major scholarly effort to account for it. For Western scholars, the puzzle to be solved went beyond the apparent influence and success of some seemingly archaic cultural movements. The very way in which those labelled 'fundamentalist' tried to bring a sacred tradition to bear on the public affairs

From: Global Fundamentalism, by F. J. Lechner, in *A Future for Religion*, edited by W. Swatos, Sage, 1993.

of their societies compelled scholars to re-examine their assumptions about the 'normal' role of religion in modern societies and about the continued viability of religious traditions themselves. By virtue of its public character, fundamentalism seemed to point to a different future for religion from what many scholars had assumed . . .

Global Perspectives

The 'global turn' in Sociology consists of sustained efforts by a number of researchers over the past few decades to treat the world as a social system in its own right. These efforts were obviously inspired by the simple realization that societies were becoming highly interdependent. Moreover, it became clear that the very processes in which sociologists were interested had an inherently global dimension. Nettl and Robertson argued, for example, that modernization consisted not of processes that simply occurred in similar fashion across the globe, but rather of deliberate attempts by societal elites to place their society in a global hierarchy. Wallerstein saw this hierarchy as the product of long-term changes in the capitalist world economy, which had brought about not only a global division of labour but also a dominant world culture. This world culture became the primary concern of Meyer and his associates, who argued that modern institutions function according to global standards that are part of a 'world polity'. Robertson described such phenomena as aspects of globalization and specifically called attention to the importance of religious reactions against this process, brought forth by the tensions it has produced. An early attempt to link socio-cultural movements to world-level changes was made by Wuthnow.

Given these scholarly precedents, what does it mean to speak of 'global fundamentalism'? It means first of all that the predicament addressed by fundamentalist movements is a global one. Modernity is no longer a societal phenomenon, if it ever was. A reaction against modernity, therefore, necessarily has global implications: it entails a world-view in the literal sense of advocating a distinct view of 'the world'. For Islamic militants this includes an oblig-ation to spread the Islamic Revolution and defeat the dominant Western Satan. A global culture, not simply local circumstances, becomes the target of fundamentalist movements. The defenders of God aspire to bringing the kingdom of God to the earth as a whole and, in this sense, they become important actors on the global scene. As global anti-systemic movements, they attempt to resolve literally world-wide problems in global fashion – changing both the actual balance of power in the world and the cultural terms on which global actors operate. The struggle in which they are engaged is not, or not only, against modernity abstractly defined, but also for a particular shape of the globe. The extent to which they pursue this ambition depends in large part on variations in global change, on the extent to which particular societies or regions are socially or culturally unsettled by forces beyond their control.

The changing global condition not only becomes a context and target of fundamentalism, but also serves as its primary precipitating factor. Yet apart from globally induced variations in the strength of fundamentalism, the very attempt to restore a sacred tradition as a basis for a meaningful social order is globally significant, as one effort among others to preserve or achieve a certain cultural authenticity in the face of a greedy, universalizing global culture. It is, in other words, a particular, albeit radical and problematic, form of striving for communal and societal identity under circumstances that make such deliberate identification a global expectation – a point Robertson has repeatedly emphasized. Indeed, fundamentalism itself has become a global category, part of the global repertoire of collective action available to discontented groups, but also a symbol in a global discourse about the shape of the world. For liberal Westerners concerned about further 'progressive' change, fundamentalism is the 'global other', that which 'we' are not; for those taking issue with the meaning and structure of current, Western-inspired global culture, fundamentalism becomes a most radical form of resistance, a symbolic vehicle. Interpreting fundamentalism in this global fashion is to subsume, not to discard, the treatment of fundamentalism as a form of anti-modernism. Indeed, of all the conventional approaches to fundamentalism, this may well have the most lasting value: global culture, after all, is still (though not only) the culture of modernity. Standard criticisms of this approach as ethnocentric appear increasingly misplaced, for it is one that touches on crucial features of the global condition and represents a form of sociological realism rather than Western wishful thinking. To see fundamentalists locked in a struggle about the shape of the world is to recognize part of their actual predicament, not to deny their particularity in imperialist fashion. In fact, those advocating a less analytical, more subjective approach to fundamentalism, as well as other manifestations of religiosity or cultural difference, now face the difficulty that doing justice to the other in his or her particularity forces one to take into account the other's relation to universal structures, the other's reaction to alien penetration, the other's distinctly modern assertions of particularity.

In other words, the 'otherness' of the other is increasingly problematic as a consequence of globalization; fundamentalism, to put it most simply, is inevitably contaminated by the culture it opposes. Just as in any pluralistic culture, the other is always already within us, we are also already in the other, even when she or he puts forth a grand display of anti-pluralist authenticity. In the modern world system, no fundamentalist can simply re-appropriate the sacred and live by its divine lights. The very re-appropriation is a modern, global phenomenon, part of the shared experience of 'creolization'. To see it as such is to include the other as full participant in a common discourse, a common society, rather than to relegate him or her to the iron cage of otherness.

The global perspective on fundamentalism also makes comparisons in the conventional sense problematic. Such comparisons, after all, presuppose that one can isolate the units to be compared, in order to examine the differential effects of similar but independently occurring processes. Often carried out for the sake of historical sensitivity, such an exercise increasingly comes to seem artificially abstract. Societies are now inherently oriented toward each other; they are involved in processes that encompass all; even the object of the comparison, namely the propensity to engage in fundamentalism, is no longer an indigenously arising phenomenon. Of course, careful comparisons can still help to determine the causal weight of particular factors in social movements. But, beyond that, the new global condition has changed the terms of scholarly analysis as much as it has the terms of actual social action.

A Future for Fundamentalism?

The global turn in the study of fundamentalism was partly inspired by the concern about the possible public influence of fundamentalism mentioned at the outset. In the end, the scholarly and the public interest in fundamentalism converge on the question about the likely extent of this influence. I will briefly offer grounds for judging this influence relatively minor and for skepticism about the overall future of fundamentalism as we know it.

Of course, assessing the future of fundamentalism, a hazardous undertaking in any case, by no means exhausts the question of the future of religion as a whole. Indeed, from the point of view of non-fundamentalist believers, it may well be the case that the demise of fundamentalism is a condition for the revitalization of serious religiosity. Expressing scepticism about the future of fundamentalism also does not imply that there is no future for research about fundamentalism. There is work to be done, if only because the trends in social analysis sketched above have improved our understanding but not answered all questions. And precisely because its future is problematic and conflicted, fundamentalism will remain a fruitful subject for research.

Turning to substance: as I and others have argued over the years, fundamentalism is a quintessentially modern phenomenon. It actively strives to re-order society; it re-asserts the validity of a tradition and uses it in new ways; it operates in a context that sets non-traditional standards; where it does not take decisive control, it reproduces the dilemmas it sets out to resolve; as one active force among others, it affirms the depth of modern pluralism; it takes on the tensions produced by the clash between a universalizing global culture and particular local conditions; it expresses fundamental uncertainty in a crisis setting, not traditional confidence about taken-for-granted truths; by defending God, who formerly needed no defense, it creates and re-creates difference as part of a global cultural struggle. So compromised, fundamentalism becomes part of the fabric of modernity.

Being compromised in this way portends a problematic future for fundamentalism – problematic, that is, from a fundamentalist point of view. It indicates one of the ways in which fundamentalism, like any other cultural movement, engages and must engage in creolization, juxtaposing the seemingly alien and the seemingly indigenous into a worldview and identity that combine both in new seamless wholes. Of course, upon inspection, traditions often display a hybrid character. But if Robertson is right, such hybridization now becomes a normal feature of globalization, robbing cultures of easy authenticity while making the search for the authentic a virtual obligation. If the point of fundamentalism is to restore an authentic sacred tradition, this means that fundamentalism must fail.

This failure is exacerbated by the modern circumstances fundamentalism must confront. In some respects, modernity does act as a solvent, undermining the thrust of fundamentalist movements. Insofar as a society becomes structurally differentiated, religion loses social significance; once that happens, restoration is difficult, if not impossible. In differentiated, specialized institutions engaged in technical control of the world, religious distinctions have little role in any case; the very conception of infusing a perceived iron cage with religious meaning necessarily remains nebulous. If a culture becomes pluralistic and tears down its sacred canopy, those who would restore it are themselves only one group among others. Making claims for a fundamentalist project requires wider legitimization, except where there is overwhelming popular support; such wider legitimization entails watering down the message. Trying to act globally with some effectiveness presupposes the use of global means, technological and institutional; but satellite dishes and fighter planes and nation-states draw the would-be opposition farther into the culture it claims to disdain. Although its relative success varies according to the conditions sketched above, fundamentalism is inevitably co-opted.

But being modern and becoming co-opted presuppose that there is a viable modern order to be co-opted into. The future of fundamentalism is thus closely linked to the future of modernity. One advantage of the analytical view of fundamentalism, starting by conceptualizing it as one form of anti-modernism among others in order to expose its modern character, is that it draws research on the subject into the larger discourse about modernity, central not only to the Social Sciences but in the public arena as well. If modernity in anything like the liberal version I adopt here can be sustained, albeit transformed through globalization, then the life chances of large-scale public fundamentalism are correspondingly diminished. How strong, then, is the fabric of modernity? Contrary to conventional assertions of the imperialism inherent in modernization, or the emptiness of liberal culture, or the loss of meaning in advanced societies, liberal modernity offers a wide variety of cultural meanings. The usual jeremiads about the ills and weaknesses of imperially secular modernity notwithstanding, the latter offers considerable room for free religious expression and experience. In the actual struggles about the future direction of world society, it appears to this biased observer, the liberal-modern view of social order thus far has prevailed against challenges issued by various kinds of anti-modern movements and regimes. Even after two World Wars, the crises and conflicts of modern societies have not brought about the demise of the liberal modern project.

And yet, fundamentalism has its origins in real discontents experienced by real people; the mobilization factors that account for its relative strength in particular places have not disappeared everywhere; the tensions inherent in the globalization process cannot be resolved in any permanent fashion; in modern global culture, fundamentalism has found a place as part of a movement repertoire, to be activated when conditions are right. This does not enable us to make any clear-cut predictions about the re-emergence of fundamentalism in the twenty first century. It does enable us to say, more modestly if less informatively, that fundamentalism has a future – albeit one less bright than that of liberal modernity.

11 HUMANITY, GLOBALIZATION AND WORLD-WIDE RELIGIOUS RESURGENCE

R. Robertson and J. A. Chirico

We claim that serious social scientific discussion of religious belief and practice in a global perspective must involve a basic concern with the crystallization of the modern global circumstances. More specifically, if the 'problemstellung' consists in accounting for the near-world-wide resurgence of religious fundamentalism, the extensive development of new religious movements (including liberational– theological movements within conventional churches and denominations), and the proliferation and sharpening of church-state tensions across much of the modern world, we must at least produce a theory sketch of the contours of and processes at work in respect of the globe as a socio-cultural-phenomenon. . . .

We will argue that, given the existence of a global complex which displays both bounded societal units and a widespread sense of global continuity, a theory sketch of that complex requires the following basic components: (a) individual national societies; (b) a system of national societies; (c) individual selves; and (d) a category to which selves belong – 'man/woman' (that is, 'mankind'). We will further argue that, at a more refined level of analysis, relationships between these four components (six sets of relationships in all) may be used to characterize in minimal terms 'the modern global circumstance'. The notion which best captures this overall conceptual patterning is that of the global-human system as an historically emergent and mutable phenomenon.

A Preliminary Positioning of Religion in the Global System

The virtually world-wide eruption of religious and quasi-religious concerns and themes cannot be exhaustively comprehended in terms of focusing

on what has been happening sociologically within societies. The societies which have been affected by upsurges of religious expression during the past two decades or so are too diverse for that approach to suffice – although, undoubtedly, a number of clusters of relatively similar societies (for example, those in the North Atlantic area) may be sufficiently similar in sociological and historical terms for us to get a significant explanatory leverage by comparing societies within a cluster. Generally speaking, however, the 'worldwideness' of the religious upsurge demands that we consider the global circumstances in totality.

The only other alternative (not, incidentally, precluding the comparative, intrasocietal, or the global approaches) is the diffusionist perspective. That has at least one serious disadvantage. This is centred on the fact that the nearly global upsurge in religion of the last 15–20 years has involved a large variety of religious doctrines. More specifically, the global revival consists in large part of movements which are sometimes indifferent and frequently hostile to the fortunes of each other. This factor largely precludes explanatory tacks which emphasize the diffusion of ideas among those with shared interests. It makes the recent cross-societal religious revival sociologically unlike, for example, the very widespread student movement of the late 1960s. In the latter case (quite apart from intra-societal determinants) there was clearly a sense of an international (or a transnational) movement, with students in one society or a group of societies emulating and influencing those in another society or other societies on the basis of a perceived shared – or, at least, shareable – set of interests. That is not, however, to say that shared interests – ideal and/or material – are entirely absent on a cross-societal basis in the present global religious revival. In the case of liberation-theological movements we can see something approaching the circumstances of shared, religiously expressed interests – now that liberation theologies have appeared, often collaboratively, on a number of continents. Another, perhaps very significant, form of modern linkage across national boundaries in relation to the revival of orthodoxies and fundamentalisms is that involving some of the fundamentalist evangelicals in the US, on the one hand, and politico-religious militants in

From: Humanity, globalization and world-wide religious resurgence, by R. Robertson and J. A. Chirico, in *Sociological Analysis*, Autumn, 1985.

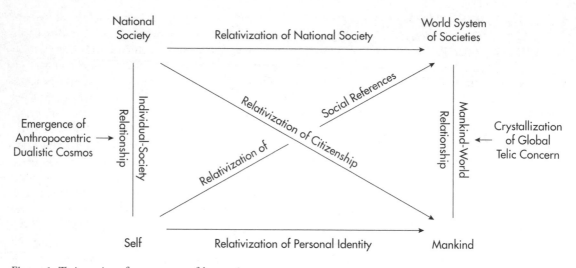

Figure 1 Trajectories of emergence of humanity

Israel, on the other. In this particular case, we have a cross-national amplification of otherwise divergent religious worldviews – the primary basis for the mutual support being the dispensationalist theology of premillennial evangelicalism (with its emphasis upon the eschatological significance of the imminent fulfilment of Jewish congregation in Israel), on the one hand, and a perceived Israeli need for politico-religious support in the US beyond the Jewish American community, on the other.

The global approach has the advantage of being able to take both intra-societal and diffusional factors into account and of incorporating them into a higher level analytic. . . .

Source and Structure of Humanitic Concern

In the present perspective modern 'humanitic concern' can be traced empirically to two major sources. First, there are aspects of the operation of modern (particularly Western) societies which generate a form of transcendence of society at the level of individuals. The combination of alienation from the state and the state's increasing concern – what we call a quasi-religious concern – with 'deep' features of life (the definition of life, the organization of death, the 'quality of life', ageing, the regulation of religion, and so on) increasingly leads to explicitness

about the attributes and raison d'être of human life beyond the particularities of social classification, voluntary religious involvement, even societal membership. The resurgence of 'fundamentalistic' promotion of particularistic ideologies and doctrines (local, ethnic national, civilizational and regional) does not by any means constitute counter-evidence. For, as we will argue more fully later, the recent globe-wide assertion of particularistic ideas is heavily contextualized by the phenomenon of increasing globality.

The second major source of humanitic concern has to do with the relations between societies. On the inter-societal front there has been, in recent years, a considerable relativization of the image of the good society. While a few scholars argued quite a long time ago that the notion of societal modernization must, in order for it to have any empirical purchase, involve a basically 'relativistic' frame of reference, the fact remains that there is much to suggest that, until quite recently, the modern system of societies operated roughly in terms of two basic images of the good society – namely the liberal-democratic industrial society and the communistic industrial society. Moreover, even in that situation of two 'northern' types of 'good society' there was clearly considerable overlap. However, it became increasingly obvious during the 1970s that the situation of relatively stable and established images and directions of societal aspirations was rapidly breaking up. Now, in the mid-1980s it seems that there is global confusion about what constitutes the ideal type of societal aspiration. If our diagnosis in this respect is cogent, it would inexorably follow – even without further empirical investigation – that there has to be 'something' resembling what Parsons analytically pinpoints as telic concern of a trans-societal kind. In other words, in a situation in which there is very little stability or security in respect of what might be called model societies, then international discourse, including heavily politico-strategic discourse, often takes place in terms of ideas, however tacitly adhered to, concerning the ends of man.

We may now schematize our thinking, with particular – but not sole – reference to the emanation of humanitic concern in Western contexts. The most basic ingredient of that process is the linkage between a situation of 'anthropocentric dualism', having to do with the relationship between individuals and societies, and a corresponding situation on a trans-societal scale. By anthropocentric dualism, we mean a human-centred world image involving a differentiation of life into two realms. On the one hand, there is the realm of societal-systemic functionality; on the other, there is the realm of individual and relational (if you will, 'life world') being. As anthropocentric, this dualistic frame is pivoted upon mankind; it being an historical transformation of a theocentric dualism.

The linkages of which we have just spoken involve four processes of relativization, two having to do with the relativization of societies ('trans-socialization') and two having to do with the relativization of persons, or selves ('trans-personalization'). By relativization we mean a process involving the placing of socio-cultural or psychic entities in larger categorical contexts, such that the relativized entities are constrained to be more self-reflexive relative to other entities in the larger context (which does not mean that they will actually be 'constructively' self-reflexive). The relativization of selves involves, along one dimension, the situating of selfhood in the more inclusive and fundamental frame of what it means to be of mankind; while the relativization of societies – along another, parallel dimension – involves

the situating of concrete societies in the context of a world complex of societies – thus constraining particular societies to judge the extent to which they exemplify principles of 'societal quality'. These are the dominant processes of relativization. There branches from each a secondary process of relativization, one having to do with the relationship between concrete societies and the category of man, the other involving a connection between selves and the global complex of societies. . . .

Our major proposition at this point is that there is an intimate link between the development of what might be called asociality – the mode of individual, 'mystical' concern with self – and the making available of individuals for concern with 'man'. In a sense this follows the line of argument of those who have spoken, in reference to the more 'advanced' societies, of individuals growing out of the nation-state shell. On the other hand, our own contentions in this regard follow a Simmel-Durkheim line of reasoning. Galtung's argument rests on the detachment of the individual from national loyalty in trans- or cross-national mode, via ideologies of professionalism which are intolerant of national loyalties by virtue of cosmopolitanism and the universalism of technological-scientific values. This we find to be unpersuasive, certainly insufficient. The process of growing out of the (state-centred) society is a much more diffuse and 'deep' process – having to do with a mixture of alienation from the state (and the economy) and a greater concern with selfhood in the mode of what is often called 'psychological man'. The development of psychological man/woman at the same time raises issues concerning the phenomenal-categorical location of selves or persons. That process of locating tends in the direction of a concern with what it means to be human in the most general terms – hence our suggestion that what is primarily involved in this form of detachment from the state-centred society may be summarized under the conceptual rubric of relativization of personal identity. A significant aspect of the latter in broad, comparative-civilizational terms is that while we see the process as 'Western-pulled', it is not confined to the 'post-industrial' societies. The nature of the modern global system is such as to place constraints relevant to the process of relativization upon nearly all societies – hence, for example, the diagnosis of the intensification of narcissistic tendencies in non-Western contexts, as a response to industrialization in these contexts relative to the global system. In other words. although third and fourth world societies do have 'problems' primarily centered upon incorporating individuals and primordial groups into the nation-state shell, the latter diffusely confronts the individual all over the contemporary world with at least some of the alienating characteristics of the modern Western model. This exacerbates the otherworldly mystical tendencies of some non-Western societies and makes the latter available as models for Western individuals, as exemplified by the diffusion of non-Western religious ideas involving a monistic resistance to Western anthropocentric dualism. The upshot is a tendency toward a near-global conception of selfhood – or at least a thematization of potentially near-global scope of the latter issue.

The second dominant process – concerning the relativization of society – involves the thematization of such issues as: what is a society? What is the purpose of societies? What does 'the good society' look like? In essence, this process of relativization – attendant upon the crystallization of a global system in which there appear to be no definite, or relatively permanent, models of 'goodness' – involves the attenuation of historically taken-for-granted assumptions about society as a mode of coherence. As suggested previously, this questioning of society is at the core of the breakdown of the circumstance which prevailed up to the 1960s – namely the situation in which it was appropriate to talk of modernization as involving a rather definite trajectory, or a very small number of possible trajectories, of societal change. Increasingly during the 1970s modernization became relativized – to the point that by now the criteria of such are being thematized. By thematization in this respect we mean that rather than small clusters of societies being regarded as clearly lead societies or global epicentres, there now obtains a situation in which the criteria for societal change themselves are matters of inter-societal, inter-continental, inter-civilizational, and inter-doctrinal interpretation and debate.

Each of our dominant processes has a secondary process. In the case of the process involving a shift along the axis self–mankind, we speak of the relativization of societal reference on the part of the individual. In the case of the shift involving relativization of society we speak of a secondary process having to do with a shift in the nature of 'citizenly involvement'. Let us consider relativization of societal reference first. In this respect detachment from society in the direction of the anthropic concern with the nature of man must, also, raise the question of the nature of orientation to the more concrete global system of inter-societal relationships. In other words, there arises the issue of the orientation on the part of individuals to societies other than their 'own' and their participation – however vicarious or empathic – in the global complex of societies, which now becomes to all intents and purposes 'the world' in the sense conveyed by theological traditions. In its extreme form, such relativization would involve looking at one's 'own' society as only one among others, but at the same time retaining a sense of membership in one's 'own' society.

The second branching process – relativization of citizenly involvement – has to do with what, in another context, has been called tertiary mobilization. Political scientists and political sociologists have tended to specify two phases of the process of political mobilization leading to the circumstance of citizenship inclusion. First, there is the phase of detachment from primordial loyalties of tribe, religion and so on – producing something like a loyalty to the political centre. Second, there is a phase of secondary mobilization, involving the inclusion of individuals as citizens with respect to law, franchise and social security. (The second phase has often been studied as a series of sub-phases). The analytical addition of a third phase of mobilization in an evolutionary perspective has to do with the process whereby citizenship is expanded so as to include both rights and duties developed in the second phase and a conception of the individual as human, with rights and needs (perhaps, ultimately, duties) which are not solely societal. Thus tertiary mobilization – the relativization of citizenly involvement – involves a realigning of the relationship between the concrete society and the individual in the form of an establishment of a new kind of differentiated attachment to man/woman. Here, again, our basic point of reference is the industrialized society. But we can also add that the process of political mobilization in other societies is certainly affected – in the sense that many individuals in those societies, for example Middle Eastern societies, are implicated in a globe-human context at the same time as they are oriented toward society centred, primary or secondary processes of mobilization.

These analytical representations of trajectories of movement away from the historical circumstances of society-centred anthropocentric dualism are intended primarily, when taken as a schematic whole, to pinpoint significant aspects of the drift toward humanitic concern in the modern world. The overall scheme characterizes an evolutionary step beyond the usual type of evolutionary stage relating to society and relationships between individuals and societies. In 'ideal-typical' form we have depicted a circumstance involving a set of processes of differentiation emanating from the anthropocentric-dualistic, individual-society context. It must be very strongly emphasized, however, that the crystallization of a new man-globe form of dualism does not entail elimination of that context. Rather, the individual-society relationship is contextualized by a much broader frame of humanitic concern. Thus, in highly ideal typical terms, the two are co-ordinated in such a way that persons are both autonomous and yet implicated in no less than three other sets of circumstances, as are societies. Finally, it must be very strongly emphasized that, even though for present purposes we have schematically indicated processes of relativization in terms of one-way arrows, the implication of our discussion is that the global-human circumstance *per se* can be most fruitfully represented analytically in terms of an entire series of two-way arrows. . . .

The globalization process itself raises religious and quasi-religious questions. Theodical and eschatological questions – or successor questions to old theodical and eschatological queries – are high on the agenda of global discourse. Religion is centred in the process of globalization by virtue of both the religious or quasi-religious matters raised as a result of universalistic tendencies involving mankind and relations between societies and by the particularizing responses to the universalistic tendencies. In the latter regard the internal-societal development of fundamentalisms is pivoted upon the perceived need for societal integrity. The extent to which would-be or actual religio-political elites are atavistic in the sense of being reactionary relative to the globalization process is a matter in need of case-by-case discussion. Some fundamentalist movements which have recently staked their claims to interpret and control the socio-cultural identities of their respective societies can, indeed, be viewed as reactionary – as sites for the expression of discontents – relative to the globalization process. At the opposite end of the spectrum, other fundamentalist movements may be viewed as merely offering – if often very militantly – new modes of particularistic societal identity relative to global universalism in more-or-less 'concultural', relatively pluralistic mode.

There are many other aspects of the ideas which we have presented here which have a direct bearing on religion and religiosity across the modern world, as well as upon arguments surrounding the secularization thesis. Our major goal here, however, has been to contribute to the task of seeing how religion may be discussed within the context of growing concern with the phenomenon of globality, which we see as a generalization and extension of the older 'gemeinscbaft-gesellschaft' problem. Direct discussion of globality and globalization is necessary before the distinctively religious aspects of such can be systematically analyzed. We should, however, emphasize in conclusion that we consider, and not only for the reasons already given, that globalization enhances, at least in the relatively short run, religion and religiosity.

PART C

GLOBALIZATION, MEDIA AND TECHNOLOGY

Part C is split into two sections, C1 and C2.

The subject of C1 is global media, including the emergence of a 'new media order' that consolidates Anglo-American corporate domination. Extracts are arranged in a number of groups, as follows:

- The content of 'global media', in particular the global appeal of soap operas (and the moralizing function of media 'scandals') and of 'global news' narrative and its reception by local audiences. Also, the Western control of global news agencies.
- Western media imperialism and the Anglo-American corporate domination of global flows of communication, media production and dissemination. Reference is also made to the Sony Company's successful global marketing of 'the Walkman'.
- A rejection of media imperialism at the level of the local reception and assimilation of global television.
- Resistance and the development of alternative media like Paper Tiger TV and clandestine video clubs in Iran. The issue of indigenous media (including Third World film) being an empowering vehicle for local communities is raised, along with the call for a more globally inclusive and democratic global media.
- Finally, the presentation of war-as-spectacle (the 'ultimate voyeurism') on global television.

The objective of C2 is to stimulate debate about the global impact of new technology and the development of evermore efficient global communicational technologies, as follows:

- The first group of extracts place the spotlight on the networked, 'informational society' and the rapidly developing 'interactive' technologies of satellite, cable, multimedia and the mobile phone upon which it is based.
- The social impact of technology is next explored and the question as to whether the full democratizing potential of 'cyber-tech' can ever be released from corporate control and the profit-motive. Included are a critique of AT&T's 'Learning Circles'; 'cyber inequities' and the disparities in technology ownership and access; a speculative design criteria for democratizing new technology; and we end with an insight into the 'digital underground' in the form of computer hacking.
- A third group of extracts take as their topic the history and development of the Internet and debates about the usefulness of the 'information superhighway', from the optimistic vision of Microsoft's Bill Gates to the more sceptical assessments of Schiller, Besser and others.
- The final group of extracts focus on the emergence of a global 'techno society', from surveillance technology in contemporary urban settings; to a critical assessment of Rheingold's notion of the 'virtual community'; on to 'virtual reality' (and 'virtual intimacy', in particular) as a means of identity reconstruction in the 'cyber age'.

PART C1

GLOBAL MEDIA AND COMMUNICATION

1 THE GLOBAL APPEAL OF SOAP OPERA

C. Barker

Anglo-American soap operas and Latin American 'telenovelas' share a number of features with each other and indeed with other soap operas around the world. These include a long-running serial form with interweaving multiple story strands mainly operating with a sense of real time and set in distinct geographical locations. While community, class and social issues all play their part in the thematic make-up of soap opera the core of the stories always revolves around interpersonal and family relationships. We also noted differences both between telenovelas and their Anglo-American counterparts and within the British, American and Latin American forms themselves. In particular, we recognized that soap operas mix the conventions of realism and melodrama in varying degrees so that British soaps are known for their realist orientation when compared to the more melodramatic form of many US soaps, and Mexican melodramatic-oriented 'telenovelas' can be contrasted with the more realist Brazilian form.

Though telenovelas share many characteristics with soap opera they are also different in some respects, notably in their commitment to a specific number of episodes in contrast to the never-ending openness of the narrative in Anglo-American soaps and in their greater stress on class, social mobility,

From: *Global Television*, by C. Barker, Blackwell, 1997.

freedom, choice, consumption and other themes of modernity. All this reminds us that genre is concerned with the management of similarity and difference wherein lies the explanation for why soap opera has emerged as one of the most popular worldwide television forms, that is to say its ability to explore apparently global themes in more specifically local ways.

Hence, the global attraction of soap opera can be partly attributed to the apparently universal appeal of particular open-ended narrative forms, the centrality of the personal and kinship relations and in some circumstances the emergence of an international style embedded in the traditions of Hollywood. Liebes and Katz identify the key cross-cultural components of 'Dallas' in terms of its primordial kinship drama and its serial narrative techniques.

We are led by viewers to two dimensions of the 'Dallas' genre, the semantic dimension, which draws so heavily on primordial themes of human relations, and the syntactic dimension of seriality, which regularly combines and recombines this set of basic relational elements to tell endless variations of the same story (Liebes and Katz, 1988, p. 117).

However, the success of the soap opera can also reflect the possibilities offered to audiences of engaging in local or regional issues and problems located in recognizable and 'real' places. The tensions between the poles of the global and the local are highlighted by, on the one hand, the enormous global popularity of soaps like 'Neighbours' and 'Dallas' and on the other hand the failure of these very same soaps in particular countries (for example, 'Neighbours' in America, 'Dallas' in Japan). Crofts' (1995) discussion of 'Global Neighbours' is illuminating in this respect since, as he argues:

> lest it be imagined that 'Neighbours' has universal popularity or even comprehensibility, there remain some 150 countries to which it has not been exported, and many in which its notions of kinship systems, gender relations and cultural spaces would appear most odd. (Crofts, 1995, p. 102)

. . . Crofts' discussion of 'Neighbours' helps us to understand that the global success, and failures, of soap opera depends on both the specificities of soap opera as a televisual form and the particularities of the conditions of reception. The dialectic of the global and local is illustrated by the fact that on the one hand there has been the emergence of an international prime-time soap opera style, while on the other many soaps retain a local setting and regional language audiences. To the degree that an international style exists it has the following characteristics:

- High production values: that is to say, a fairly glossy and expensive look.
- Pleasing visual appearances from the glamour and wealth of Dallas to the adventurous and sun-filled landscape of Australia.
- More action and physical movement than would be encountered in traditional soaps: in other words a faster-paced programme.
- Hollywood-style narrative modes with which the global audience is familiar.
- Elements of melodrama over realism as the dominant narrative style.

Nevertheless, there is widespread understanding that given a choice audiences prefer home-grown soaps to imports so that while the international soap opera makes big waves it is less impressive than an indigenous soap in local conditions. The generic soap opera form appears to have global appeal, most national television networks show soaps, but no particular soap opera has achieved such status. . . .

News narratives

A brief discussion of Anglo-American news values cannot hope to deal adequately with all the issues of news coverage or the complexities of global television news. The questions we need to ask are whether such values are globally significant and whether the essential nature of news is the same whatever its origins. Straubhaar (1992) concludes (based on a cross-cultural study involving the US, USSR, Japan, West Germany, Italy, India, Colombia and China) that 'what is news' is 'fairly consistent' from country to country and that the format of 20–40-minute programmes anchored by presenters was a common feature. In particular, 'politics' and 'economics' were consistently the main news topics. However, there were differences of emphasis in the treatment of those topics. For example, while US news contained the highest levels of criticism of government and issues of human rights they were also the most prone to 'sensationalism' and concentration on accidents, disasters and crime. Unsurprisingly, television in India and China contained more 'development news' but also, in the case of the latter, a more positive approach to science and technology. In contrast, Madden (1992) puts the case for the cultural specificity of news. Her analysis of the Inuit Broadcasting Corporation's news output suggests that it differs from Western news in both content and style. There is, in contrast to Western news, a stress on consensus over conflict, personal privacy over the public's 'right to know' and multi-vocal construction rather than the privileged voice of the news-reader. That Straubhaar should have found similarity over difference may reflect not so much a universal conception of news but 'the drift towards an international standardization of basic journalistic discourses' (Dahlgren, 1995, p. 49).

Gurevitch, Levy and Roeh (1991) carried out a study to ascertain the degree to which television news could be said to have 'gone global'. Their general case for regarding news as a global phenomenon rests on the establishment of news exchange arrangements whereby subscribing news organizations exchange news material with a particular emphasis on the sharing of visual footage. Data collected by Gurevitch *et al.*, about the Eurovision News Exchange and the thirty six countries which regularly use it suggests that the availability of common news footage and a shared professional culture led to 'substantial, but not complete' convergence of news stories. Across a two-week period up to twenty of the lead items were the same with a particular concentration in relation to foreign news so that news about other countries is more uniform than domestic news. However, the fact that much of the material exchanged is visual does mean that different interpretations of events can be added leading to what Gurevitch *et al.*, call the 'domestication' of global news. They regard this as a 'countervailing force to the pull of globalization'. For example, the same footage of a speech by the then Soviet president Gorbachev was given quite different treatments by US and British television. The former was highly sceptical about the intent of Gorbachev's speech while the latter took a much more sympathetic line. The overall picture is, thus, a mixed one with a tendency towards the establishment of global news partly countered by its insertion into local meaning structures and contexts. However, the globalizing trend remains of particular significance since, as we shall see later, Western news agencies appear to dominate global news agendas.

In this respect, a trend in Western news of global significance is the elevation of 'Islam' to the role of chief bogeyman. Much recent news coverage in the West has been devoted to the Gulf War and Saddam Hussein in particular; to the states of Iran, Iraq and Libya (with a special emphasis on their alleged sponsoring of terrorism); and to Salman Rushdie's book *The Satanic Verses* and the 'fatwa' declared by Ayatollah Khomeini. As Said (1981) has argued, Western media have represented Islamic peoples as irrational fanatics led by Messianic and authoritarian leaders. While there are of course political and ethical questions to be debated around the practices of Islam, Western media coverage has not promoted the dialogic approach required for cross-cultural understanding but has taken sides against Islam with little understanding or explanation of what meanings are involved.

Television news is constituted not only by its choice of topics and stories but also by its verbal and visual idioms or modes of address. Presentational styles have always been subject to tension between an informational and educational purpose and the need to engage and entertain us televisually. While current affairs programmes are often 'serious' in tone with adherence to the 'rules' of balance, more popular programmes adopt a friendly, lighter idiom in which we are invited to consider the impact of particular news items from the perspective of the 'average person in the street'. Dahlgren (1995) argues that increased commercial competition in global television has tilted the balance in favour of the latter and cites increased use of faster editing tempos and 'flashier' presentational styles including the use of logos, sound-bites, rapid visual cuts and the 'star quality' of news-readers.

A stress on immediacy in the presentation of news is a specific and recent development in global news which can be seen most obviously in the 24-hour live coverage of CNN, though it is also a feature of routine evening news programmes. Quite apart from live broadcasts by satellite, Electronic News Gathering (ENG) technology allows television to bring edited accounts of global and local events to the screen almost as they happen while lightweight cameras, digital video editing and the multi-skilling of television personnel allow for speed and flexibility. Global television has thus shortened the 'threshold' time of what constitutes news. This stress on immediacy may, as we shall see with regard to the Gulf War, be to the detriment of context and explanation as well as furthering an ideology of transparency. For example, CNN transmits a good deal of 'live' or lightly-edited footage which depends on its mimetic quality and so obscures its construction in terms of camera angles, voice-overs and rapid editing.

Political coverage in particular has come to rely increasingly on the staged sound-bite. Politicians go to some length to provide a resonant phrase or telling image for the purposes of television. A stress on the smart, compact sound-bite arguably downplays explanation and interpretation while strengthening the hand of those able to manage the news by providing newsworthy 'events' and footage. While this would usually favour the powerful (business, politicians, lobbyists), there is some evidence of its use by 'alternative' animal rights and ecology pressure groups. Greenpeace, for example, has proved adept at providing newsworthy footage and its success against the Shell oil company over the Brent Spar oil rig owed much to the television pictures it provided to news organizations. When French marines knowingly seized Greenpeace camera equipment in the South Pacific they dealt the Greenpeace campaign against French nuclear testing a serious blow.

2 GLOBAL TELEVISION NEWS

C. Paterson

Television news has been widely ignored in the globalization literature due, in part, to rapid change in the industry and the difficulty to determine its effect. But TV news is also being seen less as a special case – a form of television which provides a needed sociopolitical function – than as just another global cultural product. With the producers of the source material for international television news and the owners of regional and global television becoming increasingly concentrated, the content of international television news is becoming increasingly homogeneous and diversity in the marketplace of ideas is diminished. When considered in conjunction with other trends of globalization – broadcast privatization, deregulation, increasing commercialization and consumerism – the potential threat to cultural and ideological plurality and thereby, local and national identify, is vast.

Local audiences and the globalization of television news

Where do local audiences fit into the globalization of TV news? The manner in which I have described

From: Global television news services, by C. Paterson, in *Media in Global Context*, edited by A. Sreberny-Mohammadi *et al.*, Arnold, 1997.

international television news here privileges the concept of news flow, in this case, from few sources to many national, regional, and global broadcasters. But as Kavoori (1994) points out, privileging flow often results in the neglect of meaning. We are left with a sense of what the audience receives, but little sense of their sense of it all. In all the discourse on the globalization of television news, the relationship between text and audience, and the particularities of such global media products, are all but ignored.

The culturally specific particularities of the reception of global media products must be properly analyzed on their own terms, and not unquestioningly identified with the nation and/or culture native to their ownership. Should Rupert Murdoch implement a global news network of his own would it be Australian, American, or English? It would more likely be a uniquely international product, produced in a great many places. CNN is such a text now, even if its producers remain predominantly American and borrow heavily from American broadcast traditions.

New and innovative analytic paradigms are required to assess the interaction of text and audience, with care taken to avoid the outdated media imperialism paradigm lurking in many contemporary critiques of news globalization. Global conglomerates create global products for an imaginary global audience. What does this mean to the very real consumers of these alien genres, audiences who may be used to a very different style of information presentation from their public broadcaster?

The trend at the wholesale tier of international television news is to try to be a diversified, multimedia news agency cum all purpose TV production company. Reuters and Associated Press have the backing of deep corporate pockets to continue in the marginally profitable field of television news gathering, providing they don't spend too much from doing it. Disney Corporation's commitment to stepchild WTN's future is far from certain.

Broadcasters, too, will continue to diversify. Large broadcasters are increasingly marketing their produced news products to smaller broadcasters around the world. For example, NBC markets a European version of its successful domestic 'Dateline' programme, combining elements of the domestic programme with specially produced international material (Westcott, 1995). The wholesale/retail distinction may become less significant as all players offer their news products directly to subscribing computer users, the form of (multi-)media consumption predicted to eventually displace television. For now, the homogeneity of international television news sources is a concern. Despite the increasing number of news services, ownership is highly concentrated, and broadcasters are becoming increasingly dependent upon a few news providers to supply the international images they use on the air, to shape our global reality.

3 GLOBAL NEWS AGENCIES

O. Boyd-Barrett

News agencies are a part of modernization, and link it with globalization: they respond to the same processes that generated newspapers, and to the needs of newspapers for a stable, reliable and relatively cheap source of international news. We do not need to assume globalization is a product of modernization. Globalization relates back to the diffusion and intercourse of ancient civilizations and cultures through military organization, population control, construction of roads, linguistic and literary practices, etc. What changes is the form of globalization. News agencies represent communication appropriate to the informational and relational needs of state, capital and civic society in modernity.

As global actors agencies emerge from modernity (viz. industrialization, universal rationality, nationalism), and reinforce it through construction of global identities. Global agencies consolidated

From: Global news wholesalers as agents of globalization, by O. Boyd-Barrett, in *Media in Global Context*, edited by A. Sreberny-Mohammadi *et al.*, Arnold, 1997.

information networks within national boundaries through support for national agencies, contributing to the rationalization of communication between state and people and discourses about nation and state. They contributed to internationalization, constructing influential international news agendas that acted upon retail media, governments and finance. They developed and exploited technologies to improve global communications networks. They brought the global to the local and incorporated the local within the global in their day-to-day news gathering and news-dissemination, selling international news to national and local media and using local and national media as sources of news for global distribution. Reuters and other financial agencies have facilitated global financial transactions, and have even created the means (Reuters transaction services) to conduct international negotiations in equities, money markets and certain commodities. They provide the data which enable news commentators to think globally by picking up on parallel processes in different nation states and relating these to actors and events at global level.

Western in origin, global agencies are nourished by the Western news ideologies which they themselves constructed in the second half of the nineteenth century in response to telegraphic economics (Shaw, 1967), the rise of 'curiosity' journalism as exemplified by Dickens' 'Household Words' and Northcliffe's 'Titbits', and the positivistic fact-privileging influence of scientism (Schudson, 1978), and infected by small town values that helped to determine what was not 'normal' (and therefore interesting: Gans, 1979). Study of news agencies confirms that globalization is Westernization. Agencies themselves infected globalization as Westernization when taking Western-interests-as-norm (for example, in their Cold War coverage, and in their skewed global maps privileging news from Western Europe, the US and theatres of activity elsewhere which had direct relevance to Western concerns) and promoted Western values of news, business and politics. They confirm globalization as a process simultaneously economic, political and cultural: it has to do with belief systems which have been commodified within a political-economic dynamic.

News agencies contribute to the homogenization of global culture in form and in source, while greatly multiplying the texts available within these standardized discourses. They contribute to the development of local forms which they then incorporate as contributors and as clients.

New global culture is not the product of an equal contribution of all who are party to it or exposed to it and is equal only in as much as all parties have equal chances to take whatever meanings they want from it (if we want to assume that users have equal access to the texts, that they are equally skilled in making such meanings, or that they have been taught, through the structure of such discourse itself, how to make and take meanings). Global culture is not the product of equal choice; few are consulted in its manufacture. Study of news agencies is a reminder not to overlook the concrete structures through which the global culture is constructed. It tells us that globalization is neither anarchic nor random; it is the outcome of cultural agencies whose operations can be traced systematically. . . .

When the Goma flyaway went online vivid pictures became available of the Goma camps minutes after they were shot, and reporters from around the world converged on Goma because the ability to reach their audience live, at relatively little cost, had now been provided. And when the EBU decided that the flyaway should fly away to another world hotspot, with it went the story of Goma's refugees. Medium became the message in Goma, as the realities of modern television news overshadowed the realities of the Rwandan tragedy, and reinforced the confusing world of fleeting and incomprehensible disaster that is the world's image of Africa.

This case demonstrates how technological factors involving resource allocation combined with an accumulation of demand for visuals of what had, up until then, been a mostly non-visual story (and thus for TV, a non-story). Such instances are common. Television tells stories best when it can illustrate them with exciting and graphic pictures, but such pictures cost more to provide from Africa than they do from Chicago or London.

In developing world coverage, the issues are harder to illustrate and the costs are higher than anywhere else, and often so are risks to personnel and equipment, so the benefit of coverage must be concurrently higher as well. As the Goma story illustrates, rarely do the providers of international television visuals find the benefit sufficient. Exceptions generally exist only where costs have already been subsidized and facilitated through the prior existence of reliable satellite facilities, a measure of security, and a comfortable pillow for a reporter's head. Such has been the case with South Africa (South Africa's neighbours were deemed not to have these attributes: Paterson, 1992), or Somalia, where coverage facilitated by the public relations expertise of the US military ensured that the right story would make it home (Ottosen, 1994).

The coverage decisions of the international television news agencies are based largely upon client interest, what their rival company is doing, and the costs of allocating resources to areas which are expensive to provide coverage from. Do economic and technological considerations prevail in determining Developing World coverage, or do the gatekeepers possess ethnocentric biases which decrease the priority given to covering poor countries and dark people? Or, do the international services simply respond to the will of international broadcasters? There is not enough data on these aspects of international news to answer these questions, but by identifying the key players and understanding the system in which they operate, we can at least ask more appropriate questions.

4 LONG-DISTANCE MORALITY AND CULTURAL RE-EMBEDDING
J. Lull and S. Hinerman

What I have mainly tried to argue is that, when we engage with scandals that have their origin in other

From: *Media Scandals*, by J. Lull and S. Hinerman, Polity, 1997.

countries, we do so largely by assimilating them to the relevances of our everyday 'lifeworld'. The aspects of a scandal that resonate with our own moral, existential concerns are the ones that best capture our imagination, and these concerns are, of their nature, locally situated – formed out of the day-to-day, culturally specific experiences through which we elaborate our sense of self. Thus a successful 'global scandal' is one that can be, to borrow Giddens's terms (Giddens 1990), 'disembedded' from its local context and 're-embedded' into a multitude of other culturally distinct contexts. To put this proposal in its most challenging form would, indeed, be to say that there are no global scandals but only re-embedded local ones, This does not mean that scandals never achieve global scale or have global moral-political implications. But it would be a defensible claim in respect of the way we have defined scandals, as 'middle-order moral events' which lend themselves to narration at a level at which people can imaginatively and empathetically engage with them.

What implications does this view hold for the 'higher-level' moral issues (environmental damage, racism, the poverty, illiteracy and immiseration of Third World populations, war and so forth) that, it might be argued, are the really 'scandalous' issues of our age? The context of globalization, of the increasingly complex interconnection between spatially-spread social-cultural formations, suggests that we can no longer maintain the sort of moral-cultural particularism that might have been possible in Marlowe's age. In all sorts of ways, we now live in a 'global neighborhood' that forces these moral issues upon us.

Extrapolating from the arguments I have advanced in relation to scandals might, however, suggest a pessimistic view of the possibilities of constructing a moral-political order at the global level. Thinking of moral imagination as essentially local suggests a point at which involvement vanishes, just where it might most be needed. As Zygmunt Bauman argues, 'we do not "naturally" feel responsibility for . . . faraway events, however closely they may intertwine with what we do or abstain from doing. . . . Morality which always guided us and still guides us today has powerful, but short hands' (Bauman, 1993, p. 218). The pessimistic view, then, is that our social–communicational–technological development has outstripped our moral development: the globalized social world and our moral worlds have simply become out of kilter.

Perhaps the first thing to say in this respect is that the analysis of scandals alone should not push us toward such a bleak conclusion. For scandals are, after all, rather specific contexts for the exercise of the moral faculties. Although I have argued that they do generally contain a moral element (they are not merely excuses for idle curiosity, prurience, or, worse, 'schadenfreude') scandals are obviously not the only (and certainly not the ideal) form in which moral discourse can be conducted in modern societies. Furthermore, it does not follow that because people so readily involve themselves in the 'personalized' morality of scandals, they therefore lack the capacity or the innate motivation to engage with more 'serious' moral issues: It may be a question of how these issues are presented to them.

However, I do think that the analysis of scandals may have a lesson for us about this broader moral discourse. It is this: we should not struggle to extend the 'short hands' of 'localized' morality up to the level of global abstractions. Rather we should try to pose the moral issues that globalization presents within the context of local experience. This is a lesson in moral engagement we can learn by paying attention to the moral – cultural proclivities that people actually demonstrate in their lives, rather than by expecting people to 'rise to the challenge' of remote events.

The media have a clear and crucial narrational role, and perhaps even a peculiar responsibility, in this respect. For global scandals typify broader issues of global morality in being essentially (for most of us, exclusively) mediated experiences. It is overwhelmingly as a result of our use of globalizing media technologies, particularly television, that the wider world opens up to us as 'our world'. The global media make events in distant places proximate to our local lives by bringing representations of them into our living rooms. The issue then becomes that of how these images and narratives can be made morally significant; how they can pass from the world 'out there' into our own moral life-worlds.

As we have seen in the case of media scandals, the 'popular' media are actually rather good at framing certain events so as to make them engaging at a personal level. But often, as we have also noted, they are criticized for making issues too personalized – for trivializing them, for obscuring their more challenging aspects in a blur of sentimentality or (worse) by framing them in terms of crude and ideological moral stereotypes. Often this criticism is justified. However, it seems to me that the answer is not to insist that 'serious' issues should be entirely 'de-personalized'. Of course a lot of the problems that confront us in a globalized world are large, complex, and abstract – simply not of the same moral order as those of media scandals. But if people are to engage with these issues at all, to exercise any degree of moral agency, then ways need to be found to narrate them so that they become congruent with individual, locally-situated lifeworlds. A certain degree of personalization may thus be considered an essential entry-level qualification into a moral discourse. If this is so, then the 'popular framing' of high-order moral-political issues, judiciously exercised, should be regarded as not only a legitimate media practice, but an essential one. Media scandals may not be the perfect models for global moral discourse, but they do in this respect offer some clues as to how the more difficult and 'remote' problems of our time can be 'brought home to us' as moral concerns. . . .

---

5 GLOBAL MEDIA MERCHANDISING

J. Wasko

Since 1988 the studios have intensified their marketing strategies of videos, as well, incorporating techniques similar to packaged-goods companies. Tie-ins with beverages and packaged foods mean valuable display placements in supermarkets, convenience stores and restaurants. An example is Disney's 1989 holiday campaign, which included cross-promotion of its videos with Coca-Cola, Procter & Gamble and McDonald's. Other studios made similar arrangements with other companies, allowing their products to be seen much more widely than in video rental stores.

In a new merchandising wrinkle, Paramount Pictures announced a tie-in arrangement with Kmart, which would promote all of its summer films during 1991. The promotion (entitled 'Passport to Summer Entertainment') involved scratch and win cards redeemable for prizes at the stores. While not unusual in itself, it marked the first time a complete list of summer films would be tied to a single promotional partner.

Meanwhile, 'Advertising Age' reported that home video marketers spent $85 million during the second half of 1991 to market movies to children. Distributors aligned with promotional partners to share the costs. For example, Fox Video's 'Home Alone' was backed with a $25 million promotional campaign shared by Pepsi Cola and American Airlines, while New Line Home Video, Burger King and Nabisco devoted $20 million to promoting the video release of 'Teenage Mutant Ninja Turtles II'.

In addition to specific film or character-based merchandise, some of the larger entertainment companies now offer generic movie or studio merchandise. Examples include Warner Brothers hats, jackets and mugs, miniature movie clapperboards and mock Academy Awards. These items are sold through the

---

From: Hollywood meets Madison Avenue, by J. Wasko, in *Media in Global Context*, edited by A Sreberny-Mohammadi, D. Winseck, J. McKenna and O. Boyd-Barrett, Arnold, 1997.

studios' catalogues or 'entertainment stores' such as Suncoast Motion Picture Company. The Hollywood Chamber of Commerce has joined in, marketing trading cards based on stars featured on Hollywood Boulevard's 'walk of fame'. Thus, Hollywood increasingly has been selling itself in merchandisable forms.

While movie-based merchandising can be viewed as part of the proliferation of commercialization in Hollywood, this type of activity is part of a larger merchandising and licensing trend. Licensed products represented $66.5 billion in retail sales in 1990. TV programs and characters (especially those aimed at children) are an obvious and prevalent form of merchandising, while sports teams and players, rock stars and musical groups have long histories of licensing and merchandising activities. For instance, the growing phenomenon of sports cards dates back to the 1880s, when tobacco companies included baseball heroes in packets of tobacco. These days products are based on well-known images, brands and even companies: for example, Coca-Cola clothes, Harley-Davidson sunglasses. Even non-commercial organizations in the US are now offering merchandise, such as the products available from public broadcast stations. Signals is a catalogue published by the WGBH Education Foundation, which offers videos of PBS series, plus T-shirts, mugs, books, jewellery and other educational, comic, or 'tasteful' items, sometimes, but not always, connected to PBS programming.

Movie-based merchandise is especially motivated by the proliferation of such activities, as well as the massive, co-ordinated merchandising campaigns – often started months before a film's release – associated with a few blockbuster films. This merchandising bonanza represents sizeable profits. Sales of merchandise licensed from movies and stage shows in 1985 brought in $3.5 billion, although only $2.2 billion was received in 1987–84.

Some recent examples include 'Batman', which grossed $250 million and earned $50 million in licensing fees, Rambo III, which involved fifty licensing agreements for more than 75 products and 'The Jetsons', which also attracted fifty licenses. Meanwhile, the 'Star Trek' television series and films have generated a $500 million merchandising

bonanza for the thirty five companies which produce various products. Merchandising successes have not only featured cuddly, heroic characters: Freddy Krueger of 'Nightmare in Elm Street' has generated more than $3 million in licensing fees for Freddy posters, T-shirts, and other items.

Universal's 'Jurassic Park' may represent the ultimate model (at this point in time) for blockbuster merchandising/tie-in/product placement activities. The dino-tale made over $50 million at the box-office during the first weekend of release in June, 1993, and reached $750 million in gross world-wide revenues before the year ended.

---

6 THE SONY WALKMAN

P. du Gay, S. Hall, L. Janes, H. Mackay and K. Negus

We have already seen how Sony initially launched the Walkman locally in Japan, and followed this by introducing it under different brand names into other countries. When Sony standardized the name to Walkman in the early 1980s this occurred at a moment when a number of major companies were beginning to standardize the names of products that had previously been marketed with different labels around the world (this has sometimes been spoken of as 'global' branding and 'global' advertising). However, Sony did not standardize just the name of their product, they also introduced two other significant policies at the same time, which were part of a more 'global' approach to the product and the company's operations more generally.

First, the company introduced an international warranty system which meant that Sony products, no matter where they had been purchased, could be

From: *Doing Cultural Studies: The Story of the Sony Walkman*, by P. du Gay, S. Hall, L. Janes, H. Mackay and K. Negus, Sage, 1997.

repaired or replaced by Sony service agents in other countries. Second, they standardized the cassette-player's electronics so that it would run on two dry cell batteries. This meant that different models would not be dependent upon the different electricity systems operating in different parts of the world. As ex-advertising executive Shu Ueyama (1982) recalled, 'These factors encouraged the casual purchasing of the Walkman from a discount shop in Tokyo or in New York or at an airport shop in Hong Kong.'

This 'globalizing' strategy was part of a more general approach which the company had been pursuing since Morita and Ibuka started travelling backwards and forwards between Japan and the US during the 1950s. Sony were attempting at the same time to standardize – produce the same packaging and advertise a universal 'global' brand – and to individualize – by responding to the different ways in which products were being used around the world by designing a range of models of the Walkman for different markets and lifestyles.

Sony were pursuing such aims at a moment when the term 'globalization' was gaining increasing currency among business commentators and corporate strategists and, like a number of other companies, Sony began to incorporate such discourses into their own company literature. Senior executives began referring to Sony as a 'global company'. Morita continually gave interviews in which he spoke of globalization, once explaining, 'I use the term because I don't like the word multinational. . . . If it means a company with many nationalities then that is not Sony. Sony is global' (Cope, 1990, p. 53). Such a comment led to the suggestion that Morita's talk of globalization was less about any significant organizational change, but more an attempt to shift away from the negative connotations that the term 'multinational corporation' had started to assume.

The term 'globalization' has acquired a variety of meanings within and across a number of different discourses. Although initially adopted as a buzzword for a business strategy during the 1970s, the label has come to be used more generally in intellectual debate to refer to both a process and a condition. The process of globalization refers to the way in which media texts (sounds, images, words), capital, technologies, individuals and social groups seem to be moving across the world more rapidly and in greater numbers than in the past. The condition of globalization is generally used by writers who argue that human activities are converging and being shared to the extent that the planet is becoming 'one world' (Giddens, 1990, p. 77).

However, no one person or perspective can fully know 'the world' and no company can ever actually be global in anything but a partial way. Any case study that seeks to employ the concept of globalization therefore needs to approach the issue carefully in terms of the particular 'global' processes that are relevant to the case.

In this specific study we have already referred to a number of 'global' dynamics within which the Walkman was produced, marketed and interpreted. We have highlighted how the growth of Sony as a company and its technologies occurred within a process of interaction between the US and Japan. Akio Morita and his colleagues grew up in a world in which US products and cultural forms were ever present, and in which the development of manufacturing industry in Japan was restricted and monitored by the US. As the company grew, Sony executives gained considerable knowledge from constant visits to the US, acquired the rights to produce the transistor from the US and found that North America provided a major market for their audio-visual products. We have also referred to how the label Sony and the name Walkman were adopted with the aim of being 'global' brands.

Sony's global strategy

Throughout the 1980s two important developments indicate how Sony began actively extending this and presenting the company as a global corporation. First, the company aimed to operate in 'all' markets across the world, to reach as many potential consumers as possible. Second, the company aimed to re-organize processes of production in such a way so that they would not be limited by the constraints of the nation-state. In this case, a particular concern was how the effectiveness and international competitiveness of Japanese companies were constrained by the value of the Japanese yen. This meant that goods produced in Japan were more expensive when exported and in competition with those made in other parts of the world.

To pursue these aims, Sony adopted a strategy of globalization that involved moving their manufacturing and marketing operations to different locations around the world and setting up 'local' operations in various countries. Such activities are closely related to another concept that has been part of discussions of globalization, that of global–local relationships. Globalization is here associated with dynamics of 're-localization', what Kevin Robins (1991) has called a 'new global–local nexus'. Robins has used this concept to point out how national conditions of production have become less relevant to the operations of major corporations who have become more concerned with establishing specific 'global–local' relationships. The global–local nexus becomes important for large corporations who attempt to establish a presence in a variety of strategically important localities around the world. Here we give an indication of the technological, financial and political reasons why Sony are doing this.

We have already referred to how Sony faced problems due to the high value of the yen and the cost of Japan's secure 'life-time' employment system which meant that manufacturing in Japan was increasingly expensive. In addition to this, many of Sony's competitors were producing consumer technologies in parts of the world where workers were poorly paid and had few employment rights. One motive for Sony to move its manufacturing operations was a straightforward attempt to follow suit and reduce labour costs. Although the first Walkmans were manufactured and assembled in Japan so that the company's management could be close to operations and make any necessary modifications, once up and running, and not requiring so many modifications, additional assembly factories were established in Malaysia and Taiwan.

A further reason for moving assembly and manufacturing plants to other localities was technological. When producing televisions and radios the company needed to produce equipment that could receive broadcast radio waves in particular territories. These waves could not be artificially simulated in the laboratory and at one time the company had solved this by recording hours of broadcast waves on tape and then transporting them to Tokyo where engineers could tune in the equipment and make any modifications.

However, the company began to gradually move operations so that they could respond directly to local conditions. So, for example, Teletext was developed on site in the UK and Trinitron television was developed 'locally' in France. These arrangements meant that engineers could tune in the equipment and make any necessary modifications without all the previous to-ing-and-fro-ing between one part of the world and Japan.

An additional practical consideration was that, by establishing and presenting themselves as a local company, Sony could use various national and pan-regional rules and regulations to gain the most appropriate and cost-effective environment to manufacture and produce its products. The company could exploit cheap labour in Malaysia, take advantage of grants that were available to attract new electronic industries into areas of industrial decline in the UK and lobby politically to influence regulations in specific parts of the world as a 'local' rather than a 'foreign' company.

Akio Morita has often referred to these various dynamics of the 'global–local nexus' as a process of 'global–localization'. This he has presented rather benignly as a policy in which the company makes use of local talent while being sensitive to local cultural differences. As the London Evening Standard newspaper once reported, a 'caring' and 'close involvement with staff and community in Britain' has been part of Sony's policy for many years (29th October, 1992). In addition to 'caring for the community', Sony has frequently presented 'global–localization' as involving 'decentralized management' – a practice of devolving 'investment decisions, research and development, product planning and marketing' to enable local people to do things 'on the spot' (Cope, 1990).

No doubt Sony has improved the tuning of broadcast technologies and got closer to local markets. But for some staff this has not necessarily involved large degrees of local autonomy. Despite the abstract and universal significations of the term, the 'global' still has an identifiable headquarters that continues to exert a large degree of control, particularly over budgets and financial decisions. When Rainer Kurr, the general manager of Sony's European television operation, publicly stated that this was so and that Sony's factories were still controlled from Tokyo, he was promptly removed from his post (Barnet and Cavanagh, 1994, p. 66). The dynamics of the 'global–local nexus' which we have discussed here seem to involve the global as a dominant place (Tokyo) and the local as a dependent place (the UK, France or Germany).

At the same time that Sony began presenting itself as a 'global' company, staff also began to speak of 'synergy'. This term was employed to refer to a strategy, adopted by many hardware and software producing companies, of attempting to synchronize and actively forge connections between directly related technologies and areas of entertainment. Sony's annual reports and advertising began to refer to the organization as a 'total entertainment company'. Sony was no longer simply a manufacturer of technological hardware, it was an integral part of a 'culture industry'.

7 MEDIA IMPERIALISM

L. Sklair

The cultural imperialism thesis argues that the values and beliefs of powerful societies are imposed on weak societies in an exploitative fashion. In its neo-Marxist version, this usually means that First World capitalist societies impose their values and beliefs on poor Third World societies. Similar arguments have also

From: *The Sociology of the Global System*, by L. Sklair, Harvester Wheatsheaf, 1991.

been used to try to explain the consequences of the deleterious influence of the US media on rich countries, like Canada (Lee Chin-Chuan, 1980, Chapter 4), Australia (Sinclair, 1987) and the world in general (Tunstall, 1977). Kivikuru (1988), in an interesting analysis of Finland, suggests that such countries have developed relative autonomy through a process of 'modelling' on the US.

Media imperialism follows logically from cultural imperialism. If US or Western control of culture is admitted, then it is clearly achieved through control of the mass media, which creates the conditions for conformity to the hegemon culture and limits the possibilities of effective resistance to it. These theories are strongly held (see, for example, Becker *et al.*, 1986; Mattelart, 1983; Schiller, 1981) and strongly disputed.

There are four main types of criticisms of cultural and media imperialism theories:

- First, what is often identified as 'US cultural and media imperialism' is really just advanced professional practice.
- Second, there are quite different processes at work in different countries and national variations can be more important than global patterns.
- Third, all countries develop internal cultural and media forces which counteract the external influences of US cultural products.
- Fourth, US media flows may work for as well as against national autonomy.

It will be immediately obvious that most of this debate is posed within the terms of the state-centrist paradigm and, as such, few could disagree that it is possible to challenge US hegemony successfully in a wide variety of ways. As in most industries, economies of scale tend to lead to the most efficient practices. (Let us not complicate matters at this stage by asking 'efficient for whom?' or by noting that even this truism is being challenged by new flexible production methods in some Science-based industries.) The US has the largest media industry by far and its practices are invariably taken to be state of the art. For example, in discussing the relationship between US and Third World media, Lee Chin-

Chuan asserts that 'co-production has been largely limited to Anglo-American interests ... As a mockery to cultural diffusion, the co-produced products have been deliberately Americanized' (1980, p. 82). He explains this in terms of the triumph of the US-driven commercialization of global television, one of whose consequences is 'a genuine pressure on local talents to conform to the arbitrary "world standard" of technical excellence which may be at variance with native cultural needs' (p. 102).

One can certainly find co-productions that are not particularly Americanized, some national media systems that vary significantly from others in being less Americanized, domestic elements that successfully resist Americanization attempts, and even cases where 'Americanization' does seem to promote cultural autonomy. Three interesting recent cases are the glasnost-inspired 'Americanization' of Soviet television (see Barnathan, 1989); the introduction of the VCR into Turkey (Ogan, 1988); and the purchase of a VCR system by the Kayapo people in Brazil to preserve their local culture, though some claim that it will actually destroy the culture, based as it is on oral tradition (reported in Ogan).

If we replace 'Americanization' with 'capitalist consumerism', we can see that there is a double process of cultural-ideological transformation going on here. Capitalist consumerism is mystified by reference to Americanization, while Americanization, the method of the most successfully productive society in human history, gives its imprimatur to capitalist consumerism. The centrality of the 'American dream' for the project of global capitalism was briefly discussed in Chapter 3. There the point was made that, contrary to expectations borne of the origins of capitalism in Northwest Europe, the US and not the European core became synonymous with capitalism in its global incarnation. The re-formation of capitalism, thus, is the Americanization of capitalism, the culture-ideology of consumerism its rationale. But to identify cultural and media imperialism with the US, or even with US capitalism, is a profound and a profoundly mystifying error. It implies that if American influence could be excluded then cultural and media imperialism would end. This could only be true in a purely definitional sense.

Americanization itself is a contingent form of a process that is necessary to global capitalism, the culture-ideology of consumerism.

---

8 ASSESSING MEDIA IMPERIALISM

T. O'Sullivan, B. Dutton and P. Rayner

For some writers, the model of 'one-way flow' oversimplifies what is in fact a growing and more complex set of inter-relationships, with significant internal patterns, reversals and regroupings occurring within different continental, linguistic and geographical regions. However, the main challenge to the media imperialism thesis in recent years has emerged in the form of a questioning of the limits to the evidence provided. In short, does the evidence of amounts of imported programming add up to the 'imperialist effect'? As one writer has observed:

> There is an assumption that American TV imports do have an impact whenever and wherever they are shown, but actual investigation of this seldom occurs. Much of the evidence that is offered is merely anecdotal or circumstantial. Observations of New Guinean tribesmen clustered around a set in the sweltering jungle watching Bonanza or of Algerian nomads watching Dallas in the heat of the desert are often offered as sufficient proof.

What is centrally at stake here is the way in which increasingly mobile media audiences, in a diversity of national and other cultural locations, may make sense of and relate to imported programming. Those who support the ideas of media imperialism assume that American films and programmes 'blot out' authentic and original forms of indigenous culture,

From: *Studying the Media*, By T. O'Sullivan, B. Dutton and P. Rayner, Arnold, 1994.

and replace them with the ideologies and values of American consumer capitalism. However, little actual evidence has been presented about the precise nature of the forms of reception or decoding which are in play in the world-wide situations confronted with such imported material. Some recent developments in this context are worth noting.

By the mid 1980s, many cultural critics and writers agreed with the then French Minister for Culture, Jack Lang, when he attacked the American soap opera Dallas as 'the symbol of American cultural imperialism'. Set in a world of Texan oil families and their private and public feuds and conflicts, the soap opera had enjoyed massive international popularity in over a hundred countries world-wide (see Ang, 1985; Silj, 1988). One study which set out to explore how Dallas was made sense of in a diversity of cultural and global locations was carried out by Katz and Liebes (1990). They studied a large number of groups, including, for example, newcomers to Israeli society from a diversity of ethnic and cultural contexts. They viewed the dispersed and different audience groups that formed the basis for their study as active, and as capable of negotiating a range of diverse positions with regard to the serial, its stories and characters, and its relevance to their own lives. The study offers some evidence for the need to reassess this aspect of the imperialism thesis. Audiences on the 'receiving end' of American cultural products like Dallas emerge as active agents, more complex, critical or resistant and certainly less predictable in their cultural responses than has been assumed. Certainly, as Tomlinson in his assessment points out, 'We clearly cannot assume that simply watching Dallas makes people want to be rich' (1991, p. 49). The detailed study of the uses made of television in diverse national and ethnic locations has recently been developed in a series of studies by Lull (1988). . . .

One final and related question has been posed in recent work. This first emerges in an account given by Pennachioni (1984) of some observations of television viewing she made in north-east Brazil. One of the situations she describes concerns a group of poor country people in this area who were laughing at a communally watched, televised Charlie Chaplin

film. Pennachioni noted that she and they appeared to be laughing at the same things, but that this was by no means necessarily the case. On the basis of this encounter, she suggested that Western media researchers face formidable problems of understanding and interpretation. They and their research subjects, people in Third World settings, may appear to 'laugh at the same things' – the tramp character in Chaplin's films – but within very different, even irreconcilable frames of reference. Ultimately, her study poses some important questions about the assumptions often made about Third World audiences by Western researchers and their methods.

The study also highlights some important issues about the 'universal' nature of the appeal and meanings of images like Chaplin, or even more recently, J. R. Ewing in Dallas or characters in the Australian soap opera Neighbours. Tracey (1985) has posed a number of provocative questions in this context by suggesting that the world-wide appeal of American popular culture must, in part, be explained not just by its imposition, but by understanding how it taps into certain universal feelings and 'common chords', which transcend national cultures and differences of lived, situated identity. As Tomlinson notes, however, this kind of argument comes dangerously close to ignoring the historical power of Western media systems to saturate developing cultural economics with their types of material: 'One reason why Chaplin's humour can be plausibly seen as universal is that it is universally present' (1991, p. 53).

In summary, this section has suggested that there is considerable evidence available which points to the global concentration of power over media production and distribution. This has tended to be concentrated in Western nations, states and corporations. Debates about the dynamics of media imperialism may need to address more directly questions of how international audiences for the films, channels, programmes, music, videos and so on make use of and interpret these cultural products in their daily lives. In so doing, they also need to deal with the arguments and ideas contained in recent accounts of 'globalization'. Both of these issues are centrally linked with the emergence of more complex, new, multichannel media technologies, satellite, cable, digital and video being perhaps the prime examples of the moment.

---

9 LOCAL RECEPTION OF GLOBAL TELEVISION

J. D. Straubhaar

In television and in other cultural industries as well, people use globally distributed forms to create cultural products which define and re-define what the national and the local are. Robertson observes that 'globalization has involved the reconstruction, in a sense the production, of 'home', 'community' and 'locality' (1995, p. 30). Cultural producers use forms and genres that have spread globally to express ideas of what home is like. There is a subtle interplay between the global and local in television form and content.

For example, the soap opera has distinct roots in both English and French serial novels, which were carried over time in magazines and newspapers. US radio and later television took this idea and developed a particular form of soap opera, to entertain and draw loyal audiences over time, but explicitly also to sell soap. In fact, for quite a long time, the shows were produced for radio and television networks by advertising agencies on behalf of soap manufacturers. Soap companies and advertising agencies took this successful genre abroad, particularly to Latin America. Latin American radio and television producers adapted the genre to their cultures and needs, moving it into prime time, aiming it at both men and women, changing the form of story telling, and using local motifs, characters, humour, etc.

From: Distinguishing the global, regional and national levels of world television, by J. D. Straubhaar, in *Media in Global Context*, edited by A. Sreberny-Mohammadi *et al.*, Arnold, 1997.

In a sense, then, a global form is being localized, both for purposes of global capitalist development and for expression of local identity. The soap opera genre is still used to sell soap and, even more basically, to show local people an ethic or goal of consumption. For example, in one Brazilian soap opera in the late 1970s (Fernandes, 1982), a high point in the plot came when a man asked his wife if she would like a refrigerator and she burst into tears of joy. This consumption ethic is itself localized, with a refrigerator being an almost supreme ambition, compared to, say, an automobile. . . .

While such a local soap opera is delivering an adapted underlying global message about joining the lower ranks of an emerging global consumer economy, it is primarily carrying messages about the local culture. In fact, in Brazil and India, among others, the soap opera became a prime vehicle for creating elements of a 'national' culture and spreading them among localized and regionalized audiences that had not always shared a great deal of common culture between them despite being within common national boundaries (Fadul, 1993; Mitra, 1993).

In this example, the local adaptation of an increasingly global form of television illustrates that 'the concept of globalization has involved the simultaneity of what are conventionally called the global and the local' (Robertson, 1995, p. 30). In particular, we see a diffusion of some basic global forms related to the expansion of the world economy, but those globalized forms co-exist and even promote local adaptations and the expression of unique local content. With this kind of example, we can also see that globalization is not equal to global homogenization. While cultural forms, particularly those related to consumption within capitalist societies, diffuse globally, they tend to be adapted locally. In fact, global diffusion of certain elements of consumer culture may well be more effective when those consumer elements are cast in local terms and adapted to local economic realities.

There is, also, a process of active resistance to globalization in some places. The example of popular rejection of cultural Westernization, mobilized effectively by Islamic clerics in Iran, was one of the first clear signals that not all cultures were going to easily adopt Western cultural elements. Barber speaks of two opposing trends, a 'McWorld' of global homogenization versus the 'Jihad world' of localizing or particularizing 'Lebanonization' (1992).

Film and television as global phenomena

In the current era of globalization, the audiovisual media loom very large. The presence of television now builds upon patterns laid down by film in the early part of the twentieth century. More recently, however, there is some debate and questioning about, whether US dominance is slipping in world television markets. American television programmes are facing increased competition at a variety of levels: regional, national, and local. More countries are also competing to sell programmes to others. Some, like Brazil and Hong Kong, compete world-wide (Marques de Melo, 1988).

What has happened to replace American programming in a number of countries is the local adaptation of the American commercial model and American television programme formats (Oliveira, 1990). In the process of diffusion, the American model has been generalized and adapted in a global model for commercial media. This fits the model of Robertson (1995) and others that a number of current transformations may be described as 'glocalization', the oftentimes deliberate adaptation of a foreign or global model to fit national circumstances. Robertson observes that Japan is in some ways the prototype for this approach and in fact developed the term 'glocalization'.

In some countries, the process of adaptation of global genres or formats is more formal. Some nations, particularly in Europe, have been legally licensing specific US television programme formats, like 'Wheel of Fortune,' since the local adaptation of even a specific format is more popular than the simple importation of the programme. This is most true of genres and formats which are talk or language intensive, supporting the idea that languages form a natural barrier to the straightforward importation of programmes . . .

Gillespie's (1991) ethnographic study of South London Punjabi communities' use of 'Neighbours' is arguably the most in-depth audience-use study yet conducted of Australian soaps in Britain. It is deliberately narrowly focused where the ITC research is broad. Gillespie studied groups of teenagers' use of 'Neighbours' in negotiating the relations between parental and peer cultures in an environment where much of their knowledge of white Anglo society perforce comes from television. Whereas many of the key cultural audience studies of the 1980s focused on variables of class along with gender, Gillespie focuses on ethnicity, age and gender. With regard especially to her focus on a youth demographic, Gillespie's research performs a particularly useful function in illuminating that age group which has allowed 'Neighbours' to perform so strongly in Britain.

---

10 GLOBALISM'S LOCALISMS
D. Polan

In these films, and in other recent cultural production I'll be discussing, I think we can see marks of the emergence of a new global-American culture. This cultural production is globalist in several motifs that interconnect: a concern with movement and the ease of crossing fluid frontiers (whether these be the geopolitical limits between nations or the cybernetic limits between the human cogito and the computer networks in which the subject enters); an emphasis on service occupations; the representation of human interaction as mediated forms of communication (faxes, portable telephones, computer links, television, and so on); a fascination with prostheses, as if to suggest that human corporeality extends into the network of cybernetic interaction through the interface of cyborg body parts; a relative downplay of the

---

From: Globalism's localisms, by D. Polan, in *Global–Local: Cultural Production and the Transnational Imaginary*, edited by R. Wilson and W. Dissanayake, Duke University Press, 1996.

passions of the flesh (and also, often, of plots centered on bodies in violent action or sexual activity); plots that are themselves about the mediation between various subcultures of the global economy; consequently, the directing of narrative movement toward end-of-story glimpses of new post-subject forms of agency (whether these be the figurations of new post-familial collectivities as in 'Iron Maze', or the suggestion that subjectivity itself will break up and mutate as in 'The Fly', with its scientist hero merging at the end with hi-tech machinery in a dramatic rendition of the cybernetization of the self). These cultural productions both are about and are themselves in their production figurations of the five forms of border crossing that Arjun Appadurai sees as defining the complexities of the global cultural economy: ethnoscape (the transport of people); technoscape (the transport of technologies); financescape (the movement of monies); mediascape (the movement of information-forms themselves); and the ideoscape (the floating of stereotypes, social images and concepts – for example, the regulative ideal of sexual equality at the end of 'Mr. Baseball'). But, as Appadurai reminds us, there can be all sorts of disjunctions in and between each form of global transport; for example, insofar as a film like 'Mr. Baseball' is both about equality (men and women both have the right to a career) and about finance (only those at the top of the service economy have the privilege to cross borders while maintaining control of information), the film limits the representation of equality to the well-off, suggesting they literally can afford to be progressive. . . .

What else does Michael Jackson's video 'Black or White' do but offer a virtuoso vocation of art as that of 'inventing new geo-tropical cartographies'? Neither black nor white himself (surgery having weirdly turned him a curious pink), Jackson travels boldly through multiple worlds – through ethnicities rendered as backdrops and robbed of identity through mixture (Indian dancing against the backdrop of a rust-belt factory; African tribesmen in a recording studio) – and through multiple spaces (from white suburbia to the empty detritus of the inner city rendered as spectacle for the virtuoso

dancer – Jackson treating the slum street as studio set straight out of 'Singin' in the Rain'). This is the cartography of the new globalist trans-subject – faces blurring into each other, but with one subject (the elusive Jackson) also maintaining his prodigious privilege. Here, the new professional globalism achieves perfection: no frontiers, no limits, anything becomes anything else, everyone and everything linked but, at the same time, so many frontiers (art and ordinary life, privilege and anonymity, wealth and deprivation).

---

11 ASSIMILATION AND ABSORPTION STRATEGIES

M. Featherstone

One possibility is to attempt to outline some of the absorption, assimilation and resistance strategies which peripheral cultures can adopt toward the mass and consumer culture images and goods originating from metropolitan centres. In the first place it is apparent that once we investigate actual cases the situation is exceedingly complex. It is not just a question of the everyday practical culture of local inhabitants giving way to globally marketed products. Such market culture/local culture interactions are usually mediated by the nation-state which, in the process of creating a national identity, will educate and employ its own range of cultural specialists and intermediaries. Some of these may well have been educated in world cities and have retained strong networks and lifestyle identifications with other transnational 'design professionals', managers and intellectuals and para-intellectuals. Some of these may even be official 'cultural animateurs' employed

From: Localism, globalism and cultural identity, by M. Featherstone, in *Global–Local: Cultural Production and the Transnational Imaginary*, edited by R. Wilson and W. Dissanayake, Duke University Press, 1996.

by the ministry of culture, in some cases perhaps with one eye on national cultural integration and one eye on the international tourist trade. Hence, depending on the priority it gives to the nation-forming project and the power resources that the nation-state possesses, it can re-invent memories, traditions and practices with which to resist, channel or control market penetration. Some nation states, for example, will invest in locally produced film and television programmes. Yet, as we have previously mentioned, such experiments in cultural engineering are by no means certain to succeed unless they can find a base to ground themselves in local forms of life and practices. Hence the scenario of 'cultural dumping' of obsolete American television programmes on a powerless nation-state on the periphery is only one possibility from a range of responses. It also has to be set alongside the activities of cultural gatekeepers, brokers, and entrepreneurs within the major cities of the nation state, in conjunction with colleagues abroad in the world cities collaborating upon what aspects of the local popular culture – music, food, dress, crafts, etc. – can be packaged and marketed in the metropolitan centres and elsewhere. In many cases it may be that various forms of hybridization and creolization emerge in which the meanings of externally originating goods, information and images are re-worked, syncretized and blended with existing cultural traditions and forms of life.

In the case of the effects of global television, it is important to move beyond over-simplified, oppositionally conceived formulations which stress either the manipulation or the resistance of audiences. In recent years the pendulum has swung toward the latter populist direction with its claim that a new cultural studies orthodoxy has emerged around the assumption of the creativity and skilfulness of active audiences and consumers. Television and the new communications technology are frequently presented as producing both manipulation and resistance, on the one hand, and the homogenization and fragmentation of contemporary culture, on the other hand. The new communications technology is presented as producing a global Gemeinschaft which transcends physical place through bringing together disparate groups who unite around the common experience of television to form new communities. This means that the locality is no longer the prime referent of our experiences. Rather, we can be immediately united with distant others with whom we can form a 'psychological neighbourhood' or 'personal community' through telephone, or the shared experience of the news of the 'generalized elsewhere' we get from watching television. Hence, as Morley remarks, 'Thus, it seems, locality is not simply subsumed in a national or global sphere: rather, it is increasingly by-passed in both directions. Experience is both unified beyond localities and fragmented within them.' Yet this is not to suggest that the fragmentation of experience within localities is random or unstructured. Access to power resources creates important differentials. Just as there are 'information rich' nations on a global level, there are also 'information poor' ones. Within localities there are clear differentials, with the wealthy and well-educated most likely to have access to the new forms of information and communications technology through possession of the necessary economic and cultural capital. Here we can also point to Mary Douglas and Baron Isherwood's concept of 'informational goods', goods which require a good deal of background knowledge to make their consumption meaningful and strategically useful, as is the case with personal computers. On the other hand, it is the sense of instantiation and immediacy presented by television which appears to make its messages unproblematically accessible. American soap operas, Italian football or the Olympic Games all have an apparent immediacy and intelligibility which could be misunderstood as producing a homogeneous response. Yet these global resources are often indigenized and syncretized to produce particular blends and identifications which sustain the sense of the local.

A further problem with the homogenization thesis is that it misses the ways in which transnational corporations increasingly direct advertising toward various parts of the globe which is increasingly tailored to specific differentiated audiences and markets. Hence the global and the local cannot be neatly separated as we find in the statement by Coca-Cola, 'We are not a multinational, we are a multi-local.' Here we can usefully refer to the term 'globloc', the fusion of the terms global and local to make a blend. Apparently the term is modeled on the Japanese 'dochaku', which derives from the agricultural principle of adapting one's farming techniques to local conditions and was taken up by Japanese business interests in the 1980s.

The various combinations, blends, and fusions of seemingly opposed and incompatible processes – such as homogenization and fragmentation, globalization and localization, universalism and particularism – points to the problems which are entailed in attempts to conceive the global in terms of a singular integrated and unified conceptual scheme. Appadurai has rejected such attempts at theoretical integration to argue that the global order must be understood as 'a complex, overlapping, disjunctive order'. It can be best conceived as involving five sets of non-isomorphic flows of people, technology, finance, media images and information and ideas. Individual nation states may attempt to promote, channel or block particular flows with varying degrees of success depending upon the power resources they possess and the constraints of the particular configuration of interdependencies they are locked into.

12 INTERNATIONAL COMMUNICATION: THE FIELD AND THE PLAYERS

C. J. Hamelink

World communication encompasses a variety of flows of different messages. These cross-border flows can be sub-divided into the following:

From: International communication: global market and morality, by C. J. Hamelink, in *International Communication and Globalization*, edited by A. Mohammadi, Sage, 1997.

The flows of international news that are carried across the globe by the major players for print news: Associated Press, Reuter and Agence France Press, and for visual news: the two leading agencies, the former Visnews (now Reuters Television) and World Television Network. Reuters Television supplies television news to over forty broadcasters in eighty-five countries and reaches almost a half-billion households. In 1993 the Reuters Holding (UK) had sales of US$2,831 million and profits of US$452 million. World Television Network (WTN) provides services to a hundred broadcasters in eighty-five countries with an audience of some three billion people. In 1994 there were serious speculations that Reuters was planning to acquire WTN, thus reducing the two major players to one market leader. Second in line for international television news production and distribution are BBC World Service and CNN. CNN distributes around the clock to over 200 subscribers. On an average day 160 items are broadcast, of which about thirty are international. CNN is available in over 700 million households world-wide and thousands of hotels. The Turner Broadcasting System (the parent company of CNN which is 20 per cent owned by the Time-Warner conglomerate) had sales of US$1,922 million and profits of US$72 million in 1993. In the course of 1993 the news agency Associated Press announced that it was ready to enter the television news market in 1994. APTV could become the most serious competitor for Reuters Television and WTN. Other major players in the flow of news include some large newspapers with their syndicated news services, like the *New York Times*, *Los Angeles Times*, or *Washington Post*, and the publishers of international magazines such as *Time* and *Newsweek*.

The flows of entertainment and education materials which include recorded music, feature films, textbooks, and television entertainment. The major players are the world's largest entertainment media companies. . . . The flows of promotional messages which consist mainly of commercial advertising carried by international newspapers, magazines and broadcast media across the globe. The major players are the world's largest advertising agencies. . . .

The flows of data, as in electronic data exchange, electronic funds transfers, remote resource satellite sensing, electronic mail and database searches. These flows are carried by networks such as the Internet, by the provider of financial data services such as Reuters Information Services, or by such inter-firm networks as the largest interbank network SWIFT which is now operated by some 1,000 banks and links more than 2,000 sites in sixty countries. The flows of electronic data across the globe are supported by a rapidly growing software services industry, with an estimated market value of some US$300 billion in 1995. Leading players are companies like Microsoft (US) with 1993 sales of US$3,753 million and profits of US$953 million.

The flows of voice messages, for both private and commercial applications, are facilitated by such major players as the world's largest telecommunication service providers. These are AT&T (with 1993 revenues of US$67.2 billion), the combination of British Telecommunications PLC and MCI Corp (US) (with revenues in 1993 of US$33 billion), the projected combination of Deutsche Bundespost Telekom, France Telecorn and the US-based Sprint Corporation (with combined 1993 revenues of US$69 billion), and the Japanese Nippon Telegraph & Telephone (with 1993 revenues of US$60 billion).

The flows of text messages which are transported through such media as telefax, telex and the mail services. The major players are the tele-communication service providers, the postal services around the world and the leading courier companies.

The keywords of this market-driven arrangement are deregulation, privatization and globalization. Increasingly, in many countries the political climate is very supportive of those processes. The creation of the global electronic networks, for example, is largely facilitated through the privatization of public telecommunication services, the liberalization of electronics markets and the deregulation of tariff structures. There is world-wide a trend towards a shift from public service type provision of information and telecommunication services to a competitive environment for the trading of these services to public market operators.

13 THE GLOBAL MEDIA ORDER

D. Morley and K. Robins

Herbert Schiller's interpretation of the 'new media order' differs considerably from that offered by Steven Ross. 'The actual sources of what is being called globalization are not to be found in a newly achieved harmony of interests in the international arena', Schiller argues. What he sees is 'transnational corporate cultural domination'; a world in which 'private giant economic enterprises pursue – sometimes competitively, sometimes co-operatively – historical capitalist objectives of profit making and capital accumulation, in continuously changing market and geopolitical conditions' (Schiller, 1991, pp. 20–1). What is emphasized here is the historical continuity, and consistency, in corporate motivations. What is recognized and acknowledged is that, in the 1990s, the context of this drive for market and competitive position has been significantly transformed. The struggle for power and profits is now being waged at the global scale (Aksoy and Robins, 1992).

What we are seeing is the construction of the media order through the entrepreneurial devices of a comparatively small number of global players, the likes of Time-Warner, Sony, Matsushita, Rupert Murdoch's News Corporation and the Walt Disney Company. For viewers, the new media order has become apparent through the emergence of new commercial channels, such as BSkyB, CNN, MTV or the Cartoon Network. What we are seeing is the development of a new media market characterized by new services, new delivery systems and new forms of payment. In place of the mixed-programming channels of the 'traditional' broadcasters, we now have the proliferation of generic channels (sport, news, music, movies). It is estimated that the 59 channels licensed to operate in the UK in 1992 will increase to around 130 by 2002 (Booz-Allen Hamilton, 1993, p. 9). In the US, there are soon likely to be more than two hundred channels. It is,

From: *Spaces of Identity*, by D. Morley and K. Robins, Routledge, 1995.

of course, the global media players that are investing in these channels (and the UK is only one small part in their global jigsaw).

Global corporations are presently manoeuvring for world supremacy. There are three basic options open to media corporations: 'The first is to be a studio and produce products. The second is to be a wholesale distributor of products, as MTV, CBS, and HBO are. The third is to be a hardware delivery system, whether that hardware is a cable wire or a Walkman' (Auletta, 1993, p. 81). The objective for the real global players is to operate across two or even all three of these activities. It is this ambition that motivated the take-overs of Hollywood studios (Universal by Matsushita, Columbia/TriStar by Sony, Fox by Rupert Murdoch). As Steven Ross (1990) observes, 'mass is critical, if it is combined with vertical integration and the resulting combination is intelligently managed'. The issue for media corporations now is to decide what scale of integration they need to achieve, and are capable of managing, in order to build globally.

But there is more to it than just integration within the media sector. What we are beginning to see is a much more fundamental process of transformation, in which entertainment and information businesses are converging with the telecommunications industry. A sign of things to come was the projected, but ultimately unsuccessful, merger, in 1993, of the telecommunications company Bell with the largest US cable company TCI. The new company would have become the world's largest media corporation. It was described, by Bell Atlantic's chairman, as 'a perfect information age marriage' and 'a model for communications in the next century' (Dickson, 1993). The new 'multi-media' giant would have provided not only conventional cable television, but also telecommunications services, computer games and software, home banking and shopping, video on demand, and other interactive services. The aim is still to develop information and communications 'super-highways' that will move us beyond the era of mass media and into that of personalized media and individual choice.

But it will be personalized media and individual choice, of course, on the basis of what is available and for sale. Global corporations are securing control over programming (production, archives), over distribution and over transmission systems. The flow of images and products is both more intensive and more extensive than in the past. What should also be emphasized is how much American cultural domination remains a fundamental part of this new order, though now American or American-style output is also the staple fare of non-US interests too (Schiller, 1991). As a writer in the *Financial Times* recently observed, 'soon hardly anywhere on earth will be entirely safe from at least the potential of tuning in to cheerful American voices revealing the latest news or introducing the oldest films' (Snoddy, 1993).

What corporate manoeuvres and machinations are seeking to bring into existence is a global media space and market. In the mid-1980s, Saatchi & Saatchi were talking about 'world cultural convergence', and arguing that 'convergences in demography, behaviour and shared cultural elements are creating a more favourable climate for acceptance of a single product and positioning across a wide range of geography'. Television programmes such as Dallas, or films such as Star Wars or ET were seen to 'have crossed many national boundaries to achieve world awareness for their plots, characters, etc.' (Winram, 1984, p. 21). Theodore Levitt, whose influential book, *The Marketing Imagination,* helped to shape the Saatchi outlook, was, at the same time, pointing to the increasing standardization and homogenization of markets across the world. 'The global corporation', he argued, 'looks to the nations of the world not for how they are different but for how they are alike ... it seeks constantly in every way to standardize everything into a common global mode' (Levitt, 1983, p. 28). Of course, if it is profitable to do so, global companies will respond to the demands of particular segments of the market. In so doing, however, 'they will search for opportunities to sell to similar segments throughout the globe to achieve the scale economies that keep their costs competitive' (ibid., p. 26). The strategy is to 'treat these market segments as global, not local, markets' (Winram, 1984, p. 19).

There appears to be the same logic at work in the 1990s. American movies (such as 'The Flintstones' and 'Jurassic Park') are still breaking box-office records across the world (hence the keen struggle to acquire Hollywood studios and archives). Satellite and cable channels are also making headway in marketing standardized product world-wide. MTV, recently invited into Lithuania to help promote democracy, and CNN, now on twelve satellites beaming 'global village' news the world over, seem to have come close to finding the answer to global marketing. The new 'super-highways', still in their early stages of development, seem set to push processes of standardization further. But they are also likely to add more complexity, delivering 'personalized' and 'individualized' services to specialized and 'niche' markets. Such strategies, it should be emphasized, 'are not denials or contradictions of global homogenization, but rather its confirmation ... globalization does not mean the end of segments. It means, instead, their expansion to world-wide proportions' (Levitt, 1983, pp. 30–31). . . .

Since the late 1980s, a certain level of support has been elicited from the EC, particularly through its 'Media' programme, which provides loans and support for small producers across the continent. Within the Community there has been increasing sensitivity towards cultural differences and commitment to the preservation of cultural identities in Europe.

Here again we have an example of the global–local nexus. 'Local' in this case, however, means something quite different from what it means in the corporate lexicon. In this context, it relates to the distinctive identities and interests of local and regional communities. In these global times, there are those who desire to 're-territorialize' the media, that is to re-establish a relationship between media and territory. They are determined that the media should contribute to sustaining both the distinctiveness and the integrity of local and regional cultures, against the threatening forces of 'de-territorialization' and homogenization. 'Local' in this sense constitutes a challenge to the strategies of global corporate interests.

If the processes of globalization provoke fear and resentment, these tend, for the most part, to become attached to the perceived threat of American culture and 'Americanization'. American mass culture has, for a very long time, been seen as a force that is eroding and dissolving European culture and tradition. The cultural domination of Hollywood has appeared to jeopardize the very survival of Europe's cultural industries. The culture of the continent is seen to be 'in thrall to American money – and ultimately American values'; put simply, from this perspective, 'Hollywood is the enemy' (Malcolm, 1990). The American share of the European cinema market is now 75 per cent (while the non-American share of US box-office takings stands at only 2 per cent). In consequence, quotas have been imposed on non-European (in effect American) programming, with the dual aim of protecting cultural sovereignty and enhancing the competitive position of domestic producers. This was a key issue in the last round of GATT negotiations (1993–94). While the US was calling, in the name of free trade and the free circulation of ideas, for the scrapping of quota restrictions, European interests were resolved to preserve them in order, as they saw it, to defend the cultural specificity and integrity of European civilization. In France, there has been considerable hostility to Britain, for its having afforded Ted Turner access to European audiences. According to one critic, 'Turner is only the avant-garde of the big US companies who are sitting back to see how Europe reacts. If he gets in, Disney and Time-Warner will follow' (Powell, 1993). The European stance is seen as a battle for freedom of expression: 'We want the Americans to let us survive. Ours is a struggle for the diversity of European culture, so that our children will be able to hear French and German and Italian spoken in films' (ibid.). Again, the emphasis is on particularity and difference, in the face of what seems to threaten their dissolution.

14 GLOBAL TELEVISION

C. Baker

Developments in television are part of a wider set of changes to communications industries as a whole. As Dyson and Humphreys (1990) note, four key ideas have dominated the communications sector: de-regulation, globalization, synergy and convergence. These interdependent and interconnected forces are applicable both to the manoeuvrings of corporations and the strategies of governments. They are interconnected because the forces behind the radical changes in telecommunications have been a combination of technological developments and market change. This has contributed both to the creation of global communications giants and to the convergence (or erosion of boundaries) between sectors. Thus, technological developments such as the unfolding of fibre-optic cable, satellite technology and digital-switching technology have opened up commercial possibilities which have led to telecommunications being hailed by corporation and state alike as the industry of the future.

The growth of telecommunications industries has been a matter not just of technology *per se* but of the demand for information. In particular, transnational companies have become dependent on telecommunications services to develop their own internal corporate communications on a global scale and to sell services and technology to others. The global scale of transnational capitalist organizations has put communications at the heart of world business. According to Schiller (1985), the development of the International Services Digital Network (ISDN) is a mechanism both for servicing the information and communication requirements of transnational corporations and of further incorporating developing nations into the world economic order.

Associated with transnational global corporations is the pressure to de-regulate in all aspects of communications so that the influence of private companies begins to erode and eclipse the traditional public

post and telecommunications organizations of Europe, Japan and Australia. De-regulation was seen by political forces as essential in order to compete in international markets; thus the Thatcher government in Britain and the new right of Reagan in the US gave the whole economic process political and ideological reinforcement. The US in particular has been at the forefront of such developments, not only in terms of deregulation within its own borders, but in undermining international regulatory bodies such as the International Telecommunications Union and INTELSAT.

Corporations have sought to create synergy via vertical integration drawing together equipment manufacturers, information providers and transmitters. There has been a good deal of diversification by financial, computer and data-processing companies into telecommunications creating multi-media giants who dominate sectors of the market. New digital technology is one of the mechanisms driving a global communications shake-up making mergers between companies in the computer, entertainment and telecommunications sectors far more inviting. Further, companies need the financial power that can come from mergers to undertake the massive investment needed to be players in the global market. For example, in 1989 the merger of Time and Warner created the largest media group in the world with a market capitalization of $25 billion. This was followed in 1995 by Time-Warner's acquisition of Turner Broadcasting (CNN). In late 1993 the merger of Paramount communications, maker of such films as The Firm and Indecent Proposal, and Viacom, owner of MTV among other assets, saw the emergence of a $17 billion company making it the fifth largest media group behind Time-Warner, News Corporation, Bertelsmann and Walt Disney. We may note that four out of five of these companies are based in the US, the exception being the German-based Bertelsmann. The Paramount-Viacom merger illustrates the commercial advantages of integration as it put a vast array of assets under one corporate roof: a Hollywood studio, cable systems, television and radio stations, and a book publisher. The preoccupation with combining software and hardware is well illustrated by the film Last Action Hero. This

From: *Global Television*, by C. Baker, Blackwell, 1997.

Schwarzenegger 'blockbuster' was made by Columbia Pictures, owned by the Sony Corporation. The soundtrack came from CBS, also owned by Sony and it was screened in cinemas with digital sound systems made by Sony. In addition, Sony produced virtual reality and video games based on the film.

15 GLOBAL MEDIA OWNERSHIP

R. Burnett

The trend towards concentration that characterized the take-over and fusion binge of the 1980s was also felt throughout the entire entertainment industry and especially the music industry. The Big Six major phonogram companies – Sony, Warner, Polygram, EMI, BMG and MCA – now account for over 90 per cent of US sales and an estimated 70 to 80 per cent of world-wide sales.

Japanese electronics giant Sony purchased CBS Records for $2.2 billion and then purchased Columbia Pictures for $3.4 billion. Time-Life's 1990 merger with Warner Communications created Time-Warner, the world's largest communications company and significantly, the only American enterprise of that magnitude in a world dominated by multinational communications conglomerates such as Bertelsmann (Germany), Hachette (France) and Murdoch's News Corporation. Polygram Records, itself a subsidiary of The Netherlands multinational electronics giant Philips, acquired both Island Records and A&M Records. British EMI, a division of multinational Thorn, acquired independent music publishers SBK as well as Chrysalis Records and Virgin Records. The German BMG, a division of media giant Bertelsmann, purchased both RCA Records and Arista Records. And last but not least, in 1990 Matsushita Electric Industrial, which is

From: *The Global Jukebox*, by R. Burnett, Routledge, 1996.

twice the size of Sony, purchased MCA, parent of Universal Pictures and MCA records.

It is not only the music industry which is dominated by a few firms. In the US, the motion picture industry today is ruled by seven major film studios that engage in the financing, production and distribution of films: Universal Pictures (a division of MCA which was acquired by Matsushita Electrical Industrial in December, 1990), Columbia Pictures (acquired by Sony in 1989), 20th Century Fox (now a subsidiary of Rupert Murdoch's News Corporation), MGM/UA (acquired by Pathe and presently controlled by Credit Lyonnais Netherlands), Warner Brothers (a subsidiary of Time-Warner), Paramount Pictures (a subsidiary of Paramount Communications) and The Walt Disney Company (Buena Vista). Together with Orion and TriStar, the major film companies control the distribution of American motion pictures in the US as well as throughout the rest of the world. The high cost of distributing movies to the mainstream market means that independent production companies must try to convince one of the majors to carry their output if they are to have a chance of reaching a large public.

Even though the size of the major music and film companies is quite impressive in their own right they are often buried away within much larger media and electronics conglomerates and usually only account for between 5 and 25 per cent of total company revenues. If we take for example the electronics industry who manufacture the hardware for the entertainment industry we find that General Electric, Matsushita, Philips, Sony and Siemens are the largest companies in terms of revenues. If we look to the media corporations who produce the software we find in terms of total revenues the largest ranking companies are Time-Warner, Bertelsmann, Capital Cities/ABC, News Corporation and Hachette.

Let's look a little closer at some of the companies in the media hardware and software industries. The Sony Corporation is the Japanese parent company that is currently divided into the Sony Electronics Corporation and the Sony Software Corporation. The Sony Electronics Corporation is responsible for the hardware, that is, the electronics, recording, manufacturing and marketing operations. The Sony Software Corporation consists of three different divisions: Sony Music Entertainment, Sony Pictures Entertainment and Sony Electronic Publishing. As the name implies these corporate divisions are in the business of producing software.

Sony had $26 billion in sales in 1991. It reigns unchallenged as the most consistently inventive consumer electronics enterprise in the world. Sony popularized the pocket size transistor radio, the battery-powered TV set, the VCR, the camcorder and the Walkman portable cassette player. Worldwide Sony employs 112,900 people. In 1991 the company spent $1.5 billion supporting their research and product development (R&D) efforts – roughly 5.7 per cent of revenues. Sony founder, Masaru Ibuka, explains: 'The key to success for Sony, and to everything in Business, Science, and Technology for that matter, is never to follow the others' (Schlender, 1992, p. 23). Similarly, current chairman, Akio Morita, states: 'Our basic concept has always been this – to give new convenience, or new methods, or new benefits, to the general public with our technology' (ibid., p. 23).

Sony is trying for the edge in the digital future, by selling the latest machines as well as the software they use. The digital future is simply 'computing plus entertainment', says Michael Schulhof, vice-chairman of Sony America. So the key software is movies and music, which is one reason Sony bought Columbia Pictures and CBS Records. 'I spent $8 billion of Sony's money developing this strategy', says Schulhof. 'We're the best positioned company in the world' (Neff, 1992, p. 96). Indeed, perhaps only rival Matsushita, owner of MCA, comes close to matching Sony's mix of digital hardware and entertainment software. It is supposed to all come together in a series of products on CD-ROM for storing images digitally with full colour, motion and sound. 'Our new CD medium will be used for everything: entertainment, computing, data storage, and telecommunications', says Mr Idei of Sony (ibid., p. 97). Sony is focusing on what another executive calls the 'three Ps' of the digital revolution: personal entertainment, personal information and personal communications. The same source noted

that, 'the lines between hardware and software are getting fuzzier all the time.' Sony appears to have made a strategic commitment to full integration of electronics and entertainment.

The Japanese Matsushita Corporation is the world's largest consumer electronics firm with 1990 revenues of $38 billion. Matsushita produces the JVC line of consumer electronics. Matsushita bought the MCA entertainment company and Universal Pictures for $6.1 billion in 1990. The same year the company spent $3 billion on research and development or 6.2 per cent of total sales. For an electronic hardware firm like Matsushita the MCA purchase is a way of ensuring an immensely valuable supply of software: the movies, CDs and films that can be played on the machines Matsushita sells. Matsushita hopes to put half a century's worth of MCA creative output into new CDs, videotapes, laser discs and new formats.

The American Time-Warner organization claims to be the largest media company in the world. The Time-Warner organization includes the TimeLife book and magazine publishers (*Time*, *Life*, *Fortune*, *Sports Illustrated*), Warner Brothers film studio, Lorimar Telepictures (world's largest TV production company), Warner Music company, DC Comics, and the Home Box Office cable TV channel. Time-Warner's total revenue for 1991 amounted to $12 billion. This total was divided into: film 25 per cent, music 24 per cent, magazines and books 24 per cent, cable TV systems 16 per cent and television production 11 per cent.

The German Bertelsmann company has 44,000 employees in 30 countries around the world. Bertelsmann controls the RTL-Plus and Premiere TV channels in Europe. The publishing (books, magazines, newspapers) and recording industries are its principal activities in the global marketplace. The Bertelsmann group has positioned itself well in the entertainment software business in the belief that this is where future profits are to be made. Consequently, a BMG executive expressed the international strategy; 'while increasing in complexity and becoming even more fiercely competitive, this sector of the economy will continue to grow. Success will depend on skill, experience and creativity in each market segment and to the extent that entertainment properties of international importance are involved – a global infrastructure'.

News Corporation is the company controlled by Rupert Murdoch (now an American citizen). News Corporation controls or owns the Sun, News of the World and the Sunday Times newspapers among others, as well as the TV Guide magazines. News Corporation also owns the US Fox TV network, 20th Century Fox film studios, Harper & Row Books and is part owner of Reuters news bureau. They also control the Sky satellite TV channel. News Corporation's total revenue for 1991 amounted to $8.6 billion. This was broken down as follows: Newspapers 39 per cent, films 20 per cent, book publishing 14 per cent, television 12 per cent, magazines 12 per cent and commercial printing 5 per cent.

The interesting paradox is that while the six transnationals have the money and the technology to continue to dominate the production and distribution of popular music for many years to come, the digitalization of music could give them even more control and larger profits, or it could open a Pandora's box that could ultimately destroy their own control of popular music. If the electronic, digital delivery through the Internet or cable TV becomes the dominant form of music distribution in the future, then any band will be able to distribute their music themselves, directly to their fans over the wire. If artists start self-distribution over the wire then what happens to the Big Six? The music business may well never be the same. The one thing that we can be sure of (with apologies to BTO) is that 'we ain't seen nothing yet'.

---

16 ANGLO-AMERICAN MEDIA OWNERSHIP MONOPOLY

J. van Ginneken

Today, only three agencies retain a truly global role – but they still reflect the three predominant types of client. The British (former British Empire) agency Reuters is primarily a private company, now deriving most of its considerable wealth, income and profits from its financial services. The American agency AP also runs a strong financial service (together with the Dow Jones company which also owns the *Wall Street Journal*), but it primarily remains a media co-operative. The French agency AFP thrived for a long time on generous government subscriptions, but increasingly it is trying to shift its emphasis to media clients. It is currently boosting its English-language services, in order to stay in the race. The American UPI agency went bankrupt; its remains were put up for sale, and were finally bought by an Arab media group. After the demise of the Soviet Empire, the Russian Tass agency was downgraded to an ordinary medium-sized national agency with limited overseas influence – just like the German, Spanish or Japanese agencies.

Although there have been recurrent attempts to compare the remaining three global agencies in size, this makes only limited sense with the available statistics. ... A crucial development of recent decades was the gradual emergence of global news-film agencies. Reuters took a major stake in the Visnews agency, alongside the British public service broadcaster, the BBC. UPI lined up with the Independent Television News (ITN, on the commercial ITV network) to form UPITN, the forerunner of the present WTN. Reuters/Visnews and WIN are also hung up with the major American commercial broadcasters NBC and ABC respectively. The third major US commercial general interest network CBS sells its own news-film abroad. Most of the 'exotic' news-film shown on the TV evening news in lesser countries comes from these three sources. In recent

From: *Understanding Global News*, by J. van Ginneken, Sage, 1998.

years, however, thematic channels with their own news film-gathering organizations such as CNN, have decisively entered the game as well.

This emerging Anglo-American monopoly was lamented by Herve Bourges, a former president of the French public service channels, and a central figure in audiovisual policy making. He contributed an article to *Le Monde* newspaper after the Gulf War, regretting that France had been so dependent on foreign images and foreign image making. He also suggested that some allied mis-information had contributed to spoiling the traditionally good relations with some Arab countries on this occasion (3 April 1991). If key mainstream players in such major Western countries also express concerns about the unbalanced flow of international information, then there really must be a problem.

Media ownership and concentration

Within the US and other G-7 nations themselves, the degree of media decentralization or concentration has long been a major issue of public concern. Everyone agrees that some degree of pluralism is essential to the functioning of democracy, and indeed of a highly developed society as such. But whereas some claim that a wide variety of media voices can be heard, others maintain that the actual range is relatively narrow and is narrowing even further. On the one hand, this is a question of definition: how does one delineate markets and identify competitors? On the other hand, it is a question of evolution: when does one speak of oligopolies or semi-monopolies?

At the outset, there is the matter of basic media technologies and how 'affordable' they are for individuals and groups. There are two contradictory tendencies. The first is towards decentralization. Average citizens of OECD nations do indeed have access to a wide variety of technological means, and can often communicate their news and views to others. Personal computers, word processing, graphic design and page-making programmes, electronic printers, photocopying machines and photo-offset machines make it relatively easy to produce and multiply printed matter in a more or less professional way. Fax machines make it possible to distribute messages instantaneously. Digital tapes and recorders have brought small-scale audio and video productions within easy reach. The camcorder revolution is clearly a boon to counter culture. Furthermore, there is undeniably an explosion of small-scale broadcasters on the air and on cable. The Internet is an even more eloquent illustration.

At the same time, the second and opposing tendency reflects concentration. Ever larger conglomerates control the major means of information, communication, distribution. Major data banks, electronic news processing and modern printing plants for newspapers require large initial investments. It takes many millions more to launch a new daily paper and take major initial losses, before possibly establishing it in a profitable market niche. It takes billions to set up a satellite or cable infrastructure, and wholesale access to them is not always within reach of lesser players. The production of a major television spot alone may cost a million dollars today, the production of a major mini-series may cost 10 million, the production of a major Hollywood blockbuster movie may cost up to 100 million. So, whereas some maintain that the glass of access for all is half-full, others claim it is half-empty.

---

17 ALTERNATIVES: CHANNELS OF RESISTANCE?

C. Barker

Despite the overwhelming predominance of transnational corporate control of production and distribution there are nevertheless signs of alternative productions taking place, albeit on a rather limited scale (Dowmunt, 1993). Thus, Batty (1993) describes the development of 'alternative' television in Ernabella, a remote Aboriginal community located

From: *Global Television*, by C. Barker, Blackwell, 1997.

in the semi-arid regions of northern South Australia. Here the Pitjantjatjarra people, having already some considerable experience of asserting their rights, decided to establish a media committee to monitor developments within satellite and video television.

The project began as a small-scale project producing video programmes for the Ernabella community but soon expanded to take in the surrounding Pitjantjatarra communities to become the local channel. This outlet was used to distribute news about local cultural, political and sporting events, as well as to educate the younger members of the community in the traditions of the past. As the project developed, and the members became more confident, they began to stitch together locally-produced programmes with some from the national ABC network which they accessed via a satellite dish. The success of this venture, argues Batty, is based on the adaptation of international technology by local people for local needs and funded from local sources. He contrasts this with Imparja, an Aboriginal-owned and run station set up within the context of Australian commercial television. Imparja won the franchise as the 'Remote Commercial Television Service' serving central Australia with its substantial Aboriginal population. However, the fact that a substantial part of the audience is not Aboriginal and that the station must make money through advertising has undercut its original cultural and political project and left the station with only a weak Aboriginal presence both in terms of personnel and programming.

While Ernabelia television was in the remote Australian outback, 'Deep Dish' was a project conceived in the heartland of America. Lucas and Wallner (1993) describe how, in the midst of the Gulf War, a group of media activists became discontented with the lack of serious discussion or questioning in the mainstream American media. In response they launched the 'Gulf Crisis TV Project' with the express purpose of producing alternative programmes. A core group of activists, having alerted colleagues nation-wide, were able to gather and edit a vast amount of footage shot on easily available video cameras into a series of shows critical of US-government Gulf policy. They were able to persuade

a number of access cable channels and PBS stations to screen the programmes which were distributed nationally by hiring satellite time. Thus, the very commercial availability of television technology was being put to quite a different purpose.

Conclusions: global television

The key changes in the political economy of global television as described in this chapter can be summarized as follows:

- Advances in television technology creating new distribution mechanisms.
- A weakening of national regulatory environments.
- Political and industrial support for market solutions.
- A rise in television channels and broadcasting hours.
- A degree of loss of legitimacy for public television.
- The emergence of new entrants in to the global television market creating serious competition for public service broadcasters.
- A degree of loss of audience by public television to commercial competitors.
- A rise in transnational and monopoly ownership circumventing national regulation.

These trends conjure up a picture of trans-global television dominated by commercial multinational corporations, with public service television confined to the sidelines of minority interest. There is indeed grounds for painting such a picture. However, public service television has not yet disappeared; the global television market is not yet dominated by one American corporation; and the patterns of television business are complex involving global, regional and local flows.

_____

18 DEEP DISH AND THE GULF WAR

J. Drew

The need for alternative television communications was driven home by the launching of the murderous assault by the US on the people of Iraq in 1992. In an attempt to reassert US control over Middle Eastern oil fields and divert domestic problems into flag-waving patriotic hysteria, George Bush launched Operation Desert Storm. In a display of submission and one-sidedness that would have made Joseph Goebbels envious, the US corporate media stifled alternative expression and acted as the official mouthpiece of the government.

Paper Tiger TV had created 'The Gulf Crisis TV Project' months before the war began in an effort to show an alternative view of the developing situation in the Gulf. These tapes included interviews with army deserters, anti-war veterans, and analysts like Noam Chomsky, Edward Said, and Daniel Ellsberg, and showed how different communities were organizing to resist the move to war.

By the time the first four half-hour tapes were broadcast on Deep Dish TV, war fever had already swept the country. The interest in these tapes was enormous, as evidenced by the number of requests that poured into the Gulf Crisis office in New York and the Paper Tiger TV offices in New York and San Francisco. Work began on six more half-hour programmes that documented the growing anti-war movement and included information we felt important enough to be passed around the unofficial and official censorship of the US media.

These tapes were shown to many large audiences in theaters, universities, and public spaces, which had the effect of breaking the spiral of silence that the US media was promulgating in refusing to depict any mention of domestic dissent. The tapes were heavily used by activists all across the US to help build local anti-war activities. Thousands of copies were dubbed and re-dubbed and passed between friends, relatives and co-workers.

Pressure put on the Public Broadcast System to show an alternative view allowed the Gulf Crisis TV Project to be shown in major cities such as New York and Los Angeles. When the San Francisco PBS station refused to programme the show, we held a public screening on the wall of their building by using a video projector and a portable public-address system. In San Francisco, where there had been hundreds of thousands of demonstrators and more than one thousand arrests for civil disobedience, our local Paper Tiger group started a weekly cable series as a tool for anti-war activists. We had dozens of video volunteers shooting anti-war activities on a daily basis, from blockades to teach-ins. We would end each show with announcements of all the events for the coming week. And we were able to use some of this footage as defense evidence for people arrested in police sweeps. Gulf Crisis TV material was also shown on national televisions systems in Europe, Asia, and elsewhere.

Occasionally there will be extreme situations like the Gulf War in which the advantages of alternative electronic media will leap to the fore. Of course, in comparison to the monolithic media structures erected by the Time-Warner-Viacom-TCI-GE nexus, the faint snarling of Paper Tiger TV can seem ineffective. Groups like Paper Tiger TV lack the resources for building mass audiences through traditional means such as advertising and slick production values. Furthermore, in attempting to reach an invisible audience 'out there', we lack the resources for even gauging our effectiveness. However, I believe that groups like Paper Tiger, while not close to threatening mainstream television, have developed important followings on the margins of society. Public-access and alternative viewing sites have played important roles in maintaining and cultivating appositional and minority cultures. Public-access stations, for example, frequently have a high concentration of programmes by African Americans, gay and lesbian groups, Latinos, radical groups, foreign-Language-speaking groups, and other communities ignored by mainstream media.

From: Media activism and radical democracy, by J. Drew, in *Resisting the Virtual Life: The Culture and Politics of Information*, edited by J. Brook and I. A. Boal, City Lights Books, San Francisco, 1995.

Confrontation in cyberspace

The explosive growth of the Internet and the evolution of proposals for a National Information Infrastructure have heightened the struggle between the democratic and the corporate communications models. Ironies abound: the Internet began as a Department of Defense experiment in constructing a decentralized computer network that could survive a nuclear war; but this network outgrew the experiment, to become a relatively cheap and open way of communicating between computer users. Now its low cost and ease of access have begun to seem like liabilities to the profit-seekers who dream of privatizing and 'improving' the Internet to the point of charging for every mouse click.

But then much of the hard work of laying down the initial 'trails' that led to the information superhighway was done by outcast hackers, computer hobbyists, and activists who created the bulletin board services and other refuges in cyberspace for free-thinking people. Many of these computer bulletin boards served as transit points around which the current Internet system grew. Indeed, the foundations of microcomputing itself can be attributed to this community of hackers, whose members thought they saw in the microcomputer a more democratic and decentralized response to the monolithic nightmare of IBM mainframes and Orwellian information databases.

The computer subculture spawned by the microcomputer created a hacker's code of ethics, based on the ideas of 'shareware' and freedom to access information, ideas antithetical to the kind of commercial development now planned by corporate entrepreneurs. Thus the early slogan of hacking: 'Information wants to be free'. There are hundreds if not thousands of bulletin board services, Freenets, and other computer sites that, along with such established progressive sites as 'PeaceNet' and 'The Well' make up an informal alternative information structure.

The prospects for democratic media

Whatever the origins of the technologies employed, the fundamental questions about design and use remain. Will the information superhighway be decentralized, inexpensive, and open? Will it facilitate grassroots production and distribution? Or will it permit the media giants to establish a one-way flow of home shopping and movies-on-demand?

Engineering decisions are rarely based on public need and improving our quality of life; they are usually made with considerations of profit in mind. Only seldom does the public get involved in technological decisions, and this is normally in a reactive fashion when people are trying to stop something that has already been put into use, such as nuclear power and pesticides.

Critical engineering decisions being made right now will have dramatic repercussions on whether communications will help to democratize collective life. The nature of the coming information superhighway will powerfully affect our future, yet discussion and planning for it take place mostly behind closed doors. Decisions about privacy on line – of great concern to many citizens who want their computer communications to be secure – are made behind a veil of secrecy.

19 FIRST AND THIRD WORLD CINEMA

E. Showat and R. Stam

Although arguably the majority cinema, Third World cinema is rarely featured in cinemas, video stores or even in academic film courses. The yearly Oscar ceremonies inscribe Hollywood's arrogant provincialism: the audience is global, yet the product promoted is almost always American, the 'rest of the world' being corralled into the restricted category of

From: From the imperial family and the transnational imaginary: media spectatorship in the age of globalization, by E. Showat and R. Stam, in *Global–Local: Cultural Production and the Transnational Imaginary*, edited by R. Wilson and W. Dissanayake, Duke University Press, 1996.

the 'foreign film'. In this sense, the cinema inherits the structures laid down by the communication infrastructure of Empire, the networks of telegraph and telephone lines and information apparatuses which literally wired colonial territories to the metropole, enabling the imperial countries to monitor global communications and shape the image of world events. In the cinema, this hegemonizing process intensified shortly after World War I, when US film distribution companies (and secondarily European companies) began to dominate Third World markets and was further accelerated after World War II with the growth of transnational media corporations. The continuing economic dependency of Third World cinemas makes them vulnerable to neo-colonial pressures. When dependent countries try to strengthen their own film industries by setting up trade barriers to foreign films, for example, First World countries can threaten retaliation in some other economic area such as the pricing or purchase of raw materials. Hollywood films, furthermore, often cover their costs in the domestic market and can, therefore, be profitably 'dumped' on Third World markets at very low prices.

While the Third World is inundated with North American films, TV series, popular music and news programmes, the First World receives precious little of the vast cultural production of the Third World, and what it does receive is usually mediated by transnational corporations. One telling index of this global Americanization is that even Third World airlines programme Hollywood comedies, so that a Thai Air jet en route to India, packed with Muslims, Hindus and Sikhs, screens 'Honey, I Shrunk the Kids' as the airline's idea of 'universal' fare. Another index of this phenomenon is that Brazilian popular music, widely recognized as among the world's most vibrant musical traditions, is rarely heard on radios in the US, while American top-forty music is constantly heard on radios in Brazil. These processes are not entirely negative, of course. The same multinational corporations that disseminate inane blockbusters and canned sitcoms also spread Afro-diasporic music such as reggae and rap around the globe. The problem lies not in the exchange, but in the unequal terms on which the exchange take place.

At the same time, the media imperialism thesis needs drastic re-tooling in the contemporary area. First, it is simplistic to imagine an active First World simply forcing its products on a passive Third World. Second, global mass culture does not so much replace local culture as co-exist with it, providing a cultural lingua franca. Third, the imported mass culture can also be indigenized, put to local use, given a local accent. Fourth, there are powerful reverse currents as a number of Third World countries (Mexico, Brazil, India, Egypt) dominate their own markets and even become cultural exporters. The Indian TV version of the 'Mahabharata' won a 90 per cent domestic viewer share during a three-year run; and Brazil's Rede Globo now exports its telenovelas to more than eighty countries around the world. One of the biggest TV hits in the new Russia is a venerable Mexican soap opera called 'Los Ricos Tambien Lloran' ('The Rich Also Cry'). We must distinguish, furthermore, between the ownership and control of the media – an issue of political economy – and the specifically cultural issue of the implications of this domination for the people on the receiving end. The 'hypodermic needle' theory is as inadequate for the Third World as it is for the First: everywhere spectators actively engage with texts and specific communities both incorporate and transform foreign influences. For Appadurai, the global cultural situation is now more interactive; the US is no longer the puppeteer of a world system of images, but only one mode of a complex transnational construction of 'imaginary landscapes'. In this new conjuncture, he argues, the invention of tradition, ethnicity and other identity markers becomes 'slippery, as the search for certainties is regularly frustrated by the fluidities of transnational communication'. Now the central problem becomes one of tension between cultural homogenization and cultural heterogenization, in which hegemonic tendencies, well-documented by Marxist analysts like Mattelart and Schiller, are simultaneously 'indigenized' within a complex; disjunctive global cultural economy. At the same time, we would add, discernible patterns of domination channel the 'fluidities' even of a 'multipolar' world; the same hegemony that unifies the world through global networks of circulating goods and information also distributes them according to hierarchical structures of power, even if these hegemonies are now more subtle and dispersed.

'Indigenous media'

Some of the paradoxes of the global–local become manifest in the recent practices of 'indigenous media': that is, the use of audiovisual technology (camcorders, VCRs) for the cultural and political purposes of indigenous or 'Fourth World' peoples. The phrase itself, as Faye Ginsburg points out, is oxymoronic, evoking both the self understanding of aboriginal groups and the vast institutional structures of TV and cinema. Within 'indigenous media' the producers are themselves the receivers, along with neighbouring communities and, occasionally, distant cultural institutions or festivals.

Indigenous media is an empowering vehicle for communities struggling against geographical displacement; ecological and economic deterioration; and cultural annihilation. Although occasionally supported by liberal governments or international support groups, these efforts are generally small-scale, low-budget and locally based. Indigenous film and video-makers confront what Ginsburg calls a 'Faustian dilemma': on the one hand, they use new technologies for cultural self-assertion; and on the other they spread a technology that might ultimately only foster their own disintegration. Analysts of indigenous media such as Ginsburg and Terence Turner see such work not as locked into a bound traditional world but rather as concerned with 'mediating across boundaries, mediating ruptures of time and history', and advancing the process of identity construction by negotiating 'powerful relationships to land, myth and ritual'. At times, the work goes beyond merely asserting an existing identity to become 'a means of cultural invention that refracts and re-combines elements from both the dominant and minority societies'. Indigenous media thus bypasses the usual anthropological hierarchy between the 'local' object of study/spectacle, on the one hand, and the global/universal anthropologist/filmmaker,

on the other. At the same time, 'indigenous media' should not be seen as a magical panacea either for the concrete problems faced by indigenous peoples or for the aporias of anthropology. Such work can provoke factional divisions within indigenous communities and can be appropriated by international media as facile symbols of the ironies of the postmodern age.

---

20 IRAN IN THE AGE OF SATELLITE COMMUNICATION
A. Mohammadi

Since 1988 the Iranian government has started to follow the development projects of the previous regime without the help of foreign consultants. Companies have been faced with the hardship of finding necessary hardware at inflated prices and without enough technical 'know-how'. The Ministry of PTT is now far behind the demands of today's market at a time of rapid development in communication services. Iran, with a population roughly over 60 million in 1995, had only 4 million telephones, and there is increasing demand. PTT, however, has been able to decrease waiting lists from five years to three years in the urban areas, and increase the capacity of the telephone services by one million. Consequently, there are now five million telephones in use in the entire country. PTT's aim is to double this number in the next five-year development plan (1994–95, 1999–2000). As a consequence of the communication technology explosion and rapid globalization of communication and information technology, PTT will be able to provide

From: Communication and the globalization process in the Developing World, by A. Mohammadi, in *International Communication and Globalization*, edited by A. Mohammadi *et al.*, University of Minnesota Press, 1997.

services for up to 10,000 mobile telephones in the first stage.

However, with the present population growth rate of 2.97 per cent and the extensive expansion of housing and urban development, the growing demand of telephone services will be much higher than PTT had previously estimated. At the present time, the demand is four times more than what is currently available. In the area of broadcasting, Iran is struggling to keep up with the rapid mode of development in the region. Technological change in the form of satellite, computer-based information technology and, most crucially, the liberalization of the market and market forces, altogether allowed the expansion of television programmes as well as other cultural commodities such as books, music disks, cassettes and video tapes.

During the previous regime, Iranian National Radio and Television was the second largest broadcasting institution in Asia; however, after the revolution in 1979, because of the devastating purge with its enforcement of an Islamic ethic and code of appearance and conduct in all aspects of life, the process of Islamization became a first priority. The outcome of this harsh process was undoubtedly to have a devastating effect on the quality of broadcast programmes on radio and television in particular, and throughout the media generally. The stricter Islamization of popular culture included the enforcement of veil-wearing for women on television, tough censorship of film and television programmes and a drastic change in media content. Instead of promoting a progressive Islam (enforcement of social justice, re-distribution of wealth, national health and equal access to higher education) and supporting domestic programming, Islamization brought the whole development of radio and television to a halt. The new cadre of Islamic television and radio producers, having no background in radio and television production and lacking 'know-how', had also a drastic impact on the quality and quantity of television and radio programmes. Approximately 47 per cent of radio and television employees are high-school graduates, with no experience or proper training in the industry (VVIR Report, 1994). The restriction of programme

contents of radio and television and eventually the change of broadcasting policy resulted in people no longer wanting to use Islamic radio and television.

Clandestine video clubs

The continuation of control over Iranian people's ways of life has caused further resistance to the total Islamization of culture. Gradually, a few entrepreneurs started to develop underground video clubs in Tehran and major provincial capital centres throughout the country. Young high-school graduates who were living in the south or Northwest of the country, started to make pirate video recordings of interesting films or television shows from neighbouring countries. These were further copied and hired out for a small fee to neighbours or friends. The business of video piracy gradually became a very lucrative business. Within a short period of time, it had developed to such an extent that the government unleashed a group of Bassijis in order to stop the penetration of Western culture into the Islamic Republic of Iran.

Originally formed in 1980 to help in the war with Iraq, Bassijis are groups of bearded men or boys between the ages of fourteen and twenty who are now fighting against Western culture and its effects on Islamic life in Iran. They have the authority to confiscate and arrest anyone who carries video-cassettes or audio-cassettes with Western contents. The sudden re-emergence of the threat of Bassijis crushed the hopes of many Iranians of an opening to the West after parliamentary elections removed extremist deputies who opposed the president and argued for free-market reforms. (*New York Times*, 21 July, 1993).

The protection of Islamic culture by force

Since the establishment of the Islamic Republic in Iran, the major concern of the government was the protection of Islamic culture from Western influence. Consequently, the policy-makers of the Islamic Republic have employed various measures of cultural protectionism in order to halt the flood of Western cultural commodities. Surveys show that all of the harsh cultural measures of protectionism have failed – video piracy and the sale of illegal satellite dishes are booming to an extent that the government is not able to control. This is particularly the case in the 1990s since the expansion of television satellite broadcasting has increased the potential access to international television. Iranians now have access to 129 television channels (Sorush, 1993). People gradually became more aware of the availability of alternative entertainment channels, and at the same time the government failed to see that international television, with a variety of interesting programmes on one hand and easy access by satellite dish on the other, made connection to international television a lucrative business for black-marketeers. Cultural policy-makers of the Islamic Republic were not aware of the internationalization of television and the rapid technological change in television broadcasting around the world; but even if they had been aware, they would not have been able to exercise control over such television programmes.

It was when the Islamic government realized it was powerless that it started to employ various methods of coercion. The fundamentalist group in the Islamic Council Assembly (Majlis) persuaded the religious seminaries of the Holy City of Qom to ask senior religious leaders to ban the use of satellite dishes on the grounds that the content of the international television programmes was ill-suited to the Muslim people of Iran. Among all the religious leaders only the very old and fragile Grand Ayatollah Arakey issued a communique based on the information that the fundamentalist group made available to him about banning the satellite dishes.

After this smart move, banning satellite dishes became the duty of the Islamic Council Assembly (ICA) which decreed that watching international television was 'a sinful act'. In December, 1994, the ICA, after a long debate in several sessions, finally made a law banning the import, manufacture and the use of satellite dishes. Meanwhile, in an interview, the head of radio and television of the Islamic Republic indicated that the Voice and Vision of the Islamic Republic (VVIR) was in the process of monitoring between fifty and sixty channels of inter-

national television, in order to select and dub some for re-broadcasting, pending the successful negotiation of copyright permission. He also gave priority to the privatization of television programmes and indicated that he had agreed to more than 750 private television production groups.

***

21 WAR AND TELEVISION
B. Cumings

If you have nose-cone cameras, laser-guided weapons, infra-red beams, terrain-mapping cruise missiles, AWACS surveillance aircraft, high-resolution spy satellites, Patriot anti-missile missiles, and a Telestrator to explain it all on TV, realizing 'ubiquitous orbital vision of enemy territory', what need have you for morality, or empathetic knowledge of the 'other'? If you have co-operative TV networks that limit debate to fleeting soundbites and a constrained, consensual politics, with anchors who patriotically rejoice in their own impotence and irrelevance to the very war they are reporting, who dutifully black themselves out and then celebrate (and help to create) a victorious national community, why worry about 'living room wars'?

Here television becomes not just an accomplice, but a two-way panopticon: from the battlefield, through the Pentagon, into the home and back again – ubiquitous orbital vision of the enemy and the living room, a magical Stealth weapon of our own making. The state succeeds in realizing the 'armed eye' Verrov imagined: 'I am the camera's eye. I am the machine which shows you the world as I alone see it.' And the TV Cyclops doesn't get to see the war: the medium is the only message.

Was this Fiske's 'reflexive', 'interactive' viewing experience? I think not. In Signatures of the Visible Jameson writes a great deal about how the photo

From: *War and Television*, by B. Cumings, Verso, 1992.

registers the event, and how film as a medium alters the event historically and dialectically, as 'the production process becomes an event in its own right and comes to include its own reception of it'. What was the event of the Gulf War? It cannot have been the war. It was not the photo or the film. It was television itself, but then we can only intuit its production processes, particularly in regard to a Pentavision shrouded in secrecy. All that is left, therefore, is 'the reception of it', the passive, easy-chair apprehension of an 'event' so many times removed as to be incomprehensible. This event than passes quickly as memory, because there is no recess in the brain to locate it as 'what I saw in the war', or as 'what I thought about it', but only as 'identity', as 'facsimile', as simulacrum: and thus it locates alongside M*A*S*H, Hogan's Heroes, and other military sitcoms last year's hit series.

The postmodern facsimile procreated and recombined and spawned again in the months after the war, too, while television memory still had its quickly disappearing half-life, with Desert Storm: The Miniseries on the 'Arts and Entertainment' network, CNN videocassettes on sale in supermarkets (videos of the videos as it were), video biographies of Stormin' Norman for rent in the video stores, comedian Jonathan Winters cloning Schwarzkopf in TV commercials (equally portly in his Desert Storm fatigues), and everyone but everyone draping themselves in the American logo, otherwise known as Old Glory.

The victory celebration in New York was distinctly postmodern, befitting our first postmodern war. First came theme music from the film 'Star Wars', then a sky battle between simulated Scuds and Patriots over the East River, than a colossal fireworks display inaugurated with the stirring tunes of 'Thus Spake Zarathustra', which Americans knew only as the music from Kubrick's '2001'. Our paper of record foregrounded the megashow with an entire separate section, featuring on the cover a wife welcoming her soldier-husband home, Old Glory hanging in the background and he tightly gripping in his fist a small reproduction of same. They were African-Americans, limbing a new multi-cultural and multi-ethnic ventriloquy that had its greater symbols in Supreme Court nominee Clarence Thomas and celebrated intellectuals Fukuyama and D'Souza: behold, even the disadvantaged ethnics celebrate America and above all its New Right climate (so who are you to protest this war)? Although The Times labelled this section an advertisement, it allowed many of its own Gulf War articles to be reproduced throughout.

Soon, however, it became last season's hit show, a mere summer re-run, and by the Fall it was another in a lengthening list of America's 'forgotten wars'. More troops came home, more parades, more hoopla, and television duly covered it – but in a curiously attenuated and slightly bored way. It all seemed vaguely anachronistic, like something consumed and digested already. Memory was receding with the speed of (television) light. We now can appreciate the new principles of television war: crank up the hoopla and open the television window, whereupon the hoopla is magnified and the war (because censored) is unseen, and the party of forgetting wins an instant victory. Who can remember the Falklands or Grenada or Panama? Does anyone still remember the Gulf War? Memory cannot form amid the unseen, the images cannot become 'indelible'. This, in essence, was the formula for the Gulf War.

---

22 THE CYBORG SELF
K. Robins and L. Levidow

The cyborg self can be characterized as follows: through a paranoid rationality, expressed in the machine-like self, we combine an omnipotent phantasy of self-control with fear and aggression directed against the emotional and bodily limitations of mere mortals. Through regression to a phantasy

From: Soldier, Cyborg, Citizen, by K. Robins and L. Levidow, in *Resisting the Virtual: The Culture and Politics of Information*, edited by J. Brook and I. A. Boal, City Lights Books, San Francisco, 1995.

of infantile omnipotence, we deny our dependency upon nature, upon our own nature, upon the 'bloody mess' of organic nature. We phantasize about controlling the world, freezing historical forces, and, if necessary, even destroying them in rage; we thereby contain our anxiety in the name of maintaining rational control (Levidow and Robins, 1989, p. 172).

Vision and image technologies mediate the construction of the cyborg self. The so-called Gulf War highlighted their role. In a very real sense, the screen became the scene of the war: the military encountered its enemy targets in the form of electronic images. The world of simulation somehow screened out the catastrophic dimension of the real and murderous attack.

As the Gulf War also brought home to us, it was not just military personnel who became caught up in this technological psychosis. The 'Nintendo war' involved and implicated home audiences, who took pleasure in watching the official images of war, often compulsively so. How was it possible to achieve this popular engagement? How were viewers locked into the war through their TV screens? How is the cyborg self generalized to the society at large?

The military cyborg

War converts fear and anxiety into perceptions of external threat; it then mobilizes defenses against alien and thing-like enemies. In this process, new image and vision technologies can play a central role. Combat is increasingly mediated through the computer screen. Combatants are involved in a kind of remotely exhilarating tele-action – tele-present and tele-engaged in the theatre of war, sanitized of its bloody reality. Killing is done 'at a distance', through technological mediation, without the shock of direct confrontation. The victims become psychologically invisible. The soldier appears to achieve a moral dissociation; the targeted 'things' on the screen do not seem to implicate him in a moral relationship.

Moreover, by fetishizing electronic 'information' for its precision and omniscience, military force comes to imagine itself in terms of the mechanical or cybernetic qualities that are designed into computers. The operator behaves as a virtual cyborg in the real-time, man-machine interface that structures military weapons systems. A new 'cyborg soldier' is constructed and programmed to fit integrally into weapons systems. By training for endurance, the soldier attempts to overcome biological limits, to better respond to real-time 'information' about enemy movements. By disciplining his 'mindware' and acting on the world through computer simulations, the soldier can remain all the more removed from the bloody consequences of his actions (Gray, 1989).

In the Gulf War, the cyborg soldier was complemented by new, 'smart' weapons. Although the view from a B-52 bomb bay already distanced the attacker from any human victims, new weapons rationalized military vision even further. Paradoxically, the Gulf video images gave us closer visual proximity between weapon and target, but at the same time greater psychological distance. The missile-nose view of the target simulated a super-real closeness that no human being could ever attain. This remote-intimate viewing extended the moral detachment that characterized earlier military technologies (Robins and Levidow, 1991).

It was the ultimate voyeurism: to see the target hit from the vantage point of the weapon. An inhuman perspective. Yet this kind of watching could sustain the moral detachment of earlier military technologies. Seeing was split off from feeling; the visible was separated from the sense of pain and death. Through the long lens the enemy remained a faceless alien. Her and his bodily existence was derealized (Robins and Levidow, 1991). Military attack took the form of thing-like relations between people and social relations between things, as if destroying inanimate objects. Perversely, war appeared as it was (Levidow, 1994).

In targeting and monitoring the attack, a real-time simulation depended upon prior surveillance of the enemy, conceptualized as a 'target-rich environment'. In the five months preceding the January, 1991, attack on Iraq, the US war machine devoted laborious 'software work' to mapping and plotting strategic installations there. The concept of 'legitimate military target' extended from military bases and the presidential palace, to major highways, factories, water supplies, and power stations. The basic means of survival for an entire population were reduced to 'targeting information'. Enemy threats – real or imaginary, human or machine – became precise grid locations, abstracted from their human context.

This computer simulation prepared and encouraged an omnipotence phantasy, a phantasy of total control over things. At the same time, the phantasized omnipotence required the containment of anxieties about impotence and vulnerability. The drive for electronic omniscience both evoked and contained anxiety about unseen threats. Designed to prepare real-time attacks, an electronic panopticon intensified the paranoiac features of earlier omnipotence phantasies. Through these technological attempts at ordering a disorderly world, uncertainty was rendered intolerable.

Any attempt to evade penetration by the West's high-tech panopticon simply confirmed the guilt and irrationality of the devious Arab enemy. Any optical evasion became an omnipresent, unseen threat of the unknown that must be exterminated. This paranoid logic complemented the US's tendency to abandon the Cold War rationales for its electronic surveillance and weaponry, now being redesigned explicitly for attacking the Third World (Klare, 1991).

In the Gulf episode, the US military portrayed the Iraqi forces as in hiding. When Saddam decided to avoid a direct military confrontation with the US coalition's air force, he was described as 'hunkering down', almost cheating the surveillance systems of the West's rational game plan (Levidow and Robins, 1991). Iraq's caution was personified as the backward Arab playing the coy virgin: 'Saddam's armies last week seemed to be enacting a travesty of the Arab motif of veiling and concealment . . . Saddam makes a fairly gaudy display of mystique' (*Time*, February 4th, 1991). Such language updated an earlier cultural stereotyping of the mysterious Orient (Said, 1985).

The racist logic emerged more clearly after the US massacre of civilians in the Amariya air-raid shelter. In this case, unusually, TV pictures showed us hundreds of shrouded corpses. In response, the US authorities insisted that they had recorded a precise hit on a 'positively identified military target'; they even blamed Saddam for putting civilians in the bunker (Kellner, 1992, pp. 297–309). The US continued to cite its surgical precision as moral legitimation – even though it was the precise targeting that allowed the missile to enter the ventilation shaft and incinerate all the people inside the shelter.

Constructing the viewer

This combined logic of fear and aggression is not just a military phenomenon. The Gulf War showed how much we, the home viewers of the Nintendo war, were also implicated in the logic of fear, paranoia, and aggression. As seen on network TV, the video-game images were crucial in recruiting support for the US-led attack.

The images evoked an audience familiarity with video games, thus offering a vicarious real-time participation. Video games in the wider culture are also about the mastery of anxiety and the mobilization of omnipotence phantasies; these psychic dimensions correspond to the cyborg logic of the military 'game'. The parallel with weapons systems runs deep; after all, some innovators have alternated between designing military and entertainment versions of interactive simulation technology.

Where the Gulf massacre publicly enacted phantasies, video games privatize them. The processes of anxiety and control are actively structured by the computer-video microworld, with its compulsive task of achieving 'perfect mastery' (Levidow and Robins, 1989, pp. 172–75). In particular, the video game is a psycho-dynamic process of projecting and managing internal threats: 'The actual performance required of us in the video game is like being permanently connected to broadcast television's exciting live event.' Video games elicit young boys' phantasies of exploring the damage done inside the mother's body; here the male 'fears both his own destructiveness and a fantasied retaliation from the object of his destructive fantasies'. (Skirrow, 1986, pp. 121–2).

Video games can thus be understood as a paranoiac environment that induces a sense of paranoia by dissolving any distinction between the doer and the viewer. Driven by the structure of the video game, the player is constantly defending himself, or the entire universe, from destructive forces. The play becomes a compulsive, pleasurable repetition of a life-and-death performance. Yet the player's anxiety can never be finally mastered by that vicariously dangerous play. He engages in a characteristic repetition, often described as 'video-game addiction' (pp. 129–33).

While the video game simulates a real-time event, the Gulf episode took such images as its reality. The Gulf War was 'total television', an entertainment form that merged military and media planning.

PART C2

THE GLOBAL IMPACT OF NEW TECHNOLOGIES

1 THE INFORMATION SOCIETY

D. Lyon

Any concept of the Information Society must be global in scope; informatization is nowhere a merely local process. The notion of a 'global village', however, should be treated with caution. The international telecomunication web of satellites, cables, and broadcasting frequencies seems far from producing the 'one world' hinted at by that phrase. Indeed, given the inter-connections between states, TNCs and military interests involved in IT, the 'global village' is a pathetically hollow concept. Recognition of the technological potential for worldwide development too frequently ignores or glosses over the deep-seated divisions and conflicts between countries possessing IT capabilities and others which do not.

The forces which created these divisions are found in the legacy of colonialism which, though formally abandoned on a large scale after the World War II, is perpetuated by economic ties of dependence. While some countries – such as India, Singapore and Nigeria – have managed to take advantage of their relationships with former colonial powers, and have begun building the informatics infrastructures which are crucial to future development, others find themselves rapidly falling behind.

The main reason for this is found in the way transnational corporations operate. However well-intentioned their policies, they tend to have a negative effect on the indigenous development of Third World countries. Their presence all too often benefits only metropolitan elites rather than rural subsistence farmers or migrant shanty town dwellers. They offer manufacturing assembly jobs, and Western-style clothes and television shows, but do little to transfer technical expertise which would enable receiving countries to develop their own industries and culture.

Operating outside the jurisdiction of either their own governments, or those of the less developed nations, they exploit to the full the new communications technologies. They may move capital with ever-increasing ease to where labour is cheapest, advertise wares and sell cultural commodities directly to consumers, and remotely monitor by satellite crops, minerals or fish and animals to the advantage of Western commodity markets.

Recognition of this process has prompted efforts at resistance and local development on the part of Third World countries. The UNESCO-sponsored call for a New World Information and Communication Order, alongside pressures for an International Economic Order and for Technical Co-operation among Developing Countries symbolizes this. American and British withdrawal from UNESCO equally symbolizes Western unwillingness to confront responsibly the realities of electronic colonialism.

From: *The Information Society: Issues and Illusions*, by D. Lyon, Polity Press, 1988.

Despite this, evidence from different sources is not overwhelmingly negative from the viewpoint of the developing countries. In 1982 a joint communique signed by Mexican and French government officials pledged to protect each others' national identity, especially where communication languages in information systems are concerned. They also noted that major data-bases and -banks used criteria not always appropriate to the needs of developing nations. Another example is the way in which transnational corporations have been successfully established in the Third World. 'Brazil's Petrobras and Kuwait Petroleum already rank among the world's top manufacturing companies, while Hyundai (Republic of Korea) has grown bigger than France's Michelin and Britain's Rio Tinto-Zinc.' Admittedly, they do not yet offer much by way of technology, and are far less sophisticated than their Western counterparts.

Within some Third World countries renewed energy is directed towards providing alternative forms of communication and information flows at a local grass-roots level. While this may appear to be a puny response to the might of the TNCs, the long-term effects may not be negligible. Indeed the efficacy of such projects could well be enhanced if combined with efforts in the North to restrict the steamrollering of cultures which is a current effect of TNC operation. Despite US attempts to shift the balance of communication more in its favour (while simultaneously upholding 'free-flow' principles) the UN General Assembly passed a resolution in 1982 which obliges satellite owners to obtain 'prior consent' before broadcasting messages over others' borders. How this call be enforced is another question.

The growth of informatics on a global scale means that what were once issues of 'communication and cultural autonomy' (and highly significant in their own right) now also crucially affect the chances of economic and political as well as cultural development in the nations of the Southern hemisphere. Analytical problems of this new and unfolding situation are chronically intertwined with ethical and policy issues of great complexity and urgency. Given the current debt crises, alongside famine and hardship for millions, and increased military capabilities of the South as well as East and West, ignoring the issues or withdrawing from the debate are options which are neither safe nor responsible.

---

2 SATELLITES AND CABLE: THE 'NEW MEDIA'

R. Negrine

The use of satellites for television traffic is perhaps the most obvious feature of the 'revolution' in communications in recent years. This traffic is carried on the 147 or so active satellites currently in geo-stationary orbit (Wilson, 1990, p. 46) and this is partly reflected in the explosion in the numbers of television services delivered by satellite, particularly across Europe. Whereas in 1988 one could identify around 35 to 40 satellite-delivered services across Europe, by 1993 that figure stood at nearer 130 (*Screen Digest*, May, 1993, p. 105; Cable and Satellite Europe, September, 1993). Not surprisingly, many of these services use imported material, usually but not always from the US. Though detailed breakdowns are notoriously difficult to construct, and very recent ones are unavailable, *Screen Digest* felt secure enough in its analysis to note that of the 122 new television services started in the last decade, the vast majority of these being satellite-delivered services, only four 'claimed to have no imported material, one has two per cent and three have 10 per cent imports'. But, as it pointed out, 'as many as 75 per cent of new services rely on imports to fill at least half their screen time ... almost half of new services use imports for upwards of 80 per cent of their output' (*Screen Digest*, 1992, p. 40).

The implications of this for cultural and political sovereignty, and cultural integrity in the European context, have been widely discussed elsewhere, as well

From: R. Negrine, Communications technologies: an overview, in *From International Communication and Globalization*, edited by A. Mohammadi, Sage, 1997.

as in the context of the Council of Europe and the European Commission (see, for example, Negrine and Papathanassopoulos, 1990; Schlesinger, 1991; Sepstrup, 1991). Interestingly, similar changes and concerns have also been identified in relation to the development of satellite services in the Pacific region. Rupert Murdoch's take-over of the Hong Kong-based Star TV on Asia Sat in 1993 not only increases his control of media operations world-wide, but also allows him to enter markets to which he had previously had no access. Asia Sat's footprint covers some 38 nations from Egypt to Japan and from Indonesia to Siberia: a diverse collection of nations which operate different regulatory systems to direct the development of their domestic media. But with the advent of Asia Sat, the sometimes restrictive practices and broadcasting regulations operated by some countries (for example Korea and China with respect to satellite television reception) may need to be adapted to meet the challenge of programming from the Murdoch satellite system. Will they permit their citizens to install dishes to view broadcast material from outside and so risk the danger of exposure to undesirable influences? Will they seek compromises with satellite operators so as to minimize points of conflict vis-à-vis content? And how will they generally cope with the media 'explosion'?

The exploitation of satellite communications by commercial interests parallels the exploitation of other communications facilities. In this respect, the concerns of commentators such as Schiller and Nordenstreng are not misplaced since they point to the ways in which the less developed countries are unable to make a significant impact on the development of international systems of communications. Though such countries are able to exert pressure on decision-making bodies like the International Telecommunications Union (ITU), they lack the means by which to alter the agenda, an agenda set by commercial bodies.

Writing about the latest round of meetings to determine world allocations of radio frequencies, Liching Sung observed that

WARC-92 was more heavily influenced by commercial concerns than any other radio conference at the ITU (International Telecommunications Union). It was the first such conference wherein commercial interests and private sector initiatives dominated the issues addressed. The increased role that the private sector plays in telecommunication policy making largely reflects the global telecommunications and privatization trends. (Sung, 1992, p. 625)

Indeed, any description of current developments in international communication supports this view. The next section identifies some of the contemporary changes which are re-fashioning the world of communications.

The promise of the new

One of the easiest ways of making sense of contemporary developments in national and international communications is by utilizing Noam's idea of 'plural networks'. Thus, a company's head office may want to communicate with its subsidiaries across the globe; companies may wish to communicate with their clients speedily across the globe; banks may need to transfer data to other banks swiftly; and academics may want to contact others in other continents. Such examples can be multiplied yet they all emphasize two things: the existence of functional relationships for the heavy users of communication networks, and the diminution of the importance of delivering universal services to everyone.

While it is comparatively simple to plan for a universal network providing basic communications for all, the prospect, and the advent, of 'plural networks' is problematic: they cannot be planned for in advance. Their development depends on many factors, including pricing, the availability of appropriate technologies, individual and company demand, and the like. One response to this regulatory dilemma – and it is a response implicit in the liberalization philosophy of the 1980s – has been to let the market decide the pattern of developments.

According to the consultancy discussion paper 'Evolution of the UK Communications Infrastructure', produced for the British Government, 'developments in basic communications technologies are driven by world-wide trends, and that cost trends are driven by world-wide production volumes of which the UK forms only a small part' (PA Consultancy, 1987, p. 10). Indeed, there may be cost disadvantages in any one particular country 'going it alone': such an action may, in fact, be undesirable, since it may be too costly, it may lead to incompatibility, and it may close foreign markets to domestic producers. Although this is not quite a full return to Adam Smith's 'hidden hand' of the market, there is a sense in which this assumption plays with the notion of global trends narrowing available options in part by setting international technical standards, and dictating the pace of change. Yet, as the discussion paper also admits, 'global trends' are related to developments in specific, and powerful, producer countries which can effect changes by, say, shifting the scale of investment in specific technologies (PA Consultancy, 1987, p. 14). Japan, which produces most of the world's fax machines, is thus in a critical position.

Evolution of the mobile telephone

Many of these factors are at play in the evolution of the mobile telephone. The mobile phone provides flexibility and mobility to all those who need to be in permanent contact with a specific base, or a clientele. Although it was a crucial accessory to the 1980s 'Yuppie', particularly if s/he was working in a financial institution, it soon spread across into other areas. There are currently some two million mobile phone users in the UK – 23 million world-wide (Taylor, 1993, p. 11) – and it is estimated that this will increase to 5.6 million, or 10 per cent of the population, by the year 2000 (Bannister, 1993, p. 11).

But it is short-sighted to conceive of the mobile phone only as a fashion accessory or as merely providing greater flexibility. The mobile phone represents an important shift in the nature of communications away from fixed connections. According to Paul Taylor, 'By the end of the decade half of all telephone calls world-wide are expected to originate or terminate on a mobile phone' (Taylor, 1993, p. 11).

This not only has significant implications for technical standards world-wide, but it also impacts on thinking about the provision of communication facilities for the future. As regards the former, it is interesting to note that European telecommunications organizations have agreed upon a common digital telecommunications standard (GSM) which will permit mobile communications across the continent. As regards the latter, it is now possible to conceive of an enormous expansion of mobile communication which side-steps the need for a full-wired network. Indeed, one project currently being developed by the American company Motorola, and named Iridium, proposes to use a series of low earth orbit satellites (LEOs) to provide a global mobile telecommunications network. The benefits of such a system for less developed countries which do not have an existing wired network are obviously great.

The mobile phone, like the fax machine – currently with an installed base of some 20–30 million (Harnett, 1992, p. 7) – and the 'plural networks', all belong to a compendium of change which has provided flexibility of communications for, in the first instance, the business community. Other interests, like the academic community, have hung on to the coat-tails of these developments.

The 'well-connected'

A roster of names and systems easily illustrates the greater flexibility which has become standard for the well-connected. These include:

- Electronic mail which allows for communication via computer, wire network and satellites.
- Value added networks (VANs) which combine telecommunications and computing facilities to re-sell services by, say, processing data.
- Video conferencing.
- Electronic data interchange (EDI), allowing companies to have immediate access to all transactions across their branches.
- Virtual private networks (VPNs) which have the semblance of a private communications network but which are based on leased circuits. Companies can thus link up with their subsidiaries without having to create and install their own private network.

● Very small aperture terminals (VSATs) represent the creation of private satellite communications networks whereby signals are received and transmitted via small terminals installed by specific corporations. Such systems of communication bypass the PTTs which usually regulate or control the uplinking of signals to satellites. One example would be the use of VSATs by Volkswagen to connect all its dealers in different countries.

While each of these represents technical developments which allow for greater communication flexibility, underlying them is a pattern which reinforces the view that systems of communication are fragmenting in ways which mirror or 'connect' functioning groupings. Whereas twenty years ago, every communication had to be made via the public network, today it is possible to make connections in a number of different ways. In this respect, the role of the traditional centralized posts and telecommunications entity as a gatekeeper is not only under attack, but under threat.

The advent of satellite communications offers a good example of this. The exploitation of the geostationary orbit, in which the satellite orbits above the earth at 12,000 miles and so has the appearance of remaining stationary, therefore offering continuous communications facilities, opened up the prospect of 'nations being able to speak unto nations', as well as of an instant and inexpensive way for a centre to reach a population spread thinly across a large land mass. The prospect of an ever-increasing stream of communication – of images and of voices – was, to many, very exciting. Others, however, viewed the matter quite differently. In an early discussion of the development of satellite communication, Herbert Schiller highlighted the emergence and consolidation of American interests and the implications of this for both developed and developing economies (Schiller, 1970). This general critique, and in particular its relevance to developing countries, was much more focused in a later piece on the implications of satellite communications. As Schiller and Nordenstreng were careful to stress:

the informational facilities and the flows that circulate, locally and internationally, are, with few and generally trifling exceptions, responsive to, if not at the disposal of, the power centres in the dominant national states ... in this historical period, then, the preservation of national sovereignty may be understood best as a step in the still larger struggle to break the domination of the world business system. (Schiller and Nordenstreng, 1979, p. 12)

the 'new international information order' ... is ultimately aiming at the 'decolonization' of information conditions in the developing countries, and in general advocating respect for the cultural and political sovereignty of all nations. (ibid., xiv)

3 MULTIMEDIA

M. Castells

Overall, in Europe as in America or in Asia, multimedia appear to be supporting, even in their early stage, a social/cultural pattern characterized by the following features.

First, widespread social and cultural differentiation, leading to the segmentation of the users/ viewers/readers/listeners. Not only are the messages segmented by markets following senders' strategies, but they are also increasingly diversified by users of the media, according to their interests, taking advantage of interactive capacities. As some experts put it, in the new system, 'prime time is my time.' The formation of virtual communities is but one of the expressions of such differentiation.

Second, increasing social stratification among the users. Not only will choice of multimedia be restrained to those with time and money to access,

From: *The Rise of the Network Society*, M. Castells, Blackwell, 1996.

and to countries and regions with enough market potential, but cultural/educational differences will be decisive in using interaction to the advantage of each user. The information about what to look for and the knowledge about how to use the message will be essential to truly experience a system different from standard customized mass media. Thus, the multimedia world will be populated by two essentially distinct populations: the interacting and the interacted, meaning those who are able to select their multi-directional circuits of communication, and those who are provided with a restricted number of pre-packaged choices. And who is what will be largely determined by class, race, gender, and country. The unifying cultural power of mass television (from which only a tiny cultural elite had escaped in the past) is now replaced by a socially stratified differentiation, leading to the co-existence of a customized mass media culture and an interactive electronic communication network of self-selected communes.

Third, the communication of all kinds of messages in the same system, even if the system is interactive and selective (in fact, precisely because of this), induces an integration of all messages in a common cognitive pattern. Accessing audiovisual news, education, and shows on the same medium, even from different sources, takes one step further the blurring of contents that was already taking place in mass television. From the perspective of the medium, different communication modes tend to borrow codes from each other: interactive educational programs look like video-games; newscasts are constructed as audiovisual shows; trial cases are broadcast as soap operas; pop music is composed for MTV; sports games are choreographed for their distant viewers, so that their messages becomes less and less distinguishable from action movies; and the like. From the perspective of the user (both as receiver and sender, in an interactive system), the choice of various messages under the same communication mode, with easy switching from one to the other, reduces the mental distance between various sources of cognitive and sensorial involvement. The issue at stake is not that the medium is the message: messages are messages. And because they keep their

distinctiveness as messages, while being mixed in their symbolic communication process, they blur their codes in this process, creating a multi-faceted semantic context made of a random mixture of various meanings.

Finally, perhaps the most important feature of multimedia is that they capture within their domain most cultural expressions, in all their diversity. Their advent is tantamount to ending the separation, and even the distinction, between audiovisual media and printed media, popular culture and learned culture, entertainment and information, education and persuasion. Every cultural expression, from the worst to the best, from the most elitist to the most popular, comes together in this digital universe that links up in a giant, a historical supertext, past, present, and future manifestations of the communicative mind. By so doing, they construct a new symbolic environment. They make virtuality our reality.

---

4 A CRITIQUE OF AT&T'S 'LEARNING CIRCLES'
G. Dimitriadis and G. Kamberelis

Appadurai's second scape is the technoscape, or 'the global configuration . . . ever fluid, of technology, and of the fact that technology, both high and low, both mechanical and informational, now moves at high speeds across various kinds of previously impervious boundaries.' Indeed, we have entered an information age, a time when physical labor is being elbowed out by technology in an increasingly competitive global sphere. Schools – in their efforts to prepare citizen-workers for their societal roles and

From: Shifting terrains: mapping education within a global landscape by G. Dimitriadis and G. Kamberelis, in *Globalization and the Changing US City*, edited by D. Wilson, The Annals of the American Academy of Political and Social Science, Sage Periodicals Press, May 1997.

functions – have tried to respond to these economic shifts. Corporations have intervened in such efforts, forging coalitions with schools to help them prepare students for the demands of international competition. In fact, Education is becoming increasingly linked with business interests as institutions are embracing – often as a last resort – the promise of Technology in an uncritical fashion.

A key example here is AT&T's Learning Circles (part of the AT&T Learning Network). According to Margaret Riel, 'a Learning Circle is a small number of classrooms that interact electronically to accomplish a shared goal. Each classroom in a Learning Circle is a team that contributes to the overall end product [of any project]. Connecting students from different geographic, social and cultural regions creates a rich diversity of knowledge, skills, and abilities not found in single classrooms'. Learning Circles foreground many of the skills that students will need to develop for information-age success, including small-group work, collaboration and interdependence. Yet the discourse of AT&T's Learning Circles betrays a disjunctive mingling of Progressive Era educational rhetoric and post-industrial rhetoric. Learning Circles capitalize on liberal-humanistic discourse about shared ideals to promote an almost unbridled faith in technology to overcome cultural, social, political and economic differences. Yet Riel stresses that the manipulation of information allows participants to be faceless, to focus on tasks instead of on personalities or cultures. She notes that the Learning Circles' 'human and technical support systems', which help students with their work, are invisible to other participants, making it 'easier for diverse groups to work together'.

There is something terribly wrong with this picture. Making various 'support systems' invisible as individuals reach out to share perspectives and solve problems divorced from social and political contexts also functions to blur or mask questions of power and its effects. For example, what role has AT&T played in creating the global cultural economy that schools must now prepare students to face? Shifting technoscapes have made companies globally competitive and able to access the cheapest labour possible on a global scale. This labour is, paradoxically, often

demobilized by such processes. Riel optimistically notes that 'physical walls, special needs, socio-economic barriers and geographic distances are not absolute boundaries'. Yet such constraints, most especially socio-economic and geographic ones, are becoming more profound for those in increasingly segregated and economically depressed inner cities. Global economic processes, enabled through such technologies, have also created a plethora of minimum-wage service sector jobs for those stuck in these areas. These constraints are real and cannot be wished away by evoking the utopian potential of technology and its ability to constitute virtual communities. Such rhetoric hides some of the most pressing questions facing educators today – basic questions about equity and access.

While providing technological support to education programs and projects like AT&T's Learning Circles ... also divert attention from corporate investments in a radically shifting economic terrain. One effect of this diversion is that companies can draw students into a constructed set of cultural and economic circumstances as if these circumstances were both neutral and inevitable. In a critique of the inclusion of technology in the National Curriculum of Wales and England, Naz Rassool notes that 'the continuing neutral treatment of technology as a subject within the National Curriculum framework neatly avoids addressing those impacts of technology that include dominant power interests'. Although education's engagement with technoscapes through the appropriation and use of information technologies has indeed yielded positive outcomes for some students, these technologies have typically been constructed as deceptively neutral. Most efforts to integrate technology into the curriculum have neither acknowledged nor appreciated the ways in which these same technologies are part of a larger hegemonic project that is restructuring the economies in and through which these students will structure their lives. Technology, and (concurrently) the bottom-line interests of multinational corporations (as they are inflected through technology), are naturalized, thus appearing as immutable dimensions of reality. In turn, people feel increasingly disenfranchised, powerless to contest these seemingly immanent forces. The heightened political apathy of students on campuses across the nation is only one example of how this particular ideology has affected popular consciousness.

---

5 'CYBER INEQUITIES'

Z. Eisenstein

Cyberspace is accessible to only a small fraction of people outside the West. 84 per cent of computer users are found in North America and Northern Europe. 69 per cent are male, average age thirty-three, with an average household income of $59,000. The top twenty Internet-connected computer countries are significantly homogeneous. They are First World, except for Singapore. Finland leads the list, followed by Iceland, the US, Norway and Australia, with Sweden, Switzerland and the Netherlands not far behind. One-third of Finland's people carry mobile phones, many of which have e-mail and World Wide Web (WWW) access.

The racial elitism of cyber communities is palpable. In the US, only 20 per cent of African-Americans have home computers, and a mere 3 per cent subscribe to online services. Rather than a highway, the Internet seems like a segregated private road. This newest form of 'white flight' has white men retreating to their computer screens. In the 1950s, highways connecting the city to the suburbs were built to allow escape. In the 1990s it is digitised wiring.

Approximately 80 per cent of the world's population still lacks basic telecommunications access. Nevertheless, more than 160 countries outside North America and Western Europe have links to the Internet, with some 20–30 million users. Asia has

From: *Global Obscenities: Patriarchy, Capitalism and the Lure of Cyberfantasy*, by Z. Eisenstein, New York University Press, 1998.

1.5 million users, two-thirds of whom are in Japan. There are more telephone lines in Manhattan than in all of sub-Saharan Africa. The US has thirty-five computers per hundred people, Japan has sixteen; Taiwan has nine. Ghana, on the other hand, has one computer per thousand people. In France, where there has been open hostility to the global market, fewer than 15 per cent of homes have PCs and fewer than 1 per cent of them are connected to the Internet.

The infrastructure of Information Technology is spotty at best. Nearly fifty countries have fewer than one telephone line per hundred people. In Bangladesh, a computer costs as much as half a year's average salary and a modem costs more than a cow. In China, PCs priced at $2,000 are more than four times the average urban annual income of $480. The PC, modem, software and monthly access fee needed to access the Internet remain out of reach for most. Only 150,000 Chinese – barely one in ten thousand – are actually wired. On average, there are seventeen Chinese for every phone line. In contrast, 35 per cent of US families have a PC at home, and 30 million people were on-line in 1997. This means that about 115 of US households subscribe to an on-line service and about 16 per cent have modems. Many people still cannot afford a computer and the twenty dollar monthly access fee. Electronic information constructs an information hierarchy of haves, have-nots, and have-lates, which mediates access, privilege and power. Nevertheless, 66 million users are projected for the year 2000.

Cyber-discourse fashions an imaginary vision of an interconnected world that is only part true. The phrase 'World Wide Web' images the world about as accurately as the baseball phrase 'The World Series'. In the latter case, only US baseball teams compete. In the former case, only about 40 per cent of the world's population even has daily access to electricity.

'Cyber imaginings'

In spite of the inequity, and maybe even because of it, cyberspace functions as a new imaginary location of escape, promise, and profit. Cyberspace becomes a whole new arena to conquer where privatization openly seduces some, but silently punishes those who are excluded.

'Cyber-imaginings' allow communication with people in other countries, while one's neighbors can be ignored. Speech takes place between people who have no initial responsibility for one another. New rules define the modes of interaction. E-mail allows one to communicate with others on one's own terms, according to one's own needs of time and availability. One can ignore e-mail correspondence, respond at will, send and receive messages at any time. E-mail also allows mobile populations easy connection to their original homelands, a kind of alternative homeland and multiple identity.

Corporate and government voices relentlessly hype the Internet. Clinton and Gore repeat, mantra-like, their commitment to Internet availability and access. Meanwhile, poverty rates soar and much of the working poor are forced to rely on understocked food pantries to feed their families. Public schools and public libraries are downsized along with the tax base that once subsidized the purchase of computers at these locations.

It could cost upwards of $100 billion dollars to wire and equip US schools. Clearly this is a 'boon-doggle' for computer corporations, but it is less clear if computerization is what public schools today need most. Studies are beginning to challenge the relationship between cognitive skills and computer use. Some educators argue that there is a loss of creativity and cognitive development as a result of learning through computer programs. These educators say that class size should be reduced and teachers' salaries be increased before students go online.

Conflicting interests between 'cybertech' and people's access mirror the tensions between the profit motive and people's needs. The transnational corporate commitment to privatization stands in stark contrast to the seductive democratic technological potential of computer-mediated dialogue. Online anonymity can challenge and/or displace established sexual/racial hierarchies; gender swapping can liberate teenagers from traditional sex-role expectations; cyberskills can reposition people in the world; and e-mail can side-step authoritarian regimes. Obviously,

the outcome of this struggle between transnational capital's control of telecom-cyber networks and the democratic potentials of cyber-technology is not yet decided.

---

6 THE VILLAGE OF IBIECA

R. E. Sclove

During the early 1970s running water was installed in the houses of Ibieca, a small village in north eastern Spain. With pipes running directly to their homes, Ibiecans no longer had to fetch water from the village fountain. As families gradually purchased washing machines, fewer women gathered to scrub laundry by hand at the village washbasin. Arduous tasks were rendered technologically superfluous, but village social life unexpectedly changed. The public fountain and washbasin, once scenes of vigorous social interaction, became nearly deserted. Men began losing their sense of easy familiarity with the children and donkeys that formerly helped them haul water. Women stopped gathering at the wash-basin to intermix scrubbing with politically empowering gossip about men and village life. In hindsight this emerges as a crucial step in a broader process through which Ibiecans came to relinquish the strong bonds – with one another, animals, and the land – that had knit them into a community (Harding, 1984). Painful in itself, such loss of community carries a specific political risk as well: as social ties weaken, so does a people's capacity to mobilize for political action (Bowles and Gintis, 1986).

Like Ibiecans, we acquiesce in seemingly benign or innocuous technological changes. Ibiecans opted

---

From: Making technology democratic, by R. E. Sclove, in *Resisting the Virtual Life: the Culture and Politics of Information*, edited by J. Brook and I. A. Boal, City Lights Press, San Francisco, 1995.

for technological innovations promising convenience, productivity, and economic growth. But they didn't reckon on the hidden costs: deepening inequality, social alienation, and community dissolution and political disempowerment.

Technology as social structure

A crucial step toward grasping the need for a democratic politics of technology thus involves learning to see technologies as more than mere tools for accomplishing narrowly defined objectives. Technologies also represent an important kind of social structure. By 'social structure' I mean the background features that help define and regulate social life. Familiar examples include laws, dominant political and economic institutions (such as legislatures, courts, and corporations), and systems of cultural belief. All of these – like technologies – qualify as social structures by virtue of being social creations that profoundly influence one another's evolution, as well as the course of history and texture of daily life. In so doing, social structures shape and help constitute a society's fundamental political relationships and processes. To appreciate the subtle means through which technologies can exert structural influence, reconsider Ibieca.

First, upsetting Ibieca's traditional pattern of water use compromised important means through which the village perpetuated itself as a self-conscious community. Thus technologies indeed help structure social relations. But notice that technologies tend to do this independently of their nominally intended (or 'focal') purposes. We do not normally regard fountains, pipes (or, for that matter, microwave ovens, hypodermic syringes, garden hoses, or numerically controlled machine tools) as devices that shape patterns of human relationship, but that is nevertheless one of their pervasive latent (or 'non-focal') tendencies.

Second, clusters of focally unrelated technologies often interact to produce structural results that no one technology would produce alone. In Ibieca, introducing water pipes added incentive for also replacing donkeys with tractors in field work. (The fewer tasks a donkey is asked to perform, the less

economical it is to maintain it.) This eliminated any remaining practical use for donkeys, while increasing villagers' dependence on outside jobs for the cash needed to finance and operate their new tractors and washing machines. Thus it's not enough to consider just one kind of technology at a time (water pipes); we must analyze all the different artefacts, practices, and systems that jointly comprise a society's entire technological order (water pipes, washing machines, and tractors as an interdependent system).

Design criteria for democratic technologies

The following outline presents some criteria for distinguishing among technologies based on their structural compatibility with democracy. I characterize these criteria as 'provisional' because this list is neither complete nor definitive. Rather, I hope to provoke political discussion that can gradually issue in a broadened and improved set of criteria.

- Toward democratic community:
  A. Seek balance between communitarian/cooperative, individualized, and intercommunity technologies. Avoid technologies that establish authoritarian social relationships.
- Toward democratic work:
  B. Seek a diverse array of flexibly schedulable, self-actualizing technological practices. Avoid meaningless, debilitating, or otherwise autonomy-impairing technological practices.
- Toward democratic politics:
  C. Seek technologies that can help enable disadvantaged individuals and groups to participate fully in social and political life. Avoid technologies that support illegitimately hierarchical power relations between groups, organizations, or polities.
- To help secure democratic self-governance:
  D. Restrict the distribution of potentially adverse consequences (for example, environmental or social harms) to within the boundaries of local political jurisdictions.
  E. Seek relative local economic self-reliance. Avoid technologies that promote dependency and loss of local autonomy.

F. Seek technologies (including an architecture of public space) compatible with globally aware, egalitarian political decentralization and federation.

- To help perpetuate democratic social structures:
  G. Seek ecological sustainability. Avoid technologies that are ecologically destructive of human health, survival, and the perpetuation of democratic institutions.
  H. Seek local technological flexibility and global technological pluralism.

As the outline indicates, each of these criteria is intended to have some direct and important bearing upon one of strong democracy's three general institutional requirements: democratic community, democratic work, or democratic politics (for examples illustrating the practical significance of these criteria, see Sclove, 1993). In making technological decisions, there are of course many other issues that we might want to address. But we should attend first and especially to democracy because it enables us to freely and fairly decide what other considerations to take into account in our technological (and nontechnological) decision making. Until we do this, current technologies will continue to hinder the advancement of other social objectives.

---

7 THE 'DIGITAL UNDERGROUND'

T. Jordan and P. Taylor

The nature of the hacking community needs to be explored in order to grasp the social basis that produces hacking as a facet of computer networks. The figures given previously and the rise of the World Wide Web hack, offering as it does both

From: The sociology of hackers, by T. Jordan, and P. Taylor, in *The Sociological Review*, Vol. 46, No. 4, Blackwell Publishers (for Keele University), November 1998.

spectacular publicity and anonymity, point to the endemic nature of hackers now that world-wide computer networks are an inescapable reality. Hackers show that living in a networked world means living in a risky world. The community found by this research articulates itself in two key directions. First, there are a number of components that are the subject of ongoing discussion and negotiation by hackers with other hackers. In defining and re-defining their attitudes to technology, secrecy, anonymity, membership change, male dominance and personal motivations, hackers create an imagined community. Second, hackers define the boundaries of their community primarily in relation to the computer security industry. These boundaries stress an ethical interpretation of hacking because it can be difficult to clearly distinguish the activities or membership of the two communities. Such ethics emerge most clearly through analogies used by members of each community to explain hacking.

Hackers are often pathologized as obsessed, isolated young men. The alien nature of online life allows people to believe hackers more easily communicate with machines than humans, despite hackers' constant use of computers to communicate with other humans. Fear of the power of computers over our own lives underpins this terror. The very anonymity that makes their community difficult to study, equally makes hackers an easy target for pathologizing. For example, Gilboa's experience of harassment outlined earlier led her to pathologize hackers, suggesting work must be done exploring the characteristics of hackers she identified – such as lack of fathers or parental figures, severe depression and admittance to mental institutions (Gilboa, 1996, p. 112). Similar interpretations of hackers are offered from within their community: 'All the hackers I know in France have (or have had) serious problems with their parents' (Condat, hacker, interview). Our research strongly suggests that psychological interpretations of hackers that individualize hackers as mentally unstable are severely limited because they miss the social basis of hacking. Gilboa's experience is no less unpleasant but all the more understandable when the male dominance of the hacking community is grasped.

The fear many have of the power of computers over their lives easily translates into the demonization of those who manipulate computers outside of society's legitimate institutions. Journalist Jon Littman once asked hacker Kevin Mitnick if he thought he was being demonized because new and different fears had arisen with society becoming increasingly dependent on computers and communications. Mitnick replied: 'Yeah. . . . That's why they're instilling fear of the unknown. That's why they're scared of me. Not because of what I've done, but because I have the capability to wreak havoc' (Mitnick, cited in Littman, 1996, p. 205). The pathological interpretation of hackers is attractive because it is based on the fear of computers controlling our lives. What else could someone be but mad, if s/he is willing to play for fun on computer systems that control air traffic, dams or emergency phones? The interpretation of hackers as members of an outlaw community that negotiates its collective identity through a range of clearly recognizable resources does not submit to the fear of computers. It gains a clearer view of hackers, who have become the nightmare of information societies despite very few documented cases of upheaval caused by hackers. Hacking cannot be clearly grasped unless fears are put aside to try and understand the community of hackers, the digital underground. From within this community, hackers begin to lose their pathological features in favour of collective principles, allegiances and identities.

8 THE NETWORK

B. Gates

The network, and the computer-based machines connected to it, will form society's new playground, new workplace, and new classroom. It will replace

From: *The Road Ahead*, by B. Gates, Viking Press, 1995.

physical tender. It will subsume most existing forms of communication. It will be our photo album, our diary, our boom box. This versatility will be the strength of the network, but it will also mean we will become reliant on it.

Reliance can be dangerous. During the New York City blackouts in 1965 and 1977, millions of people were in trouble – at least for a few hours – because of their dependence on electricity. They counted on electric power for light, heat, transport and security. When electricity failed, people were trapped in elevators, traffic lights stopped working, and electric water pumps quit. Anything really useful is missed when you lose it.

A complete failure of the information highway is worth worrying about. Because the system will be thoroughly decentralized, any single outage is unlikely to have a widespread effect. If an individual server fails, it will be replaced and its data restored. But the system could be susceptible to assault. As the system becomes more important, we will have to design in more redundancy. One area of vulnerability is the system's reliance on cryptography – the mathematical locks that keep information safe.

None of the protection systems that exist today, whether steering wheel locks or steel vaults, are completely fail-safe. The best we can do is make it as difficult as possible for somebody to break in. Despite popular opinions to the contrary, computer security has a very good record. Computers are capable of protecting information in such a way that even the smartest hackers can't get at it readily unless someone entrusted with information makes a mistake. Sloppiness is the main reason computer security gets breached. On the information highway there will be mistakes, and too much information will get passed along. Someone will issue digital concert tickets that prove to be forgeable, and too many people will show up. Whenever this sort of thing happens, the system will have to be reworked and laws may have to be revised.

Because both the mysteries privacy and the security of digital money depend on encryption, a breakthrough in mathematics or computer science that defeats the cryptographic system could be a disaster. The obvious mathematical breakthrough would be development of an easy way to factor large prime numbers. Any person or organization possessing this power could counterfeit money, penetrate any personal, corporate or governmental file, and possibly even undermine the security of nations, which is why we have to be so careful in designing the system. We have to ensure that if any particular encryption technique proves fallible, there is a way to make an immediate transition to an alternate technique. There's a little bit of inventing still to be done before we have that perfected. It is particularly hard to guarantee security for information you want kept private for a decade or more.

Loss of privacy is another major concern about the highway. A great deal of information is already being gathered about each of us, by private companies as well as by government agencies, and we often have no idea how it is used or whether it is accurate. Census Bureau statistics contain great amounts of detail. Medical records, driving records, library records, school records, court records, credit histories, tax records, financial records, employment reviews, and charge-card bills all profile you. The fact that you call a lot of motor cycle shops, and might be susceptible to motor cycle advertising, is commercial information that a telephone company theoretically could sell. Information about us is routinely compiled into direct-marketing mailing lists and credit reports. Errors and abuses have already fostered legislation regulating the use of these databases. In the US, you are entitled to see certain kinds of information stored about you, and you may have the right to be notified when someone looks at it. The scattered nature of information protects your privacy in an informal way, but when the repositories are all connected together on the highway, it will be possible to use computers to correlate it. Credit data could be linked with employment records and sales transaction records to construct an intrusively accurate picture of your personal activities.

As more business is transacted using the highway and the amount of information stored there accrues, governments will consciously set policies regarding privacy and access to information. The network itself will then administer those policies, ensuring that a doctor does not get access to a patient's tax records, a government auditor is not able to look at a taxpayer's scholastic record, and a teacher is not permitted to browse a student's medical record. The potential problem is abuse, not the mere existence of information.

We now allow a life insurance company to examine our medical records before determining whether it chooses to insure our mortality. These companies may also want to know if we indulge in any dangerous pastimes, such as hang gliding, smoking, or stock car racing. Should an insurer's computer be allowed to examine the information highway for records of our purchases to see if there are any that might indicate risky behaviour on our part? Should a prospective employer's computer be allowed to examine our communications or entertainment records to develop a psychological profile? How much information should a federal state, or city agency be allowed to see? What should a potential landlord be able to learn about you? What information should a potential spouse have access to? We will need to define both the legal and practical limits of privacy.

---

9 THE INFORMATION SUPERHIGHWAY: LATEST BLIND ALLEY?

H. I. Schiller

American experience with the waves of new communication technology in the twentieth century reveals at least two characteristics present over the decades: one is the overblown promise greeting its appearance; the other is the rapid assumption by corporate custodians of the new instrumentation and processes for commercial ends, that is, profit making. The high expectations for the new means of transmitting

From: *Information Inequality: The Deepening Social Crisis in America*, by H. I. Schiller, Routledge, 1996.

messages and images are invariably thwarted by the institutional arrangements that quickly enfold the new instrumentation. This has been the fate, successively, of radio, television, cable, satellite communication and, still under way, digitized electronic transmission.

In the 1990s the new and advanced information technologies – computers, fiber optics, personal communications products, cyberspace networks are extolled as 'empowering'. They are described as the instrumentation that will provide individual autonomy and, no less important, that they will afford a competitive edge to those who employ them. It is surely a historical irony that as substantive content disappears in much of the media product, a varied range of media technologies are coming on-line (literally), to provide means of producing and transporting a growing volume of new media products to audiences.

---

10 THE INTERNET

H. Besser

Producers vs. Consumers

On the Internet anyone can be an information provider or an information consumer. On the information superhighway most people will be relegated to the role of information consumer.

Because services like movies-on-demand will drive the technological development of the information superhighway, movies' need for high bandwidth into the home and only narrow bandwidth coming back out will likely dominate. Metaphorically, this will be like a ten-lane highway coming into the home, with

From: Internet to information superhighway, by H. Besser, in *Resisting the Virtual: the Culture and Politics of Information*, edited by J. Brook and I. A. Boal, City Lights Press, San Francisco, 1995.

only a tiny path leading back out – just wide enough to take a credit card number or to answer multiple-choice questions.

Information vs. Entertainment

The telecommunications industry continues to insist that functions such as entertainment and shopping will be the driving forces behind the construction of the information superhighway. Yet there is a growing body of evidence that suggests that consumers want more information-related services, and would be more willing to pay for these than for movies-on-demand, video games, or home-shopping services.

If people say they desire informational services more than entertainment and shopping (and say that they're willing to pay for it), why does the telecommunications industry continue to focus on plans oriented toward entertainment and shopping? Because the industry believes that, in the long run, this other set of services will prove more lucrative. After all, there are numerous examples in other domains of large profits made from entertainment and shopping services but very few such examples from informational services.

Mass Audience

A significant amount of material placed on the Internet is designed to reach a single person, a handful of people, or a group of less than 1,000. Yet commercial distributors planning to use the information superhighway will have to reach tens (or more likely hundreds) of thousands of users merely to justify the costs of mounting multimedia servers and programmes. This will inevitably result in a shifting away from the Internet's orientation towards small niche audiences; the information superhighway will be designed for a mass audience (and even niche markets will be mass markets created by joining enough small regional groups together to form a national or international mass market).

As it becomes easier and easier to obtain images and documents on line in the home, it is possible that people will download and copy these somewhat indiscriminately. The advent of the photocopy machine led researchers to become less discriminating and to copy articles of only marginal interest. This led to a glut of paper in researchers' homes and offices. Word processing led to the generation of paper drafts each time a slight change to the text was made. In a similar way, on-line access to full-text documents and digital images may lead people to accumulate items of only marginal interest. And the proliferation of images (both those available and those accumulated) may lead to a reduction in meaning and context for all of them. This leveling effect (floating in an infinite sea of images) is a likely result of information overload – we are already seeing traces of it as people are caught in the web of the Internet, not being able to discriminate between valuable and worthless information, and not seeing the context of any given piece of information.

In a way, the on-line environment of the future is the logical extension of postmodernism. As in previous incarnations (like MTV), most of our images come from the media. The images are reprocessed and recycled. In the postmodern tradition, all images (and viewpoints) have equal value; in an on-line world they're all ultimately bits and bytes. Everything is ahistorical and has no context.

---

11 THE ORIGINS OF THE INTERNET

M. Castells

The Internet network is the backbone of global computer-mediated communication (CMC) in the 1990s, since it gradually links up most networks. In the mid-1990s it connected 44,000 computer networks and about 3.2 million host computers world-wide with an estimated 25 million users, and it was expanding rapidly. According to a survey of

From : *The Rise of the Network Society*, M. Castells, Blackwell 1996.

the US conducted in August, 1995, by Nielsen Media Research, 24 million people were Internet users, and 36 million had access to it. However, a different survey, conducted by the Emerging Technologies Research Group in November–December 1995, evaluated the number of Americans that used Internet regularly at only 9.5 million, of whom two-thirds signed on only once a week. Yet the projections were for the number of users to double in a year. Overall, while there is wide disagreement about how many users are currently connected to Internet, there is a convergence of opinion that it has the potential to explode into hundreds of millions of users by early in the twenty first century. Experts consider that, technically, Internet could one day link up 600 million computer networks. This is to be compared with its size in earlier stages of development: in 1973, there were 25 computers in the network; through the 1970s, it could only support 256 computers; in the early 1980s, after substantial enhancement, it was still limited to about 25 networks with only a few hundred primary computers and a few thousand users. The history of Internet's development and of the convergence of other communication networks into the Net provides essential material to understanding the technical, organizational and cultural characteristics of this Net, thus opening the way for assessing its social impact.

It is indeed a unique blending of military strategy, big science co-operation, and countercultural innovation. At the origins of Internet is the work of one of the most innovative research institutions in the world: the US Defense Department's Advanced Research Projects Agency (DARPA). When in the late 1950s the launching of the first Sputnik alarmed the American high-tech military establishment, DARPA undertook a number of bold initiatives, some of which changed the history of technology and ushered in the information age on a grand scale. One of these strategies, developing an idea conceived by Paul Baran at Rand Corporation, was to design a communications system invulnerable to nuclear attack. Based on packet-switching communication technology, the system made the network independent of command and control centres, so that message units would find their own routes along the network, being reassembled in coherent meaning at any point in the network.

When, later on, digital technology allowed the packaging of all kinds of messages, including sound, images, and data, a network was formed that was able to communicate all kinds of symbols without using control centres. The universality of digital language and the pure networking logic of the communication system created the technological conditions for horizontal, global communication. Furthermore, the architecture of this network technology is such that it is very difficult to censor or control it. The only way to control the network is not to be into it, and this is a high price to pay for any institution or organization once the network becomes pervasive and channels all kinds of information around the world.

But this is only one side of the story; because in parallel to the efforts by the Pentagon and 'Big Science' to establish a universal computer network with public access, within 'acceptable use' norms, a sprawling computer counter-culture emerged in the US, often mentally associated with the aftershocks of the 1960s movements, in their most libertarian/utopian version. An important element of the system, the modem, was one of the technological breakthroughs emerging from the pioneers of this counter-culture, originally labelled 'the hackers' before the term took on its malignant connotation. The modem was invented by two Chicago students, Ward Christensen and Randy Suess, in 1978, when they were trying to find a system to transfer microcomputer programs to each other through the telephone to avoid travelling in the Chicago winter between their distant locations. In 1979 they diffused the X-modem protocol that allowed computers to transfer files directly without going through a host system. And they diffused the technology at no cost, because their purpose was to spread communication capabilities as much as possible. Computer networks that were excluded from ARPANET (reserved to elite Science universities in its early stages) found their way to start communicating with each other on their own. In 1979, three students at Duke University and University of North Carolina, not included in ARPANET, created a modified version of the Unix protocol that made it possible to link up computers over the regular telephone line. They used it to start a forum of on-line computer discussion, Usenet, that quickly became one of the first large-scale electronic conversation systems. The inventors of Usenet News also diffused freely their software in a leaflet circulated at the Unix users conference.

Ironically, this counter-cultural approach to technology had a similar effect to the military-inspired strategy of horizontal networking: it made available technological means to whoever had the technical knowledge and a computing tool, the PC, which soon would start a spectacular progression of increasing power and decreasing price at the same time. The advent of personal computing and the communicability of networks spurred the development of Bulletin Board Systems (BBS), first in the US, then world-wide: the electronic protests to the Tiananmen Square events in China in 1989 via computer networks operated by Chinese students abroad were one of the most notorious manifestations of the potential of the new communication devices. Bulletin Board Systems did not need sophisticated computer networks, just PCs, modems, and the telephone line. Thus, they became the electronic notice-boards of all kinds of interests and affinities, creating what Howard Rheingold names 'virtual communities'.

The Internet today

Thousands and thousands of such micro-networks exist today around the world, covering the whole spectrum of human communication, from politics and religion to sex and research. By the mid-1990s, the majority of them were also connected to Internet, but they were keeping their own identity and enforcing their own rules of behavior. One of the most important rules was (and is) the rejection of the intrusion into BBS of undeclared commercial interests. While it is considered legitimate to create commercial BBS or business-oriented networks, it is not legitimate to invade cyberspaces created for other purposes. The sanction against intruders is devastating: thousands of hostile messages 'flame' the bad electronic citizen. When the fault is particularly serious, huge files are dumped onto the guilty system, bringing it to a halt, and usually provoking the expulsion of the culprit from the network of its host computer. This electronics grass-roots culture marked for ever the evolution and use of the net. While its most heroic tones and its countercultural ideology fade away with the generalization of the medium on a global scale, the technological features and social codes that developed from the original free use of the network have framed its utilization.

In the 1990s, business has realized the extraordinary potential of Internet, as the National Science Foundation decided to privatize some of the major operations of the network to the usual large corporation consortiums (ATT, MCI-IBM, and so on). The commercialization of Internet grew at a fast rate: while in 1991 there were about 9,000 commercial domains (or sub-networks), by the end of 1994 they had increased to 21,700. Several commercial computer services networks were created, providing services on the basis of an organized grid, with adjusted pricing. Yet the capacity of the network is such that the majority of the communication process was, and still is, largely spontaneous, unorganized, and diversified in purpose and membership. In fact, commercial and government interests coincide in favoring the expanding use of the network: the greater the diversity of messages and participants, the higher the critical mass in the network, and the higher the value. The peaceful co-existence of various interests and cultures in the net took the form of the World Wide Web (WWW), a flexible network of networks within the Internet where institutions, businesses, associations, and individuals create their own 'sites' on the basis of which everybody with access can produce her/his/its 'home page', made of a variable collage of text and images. Helped by software technology first developed in Mosaic (a Web browser software program invented in 1992 by students in Illinois, at the National Center for Supercomputing Applications, the Web allowed for groupings of interests and projects in the net, overcoming the time-costly chaotic browsing of pre-WWW Internet. On the basis of these groupings,

individuals and organizations were able to interact meaningfully on what has become, literally, a World Wide Web of individualized, interactive communication. The price to pay for such diverse and widespread participation is to let spontaneous, informal communication flourish at the same time. The commercialization of cyberspace will be closer to the historical experience of merchant streets that sprout out from vibrant urban culture, than to the shopping centers spread in the dullness of anonymous suburbs.

The two sources of the Net, the military/science establishment and the personal computing counterculture, did have a common ground: the university world. The first ARPANET mode was set up in 1969 at UCLA, and six other nodes were added in 1970–1 at UC Santa Barbara, SRI, University of Utah, BDN, MIT, and Harvard. From there, they spread primarily over the academic community, with the exception of the internal networks of large electronic corporations. This university origin of the Net has been, and is, decisive for the development and diffusion of electronic communication.

The culture of first-generation users, with its utopian, communal, and libertarian undercurrents, shaped the Net in two opposite directions. On the one hand, it tended to restrict access to a minority of computer hobbyists, the only people able and willing to spend time and energy living in cyberspace. From this era there remains a pioneering spirit that looks with distrust at the commercialization of the network, and watches with apprehension how the realization of the dream of generalized communication for the people brings with it the limits and misery of humankind as it is. But as the heroics of early computer tribes recedes under the relentless flow of 'newbies', what remains from the counter-cultural origins of the network is the informality and self-directedness of communication, the idea that many contribute to many, and yet each one has her own voice and expects an individualized answer. The multi-personalization of CMC does express to some extent the same tension that arose in the 1960s between the 'me culture' and the communal dreams of each individual. In fact, there are more bridges than communication experts usually acknowledged between the countercultural origins of CMC and the mainstream Internetters of the 1990s, as is shown by the business acceptance of Wired magazine, created as a counter-cultural outfit, but to become the hottest expression of Internet culture and how-to advice in the mid-1990s.

Thus, in spite of all efforts to regulate, privatize, and commercialize Internet and its tributary systems, CMC networks, inside and outside Internet, are characterized by their pervasiveness, their multi-faceted decentralization, and their flexibility. They sprawl as colonies of micro-organisms, to follow Rheingold's biological image. They will certainly reflect commercial interests, as they will extend the controlling logic of major public and private organizations into the whole realm of communication. But unlike the mass media of the McLuhan Galaxy, they have technologically and culturally embedded properties of interactivity and individualization. However, do these potentialities translate into new patterns of communication? Which are the cultural attributes emerging from the process of electronic interaction?

---

12 THE INTERNET

M. Tehranian and K. K. Tehranian

The Internet is another fast-growing transnational network that connects an estimated 30 million people around the world via over 1 million main-frame computers in a global network of networks. One million new users are estimated to be joining the network each month. At that rate, the network will have about 100 million users by the year 2000. If we count the members of such major commercial, on-line services as Prodigy, America Online, Delphi,

From: Taming Modernity: toward a new paradigm, by M. Tehranian and K. K. Tehranian, in *International Communication and Globalization*, edited by A. Mohammadi, 1997.

Dialogue and Compuserve logging into the Internet, that figure will be probably soon surpassed. In 1992, the *Whole Internet Users' Guide and Catalogue* sold 125,000 copies. A dozen other guides currently compete for the market, including *Zen and the Art of Internet* (Anon., 1994). It is no wonder that marketers are viewing the network as a potential electronic gold mine. However, attempts at commercializing the network have faced resistance by the current users. As Stecklow notes,

> residents of 'cyberspace', as the on-line computer galaxy is known, are a world apart. They do not take kindly to sales pitches or electronic cold calling. Many view themselves as pioneers of a new and better vehicle for free speech. Unlike television viewers, radio listeners or newspaper readers, they are hooked up to the message sender and other Internet parties interactively – meaning that an offense to their sensibilities can result in quick, embarrassing reports viewed by countless of the network's estimated 15 million users. (Stecklow, 1993)

The new global information market place

This new Network Nation consists of computer-literate professionals from all continents and all fields, united in the fine arts of chatting, gossiping, exchanging information and collaborating in a variety of projects from scientific research to lifestyle preferences, dating, financial transactions and social movements. The National Science Foundation (NSF), which subsidizes the network, has no control over a number of other data lines that are also part of the web. The NSF started phasing out its US $11.5 million annual subsidy in 1994. However, the US government and businesses are stepping in. Rupert Murdoch's News Corporation has announced it will acquire Delphi Internet Services Inc., an on-line service that provides Internet access to consumers; Continental Cablevision, the third-largest cable-television company in the US, is offering Internet access to its cable subscribers; and American Telephone and Telegraph Co. has made Internet available to some data communication customers via a nation-wide, toll-free telephone number (Stecklow, 1993).

Without telephones, the less developed countries and regions of the world would not be able to log into the global electronic superhighways. Telephones are the linchpin of the new integrated telecommunication systems. Without them it would be impossible to log-in the new data-bases and networks. Yet, the global distribution of telephony is more lopsided than any other modern media. In 1992, some fifty countries, accounting for over half the world's population, had a teledensity of less than one, that is less than one telephone line per 100 inhabitants. While the high-income countries have 71 per cent of the world's 575 million phone main lines, upper middle-income countries control 15 per cent, lower middle-income 10 per cent, and low income only 4 per cent (Tarjanne, 1994). Some newly industrializing countries in East Asia are, however, closing the gap, but many other LDCs are falling behind. On the whole, world telephone distribution patterns have remained relatively unchanged in the last 100 years. In the light of this fact, is information hegemony to replace military domination and repression? Or will the two be mutually reinforcing as in the past?

The new global information market-place includes four major components: (1) the owners of the highways, the common carriers, paid for by the private or public sectors; (2) the producers of information hardware such as telephones, televisions, and computers; (3) the producers of information software such as the press, broadcasters, libraries and infopreneurs; and (4) information consumers who demand efficiency, equity, privacy, affordability and choice. In response to the convergence of information and communication technologies, the US government aims at the removal of all barriers to entry into any particular sector of the market. This will eventually lead to the full technological and economic integration of the print, film, broadcasting, cable, telephone, cellular phone, computer and data-base industries – a process that has already begun by the emergence of giant, multi-media conglomerates.

13 THE INFORMATION SUPERHIGHWAY

H. I. Schiller

Current plans to construct an information superhighway closely follow the historical model of the US development and deployment of the communication satellite. The satellite project had a single unambiguous goal: capturing control of international communication circuits from British cable interests. The imperial rule of Great Britain in the nineteenth and early twentieth centuries had been facilitated greatly by control of the underwater message flow between the colonies and London. The American-built and -controlled satellite by-passed the cable and helped break the Empire's monopoly on trade and investment and to reduce the British role in international communication (Schiller, 1992).

Control of information instrumentation invariably goes hand-in-hand with control of the message flow and its content, surveillance capability and all forms of information intelligence. To be sure, the revenues from such control are hardly afterthoughts in the minds of the builders and owners of the information superhighway.

The recent rush to integration in the media-communication sector is itself a remarkable development. What can only be described as total communication capability – sometimes called 'one-stop communication' – has become a short-term goal of the major firms in this sector. This translates into giant companies that possess the hardware and software to fully control messages and images from the conceptual stage to their ultimate delivery to users and audiences.

In brief, what is intended is the creation of private domains that will produce data and entertainment (films, interactive TV programs and video games, recordings, news), package them, and transmit them

From: The global information highway, by H. I. Schiller, in *Resisting the Virtual Life: the Culture and Politics of Information*, edited by J. Brook and I. A. Boal, City Lights Press, San Francisco, 1995.

through satellite, cable, and telephone lines into living rooms and offices. Which companies ultimately will dominate the world and domestic markets is still uncertain. Time-Warner, Viacom, Hearst, Bell Atlantic, Sega, US West, Microsoft, AT&T, IBM, Comcast, Tele-Communications, Inc., are a few of the big players that are experimenting with different systems of 'full-service' communication and vying with each other for advantageous market position (Ken Auletta, The Magic Box, *The New Yorker*, April 11th, 1994).

Those who believe state power will be enhanced by the new information technologies and expanded information flows may be overlooking one critical point. The main beneficiaries of the new instrumentation and its product are likely to be the transnational corporations. They will always be the first to install and use these advanced communication technologies.

The strength, flexibility, and range of global business will become more remarkable. The capability of the state, including the still very powerful US, to enforce its will on the economy, domestic or international, will be further diminished. This may be partly obscured for a time because the national security state will have at its disposal an enhanced military and intelligence capability, derived from the new information technologies.

Interest rates, capital investment, employment, business-cycle policy, local working conditions, education and entertainment increasingly elude national jurisdiction. Creation of a far-flung information superhighway will accelerate the process.

---

14 TELEVISION AND SURVEILLANCE DEVICES

M. C. Boyer

Because of the dangers of downtown, eyewitness accounts of city events have declined, and vision itself is increasingly mechanized. No small wonder, then, that the image of the city has dematerialized right before our eyes. With surveillance video cameras scanning and interpreting more and more parking lots, hallways, entrances, banks, supermarkets, malls, theatres, and ballparks, our everyday environments are generally usurped by technological devices that see in our place. Television in public space – so Virilio claims – is

> tirelessly on the lookout for the unexpected, the impromptu, whatever might suddenly crop up, anywhere, any day. . . . This is the industrialization of prevention, or prediction: a sort of panic anticipation that commits the future and prolongs 'the industrialization of simulation', a simulation which more often than not involves the probable breakdown of and damage to the systems in question. . . . This doubling up of monitoring and surveillance clearly indicates the trend in public representation. It is a mutation that not only affects civilian life and crime, but also the military and strategic areas of defense.

The over-exposed city now becomes the city of concealment, revealing more and more of its crime and violence through surveillance devices, but less and less of anything else. It is a city of deterrence machines that are looking, assessing, weighing every event, in order to deploy police forces and vigilantes to avert a crime, drug sale, sexual assault, burglary, illegal entry, or accident. Consequently, we find the contemporary city to be absent of community, and urban space becomes a metaphor for a disembodied, computerized cyberspace. . . . In addition, e-mail,

From: *Cybercities: Visual Perception in the Age of Electronic Communication*, by M. C. Boyer, Princeton University Press, 1996.

voicemail and telephone messages seem to be replacing person-to-person interaction.

To return to the computer's effect on the city, we have to acknowledge that the structure of the public sphere is undergoing profound changes, not only as telecommunications increase personal choices over a variety of public communication systems, but also as these same technologies are consumed increasingly in privatized and domesticated forms. The Internet is perhaps the best example of the reach of the new communications web: accessed by more than two million computers, it is world-wide and open twenty-four hours a day, and it represents both a vast new marketplace for the future and a new public sphere for debate and argumentation. As one enthusiastic user relates, 'Internet is a sort of international cocktail party where you can talk to people from all over the world about all sorts of things . . .'

Essentially free to approximately twenty-five million people in 135 countries who have access to one of the 32,400 connected computer networks sponsored by governments and universities, it is not a service open to everyone. . . . At the same time that cities and regions of this country are being divided into homes that have access to the information highway and those that do not, some districts of the city are being prepared to receive advanced communication services such as video, voice, and computer communications while others are experiencing what has been called 'electronic redlining'. Thus the city, the region, and even the world can be grouped into information-rich or information-poor societies in the same manner as there were once societies with history and those without. . . . Projecting on present trends, futurists foresee that by the turn of the twenty-first century, five to ten corporate giants will control most of the world's important newspapers, magazines, books, broadcast stations, movies, recordings, and video cassettes.

This gloomy account also includes telecommunication infrastructures and data networks. The privatization of public television, school systems, research institutes, and communication networks means that market profitability becomes the sole criterion for the production of culture. Public access to these channels of telecommunication is far from guaranteed, and their content and subject matter are most often mediated or constructed by the programme formats of serial soap operas, news broadcasts, or advertising messages. Telecommunications are being orchestrated by interest-specific market niches at the expense of more generalized commentary and their former collective nature is being further eroded by commercialization and corporate control.

In consequence, the city and its public sphere become increasingly virtual as we move toward interpersonal systems of communication and the 'metropolis' at the expense of face-to-face communication in physical and public space . . . this virtual space has the capacity to join and yet simultaneously separate individual viewers. . . . 'Subscribers who dial up America Online find themselves in the most familiar of settings, navigating with a computer interface that is meant to look like a mall. But to some, that sense of Anytown, USA, a faceless environment that reflects mass tastes, is exactly what is wrong with cyberspace.'

Cyberspace is a new electronic, invisible space that allows the computer or television screen to substitute for urban space and urban experience. That our perception of space has become increasingly dependent on the simulated zone – a predigested, encoded digital box of algorithms – is evident in the manner in which the physical form of the city is displayed, in the mode in which information is formatted, and in the patterns in which televisual episodes are serially portrayed. In the disappearing city that has been fragmented into pieces, gaps, and holes and where reality is no longer used as a referent, space and time take on multiple profiles, non-linear relations, and recursive linkages. There is an instantaneous dispersion and regrouping of fragmented bits of information and images, as telecommunications enable these to be projected and rearranged under new laws of transmission. Time shifts away from the linearity of past-present-future, becoming either a static, frozen moment that breaks time down into discrete instances, or an automatic, continuous flow, similar to a video monitor with its screen switched on and waiting for an event to happen.

15 RHEINGOLD AND THE ILLUSION OF 'COMMUNITY'

S. G. Jones

Rheingold (1993) attempts to define how identity will be constructed via computer mediated communication (CMC):

> We reduce and encode our identities as words on a screen, decode and unpack the identities of others. The way we use these words, the stories (true and false) we tell about ourselves (or about the identity we want people to believe us to be) is what determines our identities in cyberspace. The aggregation of personae, interacting with each other, determines the nature of the collective culture. (p. 61)

One might suppose the same is true as to the aggregation of particular traits that determine the nature of the individual. However, the symbolic processes that Rheingold elides through use of such words as 'encode' and 'unpack' (themselves taken from the language of computer software) are fraught with unproblematized assumptions about the work that humans perform in search of their own identities and those of others. Interaction ought not be substituted for community, or, for that matter, for communication, and to accept uncritically connections between personae, individuals and community inadvisable. It will be unfortunate, too, if we uncritically accept that CMC will usher in the great new era that other media of communication have failed to bring us. It is not, as virtual reality pioneer Jaron Lanier says, that television has failed us because it 'wasn't planned well enough' (*Virtual Reality*, 1992, p. 6); it is that organization and planning are not necessarily appropriate processes for constructing or recapturing the sense of community for which we are nostalgic. Bender (1978) sharply criticizes those who seek 'to recapture community by imputing it to

From: Understanding community in the information age, by S. G. Jones, in *Cybersociety: Computer Mediated Communication and Community*, edited by S. G. Jones, Sage, 1995.

large-scale organizations and to locality-based social activity regardless of the quality of human relationships that characterize these contexts' (p. 143). Instead, Bender finds community in the midst of a transformation and asks us to heed his call that we not, by way of our nostalgia, limit definitions of community to that which 'seventeenth century New Englanders knew' (p. 146), although with electronic town hall meetings and the like we seem to be doing precisely that. One example can be found in Rheingold's work. Although often critical in much of his writing, it is clear from the comparisons that Rheingold (1993) makes to other forms of community that what he calls 'virtual communities' are predicated on nostalgic (and romantic) ideals:

> It's a bit like a neighborhood pub or coffee shop. It's a little like a salon, where I can participate in a hundred ongoing conversations with people who don't care what I look like or sound like, but who do care how I think and communicate. There are seminars and word fights in different corners. (p. 66)

> Virtual communities might be real communities, they might be pseudo communities, or they might be something entirely new in the realm of social contracts, but I believe they are in part a response to the hunger for community that has followed the disintegration of traditional communities around the world. (p. 62)

Of course, it is difficult to imagine what new online communities may be like, and it is far easier to use our memories and myths as we construct them. What is more important than simply understanding the construction we are undertaking is to notice that it is peculiar and particular to the computer. Because these machines are seen as 'linking' machines (they link information, data, communication, sound, and image through the common language of digital encoding), to borrow from Jensen (1990), they inherently affect the ways we think of linking up to each other, and thus they fit squarely into our concerns about community. Media technologies that have largely been tied to the 'transportation' view of communication mentioned earlier were developed to overcome space and time. The computer, in particular, is an 'efficiency' machine, purporting to ever increase its speed. But unlike those technologies, the computer used for communication is a technology to be understood from the 'ritual' view of communication, for once time and space have been overcome (or at least rendered surmountable) the spur for development is connection, linkage. Once we can surmount time and space and 'be' anywhere, we must choose a 'where' at which to be, and the computer's functionality lies in its power to make us organize our desires about the spaces we visit and stay in.

The question remains, though, whether or not the communities we may form by way of CMC will, or even ought to, be part of our public culture. If so, then perhaps it would be best to not understand them as communities. As Bender (1978) writes, 'Our public lives do not provide an experience of community. The mutuality and sentiment characteristic of community cannot and need not be achieved in public. We must be careful to distinguish between these two contexts of social experience' (p. 148).

The manner in which we seek to find community, empowerment, and political action all embedded in our ability to use CMC, is thereby troubling. No one medium, no one technology, has been able to provide those elements in combination, and often we have been unable to find them in any media. CMC has potential for a variety of consequences, some anticipated, some not. A critical awareness of the social transformations that have occurred and continue to occur with or without technology will be our best ally as we incorporate CMC into contemporary social life.

---

16 VIRTUAL REALITY

S. G. Jones

Timothy Leary says we have been living in virtual reality since the proliferation of television sets. VR differs primarily from TV in that VR makes the experience interactive rather than passive (cited in Mondo, 1992, p. 262). Howard Rheingold (1991) asks us to:

> imagine a wrap-around television with three-dimensional programmes, including three-dimensional sounds and solid objects that you can pick up and manipulate, even feel with your fingers and hands. . . . Imagine that you are the creator as well as the consumer of your artificial experience, with the power to use a gesture or word to remold the world you see and hear and feel. (p. 16)

Brenda Laurel (1991) writes that, for her, VR brings the experience of acting, a way of exploring existence from the perspectives of varied characters, situations and worlds not otherwise encountered in our everyday lives. Laurel worked on Wild Palms, which was promoted as TV's first attempt at showing virtual reality; however, she does not think that even interactive television represents the future: 'It's a dead end' (quoted in McCarthy, 1993) with a lot of scary and hopeful possible successors to it 'depending on who owns the interactive media of the future' (Antonopulos and Barnett, 1992, p. 12). Unlike most of the programmers interested in virtual reality, she is working with electronic storytelling, 'a very female-dominated' activity, with the technology as an audience (Antonopulos and Barnett, 1992, p. 12). Laurel's approach is a good illustration of the importance of paying close attention to the interests of many rather than just to the statements of those who have the loudest and best financed statements about what computers can and should be programmed to do.

From: A backstage critique of virtual reality, by C. Kramarae, in *Cybersociety: Computer Mediated Communication and Community*, edited by S. G. Jones, Sage, 1995.

VR exists in various fairly rudimentary (in terms of what is talked about as coming) forms. . . . Most VR 'entertainment' work is taking place in the US, in part because the US defense industry has invested so many (tax) dollars in VR projects and now wants to find other uses for their work (Newquist, 1993). However, in Great Britain there are also commercial applications using the technology. For example, in Nottingham, England, in a storefront in one of the city's nightclub areas, Andy and Paul Smith and Justin Webster have built one of the world's first LBE (location-based entertainment) centres. You can watch players through a large window before you walk into the office and wait for your turn. The play-room has four virtuality units. The largest depicts a medieval village and forest. The play: a new version of Dungeons and Dragons, a game played, in the past often intensively, most often by boys and men. This new game, Legend Quest, is played in virtual reality. Each player chooses from eighteen possible characters (elf, human, dwarf characters; the gender can also be chosen). The virtuality system is equipped to customize your character – the person others in the game will see and hear. After all, if you say you are an elf you need to be seen as short and to be heard as speaking in a higher voice. The goal of the game is to live rather than die from foul play or other dangers, succeed in ten challenges, and defeat the evil master of the dungeon. If this sounds familiar it's because all-too-familiar knowledges, stories, adventures, and stereotypes operate in virtual reality. The creativity does not come in the form of new legends. We can expect many more medieval imaginations, cops-and-robbers, sex, and other mayhem from other creators of VR.

Legend Quest has been hugely successful. More than 1,500 players signed up for lifetime member-ships in the first eight weeks . . . and outside of the commercial play, some of the characters meet to plan strategies and pig roasts (Delaney, 1993).

It seems to me that the potential major change here is some erosion of the classic body/mind split. VR, like all other imaginative situations, has the potential for changes in gender stereotypes, but while, as in other kinds of play-acting, women and men can temporarily change their gender, there is little to suggest major overhauls of those so-called sex roles in VR programming. As Brenda Laurel says, the guys who are designing the programmes are the guys whose business it is to sell sexual stereotypes, and so the new programs become 'another means of enforcing the gender landscape rather than a means of liberation' (Antonopulos and Barnett, 1993, p. 12).

---

17 'VIRTUAL INTIMACY' AND 'VIRTUAL VALERIE'

C. Kramarae

Rheingold (1991) writes that:

> The secondary social effects of techno-sex are potentially revolutionary. If technology enables you to experience erotic frissons or deep physical, social, emotional communication with another person with no possibility of pregnancy or sexu-ally transmitted disease, what then of conven-tional morality, and what of the social rituals and cultural codes that exist solely to enforce that morality? Is disembodiment the ultimate sexual revolution and/or the first step toward aban-doning our bodies? . . . perhaps cyberspace is a better place to keep most of the population relat-ively happy, most of the time. . . . Privacy and identity and intimacy will become tightly coupled into something we do not have a name for yet. (pp. 352–353)

This focus on intimacy as technosex is pervasive in VR discussions. For example, during a half-hour program about VR presented on PBS on May 1st, 1992, a speaker on the virtues of VR asked listeners

From: A backstage critique of virtual reality, by C. Kramarae, in *Cybersociety: Computer-Mediated Communication and Community*, edited by S. G. Jones, Sage, 1995.

to image the following: 'You are traveling. You get to the hotel and you miss your wife. You ring up your wife and then you can have sex over the glovel/phone link.'

For many men in particular, heterosexual intimacy means primarily sex, whereas women more often talk about intimacy in terms of general closeness, including sharing thoughts and discussing problems. This conflict of interests is clearly going to be played out once again in the New Media. The alt.sex. news groups on the Internet have very high traffic, with mostly men exchanging messages. . . . Sex will (has?) become another sport, like hunting and shooting tanks and hostile aliens. Collaborative interaction will likely mean it can be a men's team sport. It will again be removed from intimacy as many women know or wish it. Brenda Laurel says, 'The computer game genre has grown . . . with programmers utterly devoted to an adolescent male demographic and a very white, First World Western view of what's interesting to kids . . . shooting and killing and blowing things up . . .' (quoted in Bright, 1992, p. 66).

With VR you can also reach out and grab someone. In a passage that's been reprinted in a number of publications, Rheingold (1991) writes:

> Picture yourself a couple of decades hence, dressing for a hot night in the virtual village. Before you climb into a suitable padded chamber and put on your 3D glasses, you slip into a lightweight (eventually, one would hope, diaphanous) bodysuit, something like a body stocking, but with the kind of intimate snugness of a condom. Embedded in the inner surface of the suit, using a technology that does not yet exist, is an array of intelligent sensor-effectors – a mesh of tiny tactile detectors coupled to vibrators of varying degrees of hardness, hundreds of them per square inch. . . . Now, imagine plugging your whole sound-sight-touch tele-presence system into the telephone network. You see a lifelike but totally artificial visual representation of your own body and of your partner's. . . . Your partner(s) can move independently in the cyberspace and your representations are able to touch each other, even

though your physical bodies might be continents apart. (p. 346)

But no need to wait the decades. 'Virtual Valerie' exists. It's not called information but, rather, a game or pornography, depending on whether you think of the CD-ROM Virtual Valerie as openness and freedom or as sexist and exploitative. Because she has sold so well, she is one of the best known but still only one of a number of 'cyber-babes'.

---

18 VIRTUAL SEX
Sherry Turkle

Virtual sex, whether in MUDs (Multi-User Domains) or in a private room on a commercial Online service, consists of two or more players typing descriptions of physical actions, verbal statements and emotional reactions for their characters. In cyberspace, this activity is not only common but, for many people, it is the centrepiece of their online experience.

On MUDs, some people have sex as characters of their own gender. Others have sex as characters of the other gender. Some men play female personae to have netsex with men. And in the 'fake-lesbian syndrome', men adopt online female personae in order to have netsex with women. Although it does not seem to be as widespread, I have met several women who say they present as male characters in order to have netsex with men. Some people have sex as non-human characters, for example, it's animals on Furry MUDs. Some enjoy sex with one partner. Some use virtual reality as a place to experiment with group situations. In real life, such behavior (where possible) can create enormous practical and emotional confusion. Virtual adventures

From: *Life on the Screen: Identity in the Age of the Internet*, by Sherry Turkle, Weidenfeld and Nicolson, 1996.

may be easier to undertake, but they can also result in significant complications. Different people and different couples deal with them in very different ways . . . MUDs provide a situation in which we can play out scenarios that otherwise might have remained pure fantasy. Although they involve other people and are no longer pure fantasy, they are not 'in the world'. Their boundary status offers new possibilities. TinySex and virtual gender-bending are part of the larger story of people using virtual spaces to construct identity.

_____

PART D

GLOBALIZATION AND
THE POLITICAL ECONOMY

Part D is an important section of the book. There is often a failure to contextualize discussions of the globalization of culture and media in the rapidly evolving global political economy. Indeed, any assessment of the global media and culture industries must be rooted in the political and economic changes sweeping the planet, to which they are significant contributors. The extracts chart the new political and economic configurations that characterize the global age. Among the topics addressed are:

- Wallerstein on globalization and the capitalist world system;
- globalization as a 'grand narrative' that throws into question the future of the nation state in an increasingly 'borderless world';
- the development of an international financial system;
- the role of Europe in the light of the emergence of what has been termed a 'new world disorder';
- the role of the third world in an increasingly globalized world economy, along with debt problems and capital flows between the developed and under-developed worlds;
- world trade, global commodity chains and the positive and negative aspects of the globalizing of employment and its impact upon labour migration world-wide;
- the 'third industrial revolution', with particular reference to newly industrializing countries;
- issues of global governance and the need to ensure economic growth and reduce poverty in the least industrialized nations.

1 THE WORLD SYSTEM

Immanuel Wallerstein

We take the defining characteristic of a social system to be the existence within it of a division of labour, such that the various sectors or areas within are dependent upon economic exchange with others for the smooth and continuous provisioning of the needs of the area. Such economic exchange can clearly exist without a common political structure and even more obviously without sharing the same culture.

A mini-system is an entity that has within it a complete division of labour and a single cultural framework. Such systems are found only in very simple agricultural or hunting and gathering societies. Such mini-systems no longer exist in the world. Furthermore, there were fewer in the past than is often asserted, since any such system that became tied to an empire by the payment of tribute as 'protection costs' ceased by that fact to be a 'system', no longer having a self-contained division of labour. For such an area, the payment of tribute marked a shift, in Polanyi's language, from being a reciprocal economy to participating in a larger redistributive economy.

Leaving aside the now defunct mini-systems, the only kind of social system is a world-system, which we define quite simply as a unit with a single division of labour and multiple cultural systems. It follows logically that there can, however, be two varieties of such world-systems, one with a common political system and one without. We shall designate these respectively as 'world-empires' and 'world economies'.

It turns out empirically that world-economies have historically been unstable structures leading either towards disintegration or conquest by one group and, hence, transformation into a world-empire. Examples of such world-empires emerging from world-economies are all the so-called great civilizations of pre-modern times, such as China,

Egypt, Rome (each at appropriate periods of its history). On the other hand, the so-called nineteenth-century empires, such as Great Britain or France, were not world-empires at all, but nation-states with colonial appendages operating within the framework of a world-economy.

World-empires were basically redistributive in economic form. No doubt they bred clusters of merchants who engaged in economic exchange (primarily long distance trade), but such clusters, however large, were a minor part of the total economy and not fundamentally determinative of its fate. Such long-distance trade tended to be, as Polanyi argues, 'administered trade' and not market trade, utilizing 'ports of trade'.

It was only with the emergence of the modern-world-economy in sixteenth-century Europe that we saw the full development and economic predominance of market trade. This was the system called capitalism. Capitalism and a world economy (that is, a single division of labour but multiple polities and cultures) are obverse sides of the same coin. One does not cause the other. We are merely defining the same indivisible phenomenon by different characteristics.

How and why it came about that this particular European world-economy of the sixteenth century did not become transformed into a redistributive world-empire but developed definitively as a capitalist world-economy has been explained elsewhere. The genesis of this world-historical turning-point is marginal to the issues under discussion in this paper, which is rather what conceptual apparatus one brings to bear on the analysis of developments within the framework of precisely such a capitalist world-economy.

Let us, therefore, turn to the capitalist world-economy. We shall seek to deal with two pseudo-problems, created by the trap of not analyzing totalities: the so-called persistence of feudal forms; and the so-called creation of socialist systems. In doing this, we shall offer an alternative model with which to engage in comparative analysis, one rooted in the historically specific totality which is the world capitalist economy. We hope to demonstrate thereby that to be historically specific is not to fail to be

From: The rise and future demise of the capitalist world system, by Immanuel Wallerstein, in *Comparative Studies in Society and History*, Vol. 16, 1974.

analytically universal. On the contrary, the only road to nomothetic propositions is through the historically concrete, just as in cosmology the only road to a theory of the laws governing the universe is through the concrete analysis of the historical evolution of this same universe.

On the 'feudalism' debate, we take as a starting-point Frank's concept of 'the development of under-development', that is, the view that the economic structure of contemporary under-developed countries is not the form which a 'traditional' society takes upon contact with 'developed' societies, not an earlier stage in the 'transition' to industrialization. It is, rather, the result of being involved in the world economy as a peripheral, raw material-producing area, or as Frank puts it for Chile, 'underdevelopment . . . is the necessary product of four centuries of capitalism itself'.

This formulation runs counter to a large body of writing concerning the under-developed countries that was produced in the period 1950–70, a literature which sought the factors that explained 'development' within non-systems such as 'states' or 'cultures' and, once having presumably discovered these factors, urged their reproduction in under-developed areas as the road to salvation

What was happening in Europe from the sixteenth to the eighteenth centuries is that over a large geographical area going from Poland in the northeast westwards and southwards throughout Europe and including large parts of the Western Hemisphere as well, there grew up a world-economy with a single division of labour within which there was a world market, for which men produced largely agricultural products for sale and profit. I would think the simplest thing to do would be to call this 'agricultural capitalism'.

This then resolves the problems incurred by using the pervasiveness of wage labour as a defining characteristic of capitalism. An individual is no less a capitalist exploiting labour because the state assists him to pay his labourers low wages (including wages in kind) and denies these labourers the right to change employment. Slavery and so-called 'second serfdom' are not to be regarded as anomalies in a capitalist system. Rather the so-called serf in Poland,

or the Indian on a Spanish 'encomienda' in New Spain in this sixteenth-century world-economy were working for landlords who 'paid' them (however euphemistic this term) for cash-crop production. This is a relationship in which labour-power is a commodity (how could it ever be more so than under slavery?), quite different from the relationship of a feudal serf to his lord in eleventh-century Burgundy, where the economy was not oriented to a world market, and where labour-power was, therefore, in no sense bought or sold.

Capitalism thus means labour as a commodity to be sure. But in the era of agricultural capitalism, wage-labour is only one of the modes in which labour is recruited and recompensed in the labour market. Slavery, coerced cash-crop production (my name for the so-called 'second feudalism'), share-cropping and tenancy are all alternative modes. It would be too long to develop here the conditions under which differing regions of the world-economy tend to specialize in different agricultural products.

What we must notice now is that this specialization occurs in specific and differing geographic regions of the world-economy. This regional specialization comes about by the attempts of actors in the market to avoid the normal operation of the market whenever it does not maximize their profit. The attempts of these actors to use non-market devices to ensure short-run profits makes them turn to the political entities which have, in fact, power to affect the market – the nation-states. (Again, why at this stage they could not have turned to city-states would take us into a long discursus, but it has to do with the state of military and shipping technology, the need of the European land-mass to expand overseas in the fifteenth century if it was to maintain the level of income of the various aristocracies, combined with the state of political disintegration to which Europe had fallen in the Middle Ages.)

In any case, the local capitalist classes – cash-crop landowners (often, even usually, nobility) and merchants – turned to the state, not only to liberate them from non-market constraints (as traditionally emphasized by liberal historiography), but to create new constraints on the new market, the market of the European world economy.

By a series of accidents – historical, ecological, geographic – northwest Europe was better situated in the sixteenth century to diversify its agricultural specialization and add to it certain industries (such as textiles, shipbuilding and metal wares) than were other parts of Europe. Northwest Europe emerged as the core area of this world-economy, specializing in agricultural production of higher skill levels, which favoured (again for reasons too complex to develop) tenancy and wage-labour as the modes of labour control. Eastern Europe and the Western Hemisphere became peripheral areas specializing in export of grains, bullion, wood, cotton, sugar – all of which favoured the use of slavery and coerced cash-crop labour as the modes of labour control. Mediterranean Europe emerged as the semi-peripheral area of this world-economy specializing in high-cost industrial products (for example, silks) and credit and specie transactions, which had as a consequence in the agricultural arena share-cropping as the mode of labour control and little export to other areas.

The three structural positions in a world-economy – core, periphery, and semi-periphery – had become stabilized by about 1640. How certain areas became one and not the other is a long story. The key fact is that given slightly different starting-points, the interests of various local groups converged in northwest Europe, leading to the development of strong state mechanisms, and diverged sharply in the peripheral areas, leading to very weak ones. Once we get a difference in the strength of the state-machineries, we get the operation of 'unequal exchange' which is enforced by strong states on weak ones, by core states on peripheral areas. Thus capitalism involves not only appropriation of the surplus-value by an owner from a labourer, but an appropriation of surplus of the whole world-economy by core areas. And this was as true in the stage of agricultural capitalism as it is in the stage of industrial capitalism.

In the early Middle Ages, there was to be sure, trade. But it was largely either 'local', in a region that we might call the 'extended' manor, or 'long-distance', primarily of luxury goods. There was no exchange of 'bulk' goods, of 'staples' across interme-diate-size areas, and hence no production for such markets. Later on in the Middle Ages, world-economies may be said to have come into existence, one centring on Venice, a second on the cities of Flanders and the Hanse. For various reasons, these structures were hurt by the retractions (economic, demographic and ecological) of the period 1300–1450. It is only with the creating of a European division of labour after 1450 that capitalism found firm roots.

Capitalism was from the beginning an affair of the world-economy and not of nation-states. It is a misreading of the situation to claim that it is only in the twentieth century that capitalism has become 'world-wide', although this claim is frequently made in various writings, particularly by Marxists. Typical of this line of argument is Charles Bettelheim's response to Arghiri Emmanuel's discussion of un-equal exchange:

> The tendency of the capitalist mode of production to become world-wide is manifested not only through the constitution of a group of national economies forming a complex and hierarchical structure, including an imperialist pole and a dominated one, and not only through the antag-onistic relations that develop between the different 'national economies' and the different states, but also through the constant 'tran-scending' of 'national limits' by big capital (the formation of 'international' big capital, 'world firms', etc. . . .

The whole tone of these remarks ignores the fact that capital has never allowed its aspirations to be determined by national boundaries in a capitalist world-economy, and that the creation of 'national' barriers – generically, mercantilism – has historically been a defensive mechanism of capitalists located in states which are one level below the high point of strength in the system. Such was the case of England vis-à-vis the Netherlands in 1660–1715; France vis-à-vis England in 1715–1815; Germany vis-à-vis Britain in the nineteenth century; the Soviet Union vis-à-vis the US in the twentieth. In the process a large number of countries create national economic barriers whose consequences often last beyond their initial objectives. At this later point in the process the very same capitalists who pressed their national governments to impose the restrictions now find these restrictions constraining. This is not an 'internationalization' of 'national' capital. This is simply a new political demand by certain sectors of the capitalist classes who have at all points in time sought to maximize their profits within the real economic market, that of the world economy.

If this is so, then what meaning does it have to talk of structural positions within this economy and identify states as being in one of these positions? And why talk of three positions, inserting that of 'semi-periphery' in between the widely-used concepts of core and periphery? The state-machineries of the core states were strengthened to meet the needs of capitalist landowners and their merchant allies. But that does not mean that these state-machineries were manipulable puppets. Obviously any organization, once created, has a certain autonomy from those who pressed it into existence for two reasons. It creates a stratum of officials whose own careers and interests are furthered by the continued strengthening of the organization itself, however the interests of its capitalist backers may vary. Kings and bureaucrats wanted to stay in power and increase their personal gain constantly. Second, in the process of creating the strong state in the first place, certain 'constitutional' compromises had to be made with other forces within the state-boundaries and these institutionalized compromises limit, as they are designed to do, the freedom of manoeuvre of the managers of the state-machinery. The formula of the state as 'executive committee of the ruling class' is only valid, therefore, if one bears in mind that executive committees are never mere reflections of the wills of their constituents, as anyone who has ever participated in any organization knows well.

The strengthening of the state-machineries in core areas has as its direct counterpart the decline of the state-machineries in peripheral areas. The decline of the Polish monarchy in the sixteenth and seventeenth centuries is a striking example of this phenomenon. There are two reasons for this. In peripheral countries, the interests of the capitalist landowners lie in an opposite direction from those of the local commercial bourgeoisie. Their interests lie in maintaining an open economy to maximize their profit from world-market trade (no restrictions in exports and access to lower-cost industrial products from core countries) and in elimination of the commercial bourgeoisie in favour of outside merchants (who pose no local political threat). Thus, in terms of the state, the coalition which strengthened it in core countries was precisely absent.

The second reason, which has become ever more operative over the history of the modern world-system, is that the strength of the state-machinery in core states is a function of the weakness of other state-machineries. Hence intervention of outsiders via war, subversion, and diplomacy is the lot of peripheral states.

All this seems very obvious. I repeat it only in order to make clear two points. One cannot reasonably explain the strength of various state-machineries at specific moments of the history of the modern world-system primarily in terms of a genetic - cultural line of argumentation, but rather in terms of the structural role a country plays in the world-economy at that moment in time. To be sure, the initial eligibility for a particular role is often decided by an accidental edge a particular country has, and the 'accident' of which one is talking is no doubt located in part in past history, in part in current geography. But once this relatively minor accident is given, it is the operations of the world-market forces which accentuate the differences, institutionalize them, and make them impossible to surmount over the short run.

The second point we wish to make about the structural differences of core and periphery is that they are not comprehensible unless we realize that there is a third structural position: that of the semi-periphery. This is not the result merely of establishing arbitrary cutting-points on a continuum of characteristics. Our logic is not merely inductive, sensing the presence of a third category from a comparison of indicator curves. It is also deductive. The semi-periphery is needed to make a capitalist world-economy run smoothly. Both kinds of world-system, the world-empire with a redistributive economy and the world-economy with a capitalist market economy, involve markedly unequal distribution of rewards. Thus, logically, there is immediately posed the question of how it is possible politically for such a system to persist. Why do not the majority who are exploited simply overwhelm the minority who draw disproportionate benefits? The most rapid glance at the historic record shows that these world-systems have been faced rather rarely by fundamental system-wide insurrection. While internal discontent has been eternal, it has usually taken quite long before the accumulation of the erosion of power has led to the decline of a world-system and, as often as not, an external force has been a major factor in this decline.

There have been three major mechanisms that have enabled world-systems to retain relative political stability (not in terms of the particular groups who will play the leading roles in the system, but in terms of systemic survival itself). One obviously is the concentration of military strength in the hands of the dominant forces. The modalities of this obviously vary with the technology, and there are to be sure political pre-requisites for such a concentration, but nonetheless sheer force is no doubt a central consideration.

A second mechanism is the pervasiveness of an ideological commitment to the system as a whole. I do not mean what has often been termed the 'legitimation' of a system, because that term has been used to imply that the lower strata of a system feel some affinity with, or loyalty towards, the rulers, and I doubt that this has ever been a significant factor in the survival of world-systems. I mean rather the degree to which the staff or cadres of the system (and I leave this term deliberately vague) feel that their own well-being is wrapped up in the survival of the system as such and the competence of its leaders. It is this staff which not only propagates the myths; it is they who believe them.

But neither force nor the ideological commitment of the staff would suffice were it not for the division of the majority into a larger lower stratum and a smaller middle stratum. Both the revolutionary call for polarization as a strategy of change and the liberal encomium to consensus as the basis of the liberal

polity reflect this proposition. The import is far wider than its use in the analysis of contemporary political problems suggests. It is the normal condition of either kind of world-system to have a three-layered structure. When and if this ceases to be the case, the world system disintegrates.

In a world-empire, the middle stratum is in fact accorded the role of maintaining the marginally-desirable long-distance luxury trade, while the upper stratum concentrates its resources on controlling the military machinery which can collect the tribute, the crucial mode of redistributing surplus. By providing, however, for an access to a limited portion of the surplus to urbanized elements who alone, in pre-modern societies, could contribute political cohesiveness to isolated clusters of primary producers, the upper stratum effectively buys off the potential leadership of co-ordinated revolt. And by denying access to political rights for this commercial urban middle stratum, it makes them constantly vulnerable to confiscatory measures whenever their economic profits become sufficiently swollen so that they might begin to create for themselves military strength.

In a world-economy, such 'cultural' stratification is not so simple, because the absence of a single political system means the concentration of economic roles vertically rather than horizontally throughout the system. The solution then is to have three kinds of states, with pressures for cultural homogenization within each of them – thus, besides the upper stratum of core-states and the lower stratum of peripheral states, there is a middle stratum of semi-peripheral ones.

This semi-periphery is then assigned as it were a specific economic role, but the reason is less economic than political. That is to say, one might make a good case that the world-economy as an economy would function every bit as well without a semi-periphery. But it would be far less politically stable, for it would mean a polarized world-system. The existence of the third category means precisely that the upper stratum is not faced with the unified opposition of all the others because the middle stratum is both exploited and exploiter. It follows that the specific economic role is not all that important, and has thus changed through the various historical stages of the modern world-system.

Where, then, does class analysis fit in all of this? And what in such a formulation are nations, nationalities, peoples, ethnic groups? First of all, without arguing the point now, I would contend that all these latter terms denote variants of a single phenomenon which I will term 'ethno-nations'.

Both classes and ethnic groups, or status-groups, or ethno-nations are phenomena of world-economies and much of the enormous confusion that has surrounded the concrete analysis of their functioning can be attributed quite simply to the fact that they have been analyzed as though they existed within the nation-states of this world-economy, instead of within the world-economy as a whole. This has been a Procrustean bed indeed.

The range of economic activities being far wider in the core than in the periphery, the range of syndical interest groups is far wider there. Thus, it has been widely observed that there does not exist in many parts of the world today a proletariat of the kind which exists in, say, Europe or North America. But this is a confusing way to state the observation. Industrial activity being disproportionately concentrated in certain parts of the world-economy, industrial wage-workers are to be found principally in certain geographic regions. Their interests as a syndical group are determined by their collective relationship to the world-economy. Their ability to influence the political functioning of this world-economy is shaped by the fact that they command larger percentages of the population in one sovereign entity than another. The form their organizations take have, in large part, been governed too by these political boundaries. The same might be said about industrial capitalists. Class analysis is perfectly capable of accounting for the political position of, let us say, French skilled workers if we look at their structural position and interests in the world-economy. Similarly with ethno-nations. The meaning of ethnic consciousness in a core area is considerably different from that of ethnic consciousness in a peripheral area precisely because of the different class position such ethnic groups have in the world-economy.

Political struggles of ethno-nations or segments of classes within national boundaries of course are the daily bread and butter of local politics. But their significance or consequences can only be fruitfully analyzed if one spells out the implications of their organizational activity or political demands for the functioning of the world economy. This also, incidentally, makes possible more rational assessments of these politics in terms of some set of evaluative criteria such as 'left' and 'right'.

The functioning, then, of a capitalist world-economy requires that groups pursue their economic interests within a single world market while seeking to distort this market for their benefit by organizing to exert influence on states, some of which are far more powerful than others, but none of which controls the world-market in its entirety. Of course, we shall find on closer inspection that there are periods where one state is relatively quite powerful and other periods where power is more diffuse and contested, permitting weaker states broader ranges of action. We can talk, then, of the relative 'tightness' or 'looseness' of the world-system as an important variable and seek to analyze why this dimension tends to be cyclical in nature, as it seems to have been for several hundred years.

2 THE END OF THE NATION STATE
K. Ohmae

With the ending of the frigid 50 years' war between Soviet-style Communism and the West's liberal democracy, some observers – Francis Fukuyama in particular – announced that we had reached the 'end of history'. Nothing could be further from the truth. In fact, now that the bitter ideological confronta-

From: *The End of the Nation State*, by K. Ohmae, Harper Collins, 1996.

tion sparked by this century's collision of 'isms' has ended, larger numbers of people from more points on the globe than ever before have aggressively come forward to participate in history. They have left behind centuries, even millennia, of obscurity in forest and desert and rural isolation to request from the world community – and from the global economy that links it together – a decent life for themselves and a better life for their children. A generation ago, even a decade ago, most of them were as voiceless and invisible as they had always been. This is true no longer: they have entered history with a vengeance and they have demands – economic demands – to make.

But to whom or to what should they make them? Their first impulse, of course, will likely be to turn to the heads of governments of nation states. These, after all, are the leaders whose plans and schemes have long shaped the flow of public events. But, in today's more competitive world, nation states no longer possess the seemingly bottomless well of resources from which they used to draw with impunity to fund their ambitions. These days, even they have to look for assistance to the global economy and make the changes at home needed to invite it in. So these new claimants will turn to international bodies like the United Nations. But what is the UN if not a collection of nation states? So they will turn to multilateral agencies like the World Bank, but these too are the creatures of a nation state-defined and -funded universe. So they will turn to explicitly economic groupings like OPEC or G7 or ASEAN or NAFTA or the EU. But once again, all they will find behind each new acronym is a grouping of nation states. Then, if they are clever, they interrupt their quest to ask a few simple questions. Are these nation states – notwithstanding the obvious and important role they play in world affairs – really the primary actors in today's global economy? Do they provide the best window on that economy? Do they provide the best port of access to it? In a world where economic borders are progressively disappearing, are their arbitrary, historically accidental boundaries genuinely meaningful in economic terms? And if not, what kinds of boundaries do make sense? In other words, exactly what,

at bottom, are the natural business units – the sufficient, correctly-sized and scaled aggregations of people and activities – through which to tap into that economy?

The Influence of the 4 'I's'

One way to answer these questions is to observe the flows of what I call the 4 'I's' that define it. First, the capital markets in most developed countries are flush with excess cash for investment. Japan, for example, has the equivalent of US $10 trillion stored away. Even where a country itself hovers close to bankruptcy, there is often a huge accumulation of money in pension funds and life insurance programs. The problem is that suitable – and suitably large – investment opportunities are not often available in the same geographies where this money sits. As a result, the capital markets have developed a wide variety of mechanisms to transfer it across national borders. Today, nearly 10 per cent of US pension finds is invested in Asia. Ten years ago, that degree of participation in Asian markets would have been unthinkable.

Thus, investment – the first 'I' – is no longer geographically constrained. Now, wherever you sit in the world, if the opportunity is attractive, the money will come in. And it will be, for the most part, 'private' money. Again, 10 years ago, the flow of cross-border funds was primarily from government to government or from multilateral lending agency to government. There was a capital city and an army of public bureaucrats on at least one end of the transaction. That is no longer the case. Because most of the money now moving across borders is private, governments do not have to be involved at either end. All that matters is the quality of the investment opportunity. The money will go where the good opportunities are.

The second 'I' – industry – is also far more global in orientation today than it was a decade ago. In the past, with the interests of their home governments clearly in mind, companies would strike deals with host governments to bring in resources and skills in exchange for privileged access to local markets. This, too, has changed. The strategies of modern multinational corporations are no longer shaped and conditioned by reasons of state but, rather, by the desire – and the need – to serve attractive markets wherever they exist and to tap attractive pools of resources wherever they sit. Government-funded subsidies – old-fashioned tax breaks for investing in this or that location – are becoming irrelevant as a decision criterion. The Western firms now moving, say, into parts of China and India are there because that is where their fortune lies, not because the host government has suddenly dangled a carrot in front of their nose.

As corporations move, of course, they bring with them working capital. Perhaps, more important, they transfer technology and managerial know-how. These are not concessions to host governments; they are the essential raw materials these companies need to do their work. But they also bring something else. Pension fund money in the US, for example, might look for decent China-related opportunities by scouting out the possibilities on the Shanghai stock exchange. The prospects thus identified, however, will be largely unfamiliar. Money managers will do their best to provide adequate research, but everyone will admit that relevant knowledge is limited. But if it is a GE or an IBM or a Unilever or a P&G that is building a presence in China, the markets back home and elsewhere in the developed world will know how to evaluate that. They will be more comfortable with it. And that, in turn, expands the range of capital markets on which these companies can draw for resources to be used in China.

The movements of both investment and industry has been greatly facilitated by the third 'I' – information technology – which now makes it possible for a company to operate in various parts of the world without having to build up an entire business system in each of the countries where it has a presence. Engineers at workstations in Osaka can easily control plant operations in newly exciting parts of China like Dalian. Product designers in Oregon can control the activities of a network of factories throughout Asia-Pacific. Thus, the hurdles for cross-border participation and strategic alliance have come way down. Armies of experts do not have to be transferred; armies of workers do not have to be trained.

Capability can reside in the network and be made available – virtually anywhere – as needed.

Finally, individual consumers – the fourth 'I' – have also become more global in orientation. With better access to information about lifestyles around the globe, they are much less likely to want to buy – and much less conditioned by government injunctions to buy – American or French or Japanese products merely because of their national associations. Consumers increasingly want the best and cheapest products, no matter where they come from. And they have shown their willingness to vote these preferences with their pocketbooks.

Taken together, the mobility of these four 'I's' makes possible for viable economic units in any part of the world to pull in whatever is needed for development. They need not look for assistance only to pools of resources close to home. Nor need they rely on the formal efforts of governments to attract resources from elsewhere and funnel them to the ultimate users. This makes the traditional 'middleman' function of nation states – and of their governments – largely unnecessary. Because the global markets for all the I's work just fine on their own, nation states no longer have to play a market-making role. In fact, given their own troubles, which are considerable, they most often just get in the way. If allowed, global solutions will flow to where they are needed without the intervention of nation states. On current evidence, moreover, they flow better precisely because such intervention is absent.

This fundamentally changes the economic equation. If the unfettered movement of these 'I's' makes the middleman role of nation states obsolete, the qualifications needed to sit at the global table and pull in global solutions begin to correspond not to the artificial political borders of countries, but to the more focused geographical units – Hong Kong, for example, and the adjacent stretch of southern China or the Kansai region around Osaka or Catalonia. I call these units 'region states'. They may lie entirely within or across the borders of a nation state. This does not matter. It is the irrelevant result of historical accident. What defines them is not the location of their political borders but the fact that they are the right size and scale to be true, natural business units in today's global economy. Theirs are the borders – and the connections – that matter in a borderless world.

---

3 WHY THE NATION STILL MATTERS

P. Hirst

It has become a commonplace of political debate in the 1990s to assert that the role of national political institutions and the scope for ideologically based party politics are both rapidly diminishing. It would be difficult to deny that the arenas and the objectives of political action are changing, or that such changes require a radical rethinking of political ideas. These changes have been seen to affect the left above all, and to render its old certainties and solutions obsolete.

This new perception became firmly established in the 1980s with two very different but influential bodies of ideas that were directed more or less explicitly against the left. The first, that of the new right, was directed against western social democracy and liberal collectivism. The new right reacted against these forms of pragmatic politics with an ideological vehemence hitherto reserved for the critique of Soviet Communism. It was argued that Keynesian national economic management and comprehensive social welfare had produced the crisis of the 1970s. Attempts to civilize capitalism, to maintain full employment and to sustain growth had led to evils analogous to full-blooded socialism: accelerating inflation, excessive public borrowing and spending, the crowding-out of private capital, and the growth of inefficient big government. The solutions lay in rolling back the state, increasing the scope of market forces, and opening nationally regulated economies to international competitive pressures. The failure

From: *From Statism to Pluralism*, by P. Hirst, UCL Press, 1997.

of new right policies has not, however, led to a revival of social democracy. On the contrary, as a specific accommodation between labour and capital, it is seen as ineffective in a world where national-level solutions to economic problems are no longer possible.

The second argument, that of postmodernist philosophers and social theorists, occupied a more rarefied intellectual niche, but it was significant in undermining the intellectual foundations of the radical left. The postmodernists sought to replace a rhetoric of progress derived from the Enlightenment, central to Marxist beliefs, with a sceptical stance that emphasized the uncertainty of the future and the ambiguity of all meaning. and therefore, the problematic nature of political ideologies. The grand 'meta-narratives', the necessary futures, that had governed political imagination were exhausted and irrelevant. Chief among these was the socialist belief that it could replace capitalism with a new social system. Such totalizing projects inevitably led to new oppressions and made a mockery of the claim that socialism would realize human emancipation.

The collapse of the Soviet Union and its satellites seemed to confirm these very different arguments. Communism was dead and with it the political credibility of any form of Socialism. The revolutions of 1989 and after led to a brief mood of liberal capitalist euphoria. The hope of a 'New World Order' based on democracy and the market was rapidly dispelled by stubborn political realities, but this did nothing to restore the credibility of the left. The conflicts in the former Yugoslavia and the failure of the states of the former Soviet Union to make an effective transition to market economies simply confirmed to many how deep were the deformations of institutions and attitudes produced by socialism. If the old nationalist identities and antagonisms were tenacious, they were a politics for losers. Multinational states might break up, but nationalist politics were no real alternative to the need to adapt to the world market.

To these various perceptions of the limitation of national and socialist solutions must be added the newest rhetoric: that of 'globalization'. From management gurus to the ideologues of the radical left, it has become fashionable to assert that our era is witnessing the growth of a truly global economy dominated by internationalized financial markets and transnational companies. National economies are being subsumed within the global and as a result national-level solutions of any kind are ineffective in the face of the dominant world markets and international competitive pressures. States will be forced to trade down their labour market policies and social spending to a level consistent with matching the competition from the newly industrializing countries of the Pacific Rim, and will have to adapt their monetary and fiscal policies in order to avoid the defection of internationally mobile capital that is concerned only with getting the highest possible returns on a world scale. For the right the rhetoric of 'globalization' offers a whole new lease of life against the claims of nationally based labour at a time when the new right claims of the 1980s have worn thin. For the radical left, this is proof at last of the reality of the world capitalist system and the futility of national reform strategies, even if it is bought at the price of political impotence.

Globalization threatens national strategies based on the collaboration of locally organized capital and organized labour. Modern capitalism is dissolving the old allegiances of national capitalist industrialism. With occupational differentiation, the decline of mass manual employment in traditional manufacturing industry in the advanced countries, and the rise of new internationalized knowledge-based industries and mass media, class in its traditional sense is seen to be less and less relevant. The social basis of traditional party affiliations is disappearing. The role of the party is less and less significant as ideology declines and the media replaces party workers as a means of reaching the electorate. Traditional politics matters less because states can do less and can therefore offer fewer satisfactions in return for citizens' identification with them.

Sections of the reforming left have accepted these arguments as the basis for rethinking a radical politics. They have followed the logic of Robert Reich's *The Work of Nations* (1992) in claiming that the role of national governments is to ensure that their societies are internationally competitive, that they

can offer to international capital attractive locations based on efficient infrastructure at low cost and a highly trained labour force. National governments are the municipalities of the global system, they offer locally the public goods that business needs. This is in essence what much of the argument for 'supply-side Socialism' amounts to: public provision to ensure a thriving market economy.

Sections of the Left have also recognized the need to adopt a politics of democratic renewal that accepts the decline of traditional party politics and the weaknesses of centralized representative democracy. They embrace a politics in which it is claimed that the media are dominant, in which single-issue campaigns and social movements capture much of the traditional energy and idealism that once went into party politics, and in which new forms of democracy through referenda, consultation of citizens through new information technologies, and local direct democratic control become possible.

Globalization: A new grand narrative

The problem with such attempts to redefine the Left is not that new thinking and a new radicalism are not necessary – they are – but that they overemphasize the extent to which national states and the institutions of national democracy are obsolete and ineffective. The rhetoric of 'globalization' creates the belief that the world economy is beyond control and that national-level processes are increasingly being superseded by global ones. Ironically, like classical Marxists, the globalists believe that economic logics are driving us toward a necessary future, in this case one in which an unaccountable world capitalism is dominant. At its worst this is a meta-narrative of pessimism rather than progress.

'Globalization', however, remains more myth than reality. This is because the world economy is still predominantly determined by competitive pressures and products generated at the national level and dependent on national social and political institutions. Truly transnational companies are in fact few; most major companies are still nationally based even if they trade and produce internationally. These national bases contribute to the productive efficiency of these firms. This is particularly true of Germany and Japan, but it also applies to the US. Truly transnational companies would have to reproduce within the firm the advantages they obtain from national institutions, creating, for example, their own multinational, but cohesive managerial elite. As yet the institutional means to build non-national companies as the normal form of economic organization are far from clear.

Companies actually benefit from distinct national managerial styles. They also benefit from being embedded in a complex network of national relationships with central and local governments, with industry associations, with local capital suppliers, with regulatory and standard-setting institutions that help to protect their rights and interests against unfair competition, and with national systems of skill formation and labour motivation. This is as much the case for large, internationally oriented firms as it is for small and medium-scale enterprises in regional economies and industrial districts.

Unregulated global markets in national currencies and equities pose almost as great a threat to companies as they do to international trade. The international governance of major financial markets promises a stability that companies desire as much as anyone else. Calculable trade rules, settled standards for property rights, and a measure of stability in exchange rates are conducive to corporate planning, and, therefore, to investment and growth. Volatility and uncertainty are not. In response to periods of extreme volatility the major nation states of the G7 have attempted regulation, as with the Louvre and Plaza Accords. The tendencies in the governance of the world economy are still unsettled in their direction, but measures towards the reregulation of currency markets and the stabilization of key sectors through international governance are as likely as not.

In such schemes of international governance nation states retain a crucial role. Nation states were effective managers of their own national economies in the post-1945 period mainly because they could rely on a measure of exchange rate stability and trade liberalization conferred by a multilateral regime of international regulation. If a new international regulatory regime is established it will be because the major nation states agree to create it and to confer legitimacy on it by pooling sovereignty. National claims to 'sovereignty' have been more myth than fact: states have never been all-powerful or omnicompetent. If sovereignty means anything now, it is as a source of legitimacy in transferring power upwards and downwards, both through agreements between sovereign states to create international agencies and regulatory regimes and to abide by treaties, and through the constitutional ordering of power between central, regional and local government and publicly recognized bodies in civil society. Nation states are linchpins in the art of distributing power, ordering government by giving it legitimacy. They can only be effective in this if they are democratic and can credibly present such decisions as having popular support.

In a system of international regulation states become crucial agencies of representation. They are the 'global electors' and the means of ensuring that in some mediated degree such international bodies are answerable to the world's people. Such representation is far from direct, but it will be more effective to the extent that states are answerable to their populations and that those populations are informed and roused by a world 'civil society' of NGOs. States will continue to have a function: without them international regulation is inconceivable. And without international economic regulation, the majority of companies will lose rather than gain: a world of volatile markets is one in which success and failure are capriciously distributed, in which companies cannot plan (as they must if they are to develop new markets and products), and where investments and returns on capital are radically insecure. Such a world is sufficiently unsustainable that it will not persist, it will lead either to international regulation or to emerging forms of regional protectionism based on the major trading blocs.

Altered states

Paradoxically, therefore, the degree to which the world has internationalized reinforces the need for the traditional national democratic state, not as the sole or 'sovereign' political agency, but as a crucial relay between international processes and the articulate publics of the developed world. Not all states will matter in this process, which will remain confined to the great powers and the most prosperous nations. Nor will all states be able to achieve a satisfactory internal settlement that enables them to benefit from such international stability as can be created and contained. States and their economies will benefit from existing institutional inheritances that contribute to the co-operation of the major social interests and industrial sectors. Those states like the UK, which have the least social solidarity, the least commitment to major interests, to 'national' goals, the weakest institutions of informal economic co-ordination, and the least developed local and regional structures of economic governance, will tend to fail.

The odds are that relatively solidaristic countries like Germany and Japan will continue to be successful. Wealth and economic success will continue to be highly concentrated, even if new societies with strong national centres of economic co-operation like Korea and Singapore join the ranks of the successful. Macroeconomic policy continues to be crucial in promoting prosperity, at the international level by ensuring stability, and at the national and regional levels by balancing co-operation and competition. Governments are not just municipalities in a competitive global marketplace. Supply-side socialism is at best one-sided. Unless the conditions for stability and growth are created, it amounts to little more than spending public money in an attempt to attract capital. But even the best-trained labour forces can be idle in a world of radical uncertainty and instability.

Politics and governance is becoming ever more polycentric. Nation states are merely one level in a complex system of overlapping and competing governing agencies. Some of those agencies are not public bodies at all; they are private governments or voluntary bodies in civil society. Citizens in advanced countries have multiple foci of association and identification, while societies are becoming more pluralistic and their members more individuated. They are less willing to give unqualified allegiance to collec-

tivities or subordinate their own interests to a single political entity, be it a party, trade union or state. All of this is true, but it does not gainsay the continuing role of nation states. If the state retains a role because of its place in the securing of international regulation, it also retains a role within national societies because of this very polycentricity and complexity.

A weak argument?

It has become fashionable to downgrade the role of representative democracy and of central political institutions. Geoff Mulgan, for example, has been an important, and almost invariably very constructive voice pressing the Left to rethink and adapt to new realities. Yet he is strongly critical of traditional political institutions. He sees such institutions as forms of 'strong power' that developed in an era when the nation state became the central political community. In his essay *Party-free Politics*, he expresses this view very clearly, that politics and nation states have prevailed for 200 years and now their time is passing. They depended on certain historical conditions and 'our sense of politics as a formal system of activism, declarations of rights, manifestos, parliaments, constitutions and professional politicians . . . began . . . in the time of the spinning jenny, the musket and absolutist monarchy' (1994b, p. 15). 'Politics' existed when power had clear boundaries and 'the central institutions of politics, parties and parliament, remain stuck in a nineteenth-century form: centralized, pyramidal, national, with strictly defined rules of authority and sovereignty' (ibid.). These historically specific forms of 'strong power' are being replaced by 'new forms of soft or (weak power) that depend less on formally defined roles and strict rules of authority and cultivate instead greater flexibility, creativity and responsiveness' (ibid.).

The implication is that 'formal politics' is weakening and with it the traditional institutions of state, constitutions, parliaments, and strictly defined legal rules about who has power. The problem with this view is first of all that the list of elements of the old 'strong politics' – rights, manifestos, parliaments, constitutions and professional politicians – is not all of a piece. It can be broken down into at least two sub-sets. Thus parliaments, professional politicians and manifesto politics can all decline in significance without the codified rights of citizens or constitutional ordering suffering the same fate. The reason is that they relate to different aspects of governance. The former set is part of a substantive outcome-oriented politics concerned with win or lose contests within nation states, whereas the latter set is procedural and concerned with regulating social action in the widest sense.

In other words, even if nation states become less effective at deciding the affairs of their societies, national political institutions remain central in setting up the rules whereby various political bodies and social agencies play their games. This may not be 'sovereignty' in the old sense, and the state may be highly pluralistic, but such a society requires a public power that ensures the rule of law.

Rights and constitutional ordering are central to the rule of law. Modern politics has only partly been about parties and ideologues. Modern western societies have been economically successful and relatively civilized in their treatment of their members, in large measure because they provided the security and certainty of the rule of law, limiting the actions that citizens and companies could do to each other and binding the government to obey the law in its dealings with citizens. The politics of parties, parliaments and ideologies has been capable of undermining and destroying the rule of law, so respect for it has depended crucially on the idea of constitutionally ordered authority. Potentially, the two sets in the list above are thus profoundly different in their consequences, and the decline of the former, far from implying the latter's decline, may actually help to sustain and enhance it.

If we do move into a more complex and pluralistic social and political system, then the rule of law will become more, not less important. Law here is meant in two senses: as a guide to action, giving citizens some certainty of expectation and a minimum of norms of conduct in an increasingly complex world; and as a means to regulate conflict between a large number of competing public and private bodies. A society of diversifying political forces,

issues and organizations makes it necessary for there to be a core public power regulating and guiding action, and safeguarding those irreducible elements of the common good that remain. The constitution is thus a pouvoir neutre, not part of 'politics' in the old sense, but still essential to the emerging complexity of our national political systems. Thus constitutional and civil law remain central, and the former protects the latter from undue political interference. Bills of Rights that protect individuals from the state and their fellows, and constitutional ordering of the public domain, preventing the state exceeding certain limits or other bodies appropriating powers that should remain public, are therefore inescapable and continuing elements of modernity.

Because politicians can make less of a claim to legitimacy or majority support, and because the power of common ideologies is waning, it becomes more and not less essential to define and regulate constitutionally the powers they do have. Mulgan's example of the motorway protestors may be the model of new political movements but they would have been aided by a constitution that limited the powers of the executive in pushing through the rape of Twyford Down.

Legal ruling

As the world economy internationalizes and modern states are at best one level of economic regulation, so the roles of international regimes based on international law and of an international 'civil society', of organizations defending common human rights standards, become more necessary. The major national public powers and the private governments that are growing in significance must have internal constitutional limits and be capable of shaping, receiving and obeying international law. International law cannot be imposed on lawless states: it can be effective only if the members of the 'society of states' are themselves law creators and are bound by the rule of law internally.

Without formal democratic legitimacy it is difficult to see how constitutional ordering and the law-making functions of states can be maintained. New forms of direct democracy could only shape a fraction of the laws. Representative democracy will thus remain central, and indeed, needs to be re-invigorated and enhanced in countries like the UIZ, where its institutions have become a mere appendage of the executive. Representative democracy requires parties and politicians, however little we may esteem them at the moment.

If the above arguments are true, then the scope for national politics is by no means over. Nation states will continue to have three key roles, whatever other functions they may gain or lose. The first is as a source of advocacy of, and of legitimation for, international economic regulation, and specifically the stabilization of financial markets. Such stability is essential for the long-term interest of the majority of companies and for the labour forces of the advanced nations. It is, at the international level, a commonality of interest between labour and capital of the same kind that has sustained social democracy in nation states. The second is as the orchestrator of social cohesion and economic co-operation between the major social interests at national level. Such co-operation (rather than technical macroeconomic policy) is the key to economic success. The UK under the Conservatives has suffered from a combination of reckless adventurism in macroeconomic policy and a refusal to build co-operation between the social interests, a function of the maldistribution of power within the state and the dominance of the central executive. The third is as guarantor of the rule of law and of enabling plural communities to co-exist without excessive conflict.

These roles may be slightly different from those of nation states in the past, but they give a place to national-level politics and its political parties. In an obvious sense, this offers a continued place for the reforming left, which has always been nationally based and has always sought an ongoing collaborative dialogue with business. Social democracy in this sense may have a future, but only if it sees the national as a political stage from which to operate upwards, promoting international regulation, and downwards, promoting social cohesion as well as appropriate forms of regional, local and private government. This is yet to happen. The left remains convinced that the global economy is unregulatable,

and it has been too little interested in constitutional ordering and distributing power within the state, preferring to centralize power. Ideology may be unfashionable, but in an era in which the key role of the nation state is to practice the arts of government, orchestrating the power of others, ideas remain essential.

---

4 BEYOND THE NATION STATE
B. Axford

The nation-state was created by an act of will which transformed the 'aggregate of the inhabitants of a country under the direction of a single government into a community of affect' (Hirst and Thompson, 1992) and still serves as a powerful expression of political and cultural identity. In Hobsbawm's (1990) estimation, nationality is a mere parvenu in the list of more elemental attachments like the family, or ethnic, religious and local ties, but this is to underestimate the strong sense of 'belonging' to a country, or being the citizen of a state. The relocation of decisional authority from the nation-state to a growing complex of international and regional institutions still leaves most citizens unmoved, or bemused and cynical, over the antics of politicians and interest groups, even where their lives are directly touched by such changes. So the institutions of the nation-state remain the implicit and often the explicit focus of both demands and supports from citizens.

However, some strands of theorizing on the shape of Europe's 'would-be polity' in the form of the European Union have sought to trace the 'undoing' of the nation-state in the reorientation of various national actors to new centres of decision-making at the European level, thereby undermining

From: *The Global System: economics, politics and culture*, by B. Axford, Polity Press, 1995.

the exclusivity of national identity (Lindberg and Scheingold, 1970; Flaas, 1961). This 'neofunctionalist' representation of European integration predicted the 'Europeanization' of actor and interest group activity as a major factor in the creation of a viable European polity. This was not just a matter of changing behaviour, but of the redefinition of identities and interests. But the danger for this romanticized version of how a political community could be formed, and for the 'transactionalist' theories of writers like Karl Deutsch (1953; 1957), was that the 'spillover' from pragmatic accommodations by actors to shifts in the locus of decision-making, or to the growing intensity of routine communications across borders, would not lead to the emergence of a psychological community of identity based on European rather than national institutions. Both voluntarism and determinism informed these arguments, with 'spill-over' supplying the evolutionary logic of an integration process still reliant on the motivations of actors to make it tick.

Such grand theorizing came under criticism during the prolonged stagnation of Community institutional development from the early 1970s to the mid 1980s. Of late it has achieved something of a comeback by seeming to provide a purchase on the conscious shift from the 'negative' integration of the Single European Act to the 'positive' integration of the Maastricht Treaty on European Union (Hix, 1994). However, it is not necessary to embrace crass neofunctionalism to see the significance of a more determinedly European orientation on the part of various national and subnational actors. In its most instrumental form, this spatial shift of emphasis simply reflects the extent to which changes in the EU following the passing of the Single European Act have made Brussels and Strasbourg more obvious outlets for much lobbying activity previously conducted through national systems of interest representation (Mazey and Richardson, 1993). In other words, what we see is a modification in their behaviour, but not necessarily a change in their identity. In so far as they conceptualize the issue at all, actors may be genuinely ambivalent about the Europeanization of their activities and about the extent of their 'Europeanness'.

An example may help to clarify this point. The response of traditionally insular British trade unions to the 're-launch' of European integration in the Single European Act can be seen in part as a strategic, even an opportunist reaction to the decline in trade union fortunes under successive Conservative governments. But it is also a response which fundamentally 'Europeanizes' trade union identities (Rosamond, 1993). This is not the result of some neat neofunctionalist logic, but the outcome of practices in which agents are consciously choosing to enact, or being forced to come to terms with, a different institutional script. New rules, for example on public procurement or regional policy, which Searle (1965) distinguishes as regulative rules, prescribe empirical patterns of behaviour, but they may also function as constitutive frameworks for action and identity formation (Axford, 1994). Very little work on the European policy process, on interest group intermediation or on policy networks in the EU deals with the constitutive aspect of rules which, in Searle's terms, create and define new forms of practice and new kinds of identity, although there is a burgeoning literature on interest groups and the EU, some of it sensitive to the ways in which transnational networks affect interests and identity (for example Greenwood *et al.*, 1992; Kohler-Koch, 1994; Boyce, 1994).

Overall, the development of the institutional and policy framework of the EU seems to widen the scope for participation by interests representing local, regional, ethnic and corporate constituencies, and at the same time also enlarges the scope for conflict. Thus, the policy networks created do not mirror the neater and more consensual world of 'insiders' and 'outsiders' found in certain national systems of interest mediation (Grant, 1987; Marsh and Rhodes, 1992; Boyce, 1994). But these developments do not make national systems of interest representation obsolete, so much as contribute to a redefinition of national group-government relations. More and more groups are focusing on Brussels and there are an increasing number of 'Eurogroups' – transnational federations like the Committee of Common Market Automobile Constructors (CLCA) – which have achieved varying degrees of 'private-interest government' in their relationships with European institutions (Greenwood and Ronit, 1994). Rules get institutionalized when key stakeholders in the policy process co-ordinate their activities and establish networks of communication. They also begin to define themselves in relation to the new contexts, which in turn are legitimated through routine and chronic practice.

To that extent it might be said that the EU has already achieved epistemic status for many actors (Ruggie, 1993). Kohler-Koch, for example, has hinted at the transformative capacities of European oriented interest groups and trans-European political networks (1994, p. 179; also see Benington and Harvey, 1994), but it is clear that a reading of the internal market in Europe as a new sort of episteme, one in which 'the sovereign importance of place gives way to the sovereign importance of movement' (Ruggie, 1993, p. 173), has still to steer clear of any neo-functionalist 'logic'.

With suitable caution Ruggie himself says that the non-territorial form of the EU as an emergent space of signs and flows need not present any challenge to the integrity of the existing system of rule, the one based upon the centrality of member states in the decision-making process. But one need not be a whole-hearted supporter of neo-functionalism to see that Ruggie's idea of the EU as a 'non-territorial region' (1993, p. 173), complete with flows of capital, goods, people and electronic images, must contribute to the 'hollowing out' of the nation-state (Rhodes, 1994) as a place where policy is made and value is allocated. But I want to stress that this process is not just a matter of elements of control having passed to Brussels allowing groups, localities and regions to bypass national centres of decision-making, but one that involves a restructuration in the identities of the various units of the European system. Furthermore, the outcomes may not even be conventionally 'European' in the sense of instantiating a Brussels-dominated superstate, or some federal version of territorial rule.

Let me take this point a little further. Throughout its history the EU and its predecessors have been handicapped by their ambiguous political status, in which patently state-like activity in various policy areas was not matched by the popular legitimacy which undergirds most democratic national states (see the contributions in Story, 1993). The sort of European polity which emerged under these conditions reflected the relative statelessness of the EU, and more closely resembled the American system of 'disjointed pluralism' – organized over three levels, regions, states and Brussels itself – than it did the neo-corporatist versions of interest-group representation found within many of the member states (Schmitter and Streeck, 1991b, p. 159; 1991a). But while the formation of transnational coalitions or networks of interests mediated by technocrats and consultants in the Brussels 'quasi-state' was clearly in line with Jean Monnet's conception of a European space driven by the rationality of 'linkage' politics (Featherstone, 1994), the very success of this bloodless model of politics and government has only served to emphasize the gap between the Community and the rootedness of a fully developed, legitimated polity. As a system of governance and a form of civil society, the EU is only a simulacrum of national traditions of democratic, territorial rule. Indeed its major weakness as a context for identity formation is precisely that it lacks the crafted authenticity of the nation-state and the assumed 'naturalness' of national identity.

The revival of interest in questions of democracy, accountability and identity since the fall of communism have also surfaced in the debates on the process of European unity, which until recently had been notable as an almost pristine model of elite autonomy (Bachrach, 1967). The reaction of voting publics in Denmark and France in the referendums on the Maastricht Treaty on European Union (TEU) was much more critical of the overtly elitist and technocratic process of decision-making than is conveyed in anodyne notions like 'democratic deficit' (Lodge, 1993), which centres on incremental changes in the personnel and practices of European institutions (Middlemass, 1993). Such grumbling reaffirmations of the existence and power of low politics are difficult to accommodate in the Community setting. For all its state-like attributes, the EU is not a state and it is in the context of the nation-state that issues of democratic accountability and citizenship rights have been addressed. The translation of these questions to the Community level introduces problems for the relatively immature political system of the EU. Although a kind of social citizenship has been handed down through Community legislation, or mooted in pronouncements on the rights of employees or old people, more robust 'bottom-up' expressions of citizenship require the props of a functioning democracy, and therein lies the Community's 'Catch-22'. To institute a European citizenship would not only be an audacious and at this stage unthinkable step, but would also be meaningless unless tied to the creation of a European state, or – wild imagining – redefined as an attribute of people in general (in a sociological rather than a juridical sense) and not of the denizens of territorially bounded jurisdictions in particular (Niechan, 1993).

The debate on European unity has traded in familiar antinomies, where more or less intergovernmentalist positions (forms of realism, concern for national interests) vie with divers integrationist ones (neo-functionalism, forms of federalism). But these one-or-other approaches to European unity may hide messier truths and more complex visions of European 'unity'. This complexity has a number of strands, one of which is the standard claim that European integration is undoing the nation-state. An apparently straightforward demonstration of this is a provision in the Maastricht Treaty that the member states of the Union will not run up massive budget deficits, and will heed the advice of the Community on managing their economies. But while this clearly limits the autonomy of member states, it in no way undermines the claim made by Alan Milward (1992) that European integration has salvaged the nation-state in Europe from its post-war weakness. What it does show, however, is that things have changed a lot in the meantime. For one thing, post-1992 Europe is ever more clamorous on the status and claims of localities and regions versus those of the state. Indeed the EU has gone so far as to institutionalize sub-national demands in Maastricht's Committee of the Regions, and in the direct representation of cities and regions at the level of the EU.

So far, so conventional: globalizing and regionalizing forces have the power to succour localities, even where this involves diminishing their reliance on the nation-state. But this is only one half of the equation. On the other hand, cultural products and cultural communities are already established across borders in Europe and across the world: what are their effects on the nation-state? Again, we must be cautious. In many cases these networks or cultural communities ought to be understood as forms of 'third culture' (Featherstone, 1990). Third cultures – of specialists, Euromanagers, transnational professional associations, agreed professional standards and so on afford opportunities for new allegiances and identities, but without the concomitant destruction of old ones, because of their relative insulation from mainstream national, local or even Community cultures and because of their location in the hyperspace (Jameson 1961) or cyberspace of European flows. Perhaps this is the burden of Ruggie's point about the co-existence of a Europe of flows and places, which creates not a standard integrationist's Europe but a postmodern political economy.

In some measure, the completion of the internal market augurs just such a Europe, although it also requires that member states play a more developed role in regulating the flows of goods, services, capital and people. On my reading, the single market process is neither state-centric nor communitarian in the accepted sense of that term (see also Wallace, 1993). The 1992 doctrine of 'mutual recognition' both limits the ability of national administrations to intervene in attempts by their citizens to take advantage of the internal market, and carries the liberal ideology of deregulation further by reducing the need for, Community regulation, insisting only on the compatibility of national standards rather than on the elimination of differences between them. So, in principle, the need for extensive national and Community systems of regulation and policy accommodation is eliminated. The putative outcome is not only what Schmitter and Streeck call a 'formal devaluation of the vast political resources which have come to be organized in and around the nation-state' (1991b, p. 149) but a redefinition of a European polity as a space created and recreated by networks of interaction – cultural, educational, commercial and scientific – rather than a space to be governed or regulated in the conventional sense of these terms. In a further twist, Maastriches concept of subsidiarity also carries a potentially lethal charge for communitarian principles and nation-states, by suggesting, or appearing to suggest, that the Community should act only in those areas that cannot be properly dealt with at the national level or below.

In practice, most treatments of European unity have been unable to dispense with the mythology and imagery of place, which is rather strange because Europe has never been 'a' place or possessed 'an' identity, save in the imaginary of a European 'civilization'. In Balibar's (1991) phrase it is now a 'world space' caught between the messy and increasingly confused authenticity of the local, the ethnic or the national, and the hyperspace of the global. Recent developments in the EU and in the world economy include greater freedom of movement for businesses, money and goods, as well as for people, ideas and symbols. The globalization of many areas of economic life is unlikely to be matched by the creation of a world political system that is beyond the nation-state. But the future of the nation-state looks precariously balanced between the potentially bloody excesses of infranationalism or micronationalism, and the emotionally challenged arena of supranational rule through bureaucrats and regulatory regimes.

Though widely canvassed, this picture may be too stark. Morally, the nation-state does find itself strongly challenged as an effective instrument of policy-making and delivery in an increasing number of areas, but is still vital as the expression of a national identity, and of attachments to history, place and culture. Newer and older imaginings and identities constitute challenges to this paradigm status, which itself is still young in world-historical terms. Clearly, one of the major issues going into the twenty-first century will be the appropriate size and definition of units of government, and the continuing relevance and legitimacy of concepts like territoriality. My cautionary note about nation-states as expressive as well as instrumental institutions, and as being about meaning as much as materiality, provides an appropriate and timely reminder of the need to address the cultural make-up of the global system and those structures and flows which help secure and change identities.

---

5 AFTER THE NATION STATE – WHAT?

Z. Bauman

In an earlier generation, social policy was based on the belief that nations and within nations cities, could control their fortunes; now, a divide is opening between polity and economy, observes Richard Sennett. (1995, p. 13)

With the overall speed of movement gathering momentum – with time/space as such, as David Harvey points out, 'compressing' – some objects move faster than others. 'The economy' – capital, which means money and other resources needed to get things done, to make more money and more things yet – moves fast enough to keep permanently a step ahead of any (territorial, as ever) polity which may try to contain and redirect its travels. In this case, at least, the reduction of travel time to zero leads to a new quality: to a total annihilation of spatial constraints, or rather to the total 'overcoming of gravity'. Whatever moves with the speed approaching the velocity of the electronic signal, is practically free from constraints, related to the territory inside which it originated, towards which it is aimed or through which it passes on the way. A recent commentary by Martin Woollacott grasps well the consequences of that emancipation:

The Swedish-Swiss conglomerate Asea Brown Boveri announced it would be cutting its West

From: *Globalization: the Human Consequences*, by Z. Bauman, Polity Press, 1998.

European work force by 57,000, while creating other jobs in Asia. Electrolux followed with the announcement that it will cut its global work force by 11 per cent, with most of the cuts in Europe and North America. Pilkington Glass also announced significant cuts. In just ten days, three European firms had cut jobs on a scale large enough to be compared with the numbers mentioned in the new French and British Governments' proposals on job creation.

Germany, notoriously, has lost 1 million jobs in five years, and its companies are busy building plants in Eastern Europe, Asia, and Latin America. If West European industry is massively relocating outside Western Europe, then all these arguments about the best government approach to unemployment would have to be seen as of limited relevance. (Woollacott, 1997)

Balancing the books of what once seemed to be the indispensable setting for all economic thinking – the Nationalökonomie – is becoming more and more an actuarial fiction. As Vincent Cable points out in his recent Demos (1996, p. 20) pamphlet:

it is no longer obvious what it means to describe the Midland Bank or ICL as British (or for that matter companies like British Petroleum, British Airways, British Gas or British Telecom) . . . In a world where capital has no fixed abode and financial flows are largely beyond the control of national governments, many of the levers of economic policy no longer work.

And Alberto Melucci (1966, p. 150) suggests that the rapidly growing influence of supranational – 'planetary' – organizations 'has had the effect of both accelerating the exclusion of weak areas and of creating new channels for the allocation of resources, removed, at least in part, from the control of the various national states'.

In the words of G. H. von Wright, the 'nation-state, it seems, is eroding or perhaps "withering away".' The eroding forces are transnational. Since nation-states remain the sole frame for book-balancing and the sole sources of effective political initiative, the 'transnationality' of eroding forces puts them outside the realm of deliberate, purposeful and potentially rational action. As everything that elides such action, such forces, their shapes and actions are blurred in the mist of mystery; they are objects of guesses rather than reliable analysis. As von Wright (1997, p. 49) puts it,

The moulding forces of transnational character are largely anonymous and therefore difficult to identify. They do not form a unified system or order. They are an agglomeration of systems manipulated by largely 'invisible' actors . . . [there is no] unity or purposeful co-ordination of the forces in question . . . 'Market' is not a bargaining interaction of competing forces so much as the pull and push of manipulated demands, artificially created needs, and desire for quick profit.

All this surrounds the ongoing process of the 'withering away' of nation-states with an aura of a natural catastrophe. Its causes are not fully understood; it cannot be exactly predicted even if the causes are known; and it certainly cannot be prevented from happening even if predicted. The feeling of unease, an expectable response to a situation without obvious levers of control, has been pointedly and incisively captured in the title of Kenneth Jowitt's book – The New World Disorder. Throughout the modern era we have grown used to the idea that order is tantamount to 'being in control'. It is this assumption – whether well-founded or merely illusionary – of 'being in control' which we miss most.

'The new world disorder'

The present-day 'new world disorder' cannot be explained away merely by the circumstance which constitutes the most immediate and obvious reason to feel at a loss and aghast: namely, by 'the morning-after' confusion following the abrupt end of the Great Schism and the sudden collapse of the power-block political routine – even if it was indeed that collapse which triggered the 'new disorder' alert. The image of global disorder reflects, rather, the new awareness (facilitated, but not necessarily caused, by the abrupt demise of block politics) of the essentially elemental and contingent nature of the things which previously seemed to be tightly controlled or at least 'technically controllable'.

Before the collapse of the Communist bloc, the contingent, erratic and wayward nature of the global state of affairs was not so much non-existent, as it was barred from sight by the all-energy-and-thought-consuming day-to-day reproduction of the balance between the world powers. By dividing the world, power politics conjured up the image of totality. Our shared world was made whole by assigning to each nook and cranny of the globe its significance in the 'global order of things' – to wit, in the two power-camps' conflict and the meticulously guarded, though forever precarious, equilibrium. The world was a totality in as far as there was nothing in it which could escape such significance, and so nothing could be indifferent from the point of view of the balance between the two powers which appropriated a considerable part of the world and cast the rest in the shadow of that appropriation. Everything in the world had a meaning, and that meaning emanated from a split, yet single centre – from the two enormous power blocks locked up, riveted and glued to each other in an all-out combat. With the Great Schism out of the way, the world does not look a totality anymore; it looks rather like a field of scattered and disparate forces, congealing in places difficult to predict and gathering momentum which no one really knows how to arrest.

To put it in a nutshell: no one seems now to be in control. Worse still – it is not clear what 'being in control' could, under the circumstances, be like. As before, all ordering initiatives and actions are local and issue-oriented; but there is no longer a locality arrogant enough to pronounce for mankind as a whole, or to be listened to and obeyed by mankind when making the pronouncements. Neither is there a single issue which could grasp and telescope the totality of global affairs while commanding global consent.

Universalizing – or being globalized?

It is this novel and uncomfortable perception of 'things getting out of hand' which has been articulated (with little benefit to intellectual clarity) in the currently fashionable concept of globalization. The deepest meaning conveyed by the idea of globalization is that of the indeterminate, unruly and self-propelled character of world affairs; the absence of a centre, of a controlling desk, of a board of directors, of a managerial office. Globalization is Jowitt's 'new world disorder' under another name. This trait, undetachable from the image of globalization, sets it radically apart from another idea which it ostensibly replaced, that of 'universalization' – once constitutive of the modern discourse of global affairs, but by now fallen into disuse, rarely heard of, perhaps even by and large forgotten by anyone except philosophers.

Just like the concepts of 'civilization', 'development', 'convergence', 'consensus' and many other key terms of early- and classic-modern thinking, the idea of 'universalization' conveyed the hope, the intention, and the determination of order-making; on top of what the other kindred terms signalled, it meant a universal order – the order-making on a universal, truly global scale. Like the other concepts, the idea of universalization was coined on the rising tide of the modern powers' resourcefulness and the modern intellect's ambitions. The entire family of concepts announced in unison the will to make the world different from what it had been and better than it had been, and expand the change and the improvement to a global, species-wide dimension. By the same token, it declared the intention to make similar the life conditions of everyone and everywhere, and so everybody's life chances; perhaps even make them equal.

Nothing of that has been left in the meaning of globalization, as shaped by the present discourse. The new term refers primarily to the global effects, notoriously unintended and unanticipated, rather than to global initiatives and undertakings. Yes, it says: our actions may have, and often do have, global effects; but no – we do not have, nor do we know well how to obtain, the means to plan and execute actions globally. 'Globalization' is not about what we all, or at least the most resourceful and enterprising among us, wish or hope to do. It is about what is happening to us all. The idea of 'globalization' explicitly refers to von Wright's 'anonymous forces', operating in the vast – foggy and slushy, impassable and untamable – 'no man's land', stretching beyond the reach of the design-and-action capacity of anybody's in particular.

How has it come about that this vast expanse of man-made wilderness (not the 'natural' wilderness which modernity set out to conquer and tame; but, to paraphrase Anthony Giddens's felicitous phrase, a 'manufactured jungle' – the post-domestication wilderness, one that emerged after the conquest, and as its result) has sprung into vision? And why did it acquire that formidable power of obstinacy and resilience which since Durkheim is taken to be the defining mark of 'hard reality'?

A plausible explanation is the growing experience of weakness, indeed of impotence, of the habitual, taken-for-granted ordering agencies. Among the latter, pride of place throughout the modern era belonged to the state. (One is tempted to say: to the territorial state, but the ideas of the state and of 'territorial sovereignty' had become in modern practice and theory synonymous, and thus the phrase 'territorial state' became pleonastic.) The meaning of 'the state' has been precisely that of an agency claiming the legitimate right and boasting sufficient resources to set up and enforce the rules and norms binding the run of affairs within a certain territory; the rules and norms hoped and expected to turn contingency into determination, ambivalence into Eindeutigkeit, randomness into regularity – in short, the primeval forest into a carefully plotted garden, chaos into order.

To order a certain section of the world came to mean: to set up a state endowed with the sovereignty to do just that. It also necessarily meant the ambition to enforce a certain model of preferred order at the expense of other, competitive, models. This could be implemented solely through acquiring the vehicle of the state, or by capturing the driving seat of the existing one.

Max Weber defined the state as the agency claiming monopoly over the means of coercion and over their use inside its sovereign territory. Cornelius Castoriadis warns against the widespread habit of confusing the state with social power as such: 'State', he insists, refers to a particular way of distributing and condensing social power, precisely with the enhanced ability 'to order' in mind. 'The State', says Castoriadis (1990, p. 124), 'is an entity separated from the collectivity and instituted in such a manner as to secure the permanence of that separation.' One should reserve the name of 'the State' 'for such cases when it is instituted in the form of the State Apparatus – which implies a separate "bureaucracy", civil, clerical or military, even if only rudimentary: in other words, a hierarchical organization with delimited area of competence.'

Let us point out, though, that such 'separation of social power from collectivity' was by no means a chance event, lone of the vagaries of history. The task of order-making requires huge and continuous efforts of creaming-off, shifting and condensing social power, which in turn call for considerable resources that only the state, in the form of a hierarchical bureaucratic apparatus, is able to muster, focus and deploy. Of necessity, the legislative and executive sovereignty of the modern state was perched on the 'tripod' of military, economic and cultural sovereignties; in other words, on the state's dominion over the resources once deployed by the diffuse foci of social power, but now all needed to sustain the institution and maintenance of the state-administered order. An effective order-making capacity was unthinkable unless supported by the ability to defend effectively the territory against challenges of other models of order, both from outside and inside the realm; by the ability to balance the books of the Nationalökonomie; and the ability to muster enough cultural resources to sustain the state's identity and distinctiveness through distinctive identity of its subjects.

Only a few populations aspiring to state sovereignty of their own were large and resourceful enough to pass such a demanding test, and thus to contemplate sovereignty and statehood as a realistic prospect. The times when the ordering job was undertaken and performed primarily, perhaps solely, through the agency of sovereign states, were for that reason the times of relatively few states. By the same token, the establishment of any sovereign state required as a rule the suppression of state-formative ambitions of many lesser populations undermining or expropriating however little they might have possessed of inchoate military capacity, economic self-sufficiency and cultural distinctiveness.

Under such circumstances, the 'global scene' was the theatre of inter-state politics, which – through armed conflicts, bargaining or both – aimed first and foremost at the drawing and preserving ('internationally guaranteeing') of the boundaries that set apart and enclosed the territory of each state's legislative and executive sovereignty. 'Global politics', in as far as the foreign politics of sovereign states had anything like global horizons, concerned itself mostly with sustaining the principle of full and uncontested sovereignty of each state over its territory, with the effacing of the few 'blank spots' remaining on the world map, and fighting off the danger of ambivalence arising from occasional overlapping of sovereignties or from outstanding territorial claims. In an oblique, yet emphatic tribute to that vision, the main decision taken unanimously at the first, founding session of the Organization of African Unity, was to proclaim sacrosanct and unchangeable all new state boundaries – by common agreement totally artificial products of the colonial legacy. The image of the 'global order' boiled down, in short, to the sum-total of a number of local orders, each effectively maintained and efficiently policed by one, and one only, territorial state. All states were expected to rally to the defence of one another's policing rights.

Superimposed upon that parcelled-out world of sovereign states for almost half a century and until a few years ago were two power blocks. Each of the two blocks promoted a growing degree of co-ordination between the state-managed orders inside the realm of its respective 'meta-sovereignty', based on the assumption of each singular state's military, economic and cultural insufficiency. Gradually yet relentlessly, a new principle was promoted – in political practice faster than in political theory – of supra-state integration. The 'global scene' was seen increasingly as the theatre of coexistence and competition between groups of states, rather than between the states themselves.

The Bandung initiative to establish the incongruous 'nonblock block', and the ensuing, recurrent efforts of alignment undertaken by non-aligned states, was an oblique acknowledgement of that new principle. That initiative was, however, consistently and effectively sapped by the two super-blocks, which stayed unanimous on at least one point: they both treated the rest of the world as the twentieth-century equivalent of the 'blank spots' of the nineteenth-century state-building and state enclosure race. Non-alignment, refusal to join either one or the other of the two super-blocks, obstinate attachment to the old-fashioned and increasingly obsolete principle of supreme sovereignty vested with the state – was seen as the blocks-era equivalent of that 'no man's land' ambivalence which was fought off tooth and nail, competitively yet in unison, by modern states at their formative stage.

The political superstructure of the Great Schism era barred from sight the deeper, and – as it has now transpired – more seminal and lasting departures in the mechanism of order-making. The change affected above all the role of the state. All three legs of the 'sovereignty tripod' have been broken beyond repair. The military, economic and cultural self-sufficiency, indeed self-sustainability, of the state – any state – ceased to be a viable prospect. In order to retain their law-and-order policing ability, states had to seek alliances and voluntarily surrender ever larger chunks of their sovereignty. And when the curtain was eventually torn apart, it uncovered an unfamiliar scene, populated by bizarre characters.

There were now states which – far from being forced to give up their sovereign rights – actively and keenly sought to surrender them, and begged for their sovereignty to be taken away and dissolved in the supra-state formations. There were unheard-of or forgotten local 'ethnicities' – long deceased yet born again, or never previously heard of but now duly invented – often too small, hard-up and inept to pass any of the traditional tests of sovereignty, yet nevertheless demanding states of their own, states with the full trappings of political sovereignty and the right to legislate and police order on their own territory.

There were old or new nations escaping the federalist cages in which they had been incarcerated by the now extinct Communist super-power against their will – but only to use their newly acquired decision-making freedom to pursue the dissolution of their political, economic and military independence in the European Market and NATO alliance. The new chance, contained in the ignoring of the stern and demanding conditions of statehood, has found its acknowledgement in the dozens of 'new nations' rushing to install their offices inside the already overcrowded UN building, not originally expected to accommodate such huge numbers of 'equals'.

Paradoxically, it was the demise of state sovereignty, not its triumph, that made the idea of statehood so tremendously popular. In the caustic estimate of Erie Hobsbawm (1977), once the Seychelles can have a vote in the UN as good as Japan's 'the majority of the members of the UN is soon likely to consist of the late twentieth-century (republican) equivalents to Saxe-Coburg-Gotha and Schwarzburg-Sonderhausen.'

The new expropriation of the state

Indeed, the new states, just like the longer-living ones in their present condition, are no longer expected to perform most of the functions once seen as the raison d'être of the nation-state bureaucracies. The function most conspicuous for having been dropped by the orthodox state, or torn out of its hands, is the maintenance of that 'dynamic equilibrium' which Castoriadis (1996, p. 14) describes as 'approximate equality between the rhythms of the growth of consumption and the elevation of productivity' – the task which led the sovereign states at various times to impose intermittently import or export bans, customs barriers, or state-managed Keynes-style stimulation of internal demand.' Any control of such 'dynamic equilibrium' is now beyond the means, and indeed beyond the ambitions, of the overwhelming majority of the otherwise sovereign (in the strictly order-policing sense) states. The very distinction between the internal and global market, or more generally between the 'inside' and the 'outside' of the state, is exceedingly difficult to maintain in any but the most narrow, 'territory and population policing' sense.

All three legs of the sovereignty tripod have now been shattered. Arguably, the crushing of the economic leg has been most seminal. No longer capable of balancing the books while guided solely by the politically articulated interests of the population within their realm of political sovereignty, the nation-states turn more and more into the executors and plenipotentiaries of forces which they have no hope of controlling politically. In the incisive verdict of the radical Latin-American political analyst, thanks to the new 'porousness' of all allegedly 'national' economies, and to the ephemerality, elusiveness and non-territoriality of the space in which they operate, global financial markets 'impose their laws and precepts on the planet. The "globalization" is nothing more than a totalitarian extension of their logic on all aspects of life'. States have not enough resources or freedom of manoeuvre to withstand the pressure – for the simple reason that 'a few minutes is enough for enterprises and the states themselves to collapse':

> In the cabaret of globalization, the state goes through a striptease and by the end of the performance it is left with the bare necessities only: its powers of repression. With its material basis destroyed, its sovereignty and independence annulled, its political class effaced, the nation-state becomes a simple security service for the mega-companies . . .
>
> The new masters of the world have no need to govern directly. National governments are charged with the task of administering affairs on their behalf. (Marcos, 1997, pp. 14–15)

Due to the unqualified and unstoppable spread of free trade rules, and above all the free movement of capital and finances, the 'economy' is progressively exempt from political control; indeed, the prime meaning conveyed by the term 'economy' is 'the area of the non-political'. Whatever has been left of politics is expected to be dealt with, as in the good old days, by the state – but whatever is concerned with the economic life the state is not allowed to touch:

any attempt in this direction would be met with prompt and furious punitive action from the world markets. The economic impotence of the state would once more be blatantly displayed to the horror of its current governing team. According to the calculations of René Passat (1997, p. 26), purely speculative inter-currency financial transactions reach a total volume of $1,300 billion a day – fifty times greater than the volume of commercial exchanges and almost equal to the total of $1,500 billion to which all the reserves of all the 'national banks' of the world amount. 'No state', Passat concludes, 'can therefore resist for more than a few days the speculative pressures of the "markets".'

The sole economic task which the state is allowed and expected to handle is to secure 'the equilibrated budget' by policing and keeping in check the local pressures for more vigorous state intervention in the running of businesses and for the defence of the population from the more sinister consequences of market anarchy. As Jean-Paul Fitoussi (1997) has recently pointed out,

> Such a programme, though, cannot be implemented unless in one way or another the economy is taken out from the field of politics. A ministry of finances remains certainly a necessary evil, but ideally one would dispose of the ministry of economic affairs (that is, of the governing of economy). In other words, the government should be deprived of its responsibility for macroeconomic policy.

Contrary to oft-repeated (yet no more true for that reason) opinions, there is neither logical nor pragmatic contradiction between the new exterritoriality of capital (complete in the case of finances, nearly complete in the case of trade, and well advanced in the case of industrial production) and the new proliferation of feeble and impotent sovereign states. The rush to carve out ever new and ever weaker and less resourceful 'politically independent' territorial entities does not go against the grain of the globalizing economic tendencies; political fragmentation is not a 'spoke in the wheel' of the emergent 'world society', bonded by the free circulation of information. On the contrary – there seems to be an intimate kinship, mutual conditioning and reciprocal reinforcement between the 'globalization' of all aspects of the economy and the renewed emphasis on the 'territorial principle'.

For their liberty of movement and for their unconstrained freedom to pursue their ends, global finance, trade and the information industry depend on the political fragmentation the morcellement – of the world scene. They have all, one may say, developed vested interests in 'weak states' – that is, in such states as are weak but nevertheless remain states. Deliberately or subconsciously, such inter-state, supra-local institutions as have been brought into being and are allowed to act with the consent of global capital, exert co-ordinated pressures on all member or independent states to destroy systematically everything which could stem or slow down the free movement of capital and limit market liberty. Throwing wide open the gates and abandoning any thought of autonomous economic policy is the preliminary, and meekly complied with, condition of eligibility for financial assistance from world banks and monetary funds. Weak states is precisely what the New World Order, all too often looking suspiciously like a new world disorder, needs to sustain and reproduce itself. Weak, quasi-states can be easily reduced to the (useful) role of local police precincts, securing a modicum of order required for the conduct of business, but need not be feared as effective brakes on the global companies' freedom.

The separation of economy from politics and the exemption of the first from the regulatory intervention of the second, resulting in the disempowerment of politics as an effective agency, augurs much more than just a shift in the distribution of social power. As Claus Offe (1996, p. 37) points out, the political agency as such – 'the capacity to make collectively binding choices and to carry them out' – has become problematic. 'Instead of asking what is to be done, we might more fruitfully explore whether there is anybody capable of doing whatever needs to be done.' Since 'borders have become penetrable' (highly selectively, to be sure), 'sovereignties have become nominal, power anonymous, and its locus empty'. We are still far from the ultimate destination; the process goes on, seemingly unstoppably. 'The dominant pattern might be described as "releasing the brakes": deregulation, liberalization, flexibility, increasing fluidity, and facilitating the transactions on the financial real estate and labour markets, easing the tax burden, etc.' (Balls and Jenkins, 1996). The more consistently this pattern is applied, the less power remains in the hands of the agency which promotes it; and less can the increasingly resourceless agency retreat from applying it, if it so wished or if it was pressed to do so.

One of the most seminal consequences of the new global freedom of movement is that it becomes increasingly difficult, perhaps altogether impossible, to re-forge social issues into effective collective action.

The global hierarchy of mobility

Let us recall once more what Michel Crozier pointed out many years ago in his trail-blazing study of 'The Bureaucratic Phenomenon': all dominance consists in the pursuit of an essentially similar strategy – to leave as much leeway and freedom of manoeuvre to the dominant, while imposing the strictest possible constraints on the decisional freedom of the dominated side.

This strategy was once successfully applied by state governments, which now, however, find themselves on its receiving end. It is now the conduct of the 'markets' – primarily, world finances – which is the main source of surprise and uncertainty. It is not difficult to see therefore that the replacement of territorial 'weak states' by some sort of global legislative and policing powers would be detrimental to the interests of 'world markets'. And so it is easy to suspect that, far from acting at cross-purposes and being at war with each other, political fragmentation and economic globalization are close allies and fellow conspirators.

Integration and parcelling out, globalization and territorialization, are mutually complementary processes. More precisely, they are two sides of the same process: that of the world-wide redistribution of sovereignty, power and the freedom to act, triggered (though by no means determined) by the radical leap in the technology of speed. The coincidence and intertwining of synthesis and dissipation, integration and decomposition are anything but accidental; even less are they rectifiable.

It is because of this coincidence and intertwining of the two apparently opposite tendencies, both set in motion by the divisive impact of the new freedom of movement, that the so-called 'globalizing' processes rebound in the redistribution of privileges and deprivations, of wealth and poverty, of resources and impotence, of power and powerlessness, of freedom and constraint. We witness today the process of a world-wide restratification, in the course of which a new socio-cultural hierarchy, a world-wide scale, is put together.

The quasi-sovereignties, territorial divisions and segregations of identities which the globalization of markets and information promotes and renders 'a must', do not reflect diversity of equal partners. What is a free choice for some descends as cruel fate upon others. And since those 'others' tend to grow unstoppably in numbers and sink ever deeper into despair born of a prospectless existence, one will be well advised to speak of 'glocalization' (Roland Robertson's apt term, exposing the unbreakable unity between 'globalizing' and 'localizing' pressures – a phenomenon glossed over in the one-sided concept of globalization), and to define it mostly as the process of the concentration of capital, finance and all other resources of choice and effective action, but also – perhaps above all – of the concentration of freedom to move and to act (two freedoms which for all practical purposes have become synonymous).

Commenting on the findings of the UN's latest Human Development Report, that the total wealth of the top 358 'global billionaires' equals the combined incomes of 2.3 billion poorest people (45 per cent of the world's population), Victor Keegan (1996) called the present reshuffling of the world resources 'a new form of highway robbery'. Indeed, only 22 per cent of global wealth belongs to the so-called 'developing countries', which account for about 80 per cent of the world population. And yet this is by no means the limit the present polarization is likely to reach, since the share of the global income currently apportioned to the poor is smaller still: in 1991, 85 per cent of the world's population received only 15 per cent of its income. No wonder that in the abysmally meagre 2.3 per cent of global wealth owned by 20 per cent of the poorest countries thirty years ago has fallen by now still further, to 1.4 per cent.

Also the global network of communication, acclaimed as the gateway to a new and unheard of freedom, and above all as the technological foundation of imminent equality, is clearly very selectively used; a narrow cleft in the thick wall, rather than a gate. Few (and fewer) people get the passes entitling them to go through. 'All computers do for the Third World these days is to chronicle their decline more efficiently,' says Keegan. And concludes: 'If (as one American critic observed) the 358 decided to keep $5 million or so each, to tide themselves over, and give the rest away, they could virtually double the annual incomes of nearly half the people on Earth. And pigs would fly.'

In the words of John Kavanagh of the Washington Institute of Policy Research,

> Globalization has given more opportunities for the extremely wealthy to make money more quickly. These individuals have utilized the latest technology to move large sums of money around the globe extremely quickly and speculate ever more efficiently. Unfortunately, the technology makes no impact on the lives of the world poor. In fact, globalization is a paradox: while it is very beneficial to a very few, it leaves out or marginalizes two-thirds of the world's population.

As the folklore of the new generation of 'enlightened classes', gestated in the new, brave and monetarist world of nomadic capital, would have it, opening up sluices and dynamiting all state-maintained dams will make the world a free place for everybody. According to such folkloristic beliefs, freedom (of trade and capital mobility, first and foremost) is the hothouse in which wealth would grow faster than ever before; and once the wealth is multiplied, there will be more of it for everybody.

The poor of the world – whether old or new, hereditary or computer-made – would hardly recognize their plight in this folkloristic fiction. The media are the message, and the media through which the establishment of the world-wide market is being perpetrated do not facilitate, but, on the contrary, preclude the promised 'trickle-down' effect. New fortunes are born, sprout and flourish in the virtual reality, tightly isolated from the old-fashioned rough-and-ready realities of the poor. The creation of wealth is on the way to finally emancipating itself from its perennial – constraining and vexing – connections with making things, processing materials, creating jobs and managing people. The old rich needed the poor to make and keep them rich. That dependency at all times mitigated the conflict of interest and prompted some effort, however tenuous, to care. The new rich do not need the poor any more. At long last the bliss of ultimate freedom is nigh.

The lie of the free-trade promise is well covered up; the connection between the growing misery and desperation of the 'grounded' many and the new freedoms of the mobile few is difficult to spot in the reports coming from the lands cast on the receiving side of 'glocalization'. It seems, on the contrary, that the two phenomena belong to different worlds, each having its own, sharply distinct causes. One would never guess from the reports that the fast enrichment and fast impoverishment stem from the same root, that the 'grounding' of the miserable is as legitimate outcome of the 'glocalizing' pressures as are the new sky's-the-limit freedoms of the successful (as one would never guess from sociological analyses of the holocaust and other genocides that they are equally 'at home' in modern society as are economic, technological, scientific and standard-of-living progress).

As Ryszard Kapuscinski (1996), one of the most formidable chronographers of contemporary living, has recently explained, that effective cover-up is achieved by three inter-connected expedients consistently applied by the media which preside over the occasional, carnival-like outbursts of public interest in the plight of the 'poor of the world'.

First, the news of a famine – arguably the last remaining reason for breaking the day-by-day indifference – as a rule comes coupled with the emphatic reminder that the same distant lands where people 'as seen on TV' die of famine and disease, are the birthplace of 'Asian tigers', the exemplary benefic-iaries of the new imaginative and brave way of getting things done. It does not matter that all the 'tigers' together embrace no more than 1 per cent of the population of Asia alone. They are assumed to demonstrate what was to be proved – that the sorry plight of the hungry and indolent is their sui generis choice: alternatives are available, and within reach – but not taken for the lack of industry or resolve. The underlying message is that the poor themselves bear responsibility for their fate; that they could, as the 'tigers' did, choose easy prey has nothing to do with the tigers' appetites.

Second, the news is so scripted and edited as to reduce the problem of poverty and deprivation to the question of hunger alone. This stratagem achieves two effects in one go: the real scale of poverty is played down (800 million people are permanently undernourished, but something like 4 billion, two-thirds of the world population – live in poverty), and the task ahead is limited to finding food for the hungry. But, as Kapuscinski points out, such presentation of the problem of poverty (as exemplified by one of The Economist's recent issues analysing world poverty under the heading 'How to feed the world') 'terribly degrades, virtually denies full humanity to people whom we want, allegedly, to help'. What the equation 'poverty – hunger' conceals are many other and complex aspects of poverty – 'horrible living and housing conditions, illness, illiteracy, aggression, falling apart families, weakening of social bonds, lack of future and non-productiveness' afflictions which cannot be cured with high-protein biscuits and powdered milk. Kapuscinski remembers wandering through African townships and villages and meeting children 'who begged me not for bread, water, chocolate or toys, but a ballpoint, since they went to school and had nothing to write their lessons with'.

Let us add that all associations of the horrid pictures of famine, as presented by the media, with the destruction of work and work-places (that is, with the global causes of local poverty) are carefully avoided. People are shown together with their hunger – but however the viewers strain their eyes, they will not see a single work-tool, plot of arable land or head of cattle in the picture – and one hears no reference to them. As if there was no connection between the emptiness of the routine 'get up and do something' exhortations addressed to the poor in a world which needs no more labour, certainly not in the lands where people on the screen starve, and the plight of people offered as a carnival-like, 'charity fair' outlet for a pent-up moral impulse. The riches are global, the misery is local – but there is no causal link between the two; not in the spectacle of the fed and the feeding, anyway.

Victor Hugo let Enjolras, one of his characters, wistfully exclaim a moment before his death on one of the many nineteenth-century barricades: 'The twentieth century will be happy.' As it happened – René Passet comments – 'the same technologies of the immaterial which sustained that promise entail simultaneously its denial', particularly when 'coupled with the frantic policy of planetary liberalization of capital exchanges and movements'. Technologies which effectively do away with time and space need little time to denude and impoverish space. They render capital truly global; they make all those who can neither follow nor arrest capital's new nomadic habits helplessly watch their livelihood fading and vanishing and wonder from where the blight might have come. The global travels of financial resources are perhaps as immaterial as the electronic network they travel – but the local traces of their journeys are painfully tangible and real: 'qualitative depopu-lation', destruction of local economies once capable of sustaining their inhabitants, the exclusion of the millions incapable of being absorbed by the new global economy.

Third, the spectacle of disasters, as presented by the media, also support and reinforce the ordinary, daily ethical indifference in another way, apart from unloading the accumulated supplies of moral senti-ments. Their long-term effect is that 'the developed part of the world surrounds itself with a sanitary belt of uncommitment, erects a global Berlin Wall; all information coming from "out there" are pictures of war, murders, drugs, looting, contagious diseases, refugees and hunger; that is, of something threat-ening to us'. Only rarely, and invariably in a hushed tone, and in no connection with the scenes of civil wars and massacres, we hear of the murderous weapons used for that purpose. Less often yet, if at all, are we reminded of what we know but prefer not to be told about: that all those weapons used to make the far-away homelands into killing fields have been supplied by our own arms factories, jealous of their order-books and proud of their productivity and global competitiveness – that lifeblood of our own cherished prosperity. A synthetic image of the self-inflicted brutality sediments in public consciousness – an image of 'mean streets', 'no-go areas' writ large, a magnified rendition of a gangland, an alien, subhuman world beyond ethics and beyond salvation. Attempts to save that world from the worst consequences of its own brutality may bring only momentary effects and are bound in the long run to fail; all the lifelines thrown may be easily retwisted into more nooses.

There is another important role played by the association of the 'far-away locals' with murder, epidemic and looting. Given their monstrosity, one cannot but thank God for making them what they are – the far-away locals, and pray that they stay that way.

The wish of the hungry to go where food is plentiful is what one would naturally expect from rational human beings; letting them act on their wishes is also what conscience would suggest is the right, moral thing to do. It is because of its undeniable rationality and ethical correctness that the rational and ethically conscious world feels so crestfallen in the face of the prospect of the mass migration of the poor and hungry; it is so difficult, without feeling guilty, to deny the poor and hungry their right to go where food is more plentiful; and it is virtually impossible to advance convincing rational arguments proving that their migration would be, for them, an unreasonable decision to take. The challenge is truly awesome: one needs to deny the others the self-same right to freedom of movement which one eulogizes as the topmost achievement of the globalizing world and the warrant of its growing prosperity.

The pictures of inhumanity which rules the lands where prospective migrants reside therefore comes in handy. They strengthen the resolve which lacks the rational and ethical arguments to support it. They help to keep the locals local, while allowing the globals to travel with a clear conscience.

---

6 ISSUES OF GLOBAL GOVERNANCE: CONFUSION AND CONTESTATION

P. Dicken

While the world has become much more highly integrated economically, the mechanisms for managing the system in a stable, sustainable way have lagged behind (Commission on Global Governance, 1995, pp. 135–36).

More than at any time in the last fifty years, virtually the entire world economy is now a market economy. The collapse of the state socialist systems at the end of the 1980s and their headlong rush to embrace the market, together with the more controlled opening up of the Chinese economy since 1979, has created a very different global system from that which emerged after the World War II. Virtually all parts of the world are now, to a greater or lesser extent, connected into an increasingly integrated system in which the parameters of the market dominate.

The acceleration and intensification of technological change, and the emergence of transnational corporations, with their intricate internal and external networks, together ensure that what happens in one part of the world is very rapidly transmitted to other parts of the world although, as we have demonstrated, the processes of globalization are extremely uneven in both time and space. The massive international flows of goods, services and, especially, of finance in its increasingly bewildering

From: *Global Shift: transforming the world economy*, by P. Dicken, Paul Chapman, 1998.

variety, have created a real world whose rules of governance have not kept pace with such changes. As Strange (1996, p. 189) points out,

- power has shifted upwards, from weak states to stronger states with global or regional reach beyond their frontiers;
- power has shifted sideways from states to markets and, hence, to non-state authorities which derive their power from their market shares;
- some power has 'evaporated' in so far as no one exercises it.

Thus, although the nation-state remains a highly significant actor in the world economy it is abundantly clear that its role has been changing and that it faces increasingly intractable problems in regulating its domestic economy in a flow-intensive, market-dominated, globalizing world.

There is no doubt that the market can be a highly effective mechanism for facilitating economic growth and development. But that does not mean that the market operates independently of a social context. On the contrary, all markets are socially embedded and constituted; all have to operate within socially defined rules. Totally unregulated markets are neither sustainable nor socially equitable; the unfettered market cannot be relied upon to create outcomes which maximize benefits for the many rather than just the few. To do so demands a regulatory or governance system which is legitimated by individual nation-states and by the communities and interest groups which constitute them.

The current international economic governance system is, in fact, made up of several levels operating at different, but interconnected, geographical scales:

- International regulatory bodies established by agreement by nation-states to perform specific roles. Examples include the IMF and the WTO (formerly the CAT-1).
- International co-ordinating groups with a broader, but less formal, remit. Examples include the groups of leading industrialized countries (C3, G5, C7, etc.).
- Regional blocs, such as the EU or NAFTA.

- National regulatory bodies operating within individual nation-states.
- Local agencies operating at the level of the individual community.

These five levels are interdependent to a considerable degree. Effective governance of economic activities requires that mechanisms be in place at all five levels, even though the types and methods of regulation are very different at each level. However,

the different levels and functions of governance need to be tied together in a division of control that sustains the division of labour. ... The governing powers (international, national and regional) need to be 'sutured' together into a relatively well integrated system. ... The issue at stake is whether such a coherent system will develop . . . (Hirst and Thompson, 1996, pp. 122, 184)

In this discussion, we focus specifically on the international scales of governance.

Within a volatile global economy, there are many issues which pose very serious problems for all states and communities throughout the world and which need to be addressed at the international or global scale. In this section, we outline some of the problems associated with governance in two areas

- international finance
- international trade, with specific reference to labour standards and the environment.

Governing the international financial system

As we have seen, the regulatory basis of the post-war international financial system was established at Bretton Woods in the 1940s. However, through a whole series of developments the relatively stable basis of the Bretton Woods system was progressively undermined. In effect, we have moved from a 'government-led international monetary system (G-IMS) of the Bretton Woods era to the market-led international monetary system (M-IMS) of today (Hirst and Thompson, 1996, p. 130). As a result, the international financial system has become, in effect, a separate state ... we are left with a strange world, one in which money capital flows freely, and is becoming less and less regulated, while movement of goods in the 'productive' economy has become more and more negotiated and regulated. Yet, this productive economy is increasingly susceptible, in principle if not in practice, to the institutions of money capital. (Thrift, 1990b, p. 136)

Susan Strange (1986, p. 1) coined the graphic term 'casino capitalism' to describe the international financial system in which every day games are played in this casino that involve sums of money so large that they, cannot be imagined. ... At night the games go on at the other side of the world and (the players) are just like the gamblers in casinos watching the clicking spin of a silver ball on a roulette wheel and putting their chips on red or black, odd numbers or even ones.

What we do not have, therefore, is a comprehensive and integrated global system of governance of the financial system. Instead, there are various areas of regulation performed by different bodies which are strongly nationally based (Hirst and Thompson, 1996, pp. 130–32):

- The G3 (the US, Japan, EU) takes an overall view of the monetary, fiscal and exchange rate relationships between the G3 countries although, in practice, this has been confined primarily to attempts to determine the global money supply and to manipulate exchange rates. This has not resolved the basic problem of 'an institutional gap between the increasingly international nature of the financial system and the still predominantly "national" remits of the major central banks and the wider nationally located regulatory mechanisms for financial markets and institutions'. The problem is that the G3, as well as the broader G5 and G7, has no real institutional base. It is a largely informal arrangement structured around periodic summits of national leaders.
- The international payments system is operated through the national central banks rather than

through an international central bank. While this central banking function remains unfulfilled at the international level the risks of default increase and disturbances threaten to become magnified across the whole system ... [there is] ... a growing network of co-operative and coordinative institutionalized mechanisms for monitoring, codifying and regulating such transactions (centred on the BIS and headed by the Group of Experts on Payment Systems).

- The supervision of financial institutions themselves is carried out through the Bank for International Settlements (BIS), established in 1975 and now based upon the 1988 Basel Committee's Capital Accord.

Much like the monetary summits of the G3 to G7 the Basel Committee was initially designed as a forum for the exchange of ideas in an informal atmosphere with no set rules or procedures or decision making powers. But, although it maintains this original informal atmosphere, its evolution has been toward much more involvement in hardheaded rule-making and implementation monitoring.

Thus, there are several regulatory bodies in operation at the international level. Yet the fear remains that, in the absence of a more co-ordinated and institutionalized system, the international financial system could easily spiral out of control. What might be done to prevent this happening? Not surprisingly, there is no consensus. Martin (1994, pp. 274–75) sets out two broad alternatives:

One route would be to reimpose national systems of control and regulation, along the lines of those now being dismantled. However, the very fact of global financial integration renders the feasibility and effectiveness of this response highly doubtful. An alternative response would be to introduce new forms of regulation based on international co-operation: if markets have gone global in their geography, so too should the institutions of regulation. ... This might be in the form of supranational regulation involving governing bodies outside the bounds of nations, or transnational regulation, involving the co-ordination of nation state policies through multilateral agreements. Such plans have their problems, of course, not least the difficulty of securing the international Cupertino necessary for their implementation. But whatever the form, the case for re-regulation is strong: the power of global money over national economic space has already been allowed to extend too far.

Trade, labour standards and the environment

Compared with the international financial system, the governance of international trade in commodities and manufactured products is much clearer and well established. ... for the past fifty years the GATT and, since 1995, the WTO has constituted a trade regulatory regime based upon clearly defined, non discriminatory, multilateral principles. Although significant trade friction continues to exist over specific issues and between certain groups of countries, the WTO system is generally accepted by virtually all countries in the world. Indeed, the eventual agreement on the Uruguay Round substantially widened the remit of the GATT/WTO. However, apart from the need still to reach agreement on certain sectors (such as services), there are two controversial issues which have moved to the centre of the trade (and development) debate: the relationship between free trade and labour standards and between free trade and the environment.

The basic question is: to what extent do international differences in labour standards and regulations (such as the use of child labour, poor health and safety conditions, repression of labour unions and workers' rights) and in environmental standards and regulations (such as industrial pollution, the unsafe use of toxic materials in production processes) distort the trading system and create unfair advantages? In both cases, the basic argument is that firms – as well as individual countries – may be able to undercut their competitors by capitalizing on cheap and exploited labour and lax environmental standards. Much of the focus of this concern is on the export processing zones which ... have proliferated throughout the developing world.

These two issues were explicitly addressed in the negotiations for the NAFTA, in which the US insisted on the signing of two side agreements to protect its domestic firms from low labour and environmental standards in Mexico. More recently, a group of countries led primarily by the US but also including some European countries made a concerted attempt formally to incorporate the issue of labour standards into the WTO at its ministerial meeting in Singapore in December 1996. The attempt failed, partly because not all industrialized countries supported it but also because the developing countries were vehemently opposed. The argument of those opposed to its inclusion within the WTO's remit is that labour standards are the responsibility of the International Labour Organization; the counter-argument is that the ILO lacks any powers of enforcement. It is also notable that the US, despite its current position on including labour standards in trade agreements, has 'signed only one of the five core labour standards conventions issued by the International Labour Organization – and ratified only 12 of the total 176 ILO conventions. It says that though it respects their spirit, the UN body's conventions do not mesh with its own laws' (*The Financial Times*, 20 June 1996).

There is no doubt that stark differences do exist in labour standards in different parts of the world. As we have seen at various points in this book, basic workers' rights are denied in many countries. Working conditions, especially in the export processing zones (including the Mexican maquiladoras) – but not only in these zones are often appalling. As far as child labour is concerned, the ILO calculates that around 73 million children aged between 10 and 14 years are employed throughout the world, approximately 13 per cent of that age group. In Africa, one quarter of children aged 10 to 14 are working. If children under 10 are included, as well as young girls working full time at home, the ILO estimates that there are probably 'hundreds of millions' of child workers in the world. However, the ILO also points out that 90 per cent of children work in agriculture or linked activities in rural areas and that most are employed within the family rather than for outside employers. Even so, there is substantial evidence that, in many cases, young children are employed by manufacturers (whether in factories or as outworkers) in such industries as garments, footwear, toys, sports goods, artificial flowers, plastic products and the like. Their wages are a pittance and their working conditions often abysmal.

From the viewpoint of many developing countries, however, there is a strong feeling that the labour standards stance of many developed countries is merely another form of protectionism against their exports and, as such, an obstacle to their much-needed economic development. There is a suspicion, for example, that at least some of the developed country lobbies are pressing for international agreements on a minimum wage in order to lessen the low labour cost advantages of developing countries. By incorporating such labour standards criteria into the WTO framework, it is believed, developed countries could use trade regulations to enforce such indirect protectionism. There is clearly a basic dilemma for the international community. On the one hand, ethical considerations must be a basic component of international trade agreements; on the other hand, there is a real danger of threatened developed country interest groups using labour standards issues as a device to protect their own commercial interests.

A similar dilemma is central to the other trade-related question: that of the environment. To what extent should variations in environmental standards be incorporated into international trade regulations? Again, there is no doubting the existence of huge differences in the nature, scope and enforcement of environmental regulations across the world. There is no doubt, either, that the highest incidence of low environmental standards is in developing countries. The existence of such an 'environmental gradient' certainly constitutes a stimulus for some firms at least to take advantage of low standards. These may be domestic firms or they may be foreign firms.

Although it does not necessarily follow that such firms have relocated to environmentally lax areas simply to avoid more stringent regulations (and higher costs) elsewhere, the fact that they do operate there is a major problem. Again, one of the most notorious, and best-documented, cases is that of the maquiladoras of the US–Mexico border zone.

Matamoros, with more than 100 maquiladoras, has only three government health and safety inspectors, who normally give advance warning of factory visits. Air quality and industrial effluents are tested only once a year. Senator Richard Cephardt . . . [noted] . . .

21st century technology combined with 19th-century living and working conditions. We drove by industrial parks where companies continue to dump their toxic wastes at night into rivers. We saw furniture plants using highly toxic solvents and finishes that once operated in California and throughout the US, and which had moved to Mexico because of lax environmental enforcement. (*The Financial Times*, 6 June 1997)

But there are also broader environmental issues which have been associated with international trade and its governance. It is self-evident, for example, that many environmental problems are not confined within national boundaries but 'spill over'. For example, 'acid rain' produced by certain types of energy creation is carried by the wind way beyond its points of origin to create environmental damage. The damage to the ozone layer in the earth's stratosphere is caused by the use of certain chemicals (such as chlorofluorocarbons – CKs) which retain their stability over long periods of time and move upwards into the stratosphere, expelling chlorine which destroys ozone molecules. Again, such chemicals have an effect way beyond their points of use.

This is not the place to explore the details of the environmental debate as a whole. Various international environmental agreements are in place (with a greater or lesser degree of effectiveness) which are aimed at broader environmental governance. But how does the environmental issue relate specifically to the governance of international trade? At one level, the problem is exactly the same as that of labour standards. If a country allows lax environmental standards, it is argued, then it should not be able to use what is, in effect, a subsidy on firms located there to be able to sell its products more cheaply on the international market. The question then becomes one of whether the solution lies in using international trade regulations or in some other forms of sanction. The proponents and opponents of the 'trade solution' are the same as those discussed above in the case of labour standards.

However, there is an even more extreme position adopted by some environmentalists which is that the pursuit of ever-increasing international trade – which is clearly encouraged by a free-trade regime like the GATT/WTO – should be totally abandoned, not merely regulated. The argument here is basically that sustainable development is incompatible with the pursuit of further economic growth and, especially, with an economic system which is based upon very high levels of geographical specialization, since such specialization inevitably depends upon, and generates, ever-increasing trade in materials and products.

Daly (1993, p. 24, emphasis added) expresses this viewpoint as follows:

> No policy prescription commands greater consensus among economists than that of free trade based on international specialization according to comparative advantage. Free trade has long been presumed good unless proved otherwise. . . . Yet that presumption should be reversed. The default position should favour domestic production for domestic markets. When convenient, balanced international trade should be used, but it should not be allowed to govern a country's affairs at the risk of environmental and social disaster. The domestic economy should be the dog and international trade its tail. GATT seeks to tie all the dogs' tails together so tightly that the international knot would wag the separate national dogs.

One of the bases of Daly's argument is that the energy costs of transporting materials and goods across the world are not taken into account in setting the prices of traded goods and that, in effect, trade is being massively subsidized at a huge short term and long-term environmental cost. Another is that free trade injects new inefficiencies into the system: 'more than half of all international trade involves the simultaneous import and export of essentially the same goods. For example, Americans import Danish sugar cookies, and Danes import American sugar cookies. Exchanging recipes would surely be more efficient' (Daly, 1993, p. 25).

The counterview from a rather different environmentalist perspective is clearly expressed by Pearce (1995, pp. 74, 77, 78):

> Unquestionably, there are environmental problems inherent in the existing trading system. But there is also extensive confusion in the environmentalist critique of free trade. . . . Given the potentially large gains to be obtained from free trade, adopting restrictions on trade for environmental purposes is a policy that needs to be approached with caution. Most importantly, all other approaches to reducing environmental damage should be exhausted before trade policy measures are contemplated . . . the policy implication of a negative association between freer trade and environmental degradation is not that freer trade should be halted. What matters is the adoption of the most cost-effective policies to optimize the externality. Restricting trade is unlikely to be the most efficient way of controlling the problem. . . . The losses can best be minimized by firm domestic environmental policy design to uncouple the environmental impacts from economic activity. . . . The 'first' best approach to correcting externalities is to tackle them directly through implementation of the polluter pays principle (PPP), not through restrictions on the level of trade. Where the PPP is not feasible (e.g. if the exporter is a poor developing country), it is likely to be preferable to engage in co-operative policies, e.g. making clean technology transfers, assisting with clean-up policies etc., rather than adopting import restrictions.

'Through a glass darkly'

Time present and time past
Are both perhaps present in time future
And time future contained in time past
(T. S. Eliot, *Four Quartets*)

What of the future? Although 'time present' and 'time past' are indeed present in 'time future' we cannot simply extrapolate current patterns and processes into the future. The future is an amalgam of the probable and the unpredictable. Change occurs within an existing context but it also transforms that context, usually gradually, occasionally rapidly. The future, then, is a land of many questions to which there are no certain answers. What does seem certain is that the tendency towards an increasingly highly interconnected and interdependent global economy will intensify. The fortunes of nations regions, cities, neighbourhoods, families and individuals will continue to be strongly influenced by their position in the global network but in complex and highly reflexive ways. The world economy is structured as a multilayered, multiscale mosaic of activities.

In trying to understand the processes of global economic transformation in this book we have emphasized the importance of two major kinds of institution – transnational corporations and nation-states – operating in a complex and volatile technological environment. Through their strategies and interactions TNCs and states have reshaped the global economic map and contributed towards the increasing globalization of economic activities. There is every reason to believe that they will continue to be the primary forces even though their particular behaviour, and the inter-relationships between them, will certainly change. The key point is that each is both a political and an economic institution. Nation-states, while essentially political institutions, have become increasingly involved in economic matters, arguably as increasingly competitive economic actors. Transnational corporations, though fundamentally economic in function, have become increasingly political in their actions and impact.

The 'topography' of tomorrow's global economic map, like that of yesterday's and today's, will be the outcome of both economic and political forces. The two cannot properly be separated. In the end, however, the issues are not merely academic. The global economy and all its participants – from transnational corporations and national governments, to local communities and individual citizens – face a major global challenge: to meet the material needs of the world community as a whole in ways which reduce, rather than increase, inequality and which do so without destroying the environment.

---

7 WORLD ECONOMY AND GLOBAL SYSTEM

B. Axford

The character of global systemness can be seen most clearly in the development of the world economy over the last few decades, which has seen a transformation from 'organized' to 'disorganized' capitalism on a global scale (Lash and Urry, 1987) and the emergence of what Carnoy *et al.* (1993) call 'the new global information economy'. As such it affords a vantage point from which to view the 'economies of signs and space' which now are as characteristic of the global political economy as the production and movement of material goods (Lash and Urry, 1994).

Much recent discussion of the world economy has emphasized the complete 'globalization' of economic relations, so much so that there is sometimes an unquestioning certainty about the existence of a truly global economy. In part this arises from a reductionist treatment of the significance of broadly economic and technological factors relative to others, and in part because there has been a persuasive neatness about the transnationalization of production, trade and finance compared with evidence of resolute difference elsewhere (Hirst and Thompson, 1992; Campanella, 1992). There is also a casual assumption that changes in the organization of production and consumption have the power to transform meaning structures and identities in a more or less

From: *The Global System: Economics, Politics and Culture*, by B. Axford, Polity Press, 1995.

direct fashion. In short, the economic realm is said to display greater interdependence and homogeneity than the curmudgeonly and fragmented political, sphere, and certainly more than the cultural – realm with its still fragile evidence of global themes. The purpose of this chapter is to garner evidence for and against this claim, bearing in mind previous warnings on the need to treat globalization as an asymmetrical process, and to exercise some caution in assessing the power of 'diverse totalizing orders and impulsions' (Giddens, 1993, p. 8).

The asymmetrical nature of globalizing processes is very apparent in the 'turbulent' 1990s, when the multilateralist institutions most closely associated with global economic liberalization are being challenged by regional trading blocs and by forms of 'minilateralism' (Campanella, 1992; Ruggie, 1992). Even so, it is still right to see these tensions as the outcome of increasingly contested processes of globalization rather than as clear evidence of the deglobalization of the world economy. At all events, challenges to world economic integration are not new: indeed the very dynamism of the modern world economy turned on the classic antinomy between global interdependence and national autonomy. . . . Wallerstein's conception of a capitalist world economy seeks to trace the emergence and functioning of a global political economy by connecting the processes of capital accumulation on a global scale with the geopolitical rivalries of nation-states. Further evidence of tensions in the global political economy are visible in the conflicts between the relatively ordered world of multilateral institutions like the General Agreement on Tariffs and Trade (GATT) and the other pillars of the international trading order of liberalism, namely the International Monetary Fund (IMF) and the World Bank, and the rational anarchy of the money markets, the high-rollers of 'casino capitalism' (Strange, 1986; 1988).

All these tensions suggest that growing interconnectedness and interdependence produce not stability but the greater vulnerability of actors under high-risk conditions. Many of the developments in the global economy in recent years, notably the shift to forms of more managed trade, and the appeal of different forms of protectionism, can be seen as a response to endemic uncertainty and rapid change. As a result, the global economy is located somewhere between a realist set, featuring the knock-about of national competition, and a postmodern space of flows – of goods, services, people, images and information. High-tech firms or industries now require economic units that are larger than most national states, but continue to demand the protection afforded by managed trade, or the comfortable reciprocities between trading blocs. Such developments do form part of what Robertson (1992) calls the 'trend to unicity', but reinforce the idea of global systemness as being fundamentally contested.

The idea of a global economy

The imagery of a borderless world (Ohmae, 1990) is in common use as a description of the global economy. Some accounts focus on the major growth in transnational micro-economic links among the 'triad' economies of Europe, the Americas and the Pacific Rim (Ruggie, 1993) and see the processes of globalization as the wave of a post-industrial future (Drucker, 1993). Generally these accounts adopt a strongly liberal stance and point to the obvious and growing irrelevance of states and of the very idea of national economies. On the other hand, realist interpretations of the international economy still insist that economic realities are the province of the national company, and see the territorial state as the key instrument of international regulation and governance (Kapstein, 1991–2).

Between these lie a range of interpretations which recognize the transformative potential of cross-national production networks and global communication flows, but continue to believe that the nation-state is an important actor in global economic management and in both corporate and national success (Porter, 1990; Reich, 1992). Nor is this debate confined to the writings of international relations theorists and international economics. For some time now, students of strategic management have explored the phenomenon of the global company (Prahalad and Doz, 1987; Bartlett and Ghoshal, 1989; 1992; Bartlett *et al.*, 1990). By and large this debate has been conducted over the extent to which recent developments – cheap and powerful computing and communications, the breaking down of barriers to foreign direct investment (FDI) and capital raising, along with the global spread of consumerist ideologies – have turned large companies into 'world players' independent of their national origins.

The conception of a global company differs from the older though still widely used concept of the multinational corporation (MNC) which dominated the pattern of international business activity from the 1950s to the 1970s. MNCs consisted of a dominant parent company and various foreign offspring, fighting competitors in overseas markets. By the 1990s, runs the argument, the multinational corporation had given way to the phenomenon of the global corporation. Firms now locate production wherever the costs are lowest and organize on the basis of overseas transplants or through mergers and acquisitions, but increasingly through more collaborative and equal ventures involving FDI. The latter arrangements may involve spreading investment risks in the exercise of high-cost and long-term research and development programmes, or piggy-backing in new and untried markets, or may just indicate a fear of flying in the competitive world of the internal market in Europe. In some fields it is not too fanciful to suggest that the idea of separate domestic and foreign markets has become altogether redundant.

At the same time, the picture painted is seldom one of the homogenization of products. There may be global or generic strategies but, except in the case of very specialized and high value-added products, or those which by dint of marketing or serendipity achieve the status of consumer icons, for example Coca-Cola, there are unlikely to be global customers (if by that is meant consumers with uniform demands and uniform tastes). So to some extent there is a powerful mythology at work here, or at the very least a confusion over the meaning of the term 'global business'). Let me recap: there is a definitional world of difference between the concept of a multinational corporation, which implies that a corporation may be very 'national' in key aspects of its functioning and governance, and that of a transnational corporation (TNC) or global corporation, which suggests that the company has broken free from or transcended the bounds of nationality. Undoubtedly MNCs are very visible and powerful actors in the world economy, although it is only partly true that they can conduct business without regard for the sensibilities of nation-states. As we shall see, a good deal of evidence supports the claim that national factors contribute significantly to corporate success (Porter, 1990; Carnoy *et al.*, 1993).

Truly transnational actors, however, are still few and far between, and the ties that bind even the biggest corporations to particular nation-states remain strong. According to Yao-Su Hu (1992), only a very few companies, like Shell, Unilever, Nestlé, ABB and ICI, can be defined as real transnationals. This is because most very large corporations, like Du Pont or General Motors, have less than half of their operations and employees abroad, because 'foreigners' occupy only a very small proportion of senior management positions, and because they are subject to a legal and fiscal nationality which, in the last resort, is more significant than other jurisdictions within whose remit they fall. Even companies who meet these criteria, and who may have required their overseas outposts to embrace the local business culture or 'go native', still owe some debt of allegiance to the 'mother country' and are particularly sensitive to its politics and shifts in policy. They are also likely to be carrying around at least some cultural baggage which identifies them as 'foreign' and may well trade on this awareness of difference to their competitive advantage. The French hotel group Méridien, though hardly a world player, has carved useful market niches in overseas markets like the US by trading on its very Frenchness. The burden of all this is that Japanese or Korean companies in the US or Britain will remain Japanese or Korean in some fundamental sense; and, of course, the opposite is also true.

However, attention to the 'objective' or easily measurable factors of globalization may miss the point. If the global corporation is still more myth than reality, it is one which now exercises a powerful hold over the strategic vision as well as the management styles of large corporations with international connections and markets. Many such organizations are adopting a self-conscious 'global rationale' and at least the rhetoric of global management informs much of their discourse, playing a growing part in more formal schemes of management training and development as well as in marketing strategies. Managers in such organizations 'speak globally' in the sense that they have come to see the world as a putative operational whole (Wildish and Case, 1994, p. 7). This notional cultural change is in marked contrast to the received model of preparation for 'overseas' management, or even forms of cross-cultural training in which more or less sophisticated advice and schooling are offered to the novice 'expatriate' being groomed for extended periods overseas. Being a 'global manager' implies travel, but more critically it suggests that it is possible to be a 'worldwide' business without transferring staff from one country to another (p. 8).

Instead, a global mentality is instantiated through strategic networks of communication between managers as professionals, through interpersonal networks, as well as through different forms of functional integration. Thus for many writers on international management, it is the management style of an organization that is the key determinant of its taxonomic status as a global company, as opposed to the product or service which it produces or provides, or even where its key functions are located (Wildish and Case, 1994). In the new information economy, the importance of place, or of vertical integration as a means of creating an economy of scale, gives way to forms of strategic networking, where co-ordination or a 'single face' is achieved by independent companies working together. The 'globalness' of such alliances is not diminished by the rootedness of participants in particular locales. So the 'essence' of a global company may be best understood by looking at the way in which it is managed and how it identifies itself in relation to the changing competitive environments in which it is located.

Of course, in this respect the 'soft' side of the globalizing equation sometimes lags behind developments in the 'hard' indicators. The injunction to 'think globally and manage locally' has attained the status of lore, but the reality for many small to medium businesses is that local considerations and

a parochial 'mindset' remain powerful constraints on the achievement of a global mentality. The completion of the internal market in Europe, widely bruited as a fundamental fracture line in the operating environment of businesses, evoked almost universal apathy or benign optimism among the owner–managers of small businesses throughout the Community member states (Axford *et al.*, 1991). So, if it is true that organizations enact their environments in their own image (Morgan, 1986; Wendt, 1987), then many are reproducing an environment at odds with the exigencies of the contexts in which they are operating or will be operating.

A no-nonsense realist response to these sorts of arguments would point to the continuing power of states to intervene effectively in the organization of economic life and to shape or control aspects of the global cultural economy, even where these may be transmitted by the electronic impulses which carry them down wires or beam them through space. In swashbuckling style, Kapstein (1992) suggests that information satellites could be shot down by a government bent on interrupting communication flows which it deemed not in the national interest. This is good knock-about stuff but something of a limiting case, and one need not go quite this far to underscore the viability and continuing importance of national factors as the basis for corporate success. It is possible to accept the premise that markets and businesses are becoming more global and still argue, as Michael Porter (1990) does, that this makes nations more, rather than less, important. In brief, Porter's argument is that it is the national business environment which determines the competitive advantage of firms, and paradoxically the nurturing of difference, reflected in different national virtues or styles, itself becomes a means of overcoming the constraints imposed by an increasingly homogenized world.

Porter's analytical framework makes much of those domestic conditions – factors of production, the quality of home demand, the intensity of domestic competition, and the regimes under which business is conducted within a nation – which favour and promote or sustain competitiveness. His argument is that these factors become more significant as globalization proceeds and uncertainty deepens. The very appeal of the domestic sources of 'competitiveness' school of international economics and strategic management – not least their appeal to the protectionist Clinton administration in the US – is a corollary of the faltering tide of liberal-economic discourse during the early 1990s and its partial replacement by regimes of managed trade and trading blocs. For the US these developments have been attended by the clamorous rhetoric of national decline (Kennedy, 1993). But in the nature of uncertain times, none of these trends is clear cut. Thus the growth in the volume of cross-national, defensive joint ventures demonstrates that companies are aware of the threats and opportunities opened up by the liberalizing of markets, and also shows that the globalization of risk requires insurance which cannot be provided by national administrations, but is as yet unavailable through forms of international governance or regulation.

Against these views of the salience of country of origin is the argument, put most strongly by Kenichi Ohmae (1990), that the nationality of companies is irrelevant in what he terms a 'borderless world'. In the global economic space, big firms at least have to operate in many different markets and for competitive reasons they have to behave like locals wherever they find themselves. So although they may have a headquarters operation, or have most of their shares owned in one country, they have become multinational in terms of their identity, and may even have engineered or 'grown' a culture which is not tied to any one place. Nonetheless, the 'foreignness' of multinational firms, to use Michael Reich's (1992) term, remains an issue in the domestic politics of many countries which are the recipients of inward investment by such businesses, as well as a matter of concern to the stewards of national economies who see their own 'domestic' multinationals exporting jobs to locations with cheaper sources of labour supply (Carnoy et al., 1993).

At this stage of the argument we need not worry about who is right, Porter or Ohmae, because in a sense they both identify salient features of the world economy seen from the point of view of different actors – states and businesses. Moreover, both have

the same view of the nation-state, which is that it is primarily a convenient supplier of intrastructural and cultural resources which may contribute to corporate performance. The tensions, or possible tensions, between national goals and national administrations and those of private multinational corporations do not enter these discussions (Carnoy et al., 1993).

But in other respects, the sort of world economic order painted by Ohmae, and implied by Porter too, is remarkably benign. In reality the borderless world, where the only effective global actors are global companies and in which production is globalized and consumption increasingly specialized, will continue to produce winners and losers and to exacerbate the differences between haves and have-nots (Kennedy, 1993, chapters 2 and 3). The prospects for a globalized post-capitalist nirvana based upon 'knowledge' work or 'reflexive accumulation' rather than labour in the traditional sense, or a post-scarcity world economy in which industrial and agricultural production has been revolutionized by robotics and biotechnology, still look slim given the pace of the technological revolution in the developed world and the population explosion in the periphery of the world economy (Drucker, 1993, pp. 60–109; Kennedy, 1993).

Generally speaking, debate about the borderless world has been innocent of any treatment of the world-historical legacies of imperialism and of global inequalities, preferring to concentrate upon the dynamic qualities of economies like the self-styled 'intelligent island' of Singapore, or the globe-compressing power of clever machines.

8 THE CONTEMPORARY CONTEXT OF DEVELOPMENT

R. Kiely

The globalization thesis is particularly weak and cannot account for the direction of capital flows in the world economy. The direction of these flows suggests that there may be strong reasons for capital concentrating in the First World and selected parts of the former Third World. This observation could possibly support the post-Fordist claim that capital is likely to locate close to the final market. But . . . the post-Fordist thesis at best lacks clarity, and tends towards prescription rather than analysis. This section attempts an alternative analysis, which is sensitive to the changes in the world economy in terms of globalization and industrial organization, but which attempts to avoid the oversimplifications of both theses. Two factors are examined: the global hierarchy of production and the role of the nation-state, and I draw on this discussion to show the utility of an analysis rooted in the existence of 'global commodity chains' (Gereffi and Korzeniewicz, 1994).

1. Global hierarchies of production

Capital has continued to concentrate in certain parts of the world at the expense of others. In terms of domestic investment and composition of board of directors, TNCs continue to remain loyal to their country of origin. The strong globalization thesis exaggerates the mobility of productive capital, and therefore the degree to which it has been, and can be, transferred to areas of low labour costs. Capital faces a number of sunk costs, which constitute significant barriers to exit. As Wade (1996a, pp. 80–1) points out:

> These include initial start-up costs, the costs of learning over time about a particular environ-

ment, and the costs of building reputation, gaining acceptance among government, employees, and other firms regarding their reliability as producers, employers, and suppliers in each market.

Experiments in Japanese production techniques, and the volatility of markets for some goods, has reinforced the tendency towards agglomeration. Of course, as I warned in the previous section, such techniques may not be as generalized as is often claimed, but the important point is that some company officials are acting as though a Japanese model existed, and so are actively promoting local agglomeration. Thus, given a situation in which there has been some movement towards a global free market, capital will not behave in a particularly foot-loose manner. Instead, capital will accumulate in some areas and marginalize others and, given the advantages enjoyed by established producers (plus the more successful NICs), it is most likely to accumulate in these regions. These advantages include research and development in new technology, infrastructure, skills and established markets.

We are, therefore, witnessing a situation in which capital is not exploiting the so-called Third World, it is marginalizing it. One is reminded of Marx's dictum (see Kay, 1975) that if there is one thing worse than being exploited, it is (in capitalist terms) not being exploited. In practice, some parts of the old Third World are important recipients of capital investment. Strategic countries 'act as nodes in the trade and investment circuits reaching out from the key First World states' (McMichael, 1996, p. 107). Thus, China, Mexico, South Korea and Indonesia, for example, are favoured recipients of investment, due to the size of their domestic markets, and their proximity to other large, relatively affluent markets. Regionalism is thus compatible with a selective movement towards post-Fordism, as close proximity to suppliers and markets may not occur within a nation-state.

However, this concentration of capital does not occur in all industrial sectors. Particularly in labour-intensive sectors, there has been some relocation of capital in accordance with the globalization thesis.

From: Globalization, Post–Fordism and the contemporary context of development, by R. Kiely, in *International Sociology*, Vol. 13, No. 1, March 1998.

In sectors such as clothing, textiles and electronic assembly fixed costs are not too high as technology is not very advanced, and so capital is far more mobile. Labour costs constitute a higher proportion of total costs in these sectors, and so cheaper labour in the periphery can be an advantage. Those who advocate the globalization thesis, both on the left and right of the political spectrum, have pointed to the growth of the aforementioned export processing zones. The left argue that such zones facilitate the global expansion of the super-exploitation of labour, while the right regard these zones as the place where a country's comparative advantage may be secured (Frank, 1981; Little, 1981). But in fact the 200 or so zones operating in 50 countries employ only around 2 million workers, although this figure does not include the special economic zones in China (Gereffi and Hempel, 1996, p. 22). Employment in the zones rarely accounts for more than 5 per cent of total industrial employment within individual countries, and in most cases less than 10 per cent of total manufactured exports originate from the zones. Moreover, local capital is just as likely as foreign capital to be used in these zones (Jenkins, 1987, p. 132). Thus, the globalization thesis whereby mobile capital invests where labour costs are lowest applies only to a few industrial sectors.

Moreover, even in these cases, TNC investment is more complex than that allowed for by the cheap labour hypothesis. Local factors are also important. For instance, Nike, the market leader in the athletic footwear industry, draws on manufacturing subcontractors in East Asia. In recent years, this has included China, where labour costs are particularly low. This strategy is not without its problems however, as 'The advantages of lower labour costs in the developing manufacturing areas had to be weighed against disadvantages in production flexibility, quality, raw material sourcing and transportation' (Korzeniewicz, 1994, p. 259). The development of new model specifications took four months in South Korea, where labour costs are higher, compared to eight months in China; South Korea resourced 100 per cent of its raw materials compared with only 30 per cent in China; and shipping time from South Korea was 20 to 25 days compared to 35 to 40 days from Shanghai (Korzeniewicz, 1994, p. 259).

Moreover, technological change (such as automation of cutting), changes in market structure and lower labour costs and few regulations have encouraged continued production of clothing in the First World. In particular, higher value, fashion-oriented niche market products may well continue to be made in the First World, while lower cost products may be made in cheaper labour areas (Cereffi, 1994b, pp. 110–11). But there are significant exceptions to this rule, as many designer labels are 'basically a device to differentiate what are often relatively similar products' (Dicken, 1992, p. 246). On the other hand, companies using cheaper labour may not rely on the very cheapest labour, but instead draw on labour which is both cheap and skilled, and from those countries which have developed infrastructures, suppliers and transportation. The importance of these factors show that local initiatives, and in particular the role of the state, remain important.

2. The role of the state

As already argued, the success of the East Asian NICs cannot be explained as a product of the globalization of capital. Particular, contingent, international factors were important, such as geographical location (Hong Kong and Singapore), high levels of aid and relatively open access to the lucrative US market (South Korea and Taiwan). But as important was the role of the state in directing local capital into particular sectors, including heavy and high-tech industries (Amsden, 1989; Wade, 1990), and protecting local capital from foreign competition through subsidies, import controls and restrictions on foreign ownership. Such practices were (and are) too commonplace for the World Bank's position that state intervention was irrelevant to South Korea's success (World Bank, 1994; criticized in Kiely, 1998, Chapter 8). In many Third World countries state intervention has been inefficient, but the World Bank makes the far stronger (and unconvincing) claim that it is necessarily inefficient. The Bank, along with neoliberal theorists more generally, can be described as optimistic globalizers who believe that the globalization of production and markets will promote a level playing field in which all countries can equally benefit. As the previous data make clear, the 'global marketplace' does not exist, and 'late developers' face the prospect of unequal competition with established producers, both in their domestic economy – and thus the potential devastation of domestic capital faced with cheaper imports – and in breaking into new markets in the global economy (Kiely, 1994). The effectiveness of state intervention in South Korea and Taiwan is not easily replicated, as it rested on a particular history and social structure such as the elimination of unproductive agrarian classes, the development of nascent capitalist classes under Japanese colonialism, and a militarization of society (Kiely, 1998, Chapter 7). However, the point is that these too are local factors (albeit interlinked with global ones), and that, given the hierarchies that exist in the global economy, it is unlikely that potential later developers can do without state economic intervention.

These points are of increasing relevance in the era of flexible accumulation. Even optimistic accounts of the new opportunities for late developers recognize the need for the diffusion of new technology and the development of an appropriate infrastructural base, including skilled labour (Hoffman and Kaplinsky, 1988, pp. 334–5). But, while these requirements are not an impossibility, neither are they an inevitability. Even if the technology can be acquired on competitive terms from abroad, many local capitalists are likely to attempt to remain competitive through the maintenance of low wages rather than introduce the new technology. A local infrastructure may also be developed, but this is an expensive and time-consuming process, and so construction may take too long, especially given the agglomeration tendencies associated with flexible accumulation outlined earlier. It is for these reasons that a developmental state along South Korean lines is crucial but, as I have argued, the success of this state rested on specific, contingent social factors. The growing liberalization of many peripheral economies undergoing structural adjustment programmes militates further against the development of such states. Moreover, in many cases current potential developers

face less open access to First World economies than either South Korea or Taiwan in the 1960s and 1970s (Cline, 1982).

3. Global commodity chains

A commodity chains approach is one fruitful way of analysing the hierarchies of production in the global economy. I (Hopkins and Wallerstein (1986, p. 159) define a commodity chain as 'a network of labor and production processes whose end result is a finished commodity'. A global commodity chain links such processes at a global level. Gereffi (1994a, p. 219) distinguishes between two kinds of commodity chains. Producer-driven chains operate where the site of production is relatively immobile, and tend to agglomerate within established areas of accumulation. In such cases

> manufacturers making advanced products like aircraft, automobiles and computer systems are the key economic agents in these producer-driven chains not only in terms of their earnings, but also in their ability to exert control over backward linkages with raw material and component suppliers, as with forward linkages into retailing.

The second, buyer-driven commodity chains are characterized by more mobility as production is labour intensive and therefore more likely to take place in the Third World. However,

> these same industries are also design and marketing-intensive, which means that there are high barriers to entry at the brand name merchandising and retail levels where companies invest considerable sums in product development, advertising and computerized store networks to create and sell these items. Therefore, whereas producer-driven commodity chains are controlled by core firms at the point of production, control over buyer-driven commodity chains is exercised at the point of consumption. (Gereffi, 1994a, p. 219)

While recognizing the utility of the commodity chains approach, one should be careful not to assume that the world is composed of all-powerful TNCs simply deciding what role particular parts of the world play in the network of chains linking the global economy. In fact, nation-states can play a crucial role in upgrading (or indeed downgrading, as in the case of Britain) the kind of production undertaken within its still important borders.

This approach also undermines the optimistic claims of the flexible specialization school. This perspective puts forward the view that competitiveness can be reared through the development of small-scale, autonomous local industries. (Although) critical of the strong globalization thesis, I recognize that simply wishing away global actors is even less useful. The global commodity chains framework correctly recognizes the proliferation of small industries in some sectors, but unlike the flexible specialization thesis, it also recognizes that such industries are often in a subordinate relationship to large TNCs, the latter of which are happy to contract out some production activities while they maintain ultimate control.

Conclusion

Four key points can be made by way of conclusion.

Post-Fordist methods of work organization are not compatible with the strong globalization thesis. In fact the former implies the increasing localization of production, as companies locate close to suppliers and final markets.

Post-Fordism has been unevenly implemented, both across and within economic sectors. For example, the automobile industry has combined Fordist (world car) and post-Fordist (Japanese techniques) strategies. The same is also true in the clothing sector, where cheap labour is a factor in a labour-intensive industry, but so too are labour skills and close proximity to what is sometimes a highly volatile market. Thus, Fordist methods, which persist to this day, are more compatible with the globalization thesis, but even here there are some definite limits. Capital investment in the former Third World is often concerned with market access in nation-states which continue to protect national production – and so the state is far from being an anachronism.

Moreover, there remain strong incentives to maintain investment in established areas, which monopolize skills, markets and marketing, and have the most advanced infrastructures and research and development facilities. Hence, TNC investment still largely concentrates on production for home markets, and direct foreign investment focuses on the First World and selected former Third World countries.

We are, therefore, witnessing a diversity of methods of capital accumulation in the world economy. Rustin (1989, p. 305) rightly argues that 'What seems to be emerging is not one "progressive" mode of information-based production, but a plethora of co-existing and competing systems, whose ultimate relative weight in the system is impossible to predict.' However, both Fordist and post-Fordist methods show the limits of the globalization thesis, and whatever the strategy, development prospects for the former Third World occur in the context of a global hierarchy of production. There remains room for specific nation-states to alter their position in this hierarchy, as the East Asian states showed. Of course the rules of the game change over time, and state capacity in parts of the periphery is extremely limited, but this shows that the context of development is influenced by a mixture of both global and local factors, and not just the former.

Nevertheless, the tendency today is towards an increase in global hierarchies, and the maintenance/ intensification of uneven development. Without significant countervailing factors – both local and global – this trend is likely to continue.

9 PROBLEMS OF DEVELOPING COUNTRIES IN A GLOBALIZING ECONOMY

P. Dicken

Heterogeneity of the developing world

In large part, though by no means entirely, the economic progress and well-being of developing countries are linked to what happens in the developed market economies. A continuation of buoyant economic conditions in the industrialized economies, with a general expansion of demand for both primary and manufactured products, would undoubtedly help developing countries. But the notion that 'a rising tide will lift all boats', while containing some truth, ignores the enormous variations that exist between countries. The shape of the 'economic coastline' is highly irregular; some economies are beached and stranded way above the present water level. For such countries there is no automatic guarantee that a rising tide of economic activity would, on its own, do very much to refloat them.

For the developing world as a whole, the basic problem is one of poverty together with a lack of adequate employment opportunities. More than twenty years ago, the problem was described in the following terms:

> More than 700 million people live in acute poverty and are destitute. At least 460 million persons were estimated to suffer from a severe degree of protein-energy malnutrition even before the recent food crisis. Scores of millions live constantly under a threat of starvation.

> Countless millions suffer from debilitating diseases of various sorts and lack access to the most basic medical services. The squalor of urban slums is too well known to need further emphasis. The number of illiterate adults has been estimated to have

grown from 700 million in 1962 to 760 million towards 1970. The tragic waste of human resources in the Third World is symbolized by nearly 300 million persons unemployed or under-employed in the mid-1970s' (ILO, 1976, p. 3).

Twenty years later, the precise numbers may have changed but the basic dimensions of the problem surely have not. Indeed, the income gap between the rich and the poor has widened:

> In 1960, the richest 20% of the world's population had incomes 30 times greater than the poorest 20%. By 1990, the richest 20% were getting 60 times more. And this comparison is based on the distribution between rich and poor countries. Adding the maldistribution within countries, the richest 20% of the world's people get at least 150 times more than the poorest 20%. (UNDP, 1992, p. 1)

Apart from the yawning gap between developed and developing countries as a whole, however, there are enormous disparities within the developing world itself. The weighted averages of three development indicators – per capita income, life expectancy and infant mortality – give some impression of the heterogeneity within the developing world as well as a stark indication of the gap between these countries and the high-income countries of the world. The income disparities are especially marked. The average per capita income of the fifty-one poorest countries in the mid-1990s was a mere $380 compared with $4,640 in the upper middle-income group of developing countries and $23,420 for the high-income countries. This income gradient is, not surprisingly, reflected in the data for life expectancy and infant mortality.

Not only are the variations in well-being between developing countries much greater than those between industrialized countries but also variations between different parts of the same developing country tend to be much greater. In particular, the differential between urban and rural areas is especially great. United Nations data show that in Africa as a whole, 29 per cent of the urban population live in 'absolute' poverty compared with 58 per cent of

From: *Global Shift: Transforming the World Economy*, by P. Dicken, Paul Chapman, 1998.

the rural population. In Asia and Latin America the urban-rural differential is less but still substantial. In Asia, 34 per cent of the urban population and 47 per cent of the rural population live in absolute poverty – in Latin America the figures are 32 per cent and 45 per cent respectively (United Nations, 1996, p. 113).

Gilbert and Gugler (1982, pp. 23, 25) summarize the situation very concisely. On the one hand,

> Urban poverty in the Third World is on a scale quite different to that in the developed countries. . . . In the Third World city the relative poverty of the black Baltimore slum dweller is accentuated by absolute material deprivation. Some poor people in the US suffer from malnutrition. Most of the poor in Indian cities fall into this category. Overcrowded tenement slums and too few jobs are abhorrent, but the lack of fresh water, medical services, drainage, and unemployment compensation adds to this problem in most Third World cities.

On the other hand, in the developing world,

> cities are centres of power and privilege . . . Certainly, many urban dwellers live in desperate conditions . . . [but] . . . even those in the poorest trades reported that they were better off than they had been in the rural areas. . . . The urban areas, and especially the major cities, invariably offer more and better facilities than their rural hinterlands. (Gilbert and Gugler, 1982, pp. 50, 52)

Employment, unemployment and under-employment in developing countries

The basic problem is that labour force growth outstrips the growth of jobs. Although the employment structure of Third World countries has undergone marked change the fact remains that most developing countries are predominantly agricultural economies. An average of 69 per cent of the labour force in the lowest-income countries was employed in agriculture in 1990 (in some countries the figure was above 90 per cent) compared with only 5 per

cent in the industrial market economies. Even in the upper middle-income group (in which most industrial development has occurred) agriculture employed around one-fifth of the labour force. In each category the relative importance of agriculture has declined even though in absolute terms the numbers employed in agriculture continued to grow. The balance of employment has shifted towards the other sectors in the economy: industry and services.

These broad sectoral changes in employment in developing countries have to be seen within the broader context of growth in the size of the labour force. The contrast with the experience of the industrialized countries in the nineteenth century is especially sharp. During that earlier period the European labour force increased by less than 1 per cent per year on average; in today's developing countries the labour force is growing at more than 2 per cent every year. Thus, the labour force in the developing world doubles roughly every thirty years compared with the ninety years taken in the nineteenth century for the European labour force to double. Hence, it is very much more difficult to absorb the exceptionally rapid growth of the labour force into the economy. The problem is not likely to ease in the near future because labour force growth is determined mainly by past population growth with a lag of about fifteen years. Virtually all the world's population growth – more than 90 per cent of it – since around 1950 has occurred in the developing countries.

There is, therefore, an enormous difference in labour force growth between the older industrialized countries on the one hand and the developing countries on the other. But the scale of the problem also differs markedly between different parts of the developing world itself. By far the greatest problem exists in low-income Asian countries, where the projected increase of 250 million in the labour force between 1975 and 2000 is twice that of the region's labour force growth rate between 1950 and 1975. Of course, pressure on the labour market is lessened where lower population growth rates occur. The basic dilemma facing most developing countries, therefore, is that the growth of the labour force vastly exceeds the growth in the number of employment opportunities available.

Formal and informal sectors in developing country labour markets

It is extremely difficult to quantify the actual size of the unemployment problem in developing countries. There are three main reasons for this. One is the simple lack of accurate statistics. A second is the nature of the unemployment itself, which tends to be somewhat different from that in the developed economies. A third reason is the structure of most developing economies, particularly their division into two distinctive, though closely linked, sectors: formal and informal. Published figures in developing countries tend to show a very low level of unemployment, in some cases lower than those recorded in the industrial countries. But the two sets of figures are not comparable. Unemployment in developing countries is not the same as unemployment in industrial economies. To understand this we need to appreciate the strongly segmented nature of the labour market in developing countries.

The formal sector is the sector in which employment is in the form of wage labour, where jobs are (relatively) secure and hours and conditions of work clearly established. It is the kind of employment which characterizes the majority of the work force in the developed market economies. But in most developing countries the formal sector is not the dominant employer, even though it is the sector in which the modern forms of industry are found.

The informal sector encompasses both legal and illegal activities, but it is not totally separate from the formal sector: the two are inter-related in a variety of complex ways. The informal sector is especially important in urban areas; some estimates suggest that between 40 and 70 per cent of the urban labour force may work in this sector (Gilbert and Gugler, 1982). But measuring its size accurately is virtually impossible. By its very nature, the informal sector is a floating, kaleidoscopic phenomenon continually changing in response to shifting circumstances and opportunities.

In a situation where only a minority of the population of working age are employed in the sense of working for wages or salaries, defining unemployment is thus a very different issue from that in the developed economies. In fact, the major problem in developing countries is under-employment, whereby people may be able to find work of varying kinds on a transitory basis, for example, in seasonal agriculture, as casual labour in workshops or in services.

The urban–rural dimension

Under-employment and a general lack of employment opportunities are widespread in both rural and urban areas in developing countries. There is a massive under-employment and poverty crisis in rural areas arising from the inability of the agricultural sector to provide an adequate livelihood for the rapidly growing population and from the very limited development of the formal sector in rural areas. Some industrial development has occurred in rural areas, notably in those countries with a well developed transport network. Mostly this is subcontracting work to small workshops and households in industries such as garment manufacture. But the bulk of the modern industries are overwhelmingly concentrated in the major cities or in the export processing zones.

It is in the big cities that the locational needs of manufacturing firms are most easily satisfied. Yet despite the considerable growth of manufacturing and service industries in the cities the supply of jobs in no way keeps pace with the growth of the urban labour force. Not only is natural population increase very high in many developing country cities but also migration from rural areas has reached gigantic dimensions. The pull of the city for rural dwellers is directly related to the fact that urban employment opportunities, scarce as they are, are much greater than those in rural areas.

In complete contrast to the older industrialized countries, therefore, where a growing counter-urbanization trend was evident for some years, urban growth in most developing countries has continued to accelerate. The highest rates of urban growth are now in developing countries where the number of very large cities has increased enormously. The sprawling shanty towns are the physical expression of this explosive growth. In the older industrialized countries, most industrial growth now occurs away from the major urban centres. In the developing countries, the reverse is the case: virtually all industrial growth is in the big cities. Like labour force growth in general, there is a stark contrast with the experience of the growing cities of the nineteenth-century industrial revolution:

> Whereas urbanization in the industrialized countries took many decades, permitting a gradual emergence of economic, social and political institutions to deal with the problems of transformation, the process in developing countries is occurring far more rapidly, against a background of higher population growth, lower incomes, and fewer opportunities for international migration. The transformation involves enormous numbers of people: between 1950 and 1975, the urban areas of developing countries absorbed some 400 million people; between 1975 and 2000, the increase will be close to one billion people. . . . The rate of urban population growth in these countries is likely to decline after 1975, but it is expected to remain three to four times as high as the urban growth rates of the industrialized countries in this period. (World Bank 1979, p. 72)

Labour migration as a 'solution'

Despite its considerable growth in at least some developing countries, manufacturing industry has made barely a dent in the unemployment and underemployment problem of most developing countries. Only in the very small NIEs, such as Hong Kong and Singapore – essentially city states with a minuscule agricultural population – has manufacturing growth absorbed large numbers of people. Indeed, Singapore has experienced a labour shortage and has had to resort to controlled in-migration while Hong Kong firms have increasingly located manufacturing production across the border in southern China. In all other cases, however, the problem is not so much that large numbers of people have not been absorbed into employment – they have – but that the rate of absorption cannot keep pace with the growth of the labour force.

One commonly adopted solution has been to 'export' labour to foreign countries Although in general terms, labour is relatively immobile (certainly in comparison with capital) massive flows of international labour migration occur, often encouraged by developing country governments. In some cases, for example across the Mexico–US border, much of this migration is illegal. The effects of such out-migration on the countries of origin can be very substantial, although they are not necessarily all beneficial. It is certainly true that out-migration helps to reduce pressures in local labour markets. It is also true that the remittances sent home by migrant workers make a very important contribution to the home country's balance of payments position and to its foreign exchange situation (as well as to the individual recipients and their local communities). Indeed, in many cases the value of foreign remittances is equivalent to a very large share of the country's export earnings as the table below shows. Other supposed benefits of out-migration include the learning of skills which, when the migrant returns will help to upgrade the home country's economic and technological base.

The other side of the coin is less attractive for the labour-exporting countries. That migrants are often the young and most active members of the population. Further, as Jones (1990, p. 250) points out:

> Growing familiarization with foreign consumption styles leads to disdain for domestic products and a growing dependence on expensive foreign imports . . . returning migrants are rarely bearers of initiative and generators of employment. Only a small number acquire appropriate vocational training – most are trapped in dead-end jobs – and their prime interest on return is to enhance their social status. This they attempt to achieve by disdaining manual employment, by early retirement, by the construction of a new house, by the purchase of land, a car and other consumer durables, or by taking over a small service establishment like a bar or taxi business; there is also a tendency for formerly rural dwellers to settle in urban centres. There is thus a reinforcement of the very conditions that promoted emigration in the first place. It is ironic that those migrants who

are potentially most valuable for stimulating development in their home area – the minority who have acquired valuable skills abroad – are the very ones who, because of successful adaptation abroad, are least likely to return. There are also problems of demographic imbalance stemming from the selective nature of emigration. Many villages in Southern Europe have been denuded of young men, with consequences not only for family formation and maintenance but also for agricultural production.

The positive and negative effects of globalization processes on employment in developing countries can be summarized as shown in the Table below.

There is no question, therefore, that the magnitude of the employment and unemployment problem in developing countries is infinitely greater than that facing the older industrialized countries, serious as their problem undoubtedly is. The biggest problem in developing countries is under-employment and its associated poverty. The high rate of labour force growth in many developing countries continues to exert enormous pressures on the labour markets of both rural and urban areas. Such pressures are unlikely to be alleviated very much by the development of manufacturing industry alone. With one or two exceptions among the NIEs, industrial growth has done little to reduce the severe problems of unemployment and under-employment with their

POSITIVE EFFECTS	NEGATIVE EFFECTS
Higher export-generated income promotes investment in productive capacity with a potentially positive local development impact, depending on intersectoral and interfirm linkages, the ability to maintain competitiveness, etc.	The increases in employment and/or earnings are (in contradiction to the supposed positive effects) unlikely to be sufficiently large and widespread to reduce inequality. On the contrary, in most countries, inequality is likely to grow because unequal controls over profits and earnings will cause profits to grow faster.
Employment growth in relatively labour-intensive manufacturing of tradable goods, causes (1) an increase in overall employment; and/or (2) a reduction of employment in lower wage sectors. Either of these outcomes tends to drive up wages, to a point which depends on the relative international mobility of each particular industry, labour supply-demand pressure and national wage-setting/bargaining practices.	Relocations of relatively mobile, labour intensive manufacturing from industrialized to developing countries, in some conditions, can have disruptive social effects if – in the absence of effective planning and negotiations between international companies and the government and/or companies of the host country – the relocated activity promotes urban-bound migration and its length of stay is short. Especially in cases of export assembly operations with very limited participation and development of local industry and limited improvement of skills, the short-term benefits of employment creation may not offset those negative social effects.
These increases in employment and/or wages – if substantial and widespread – have the potential effect of reducing social inequality if the social structure, political institutions and social policies play a favourable role.	Pressures to create local employment, and international competition in bidding for it, often put international firms in a powerful position to impose or negotiate labour standards and labour management practices that are inferior to those of industrialized countries and, as in the case of some EPS, even inferior to the prevailing ones in the host country.
Exposure to new technology and, in some industries, a considerable absorption of technological capacity leads to improvements in skills and labour productivity, which facilitate the upgrading of industry into more value-added output, while either enabling further wage growth or relaxing the downward pressure.	

Source: Based on ILO (1996b, Table Int. 1).

resulting poverty – in developing countries. Globalizing processes, while offering some considerable employment benefits to some developing countries, are, again, a double-edged sword.

Sustaining growth and ensuring equity in the newly industrializing economies

The spectacular industrial growth of a small group of developing countries – the NIEs – has been one of the most significant developments in the world economy in recent years. Indeed, in many respects the four leading Asian NIEs – the four 'dragons' or 'tigers' – should perhaps no longer be regarded as developing countries at all. Certainly, there can be no doubting the remarkable industrial progress of this group of countries although these 'industrial miracles' are not without their serious internal difficulties. Three kinds of problem can be identified here:

- sustaining economic growth;
- ensuring that such growth is achieved with equity for the countries' own people;
- the problem of foreign debt which faces some, though not all, newly industrializing economies.

Measured in terms of increased per capita income, larger shares of world production and trade the east and southeast Asian NIEs, in particular, have been phenomenally successful. But can such spectacular growth rates be maintained in the future? Although each of the four leading NIEs has managed to sustain very high rates of growth for a very long period there were suggestions in the mid-1990s that perhaps the 'miracle' was coming to an end. Press headlines such as 'Asia's precarious miracle'; 'Is it over?'; 'Roaring tiger is running out of breath' began to appear. Even though it is difficult to avoid a feeling that the western media were engaging in a little wish fulfilment the question of the sustainability of NIE growth is a significant one.

Economic growth in the NIEs has been based primarily upon an aggressive export-oriented strategy. It is no coincidence that the take-off of the first wave of Asian NIEs occurred during the so-called 'golden age of growth' in the 1960s and early 1970s or that it was made possible by the relative openness of industrialized country markets. The growth and openness of such markets is, therefore, vital for the continued economic growth and development of the NIEs. During the 1960s the conditions were indeed favourable; future prospects look far less propitious as the older industrialized countries have reduced their demands for NIE exports, partly through the deliberate operation of protectionist trade measures. From the NIEs' viewpoint, therefore, the macroeconomic expansion of the industrialized economics is vital. But this will be effective only if trade barriers – especially non-tariff barriers are also removed or at least lowered. The present political climate in the older industrialized countries makes both possibilities somewhat remote.

Trade tensions, particularly between the US, their biggest export market, and the leading Asian NIEs are palpable and show little sign of disappearing. Countries like South Korea and Taiwan are regarded by the US as being less open to industrialized country imports than they might be. Consequently, the NIEs will need to develop further their own domestic markets although if this were to be done by raising trade barriers which are already high, the likely result would be to make the older industrialized countries even more reluctant to modify their own protectionist stance. There is also the problem that the smaller NIEs have very limited domestic markets; this was the major reason for adopting an export-oriented strategy in the first place. However, it is significant that regional markets, notably in Pacific Asia, are becoming increasingly important. This fits the policy position of UNCTAD which strongly urges NIEs to develop markets outside the older industrialized countries.

A second problem facing the leading NIEs in sustaining economic growth arises from the growing competition from other developing countries – the 'proto-NIEs'. This 'next tier' includes such countries as Malaysia, China, the Philippines, Thailand, Pakistan, Indonesia, Colombia, Chile, Peru, Turkey, and also the transitional economies of eastern Europe. Competition from these lower-wage countries has intensified as labour costs in the first tier of NIEs have risen. The competition is obviously most severe in the lower-skill, labour-intensive activities on which NIE industrialization was originally based.

Thus, the development of competition from other developing countries, together with trends in the automation of some labour-intensive processes in the industrialized countries, has added to the pressures on the leading NIEs to shift to more skill-intensive and capital-intensive products and processes. As we have seen at various points in this book, they have been very successful in making this transition so far. But the competitive pressure continues to intensify as other newly industrializing economies not only take on the less skilled functions but also, themselves, strive to upgrade their economies even further. As a result a complex intraregional division of labour has developed in east and southeast Asia with a clear hierarchical structure composed of countries at different levels of industrialization.

Prospects for the other NIEs outside Asia depend very much on their specific regional context. For Mexico, the key issue is its ability to prosper within the NAFTA. While its access to the US and Canadian markets is now guaranteed, at least over a period of time, its own economy will also feel the full force of external competition within its own borders. Similarly, the southern European NIEs (Spain, Portugal and Greece), which are full members of the EU, have unfettered access to the entire EU market. However, not only are their own economies open to the full force of competition from the industrialized economies of the EU but also they now face increasing competition from the opening up of eastern Europe (as, of course, do the NIEs in general).

How far a third or fourth tier of NIEs really will emerge to threaten the 'super league' is, however, a matter of considerable argument. In the early 1980s, Cline put forward the 'fallacy of composition' argument: that what is possible for a small number of cases is not possible for all, or even the large majority of cases. He argued that if the east Asian model of export-led development were to become characteristic of all developing countries 'it would result in untenable market penetration into industrialized

countries' (Cline, 1982, p. 88). The World Bank argues against this viewpoint.

First, the capacity of industrial nations to absorb new imports may be greater than supposed. . . . Second, the idea that a large number of economies might suddenly achieve export-to-GDP ratios for manufactures like Hong Kong, Korea or Singapore is highly implausible. . . . Third, export-oriented countries would produce different products, and intra-industry trade is likely to be important. Finally, the first wave of newly industrializing countries is already providing markets for the labour-intensive products of the countries that are following. (World Bank, 1987, p. 91)

Ensuring economic growth with equity

Sustaining economic growth is only one of the difficulties facing the NIEs (both existing and potential) in today's less favourable global environment. Sustaining growth with equity for the populations of the NIEs themselves is also a major problem. Two aspects of this issue are especially important: income distribution and the sociopolitical climate within individual countries.

A widely voiced criticism of industrialization in developing countries has been that its material benefits have not been widely diffused to the majority of the population. There is indeed evidence of highly uneven income distribution within many developing countries. In countries such as Brazil, Chile, Mexico and Malaysia, for example, the share of total household income received by the top 20 per cent of households was very much higher than that in the industrial market economies. However, this pattern does not apply in all cases. For example, India and South Korea has a household income distribution very similar to that of the industrial market economies (though at much lower levels). Of course, the question of income distribution is very much more complex than these simple figures suggest and is the subject of much disagreement among analysts. The fact remains, however, that in general the Asian NIEs have a more equitable income distribution than the Latin American countries. Without doubt this reflects the specific historical experiences of these countries and, especially, the different patterns of land ownership and reform.

Income distribution is one aspect of the 'growth with equity' question. Another is the broader social and political issue of democratic institutions, civil rights and labour freedom. Although the degree of repression and centralized control in NIEs may sometimes be exaggerated, the fact is that such conditions do exist in a number of cases. The very strong state involvement in economic management in most NIEs has brought with it often draconian measures to control the labour force. Labour laws tend to be extremely stringent and restrictive; in many instances strikes are banned:

> With regard to the maintenance of low-wage labour reserves, the proletarianized segment of labour in all Asian NIEs has suffered from state intervention to depress workers' wages below market rates in order to make exports competitive on the international market. . . . But internal conditions and state strategies varied. . . . In both Korea and Singapore, the government has been actively involved in the creation of a 'hyperproletarian' segment of the labour market that has been largely filled by women and is characterized by a high turnover of labour, institutionalized job insecurity, and low wages. . . . The absence of either state or community restraint on exploitation of workers in Korea is manifested by extremely poor working conditions for this segment. Labour laws have been arbitrarily enforced and favour employers over workers, particularly in the case of heavy industry and automobile production, the sectors in which labour has become most militant. (Douglass, 1994, p. 554)

How far the success of NIEs, particularly in attracting foreign investment, really depends on the use of strongly authoritarian measures is difficult to ascertain. But until such repressive behaviour is relaxed, the achievements of some of the NIEs in the strictly economic sphere must be regarded with some reservations. In this respect, it is significant that in the late 1980s both South Korea and Taiwan began to move along the democratization path. As the persistence of labour disturbances in South Korea shows, however, the transition is not proving to be easy.

Environmental degradation is also a major social problem facing most of the NIEs. In the cases of South Korea and Taiwan, for example, Bello and Rosenfeld write of the 'toxic trade-off' and 'the making of an environmental nightmare' respectively. Although extensive environmental damage is certainly not confined to the NIEs:

> Their single-minded pursuit of rapid economic growth has caused particularly severe environmental degradation. Much of the countryside in both South Korea and Taiwan is severely and perhaps irreparably damaged. South Korean rural areas suffer from extensive deforestation, related problems of soil erosion and flooding, and widespread chemical contamination of ground water. . . . Rising environmental costs in both urban and rural areas are materializing in poor health, physical damage, loss of amenities, and other problems that demand extensive remedial spending. . . . In order to stimulate rapid growth, the NIEs have used up significant environmental capital that can only be restored, if at all, at considerable cost to future generations. (Brohman, 1996, pp. 126, 127)

Although we have treated the questions of sustaining growth and sustaining growth with equity as separate they are, in fact, closely related. It is an open question as to how far the various forms of the developmental state which are manifested in different NIEs can continue to provide the basis for future economic development. This is an issue addressed by Douglass (1994). He concludes his analysis as follows:

> The strong state model of societal guidance that was a key feature of all of the Asian NIEs' industrialization processes is being challenged on all fronts, and whether a new complex of institutions reflecting an expanded political community that includes more democratic methods of regulation

will appear to be or be effective is one of the most important questions for the coming years. If Bello and Rosenfeld (1990) are accurate in claiming that the command economies of the Asian NIEs are obsolete and that legitimation crises can no longer be met with the stick but must instead be resolved through democratic practice, the message from the West may not be comforting. But if there is a process of 'late democratization' accompanying late industrialization, a nonauthoritarian alternative to the developmental state based on the extension of political community beyond the state itself will also be on the political agenda. (p. 563)

The debt problem

A third serious problem for the NIEs is the burden of financial debt which many have incurred, particularly since the late 1970s. Much of the industrial growth of the NIEs has been financed by overseas borrowing (as was that of the industrializing countries in the nineteenth century). Before the 'second oil shock' of 1979 there were no major problems. Exports from NIEs continued to hold up well despite the onset of recession in the older industrialized countries. Capital was needed for investment in the NIEs; after the 1973 oil crisis the huge volume of petro-dollars had to be recycled by the commercial banks to prevent the world financial system from seizing up. The banks were only too ready to lend to the more successful developing countries in order to achieve this.

The international debt crisis broke with great suddenness in the early 1980s when the first, and most spectacular, incident was the financial collapse of Mexico in August 1982. It soon became clear that a number of developing countries were in deep financial difficulty. The problem was particularly concentrated in the middle-income group of developing countries which had come to depend most heavily on commercial lending. The fact that the low-income countries were not greatly involved in no way indicates their lack of financial difficulty – on the contrary. But commercial banks have generally been unwilling to lend to the very poor countries so that most of their borrowing is in the public sector aid programmes.

In the early 1980s, therefore, the problem of recycling funds was suddenly displaced by that of rescheduling the massive debts of some developing countries. An increasing number of countries found themselves unable to repay the interest on the sums borrowed let alone reduce the basic sum. Some were having difficulty paying the interest on the interest as they had to borrow more simply to avoid going under completely. The emergence of this very serious problem reflects a whole host of factors. Some are internal to the countries involved: undoubtedly there has been some profligate spending on unnecessary prestige projects. But this is not the fundamental cause.

The most important factors relate to developments within the global economy since the late 1970s. As we have seen, demand for manufactured goods and materials in the older industrialized countries declined as recession deepened and as protectionist measures intensified. The market for NIE exports slackened very substantially. At the same time, the governments of the industrialized countries began to pursue very tight financial and fiscal policies which, while reducing price inflation in their own economies, forced up interest rates. In particular, the need for the US to finance its enormous budget deficit kept interest rates especially high. Floating interest rate debts subsequently cost far more to service than when they were initially incurred. New loans taken out became extremely expensive.

The largest debt problems are in Latin America. Brazil, Mexico and Argentina in particular have been continuously in the financial headlines since 1982 as each country seemed to be on the brink of financial collapse. Each of the major debtor nations has been forced to seek the co-operation of the international financial institutions – the IMF and the major commercial banks – in rescheduling their debts. So far, total breakdown has been averted but the very severe conditions the IMF places on the debtor countries as the price of rescue create serious social and political problems for the countries themselves. Whether the lid can be kept on such a volatile pot is by no means certain, as the collapse of the Mexican peso in December, 1994, again illustrated. Prior to 1997, the east and southeast Asian NIEs had not experienced such problems. The relative buoyancy of the Asian NICs helped to keep them out of the grip of the moneylenders. For example, although South Korea has borrowed very heavily, its continuing high-level export performance enabled it to service the debt, although concerns surfaced in the mid-1990s over its rapid growth. However, the collapse of the Thai baht in the summer of 1997 and its knock-on effects in the region demonstrated the fragility of the situation.

Ensuring survival and reducing poverty in the least industrialized countries

Although the NIEs certainly face problems, they are not of the same magnitude or seriousness as those facing the least industrialized, low-income countries. The poorest fifty or so developing countries are poor not just in terms of income but also in virtually every other aspect of material well-being. They are the countries of the deepest poverty, several of which face mass starvation. For large numbers of people in the low-income countries (and in some of the higher income countries, too) life is of the lowest material quality.

The causes of low income levels

Poverty is the most crushing burden of all. As Todaro (1989, p. 93) succinctly demonstrates, '. . . low levels of living (insufficient life-sustaining goods and inadequate or non-existent education, health, and other social services) are all related in one form or another to low incomes. These low incomes result from the low average productivity of the entire labour force, not just those working.' Todaro argues that low labour force productivity can result from a variety of factors:

- On the supply side: poor health, nutrition and work attitudes; high population growth, and high unemployment and underemployment.

- On the demand side: inadequate skills, poor managerial talents, overall low levels of worker education; the importation of developed country labour-saving techniques of production which substitute capital for labour.
- The combination of low labour demand and large supplies results in the widespread under-utilization of labour.

In addition,

- low incomes lead to low savings and investment which also restrict the total number of employment opportunities;
- low incomes are also thought to be related to large family size and high fertility since children provide one of the few sources of economic and social security in old age for very poor families:

> The important point to remember . . . is that low productivity, low incomes, and low levels of living are mutually reinforcing phenomena. They constitute what Myrdal has called a process of 'circular and cumulative causation' in which low incomes lead to low levels of living (income plus poor health, education etc.) that keeps productivity low, which in turn perpetuates low incomes, and so on. (Todaro, 1989, p. 99)

Dependence on a narrow economic base

A most important contributory factor in the poverty of low-income countries (and of some of the lower middle-income countries too) is their dependence on a very narrow economic base together with the nature of the conditions of trade. We saw earlier that the overwhelming majority of the labour force in low-income countries is employed in agriculture. This, together with the extraction of other primary products, forms the basis of these countries' involvement in the world economy. Approximately four-fifths of the exports of developing countries are of primary products compared with less than one-quarter for the developed economies.

In the classical theories of international trade, based upon the comparative advantage of different factor endowments, it is totally logical for countries to specialize in the production of those goods for which they are well endowed by nature. Thus, it is argued, countries with an abundance of particular primary materials should concentrate on producing and exporting these and import those goods in which they have a comparative disadvantage. This was the rationale underlying the 'old' international division of labour in which the core countries produced and exported manufactured goods and the countries of the global periphery supplied the basic materials. According to traditional trade theory all countries benefit from such an arrangement. But such a neat sharing of the benefits of trade presupposes some degree of equality between trading partners, some stability in the relative prices of traded goods and an efficient mechanism – the market – which ensures that, over time, the benefits are indeed shared equitably.

In the real world (and especially in the trading relationships between the industrialized countries and the low-income, primary-producing countries) these conditions do not hold. In the first place, there is a long-term tendency for the composition of demand to change as incomes rise. Thus, growth in demand for manufactured goods is greater than the growth in demand for primary products. This immediately builds a bias into trade relationships between the two groups of countries, favouring the industrialized countries at the expense of the primary producers.

Over time, these inequalities tend to be reinforced through the operation of the cumulative processes of economic growth. The prices of manufactured goods tend to increase more rapidly than those of primary products and, therefore, the terms of trade for manufactured and primary products tend to diverge. (The terms of trade are simply the ratio of export prices to import prices for any particular country or group of countries.) As the price of manufactured goods increases relative to the price of primary products, the terms of trade move against the primary producers and in favour of the industrial producers. For the primary producers it becomes necessary to export a larger quantity of goods in order to buy the same, or even a smaller, quantity of manufactured goods. Although the terms of trade do indeed fluctuate over time, there is no doubt that they have generally deteriorated for the primary producing countries.

The severity of the situation facing the developing countries in general, and the low-income, least industrialized, countries in particular, led to demands for a radical change in the workings of the world economic system. The demand by a group of developing countries was for a new international economic order (NIEO), a demand set out formally in a United Nations Declaration in 1974. The United Nations Declaration called for:

the replacement of the existing international economic order, which was characterized by inequality, domination, dependence, narrow self-interest and segmentation, by a new order based on equity, sovereign equality, interdependence, common interest and co-operation among States irrespective of their economic and social systems. (United Nations, 1982, p. 3)

The NIEO declaration set out a very ambitious and detailed agenda. Overall, the demand was for better access to world markets for both primary products and manufactured goods from developing countries. In the case of primary products a key demand was for stabilization schemes to remove the serious fluctuations in both demand and prices for them, fluctuations which have an especially severe impact on many developing countries. In the case of manufactured goods, the demand was for a reduction in protection of developed country markets, for the older industrialized countries to adopt more positive adjustment policies in their home economies to permit the expansion of developing country exports and for measures to ease the transfer of technology.

The demand for a fairer distribution of world industrial production was formulated more precisely in the 1975 Lima Declaration and Plan of Action for Industrial Co-operation. The Lima Declaration set a target for 25 per cent of world industrial production to be located in the developing countries by the year 2000. Developing countries now account for around 20 per cent of world manufacturing production. At first sight, therefore, it would seem that the Lima target is within grasp. Not so. Virtually all the manufacturing production outside the core industrial economies is located in a very small number of developing countries. For the vast majority, as we have seen, levels of industrialization remain exceptionally low.

In fact, very little progress has been made on most of these demands. The very poor developing countries, those at the bottom of the well-being league table, have benefited least from the internationalization and globalization of economic activities. Both their present and their future are dire. Ways have to be found to solve the problems of poverty and deprivation: 'No task should command a higher priority for the world's policy makers than that of reducing global poverty. In the last decade of the twentieth century it remains a problem of staggering dimensions' (World Bank, 1990, p. 5).

In such a highly interconnected world as we now inhabit, and as our children will certainly inhabit, it is difficult to believe that anything less than global solutions can deal with such global problems. But how is such collaboration to be achieved? Can a new international economic order be created or is the likely future one of international economic disorder? There can be no doubt that the present immense global inequalities are a moral outrage. The problem is one of reconciling what many perceive to be conflicting interests. For example, one of the biggest problems facing the older industrialized countries is unemployment. As we have seen, the causes of unemployment are complex but if one factor is perceived to be import penetration by developing country firms then the pressure to adopt restrictive trade policies becomes considerable.

The alternative is to adopt policies which ease the adjustment for those groups and areas adversely affected and to stimulate new sectors. But this requires a more positive attitude than most western governments have been prepared to adopt. For the poorer developing countries it is unlikely, however, that industrialization will provide the solution to their massive problems. Despite its rapid growth in

some developing countries, manufacturing industry has made barely a small dent in the unemployment and underemployment problems of developing countries as a whole. For most, the answer must lie in other sectors, particularly agriculture, but the seriousness of these countries' difficulties necessitates concerted international action. This, in turn, is part of a much larger debate about the overall governance of the world economy.

---

10 THE THIRD INDUSTRIAL REVOLUTION

J. Rifkin

The destabilizing effects of the Third Industrial Revolution are being felt all over the world. In every advanced economy, new technologies and management practices are displacing workers, creating a reserve army of contingent laborers, widening the gap between the haves and the have-nots, and creating new and dangerous levels of stress. In the Organization for Economic Cooperation and Development (OECD) countries, 35 million people are currently unemployed and an additional 15 million have either given up looking for work or unwillingly accepted a part-time job (OECD, 1994, p. 7). In Latin America, urban employment is over 8 per cent. India and Pakistan are experiencing unemployment of more than 15 per cent. Only a few East Asian nations have unemployment rates of below 3 per cent (UN, 1993, p. 35).

In Japan, where the term 'unemployment' is barely uttered, fierce new global competition is forcing companies to tighten their operations, throwing workers into unemployment lines for the first time in recent memory. Although Japan claims

From: *The End of Work: the decline of the global labour force and the dawn of the post-market era*, by J. Rifkin, 1995, Putnam, pp. 198–207.

an unemployment rate of only 2.5 per cent, some analysts point out that if the high number of discouraged unemployed workers and unrecorded jobless is added to the totals, the figure might be as high as 7.5 per cent (*Financial Times*, 22 July 1993, p. 18). The *Wall Street Journal* reported in September 1993 (p. A10) that 'fears are spreading [in Japan] that major corporations will soon be forced to lay off workers perhaps on a large scale.' Job openings have fallen by 26 per cent, and some Japanese economists predict two job applicants for every job in the next few years. Koye Koide, a senior economist at the Industrial Bank of Japan, says, 'the potential pressure of labor adjustment [in Japan] is the greatest since World War II' (*Wall Street Journal*, 5 October 1993, p. B1).

Employment prospects have dimmed in virtually every sector of the Japanese economy. Megumu Aoyana, a job placement officer at Toyo University in Tokyo, complains that corporate recruitment of college graduates is at a post-war low. Middle-management job openings in manufacturing firms are slowing, and some analysts claim that as many as 860,000 management jobs will likely be eliminated in the next wave of corporate re-engineering. In the past, says Aoyana, it was assumed that if manufacturing jobs were cut, the service sector would absorb the excess workers. Now, service-sector job offers have fallen by 34 per cent, the largest drop of any sector. Aoyana believes that Japan's giant corporations 'will never again hire a lot of people' (ibid.).

In a recent article in the *Harvard Business Review* (1994, p. 6), Shintaro Hori, a director of the consulting firm of Bain and Company, Japan, warned that Japanese companies would likely have to eliminate as much as 15 to 20 per cent of their entire white collar workforce to match the low overhead of US-based companies and remain competitive in world markets. Japanese employers, faced with the realities of a highly competitive global economy, are likely to feel increasing pressure to downsize their operations in the years immediately ahead, displacing millions of workers in the process.

While concerns over unemployment are mounting in Japan, the same fears have reached a near fever pitch in Western Europe, where one in nine workers is currently without a job. Every Western European nation is experiencing worsening unemployment. France's unemployment is at 11.5 per cent. In England it has topped 10.4 per cent. In Ireland unemployment is now over 17.5 per cent. Italy's has reached 11.1 per cent. In Belgium, unemployment stands at 11 per cent. Denmark's unemployment is approaching 11.3 per cent. In Spain, once among the fastest-growing countries in Europe, one out of five workers has no job.

German unemployment now hovers at 4 million. More than 300,000 jobs in the auto industry alone are expected to be eliminated in the coming period. Comparing the unemployment figures today with those in Germany in the early 1930s, Chancellor Helmut Schmidt recently made the chilling observation that more people are unemployed in Chemnitz, Leuna or Frankfurt and the Oder than in 1933, when people there elected the Nazis. Schmidt warned the German people and the global community of dire consequences ahead. 'If we cannot overcome this [problem]', said Schmidt, 'we must be prepared for everything'. The German situation is sending shock waves through the European economy. Germany's 80 million citizens make up 23 per cent of Europe's consumers and its $1.8 trillion economy accounts for 26 per cent of the European Union's GNP.

Industry observers claim that the number of unemployed in Europe will climb to 19 million by the beginning of 1995 and will probably continue to rise during the remainder of the decade. Drake, Beam, Morin, a consulting company, recently surveyed more than 400 European companies and reported that 52 per cent intend to cut their workforce by 1995. (In a similar survey conducted in the US, the consulting company found that 42 per cent of the firms interviewed were planning further cuts in their workforce by 1995.) The firm's chairman, William J. Morin, warns that: 'the pressures of global competition and new technology are beginning to hit hard in Europe' (*Washington Post*, 21 September 1993, p. C3).

High-tech politics in Europe

The issue of technology displacement is fast moving to the fore in European political debate. By the beginning of the 1990s, only one in five European workers was employed in manufacturing, down from one in four in 1960. The loss of manufacturing jobs is due in large part to the introduction of new labor saving, time-saving technologies and the restructuring of production practices along lines already well advanced in the US and Japan.

The European automotive components industry is illustrative of the trend. The industry currently employs more than 940,000 workers in EC countries. According to a confidential report prepared for the European Commission, in order for European firms to remain competitive and regain their market position they will need to re-engineer their operations and reduce their workforce by 400,000 by 1999. That represents a 40 per cent projected drop in employment in just one industry in less than six years.

Manufacturing industries in Europe and the other OECD countries are expected to continue to eliminate increasing numbers of workers over the next several decades as they move inexorably toward the era of the workerless factory. Whatever hope economists and policy leaders had that the service sector would provide jobs for the unemployed, as it had done in the past, is now dwindling. While the service sector in OECD countries grew by 2.3 per cent per year during the 1980s, by 1991 the rate of growth had dropped to less than 1.5 per cent. In Canada, Sweden, Finland and the UK the service sector actually declined in 1991. The ILO places the blame for the downturn on the structural changes taking place in the service sector. In its World Labour Report, 1993, pp. 19–20), the ILO noted that 'most services, from banking to retailing (with the possible exception of health care) are now restructuring in ways which the manufacturing industry adopted a decade ago'.

In Europe, the unemployment problem is likely to be further exacerbated by the drop in public employment. During the 1980s, public-sector jobs (a total of 5 million) accounted for most of the job growth in the European Union. Now, with European nations thinning their budgets in an effort to lower government deficits and debt, the prospect of governments hiring displaced manufacturing and service workers and acting as an employer of last resort is no longer politically feasible. Even more alarming is the fact that more than 45.8 per cent of the unemployed workers in Europe have been without a job for more than a year – a staggering figure compared to the US, where only 6.3 per cent have been out of a job for more than twelve months.

What employment opportunities do exist are largely limited to part-time work. As in the US, European companies are increasingly turning to temps to save on labour costs. Just-in-time employment is becoming the norm in many European countries. Temps are concentrated in the service sector, where the re-engineering phenomenon is spreading rapidly, challenging traditional notions of job security. In the Netherlands, 33 per cent of the workers are part-time, and in Norway more than 20 per cent. In Spain, one out of every three workers is now part-time. In the UK, nearly 40 per cent of the jobs are part-time.

The evidence suggests that just-in-time employment is going to play a larger and even more expanded role in the new high-tech global economy of the twenty-first century. Multinational companies, anxious to remain mobile and flexible in the face of global competition, are increasingly going to shift from permanent to contingent workforces in order to respond quickly to market fluctuations. The result is going to be increased productivity and greater job insecurity in every country of the world.

In Europe, in particular, the increasing reliance on a reserve army of contingent workers reflects the growing concern on the part of corporate management that the expensive social net erected in the EC countries in the post-war era is making their companies less competitive in the global arena. The average German manufacturing worker is much better paid than is his American counterpart. His hourly compensation costs employers approximately $26.89, with 46 per cent going to benefits. Italian manufacturing workers make more than $21 an hour, and most of their compensation comes in the form of benefits. An American manufacturing worker costs his employer only $15.89 an hour and only 28 per cent of it goes to benefits.

Europeans also enjoy longer paid vacations and work fewer hours. In 1992 the average German worker put in 1,519 hours a year and received forty days of paid vacation. Government workers averaged 1,646 hours. American employees work an average of 1,857 hours a year while Japanese workers top the list, logging more than 2,007 hours of work every year. All in all, European labour is 50 per cent more expensive than either US or Japanese labour.

Public spending in Europe is also higher than in any other industrial region of the world. Much of it goes to finance social programs to protect and enhance the well-being of workers and their families. Social security payments in Germany in 1990 were 25 per cent of the gross domestic product, compared to only 15 per cent in the US and 11 per cent in Japan. Financing social benefits for workers requires heavier taxes on corporations. The corporate tax burden in Germany now exceeds 60 per cent, and in France is approaching 52 per cent. In the US it is only 45 per cent. When all of the costs of maintaining an adequate social net are added up – including the costs of taxes, social security, unemployment compensation, pensions, and medical insurance – they amount to about 41 per cent of the total gross domestic product in Europe, compared to 30 per cent in the US and Japan.

Corporate leaders have introduced a new term, 'Euro-sclerosis', into the public dialogue in an effort to draw attention to what they consider to he bloated and unnecessary social welfare programmes. In defense of their claims, they point to the US, where the social net was stripped away during the Reagan–Bush years as part of a well-orchestrated campaign to rid companies of undue labour costs.

In August, 1993, Chancellor Helmut Kohl's government announced a $45.2 billion cut in social-benefit programs as part of an austerity drive designed to tame the escalating federal deficit. Other European countries are following suit. In France, the new conservative government enacted measures to significantly cut social programs, including a reduction in retirement payments and reimbursement for

medical expenses. The new government also shortened the number of weeks an unemployed worker can receive jobless benefits. Commenting on the changes, a French official remarked, 'We can't have people working for eight months and then receiving fifteen months of unemployment benefits, as they do today'. In the Netherlands, the conditions governing disability benefits have been tightened up in the hope of saving more than $2 billion a year in public spending. Some European officials, such as European Union (EU) Commissioner Padraig Flynn, are urging caution in the debate over lowering the social net. He warns that 'you're going to see more low-wage jobs being created ... and more part-time work'. In both cases, says Flynn, 'the key is to have a satisfactory level of social protection ... so that you're not creating working poor and increased levels of poverty'.

The lowering of the social net, at a time when growing numbers of workers are being displaced by new technologies and management restructuring, is increasing tensions throughout Europe. In March, 1994, tens of thousands of students took to the streets in cities across France to protest a government decree lowering the minimum wage for young people. With one out of four French youth already unemployed, the government is worried that increasing political unrest could lead to a repeat of the kind of violent protests that shook France in 1968, paralysing the government. In Italy, where youth unemployment has reached 30 per cent, and in England, where it now tops 17 per cent, political observers watched the events taking place in France with keen interest, worried that their countries might be the next to be rocked by militant youth protests.

Surveying the plight of European workers, researcher Heinz Werner said it's 'like a treadmill for hamsters. Anyone who gets off the treadmill will find it hard to get back on'. Once off, says labour expert Wilhelm Adamy, 'the problem of each unemployed person will worsen' (World Press Review, February, 1993, p. 40) as they find themselves facing an ever shrinking social net. More than 80 million people in the EC are already living in poverty. Their numbers are likely going to swell, perhaps to epidemic proportions, as more and more workers are displaced by new technologies and set adrift in an economic sea with fewer public lifeboats to rescue them.

Automating the third world

The Third Industrial Revolution is spreading quickly into the third world. Global companies are beginning to build sophisticated high-tech, state-of-the-art plants and facilities in countries throughout the southern hemisphere. 'In the 1970s', says Harley Shaiken, Professor of Labour and Technology at the University of California at Berkeley, 'capital intensive, highly automated production seemed to be linked to industrial economies like the US, and the jobs that went off-shore were low-tech, low productivity jobs like sewing blue jeans and assembling toys'. Now, says Shaiken, 'with computers, telecommunications and new forms of cheap transport, highly advanced production has been successfully [transplanted] to third world countries'.

As noted earlier, the wage component of the total production bill continues to shrink in proportion to other costs. That being the case, the cost advantage of cheap, third world labour is becoming increasingly less important in the overall production mix. While cheap labour might still provide a competitive edge in some industries like textiles and electronics, the advantage of human labour over machines is fast diminishing with advances in automation. Between 1960 and 1987, 'less than a third of the increase in output in developing countries . . . came from increased labour', according to a recent report by the United Nations Development Programme (1993, p. 35), and 'more than two-thirds [came] from increases in capital investment'.

Many companies in third world countries have been forced to invest heavily in automated technologies in order to ensure speed of delivery and quality control in an ever more competitive global market. Often the decision to locate a plant in a developing nation is as much influenced by the desire to be close to a potential new market as by labour cost differentials. Whether it be market performance or market location, say the editors of Fortune (14 December 1992, p. 52), 'New technology and the continuing drive for higher productivity push companies to build in less developed countries plants and offices that require only a fraction of the manpower that used to be needed in factories back home'.

Consider the case of Mexico. Global companies based in the US and Japan have been setting up plants along a 300-mile strip of border towns in northern Mexico since the late 1970s. The assembly plants, known as 'maquiladoras', include Ford, AT&T, Whirlpool, Nissan, Sony, and scores of other manufacturing giants. The newer plants are highly automated facilities requiring a much smaller workforce of skilled technicians to operate.

Companies are quickly automating their plant production process in northern Mexico more in an effort to improve quality than to save labour costs. Like other global companies operating there, Zenith has automated its manufacturing facilities and reduced its workforce from 3,300 to 2,400. Elio Bacich, the director of Zenith's Mexican operations, says that 'sixty per cent of what we once did by hand is now done by machinery' (*New York Times*, 21 March 1993, p. 4).

Machines are replacing workers in every developing country. Martin Anderson, vice president of the Gemini Consulting Firm, in New Jersey, says that when companies build new factories in developing countries they are generally far more highly automated and efficient than their counterparts back in the US. 'Some of the most Japanese-looking American plants are going up in Brazil', says Anderson. The idea that transferring production facilities to poor countries is going to mean high levels of local employment and greater prosperity is no longer necessarily true. Shaiken agrees, arguing that 'the kind of needs in the third world for jobs dwarf the number of jobs that are being created' by the new high-technology automated plants and businesses. He worries that the Third Industrial Revolution is going to mean a few high-tech jobs for the new class of elite knowledge workers and growing long-term technological unemployment for millions of others. The clear trend, says Shaiken, is 'a continuation of the extensive polarization of incomes and the marginalization of millions of people'.

The substitution of machines for human labour is leading to increased labour unrest in the third world. On 1 July 1993, workers struck at the Thai Durable Textile Company, just outside of Bangkok, shutting down production. The strike was called to protest the layoff of 376 of the company's 3,340 workers, who were let go to make room for new labour-saving technology. With more than 800,000 workers – mostly women – employed in the Thai textile industry, both labour and management view the strike as a test case that is likely to decide the fate of tens of thousands of workers caught in the throes of a technology revolution that is moving the world ever closer to the 'workerless factory'.

In neighbouring China, where cheap labour has long substituted for more expensive machine capital, government officials have announced an across-the-board restructuring of factories and upgrading of equipment to help give the world's most populous nation a competitive advantage in world markets. Chinese industry analysts predict that as many as 30 million will be let go in the current wave of corporate restructuring.

Nowhere is the contrast between the high-tech future and the low-tech past more apparent than in Bangalore, India, a city of 4.2 million that is fast becoming known as that country's Silicon Valley. Global companies like IBM, Hewlett-Packard, Motorola and Texas Instruments are flocking to this city located atop a 3,000-foot plateau some 200 miles west of Madras. In colonial times, the city, with its mild climate, tropical plants, and beautiful vistas, was a favourite vacationing spot for British civil servants. Today, it sports 'gleaming office towers blazoned with Fortune 500 logos.' In a country teeming with poverty and social unrest, Bangalore 'is an island of relative affluence and social stability'. Touting some of the best-trained scientists and engineers anywhere in the world, this Indian city has become a high-tech mecca for global electronic and computer firms eager to set up shop close to burgeoning new markets.

Bangalore is just one of a number of new high-tech enclaves being established in key regional markets around the planet. Their very existence, amidst growing squalor and despair, raises troubling questions about the high-tech future that awaits us in the coming century. Historian Paul Kennedy (1993, pp. 182–3) asks whether countries like India can 'take the strain of creating world competitive, high-tech enclaves . . . in the midst of hundreds of millions of their impoverished countrymen'? Noting the growing disparity between the new symbolic analyst class and the declining middle and working poor in countries like the US, Kennedy asks whether developing countries like India might fare even more poorly in the new high-tech world. 'Given the even greater gap in income and lifestyles that would occur in India', says Kennedy, 'how comfortable would it be to have islands of prosperity in a sea of poverty?'

Kennedy's concerns become even more compelling in light of the rising number of workers projected to enter the labor force in developing countries in the years ahead. Between now and the year 2010, the developing world is expected to add more than 700 million men and women to its labour force – a working population that is larger than the entire labour force of the industrial world in 1990. The regional figures are equally striking. In the next thirty years the labour force of Mexico, Central America, and the Caribbean is expected to grow by 52 million, or twice the number of workers as currently exist in Mexico alone. In Africa, 323 million new workers will enter the labour force over the next three decades – a working-age population larger than the current labour force of Europe.

World-wide, more than a billion jobs will have to be created over the next ten years to provide an income for all the new job entrants in both developing and developed nations. With new information and telecommunication technologies, robotics, and automation fast eliminating jobs in every industry and sector, the likelihood of finding enough work for the hundreds of millions of new job entrants appears slim. Again, Mexico offers a good case in point. Even though Mexico is better off than most developing nations, 50 per cent of the labour force is still unemployed or underemployed. Just to maintain the status quo, Mexico will need to generate more than 900,000 jobs a year during the remainder of the current decade to absorb the new workers entering the labour force.

We are rapidly approaching a historic crossroad in human history. Global corporations are now capable of producing an unprecedented volume of goods and services with an ever smaller workforce. The new technologies are bringing us into an era of near workerless production at the very moment in world history when population is surging to unprecedented levels. The clash between rising population pressures and falling job opportunities will shape the geo-politics of the emerging high-tech global economy well into the twenty-first century.

_____

QUESTIONS

General introduction

(1) List the most significant ideas and concepts in the General Introduction.
(2) What is 'globalization'? Why is it held to be so significant in the contemporary world?
(3) Is it possible to say when globalization, as we know it today, started? Discuss the main events in the history of contemporary globalization.
(4) In what sense can we talk of a 'global culture'? What are its defining features?
(5) Critically explore the principal processes behind the globalization of culture.
(6) Assess the cases for and against 'cultural homogenization'; 'cultural hybridization'; and 'media imperialism'.
(7) Critically assess the contribution made to our understanding of global culture by Jean Baudrillard, David Harvey and Paul Virilio.
(8) Critically assess the contribution made to the analysis of globalization by Roland Robertson and Arjun Appadurai.

Part A Globalization and society

(1) List the most significant ideas and concepts in Part A.
(2) In what sense are we all increasingly living in a 'global neighbourhood'?
(3) What does the slogan 'think global, act local' mean and what are its implications?

(4) Why is it no longer tenable to conceive of the global in terms of a single, integrated and unified conceptual scheme? Rather, should we conceive of globalization in the plural?
(5) What sympathy do you have with the view that 'genuine locals have ceased to exist and that the local is now, itself, a global product'?
(6) List (and discuss) the ways in which globalization has an impact on you personally? Does globalization shape your world view (that is, how you perceive the world and your place in it) in any significant way?
(7) What is meant by the description of young people today as the first truly 'global generation'? Is it equally true of all young people world-wide or only those in the (rich) West?
(8) What do you understand by a 'global city' and what are its defining features?

Part B Globalization and culture

B1 Global culture

B2 Global consumerism and tourism and identity

(1) List the most significant ideas and concepts in Part B.
(2) Critically comment upon the links between globalization, consumerism and postmodernism.

(3) What do you understand by the (local) 'cultural impact' of globalization?

(4) What is the evidence for the existence of a predominantly Americanized 'global culture' and should we be concerned?

(5) Global popular cultural production is primarily profit-driven and consumption primarily image-driven. Discuss.

(6) What are the positive and negative features of global tourism?

(7) How convincing (or otherwise) do you find the argument that we are increasingly living 'cyber-lives' in a 'cyber-world'?

(8) Research and document instances of 'local–global' and 'global–local' interactions.

Part C Globalization, media and technology

C1 Global media and communication

C2 The global impact of new technologies

(1) List the most significant ideas and concepts in Part C.

(2) Global media appears to be owned and run by a club of immensely powerful Anglo-American corporations. If this is the case then what are the dangers of such a monopoly?

(3) What do you understand by the 'global media' as a primary transmitter of 'global culture'? What do you take to be its defining features?

(4) What role does indigenous media (including 'alternative' television like 'Paper Tiger') have in the increasing globalization of television?

(5) What evidence is there to support the view that global flows of television are locally 'read', appropriated and adapted?

(6) What, if anything, is wrong with television global news? How is war now represented by global television? Has it become the 'ultimate voyeurism?

(7) Why should we be concerned about the emergence of the ' information rich' and 'information poor' (the 'interacting' and the 'interacted')?

(8) New global communicational technologies present both unique new possibilities and new threats. Discuss.

Part D Globalization and political economy

(1) List the most significant ideas and concepts in Part D.

(2) Are nations, institutions and individuals helpless in the face of the forces of globalization?

(3) Account for the momentous events in the period 1989–92 in Eastern Europe. What were their global implications?

(4) Summarize the case for and against the 'end of history'?

(5) Should we continue to think in terms of the 'nation-state' or, alternatively, is it now more realistic to consider aggregates of states within a 'global polity'?

(6) What major changes have occurred with respect to the (global) labour force over the last two decades?

(7) Outline what you understand to be 'Fordist' and 'post-Fordist' working practices. What impact has globalization had in the movement from the former to the latter?

(8) How far have we moved towards a 'post-industrial order'?

(9) Employing a variety of data-collecting methods (from the quantitative/statistical to the qualitative/ethnographic) draw up a series of research plans to investigate critically:

   (a) a particular phase in the history of globalization;

   (b) key aspects of the changing political economy;

   (c) the production and reception of 'global culture' (including 'global media');

   (d) global cultural movements, or 'flows';

   (e) the interplay between globalization, consumerism and postmodernism;

   (f) the role of rapidly developing and converging communicational technologies in the globalizing process.

ACKNOWLEDGEMENTS

We would like to thank the following:

- Our publishers, Athlone Press and Routledge, US and, especially, Tristan Palmer, our enthusiastic and ever-supportive editor;
- Penny Byrne, Alan Cotton and, in particular, Colin Gent of the University of Glamorgan: without their technical expertise, generosity of time and uncomplaining goodwill, it is unlikely that this book would have ever seen the light of day;
- Steve Lee and Bill Newman, Social Sciences librarians in the University of Glamorgan;
- Other library staff in both the University of Glamorgan and Cardiff University;
- Karl Davies of Dolphin Books, Barry;
- Helen and Teresa;

- Our warmest thanks, however, are extended to all the authors upon whose work we have extensively drawn; and to the students and colleagues who have forced us to clarify our ideas on globalization over many years;
- Finally, this book is dedicated to MAG, JS and TR in the hope that the Global Studies Project on which we worked hard in recent years (and in which this book had its origins) might now make further progress.

John Beynon and David Dunkerley,
School of Humanities and Social Sciences,
University of Glamorgan,
Wales, UK
July 2000

REFERENCES

Albrow, M (1996), *The Global Age*, Polity Press, Cambridge.

—— (1997), Travelling beyond local cultures: socioscapes in a global city, in Eade, J, ed., op. cit.

Alleyne-Dettmers, P (1997), 'Tribal arts': a case study of global compression in the Notting Hill carnival, in Eade, J ed., op. cit.

Anderson, B (1983), *Imagined Communities,* Verso, New York.

Andrews, DL (1997), The (trans) National Basketball Association: American commodity sign culture and global–local conjuncturalism, in Cvetkovich, A and Kellner, D, eds, op. cit.

Ang, I (1985), *Watching Dallas: Soap Opera and the Melodramatic Imagination,* Methuen, London.

Appadurai, A (1990), Disjuncture and difference in the global cultural economy, in *Public Culture*, Vol. 2:2, 1990.

Archer, MS (1988), *Culture and Agency: The Place of Culture in Human Agency*, Cambridge University Press, Cambridge.

—— (1990), *Theory, culture and post-industrial society*, in Featherstone, M, ed., op. cit.

Auge, M (1995), *Non-Places: An Introduction to an Anthropology of Supermodernity*, Verso, London, Verso, London.

—— (1999), *The War of Dreams: Studies in Ethno Fiction*, Verso, London.

Axford, B (1995), *The Global System*, Polity Press, Cambridge.

Axtmann R (1997), Collective identity and the democratic nation state in the age of globalization, in Cvetkovich, A and Kellner, D, eds, op. cit.

Barker, C (1999), *Television, Globalization and Cultural Identities*, Open University Press, Milton Keynes.

Barnet, RJ and Cavanagh, J (1994), *Global Dreams: Imperial Corporations and the New World Order*, Touchstone Press, New York.

Baudrillard, J (1983), *Simulations, Semiotext*, New York.

—— (1988), *America*, Verso, London.

Beck, U (1992), *Risk Society: Towards a New Modernity*, Sage, London.

—— (2000), *What is Globalization?*, Polity, Cambridge.

Bird, J, Barry, C, Putnam, T, Robertson, G and Tickner, L (1993), eds, *Mapping the Futures: Local Cultures, Global Change*, Routledge, London.

Boyd-Barrett, JO (1982), Cultural dependency and the mass media, in Gurevitch, M *et al.*, eds, Culture, Society and the Media, Methuen, London.

Bredin, M (1996), Transforming images, in Howes, D, ed., *Cross-Cultural Consumption*, Routledge, London.

Classen, C (1996), Consumption and surrealism in the Argentine North West, in Howes, D, ed., op. cit.

Classen, C and Howes, D (1996), The dynamics and ethics of cross-cultural consumption, in Howes, D, ed., op. cit.

Cook, G (1994), *The Discourse of Advertising*, Routledge, London.

Craik, J (1994), *The Face of Fashion: Cultural Studies in Fashion*, Routledge, London.

Crick, M (1989), Representations of international tourism in the social sciences, *Annual Review of Anthropology*, 18.

Crook, S, Pakulski, J and Waters, M (1992), eds, Postmodernization: change in advanced society, Sage, London.

Cvetkovich, A and Kellner, D (1997), eds, *Articulating the Global and the Local*, Westview Press, Boulder, Colorado, US.

Cvetkovich, A and Kellner, D (1997), Thinking global and local, in Cvetkovich, A and Kellner, D, eds, op. cit.

Dorfman, A and Mattelart, A (1975), *How to Read Donald Duck*, International General Editions, New York.

Douglas, M and Isherwood, B (1979), *The World of Goods: Towards an Anthropology of Consumption*, WW Norton and Company, New York.

Eade J (1997), ed., *Living the Global City: globalization as local process*, Routledge, London.

—— (1997), Identity, nation and religion: educated young Bangladeshis in London's East End, in Eade, J, ed., op. cit.

Enloe, C (1989), *Bananas, Beaches and Bases*, University of California Press.

Featherstone, M (1990), ed., *Global Culture: Nationalism, Globalization and Modernity*, Sage, London.

Featherstone, M, Lash, S and Robertson, R (1995), eds, *Global Modernities*, Sage, London.

Fejes, F (1981), Media imperialism: an assessment, in Media, Culture and Society, 3, 3, pp. 281–289, Sage, London.

Fennell, G (1997), Local lives-distant ties: researching community under globalized conditions, in Eade, J, ed., op. cit.

Fiske, J (1989), *Understanding Popular Culture*, Unwin Hyman, Boston.

Foster, H (1985), *Recodings: Art, Spectacle, Cultural Politics*, Port Townsend, Washington DC.

Friedman, J (1990), Being in the world: globalization and localisation, in Featherstone, M , ed., op. cit.

—— (1995) Global system, globalization and the parameters of modernity, in Featherstone, M *et al.,* eds, op. cit.

—— (1997), Simplifying complexity: assimilating the global in a small paradise, in Olwig, KF and Hastrup, K, eds, *Siting Culture: The Shifting Anthropological Object*, Routledge, London.

Fukuyama, F (1992), *The End of History and the Last Man*, Hamish Hamilton, London.

Gewertz, D and Errington, F (1991), *Twisted Histories, Altered Contexts*, Cambridge University Press, Cambridge.

Giddens, A (1990), *The Consequences of Modernity*, Polity Press, Cambridge.

Graburn, N (1995), The past in the present in Japan, in Butler, K and Pearce, D, eds, *Change in Tourism, People, Places, Processes*, Routledge, London.

Hall, S (1991), The local and the global: globalization and ethnicity, in King, AD, ed., *Culture, Globalization and the World System*, Macmillan, London.

—— (1992), The question of cultural identity, in Hall, S, Held, D and McGrew, T, eds, *Modernity and its Futures*, Polity Press, Cambridge.

Hamelink, CJ (1983), *Cultural Autonomy in Global Communication*, Longman, London.

Hannerz, U (1990), Cosmopolitans and locals in world culture, in Featherstone, M, ed., *Global Culture*, Sage, London.

—— (1991), Scenarios for peripheral cultures, in King, AD, ed., *Culture, Globalization and the World System*, Macmillan, London.

—— (1992), *Cultural Complexity: Studies in the Social Organization of Meaning*, Columbia University Press, New York.

Harding, S (1995), Towers of power, *Loaded Magazine*, February, pp. 50–53, Loaded Press, London.

Harvey, D (1989), *The Condition of Modernity*, Blackwell, Oxford.

Hebdige, D (1989), After the masses, in Hall, S and Jacques, M, eds, *New Times*, Lawrence and Wishart, London.

—— (1990), Fax to the future, *Marxism Today*, January, London.

Held, D, Mcgrew, A, Goldblatt, D and Perraton, J (1999), eds, *Global Transformations: Politics, Economics and Culture*, Polity, Cambridge.

Henderson, L (1993), Justify our love: Madonna and the politics of queer sex, in Schwichtenberg, C, ed., *The Maddona Connection: Representational Politics, Subcultural Identities and Cultural Theory*, Westview Press, San Francisco.

Howes, D (1996), ed., *Cross-Cultural Consumption: Global Markets, Local Realities*, Routledge, London.

—— Commodities and cultural borders, in Howes, D, ed., op. cit.

Huntington, S (1993), The clash of civilisations, *Foreign Affairs*, 72, 2, pp. 22–49.

Huyssens, A (1984), *After the Great Divide: Modernity, Mass Culture and Postmodernism*, Routledge, London.

James, A (1996), Cooking the books: global or local identities in contemporary British food culture, in Howes, D, ed., op. cit.

James, J (1993), *Consumption and Development*, St. Martins Press, New York.

Jameson, F (1984), Postmodernism or the cultural logic of late capitalism, *New Left Review*, 146, pp. 53–92.

—— (1991), *Postmodernism or The Cultural Logic of Late Capitalism*, Verso, London.

—— (1998), Preface, in Jameson, F and Miyoshi, M, eds, *The Cultures of Globalization*, Duke University Press, London and Durham.

Katz, E and Liebes, T (1985), Mutual aid in the decoding of Dallas, in Drummond, P and Paterson, R, eds, *Television in Transition*, BFI, London.

King, A (1990), *Global Cities*, Routledge, London.

Kroker, A and Cook, D (1988), *The Postmodern Scene*, Macmillan Education, London.

Laclau, E and Mouffe, C (1985), *Hegemony and Socialist Strategy*, Verso, London.

Lash, S and Urry, J (1987), *The End of Organised Capitalism*, Polity Press, Cambridge.

—— (1994), *Economies of Signs and Space*, Sage, London.

Liebes, T and Katz, E (1993), *The Export of Meaning: Cross-Cultural Readings of Dallas*, Cambridge, Polity.

Luke, TW (1995), New world order or neo-world orders, in Featherstone, M, Lash, S and Robertson, eds, op. cit.

Lull, J and Hinerman, S (1997), *Media Scandals: morality and desire in the popular culture marketplace*, Polity Press, Cambridge.

Lury, C (1996), *Consumer Culture*, Polity Press, Cambridge.

McBride, S (1980), *Many Voices, One World*, Paris, UNESCO.

Mackay, H (2000), The globalization of culture, in Held, D (ed.), *A Globalizing Society?*, Routledge, London.

Madsen, R (1993), Global monoculture, multiculture and polyculture, *Social Research*, 60, 3, pp. 493–511.

Maffesoli, M (1988), *Le Temps des Tribus*, Klincksieck, Paris.

Massey, D (1994), *Space, Place and Gender*, Polity, Cambridge.

Mattelart, A (1979) *et al.*, eds, *Communication and Class Struggle*, International General, New York.

Mattelart, A, Delacourt, X and Mattelart, M (1984), *International Image Markets*, London, Comedia.

Miller, D (1987), *Material Culture and Mass Consumption*, Blackwell, Oxford.

—— (1992), The young and restless in Trinidad: a case of the local and the global in mass consumption, in Silverstone, R and Hirsch, E, eds, *Consuming Technology*, London, Routledge.

Mohammadi, M (1997), Communication and the globalization process in the developing world, in Mohammadi, A, ed., *International Communication and Globalization*, Sage, London.

Negus, K (1992), *Producing Pop: Culture and Conflict in the Pop Music Industry*, Edward Arnold, London.

—— (1996), *Popular Music in Theory*, Polity Press, Cambridge.

O'Byrne, D (1997), Working class culture: local community and global conditions, in Eade, ed., op. cit.

Ohmae, K (1990), *Borderless World*, Collins, London.

Perry, N (1998), *Hyper-Reality and Global Culture*, Routledge, London.

Pieterse, JN (1995), Globalization as hybridization, in Featherstone, M *et al.*, eds, op. cit.

Poster, M (1986), ed., *Selected Works of Jean Baudrillard*, Polity Press, Cambridge.

Rieff, D (1993), A global culture?, *World Policy Journal*, 10, 14, pp. 73–81.

Robertson, R and Chirico, JA (1985), Humanity, globalization and world-wide religious resurgence, *Sociological Analysis*, Autumn.

Robertson, R (1990), Mapping the global condition: globalization as the central concept, in Featherstone, M, ed., op. cit.

—— (1992), *Globalization: Social Theory and Global Culture*, Sage, London.

—— (1995), Glocalization, in Featherstone, M, Lash, S and Robertson, R, eds, op. cit.

Robinson, D, Buck, E and Cuthbert, M (1991), *Music at the Margins: Popular Music and Global Cultural Diversity*, Sage, London.

Roth, L and Valaskakis, G (1989), Aboriginal broadcasting in Canada, in Raboy, M and Bruck, P, eds, *Communication For and Against Democracy*, Black Rose Books, Montreal.

Rutherford, J (1990), A place called home: identity and the cultural politics of difference, in Rutherford, J, ed., *Identity: Community, Culture and Difference*, Lawrence and Wishart, London.

Schiller, HI (1976), *Communication and Cultural Domination*, M.E. Sharpe, New York.

—— (1985), Electronic information flows as the new basis for global domination, in Drummond, P and Patterson, R, eds, *Television in Transition*, BFI, London.

—— (1991), Not yet the post-industrial era, *Critical Studies in Mass Communication*, Vol. 8, pp. 13–28.

—— (1996), *Information Inequality*, Routledge, London.

Simon, W (1996), *Postmodern Sexualities*, Routledge, London.

Sinclair, J, Jacka, A and Cunningham, S (1996), 'Peripheral vision' in Sinclair, Jacka, A and Cunningham, S, eds, *New Patterns in Global Television: Peripheral Vision*, Oxford University Press, Oxford.

Sklair, L (1991), *The Sociology of the Global System*, Harvester Wheatsheaf.

Smith, AD (1990), Towards a global culture, *Theory, Culture and Society*, 7, 2–3, Sage, London.

—— (1992), *Nationalism in the Twentieth Century*, New York University Press, New York.

Sola Pool, I de (1979), Direct broadcast satellites and the integrity of national cultures, in Nordenstreng, K and Schiller, HI, eds, National Sovereignty and International Communication, Ablex New Jersey, US

Solomon, MR (1994), *Consumer Behaviour*, Allyn and Bacon Needham Heights, MA, US.

Sparks, C (1998), Is there a global public sphere?, in Thussu, DK, ed., *Electronic Empires: Global Media and Local Resistance*, Arnold, London.

Spybey, T (1996), *Globalization and World Society*, Polity Press, Cambridge.

Thompson, K (1992), Social pluralism and Postmodernity, in Hall, S and Gieben, B, eds, *Modernity and its Futures*, Polity Press, Cambridge.

Tomlinson, J (1991), *Cultural Imperialism*, Pinter Publishers, London.

Valaskakis, G (1988), Television and cultural integration, in Lorimer, R and Wison, DC, eds, *Communication Canada: Issues in Broadcasting and New Technologies*, Kagan and Woo, Toronto.

Virilio, P (2000), *Polar Inertia*, Sage, London.

Wallerstein, I (1979), *The Capitalist World Economy*, Cambridge University Press, Cambridge.

—— (1984), *The Politics of the World Economy: the states, the movements and the civilisations*, Cambridge University Press, Cambridge.

Wark, M (1994), *Virtual Geography: Living with Media Events*, Indiana University Press, Bloomington and Indianapolis.

Waters, M (1995), *Globalization*, Routledge, London.

Weismantel, MJ (1989), Hegemony and the transfer of consumption, in Ritz, A and Orlove, B, eds, *The Social Economy of Consumption*, University Press of America.

Wilk, R (1996), Consumer goods as dialogue about development, in Friedman, J, ed., *Consumption of Identity*, Harwood Academic Publishers, Switzerland.

Williams, J (1994), The local and the global in English soccer and the rise of satellite television, *Sociology of Sport Journal*, 11, 4, pp: 376–97.

Williamson, J (1990), *Decoding Advertisements*, M. Boyars, London.

Wilson, R and Dissanayake, W (1996), *Global–Local: cultural production and the transnational imagery*, Duke University Press, London and Durham.

INDEX